BARRON'S
BUSINESS
REVIEW
SERIES

Quantitative Methods

Douglas Downing, PhD
School of Business and Economics
Seattle Pacific University

Jeffrey Clark, PhD
Research Analyst
Salomon Brothers, Inc.

Consulting Editor
G. Thomas Friedlob, PhD
College of Commerce and Industry
School of Accountancy
Clemson University

BARRON'S
New York • London • Toronto • Sydney

ACKNOWLEDGMENTS

We would like to thank Dave and Kathy Knerr, and Ruth Flohn of Barron's
for their help. Appreciation is due also to the students at Seattle Pacific who
worked some of the exercises included here.

This book is for Laura.

All inquiries should be addressed to:
Barron's Educational Series, Inc.
250 Wireless Boulevard
Hauppauge, New York 11788

Library of Congress No. 87-31676
International Standard Book No. 0-8120-3947-5

Library of Congress Cataloging-in-Publication Data
Downing, Douglas.
    Quantitative methods/by Douglas Downing and Jeffrey Clark.
    p. cm. — (Barron's business review series)
    Includes index.
    ISBN 0-8120-3947-5
    1. Mathematical optimization.   2. Linear programming.
  3. Probabilities.   I. Clark, Jeff. II. Title. III. Series.
  QA402.5.D68 1988   87-31676
  519.3—dc19   CIP

PRINTED IN THE UNITED STATES OF AMERICA
8901   800   987654321

CONTENTS

PREFACE

This is a book about decision making: how to choose the best course of action, considering the goals you are trying to achieve and the constraints that limit your action. We will cover several areas of mathematics that are applied to management decision making under the general heading of *quantitative methods* or *management science* or *operations research*. We will be discussing situations where the real world is represented by a mathematical model, consisting of variables, equations, and inequalities. In each case we will be trying to achieve a specific goal, such as choosing the optimal product mix or minimizing the cost of production. You should realize the importance of the decision-making responsibility. Nonoptimal decisions can be bad for the employees, customers, neighbors, and owners of a firm.

Chapter 1 covers methods for solving systems of equations. In many problems there are constraints that take the form of inequalities. (For example, you have only so much of a particular resource available, so your solution cannot exceed that limit in its use of that resource.) In this case the type of analysis required is called *linear programming*. Chapters 2 to 5 show how to set up and solve linear programming problems. Chapters 6 to 8 discuss applications of linear programming in areas such as shipping and production.

In the first eight chapters the focus is on linear functions. A linear function can be represented as a straight line on a graph. To analyze nonlinear functions we need to use methods from calculus, which we consider in Chapters 9 and 10.

We also face problems caused by uncertainty. We don't know what the condition of the world will be in the future. We must make decisions that involve risk, because the outcomes may be worse (or better) than we expect. The study of probability helps in analyzing these situations. The principles of probability are discussed in Chapters 11 and 12, and applications of probability are examined in the remaining chapters.

Another type of uncertainty arises when we consider the fact that we will be affected by the behavior of other people. Any move that we make can be expected to lead to a response from rivals. Because this type of situation is similar to a game, the branch of mathematics that analyzes these situations is called *game theory* (discussed in Chapter 13).

Many sections of the book start by presenting examples, and then proceed to a general statement of the problem. You should become familiar both with moving from a specific example to a general problem, and with applying a general method to a specific example. In many cases the examples in the book have been rigged so that the arithmetic works nicely. As you undoubtedly realize, this is not often the case in the real world. However, when you are working through an unfamiliar type of problem for the first time, the task is easier if complicated arithmetic does not obscure the issue.

You should be familiar with principles of algebra. We assume that linear programming and calculus are completely new to you. If you are familiar with one-variable differential calculus, the material in Chapter 9 will serve as a review.

Many questions and problems are included at the end of each chapter. You cannot learn quantitative methods without practice. Do as many exercises as required for you to feel comfortable with a topic. The answers to all of the questions and problems are included.

The "Key Terms" section (at the start of each chapter) and the Glossary contain definitions of the important terms used in the book. Terms that appear in the Glossary are printed in boldface when they first occur in the text.

Many of the problems involve tedious calculations. It helps to use a computer to perform these computations; working all of the problems in this book by hand would be a nuisance (although it can be done). Many of the problems that arise in practice are so complicated that it would be totally impracticable to solve them without computers. In fact, the growth of the entire subject of management science became possible only after the development of computers in the late 1940s. If your office or school has management-decision-making software available, you will find it beneficial to learn how to use it.

Another option for working the problems in the book is to use the computer programs included in Appendix 2. These programs, which can be used to solve small-scale equation systems or linear programming problems, are written in the BASIC programming language. (The specific version is Microsoft BASIC, which is commonly used on IBM-PCs and compatibles. The programs can be adapted for other versions of BASIC.)

Even when a computer performs the calculations for you, you should understand what it is doing. Since the computer does only what it is told, it will give you an incorrect result if you do not understand how to specify a problem correctly.

The use of mathematical techniques is only part of management decision making. Much of the work in decision making involves setting up an applicable model and reviewing data to verify that the model is appropriate. When developing a model, it is essential to include all factors, even those that are very difficult to measure, such as employee morale. As valuable as mathematical optimization procedures can be, keep in mind that any mathematical model can be no better than the data used to construct it.

Douglas Downing
Jeffrey Clark

LIST OF SYMBOLS AND ABBREVIATIONS

MATRICES

Boldface quantities, such as **A** and **x**, represent matrices.

I	identity matrix
AB	matrix product of **A** and **B**
$\mathbf{A}^{-1}$	inverse of matrix **A**
$\mathbf{A}'$ or $\mathbf{A}^T$	transpose of matrix **A**

$$\begin{vmatrix} a & b \\ c & d \end{vmatrix}$$ determinant of the matrix whose elements are shown

det **A**   determinant of **A**

CALCULUS

$\dfrac{dy}{dx}$ or y'	derivative of y with respect to x
$\dfrac{d^2y}{dx^2}$ or y''	second derivative of y with respect to x
$\dfrac{\partial z}{\partial x}$ or z_x	partial derivative of z with respect to x
$\dfrac{\partial^2 z}{\partial x^2}$ or z_{xx}	second partial derivative of z with respect to x
$\dfrac{\partial^2 z}{\partial x\,\partial y}$ or z_{xy}	cross partial derivative

GREEK LETTERS

Δ	upper-case delta (change in)
δ	lower-case delta
λ	lambda (Lagrange multipliers; parameters for Poisson and exponential distribution; arrival rate)
μ	mu (mean; service rate)
ω	omega (value of a game)
ρ	rho
σ	lower-case sigma (standard deviation)

GREEK LETTERS

Σ upper-case sigma (summation) for example:

$$\sum_{i=1}^{n} x_i \text{ means "Add up } x_1 \text{ to } x_n\text{"}$$

$$\sum_{k} A_{kj} \text{ means "Add up all values of } A \text{ where second subscript is } i\text{"}$$

PROBABILITY

$\Pr(A)$	probability that event A will occur
$\Pr(A \mid B)$	conditional probability that A will occur, given that B has occurred
!	factorial (product of all whole numbers from 1 up to the given number)
$\dbinom{n}{j}$	number of combinations of n things taken i at a time:

$$\binom{n}{j} = \frac{n!}{j!(n-j)!}$$

RANDOM VARIABLES

Capital letters are used to represent random variables.

$E(X)$	expectation of X
$\mathrm{Var}(X)$	variance of X
$\mathrm{Cov}(X, Y)$	covariance of X and Y

ABBREVIATIONS

CSE	constraint simultaneous equation system
EOQ	economic order quantity
MNG	marginal net gain
ROP	reorder point
SES	standard easily solvable form
SS	safety stock

1

SOLVING EQUATIONS

KEY TERMS

determinant a quantity that characterizes the nature of a matrix; if the determinant of the matrix of coefficients for an equation system is zero, then the matrix does not have an inverse and the equation system is either redundant or contradictory

linear equation an equation in which no variable is raised to any power other than 1, and no variables are multiplied together; the general form for a linear equation in one variable x is $ax + b = 0$

matrix a rectangular table of numbers or variables arranged in rows and columns

slope a quantity that measures the steepness of a line; the absolute value of the slope of a line is equal to the vertical distance between any two points on the line divided by the horizontal distance between those two points; if you move along the line from left to right and the line slopes upward, then the slope is positive; if the line slopes downward, then the slope is negative

Many practical problems involve solving equations or systems of equations. The early part of this chapter should be mostly review. The second part of the chapter covers the application of matrices for help in understanding and solving equation systems.

ONE-VARIABLE EQUATIONS

Example: Calculating the Break-even Quantity

PROBLEM   An ice cream shop sells sundaes for a price of $1.60. There are two kinds of costs: variable costs, which include items such as the cost of the ice cream itself and the cherry that tops each sundae; and fixed costs, which include items, such as interest payments and insurance, that do not depend on the number of sundaes sold. The average variable cost for each sundae is $1.20. The fixed costs total $120,000 per year.

How many sundaes must the shop sell every year in order to break even?

SOLUTION Let Q represent the quantity of sundaes sold. Then the total revenue (TR) is

$$TR = 1.60 \times Q = 1.60Q$$

(Note that the multiplication sign is usually omitted.)
The total variable cost (VC) is

$$VC = 1.20Q$$

The total cost (TC) is the sum of the fixed cost plus the variable cost:

$$TC = 120{,}000 + 1.20Q$$

The break-even quantity will occur where $TR = TC$:

$$1.60Q = 120{,}000 + 1.20Q$$

Now we have expressed the problem as a single equation with one variable. This type of equation is called a **linear equation** because the variable does not occur raised to any power, such as Q^2 or $Q^{1/3}$. A linear equation can be solved fairly easily by following what we will call the Golden Rule of Equations.

Golden Rule of Equations
   Whatever you do to one side of an equation, do exactly the same thing to the other side of the equation. Then the equation will still be a true equation (provided that it was true to begin with). There is one exception: you cannot divide both sides of an equation by zero.

To solve the equation

$$1.60Q = 120{,}000 + 1.20Q$$

we first subtract 1.20Q from both sides:

$$1.60Q - 1.20Q = 120{,}000 + 1.20Q - 1.20Q$$
$$0.40Q = 120{,}000$$

Then we divide both sides of the equation by 0.40:

$$\frac{0.40Q}{0.40} = \frac{120{,}000}{0.40}$$
$$Q = 300{,}000$$

Therefore, the ice cream shop must sell 300,000 sundaes in a year in order to break even.

Note that we managed to solve the equation after we converted it into an equivalent equation that contains the variable (and nothing but the variable) on one side, and a known quantity (and nothing but a known quantity) on the other side. Therefore, our procedure to solve a linear equation in one variable is to perform operations on the equation (making sure to perform exactly the same operation on both sides) until we have transformed the equation into a form with the variable on only one side.

Example: Calculating Quantity when Selling Price = Marginal Cost

PROBLEM   A company sells toothpicks in a perfectly competitive market. The price of each case of toothpicks is constant at $36. The marginal cost of producing each case is given by the formula

$$MC = 6 + \frac{1}{12}Q$$

where Q represents the quantity of cases produced. (The **marginal cost** is the amount by which cost increases when one more unit of the good is produced.)

How many toothpicks should the company produce to maximize profit?

SOLUTION   The profit-maximizing quantity of output occurs at the quantity of output where the price is equal to the marginal cost. (If the price is greater than the marginal cost, you can increase your profits by producing more. If you sell one more good, your revenue will go up by the amount of the price; your cost will go up by the amount of the marginal cost.)

Therefore, the profit-maximizing quantity of output can be found by setting $P = MC$:

$$36 = 6 + \frac{1}{12} Q$$

To solve this equation, subtract 6 from both sides:

$$30 = \frac{1}{12} Q$$

Multiply both sides by 12:

$$360 = Q$$

Therefore, the profit-maximizing quantity of output occurs when a quantity of 360 is produced. (Chapter 10 will include more discussion of marginal cost.)

YOU SHOULD REMEMBER

If an equation contains one variable that is not raised to any power (other than 1), it is called a **linear equation**. It is possible to perform operations on the equation to transform it into this general form:

$$ax + b = 0$$

where x represents the variable and a and b represent known quantities. Then the solution (assuming that $a \neq 0$) is

$$x = -\frac{b}{a}$$

EQUATIONS WITH TWO VARIABLES

Example: Truck Purchasing

PROBLEM   The Helpful Delivery Company, which needs to buy several trucks, has asked us for advice. Trucks come in two sizes: big trucks, which have a capacity of two containers, and small trucks, which have a capacity of one container. We need enough trucks to have a total capacity of 20 containers.

How many trucks of each type do we need?

SOLUTION   This problem can be set up as an equation. We will use x to represent the quantity of small trucks, and y to represent the quantity of big trucks. Then we must satisfy this equation:

$$x + 2y = 20$$

Here is one solution: buy 20 small trucks. Then $x = 20$, $y = 0$. The solution can be written as the ordered pair $(20, 0)$. It is traditional that the value of x is listed first and the value of y is listed second. However, that is not the only solution. We could also buy 10 big trucks ($x = 0, y = 10$). In fact, there are several possible solutions: $(x = 16, y = 2)$; $(x = 10, y = 5)$; and $(x = 4, y = 8)$, for example.

In general, if an equation system contains more variables than equations, there will often be an infinite number of solutions.

Which is the best solution? We cannot tell, given the available information. For all we know, any solution that satisfies the equation $x + 2y = 20$ is acceptable.

It is often helpful to draw pictures that represent algebraic equations. As the saying goes, "One picture is worth a thousand words." Figure 1-1 shows a graph of all solutions to the equation $x + 2y = 20$. It is traditional that x is measured along the horizontal axis and y is measured along the vertical axis. For the present we will not worry about the fact that in practice the number of trucks must be a whole number.

The graph of a line can be characterized by two numbers: the slope and the vertical intercept. The **vertical intercept** of a line is the point where the line crosses the vertical axis. For the line in Figure 1-1, the vertical intercept is 10.

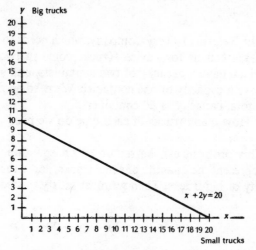

Figure 1-1

The **slope** measures the steepness of the line. To calculate the slope, choose any two points on the line. Suppose that the first point is represented by the coordinates (x_1, y_1) and the second point is represented by the coordinates (x_2, y_2). Then calculate the difference between the vertical coordinates $(y_2 - y_1)$, and the horizontal difference $(x_2 - x_1)$. (See Figure 1-2.) The slope is equal to

$$\text{slope} = \frac{y_2 - y_1}{x_2 - x_1}$$

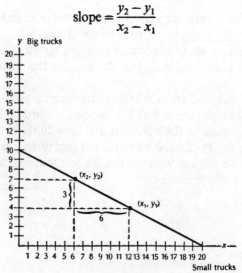

Figure 1-2

Since a straight line has a constant slope, the numerical value of the slope will be the same no matter which two points on the line you choose. In Chapter 10 we will use calculus to investigate the slope of a curve, which changes when you move to different points along the curve.

The absolute value of the slope is equal to the vertical distance between the two points divided by the horizontal distance. The sign of the slope tells whether the line is upward sloping or downward sloping.

The graph of the line representing the equation $x + 2y = 20$ has a slope of $-3/6 = -1/2$. Note that the slope of the line is negative. Imagine that you are on a pair of skiis traveling along the line from left to right. Clearly the line is going down, as is reflected in the negative slope. If the line goes up as you move along it from left to right, it has a positive slope. Figure 1-3 shows several lines with different slopes.

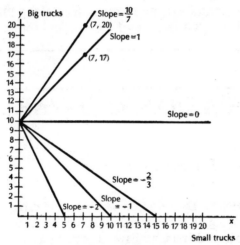

Figure 1-3

The equation $x + 2y = 20$ can also be written in the form

$$y = -\frac{1}{2}x + 10$$

Remember that $-1/2$ is the slope of the line represented by this equation, and 10 is the vertical intercept. In general, if the equation of a line is written in the form

$$y = mx + b$$

then m represents the slope of the line and b represents the value of the vertical intercept. (If $m = 0$, then the line is horizontal.)

YOU SHOULD REMEMBER

To calculate the slope of a line, choose any two points on the line: (x_1, y_1) and (x_2, y_2). Then:

$$\text{slope} = \frac{\text{(vertical distance)}}{\text{(horizontal distance)}} = \frac{y_2 - y_1}{x_2 - x_1}$$

If an equation is written in this form:

$$y = mx + b$$

then it can be represented as a line on a diagram with x measured along the horizontal axis and y measured along the vertical axis. The slope of the line is m, and the vertical intercept is b.

TWO-EQUATION, ONE-VARIABLE SYSTEMS

Example: Determining the Number of Drivers

PROBLEM The Helpful Delivery Company needs 14 drivers to cover all of the routes. Again it has asked us for advice. Using n to represent the number of drivers, we have the equation $n = 14$.

Each driver is paid $10 per hour. (If the drivers were offered any less, they would work somewhere else.) A naive consultant tells us that we should make sure that our total wage cost is $70 per hour. How many drivers should be hired?

SOLUTION The total labor cost per hour is equal to 10 times the number of drivers, so we have these two equations:

$$n = 14 \qquad\qquad n = 14$$
$$10n = 70 \qquad\qquad n = 7$$

The second equation can be rewritten as the equivalent equation $n = 7$, so we have this two-equation, one-variable system:

These equations clearly are contradictory; we cannot have *n* equal to both 14 and 7 simultaneously. Quite likely there will be no solutions for an equation system if there are more equations than there are variables in the system. If this situation happens in a practical problem, it means that it is impossible to satisfy all of the constraints that have been established for the problem. At least one of the constraints will not be satisfied. In this case we can either hire 14 drivers, or have the total wage cost equal to 70, but we cannot have both.

YOU SHOULD REMEMBER

If a simultaneous equation system contains more variables than equations, it is likely that there will be an infinite number of solutions for the system.

If a simultaneous equation system contains more equations than variables, it is likely that a contradiction will occur, meaning that it is impossible to find a solution that will satisfy all of the equations simultaneously.

Is it ever possible that there can be a solution if there are more equations than variables? Yes, provided that some of the equations are redundant. We'll come to that later.

SOLVING TWO-EQUATION, TWO-VARIABLE SYSTEMS BY GRAPHING

Example: Making a Truck Selection Decision

Earlier we found that our truck selection decision must satisfy this equation:

$$x + 2y = 20$$

where x = number of small trucks and y = number of big trucks.

Now suppose we have decided that we will need exactly 14 drivers, so we will purchase exactly 14 trucks. Therefore, the total number of trucks must satisfy this equation:

$$x + y = 14$$

The constraint again takes the form of an equation. However, in many realistic cases the constraints will take the form of inequalities. For example, suppose that we knew that we needed at least 14 trucks, but it was acceptable to have more than 14. In that case our constraint would be written as an inequality:

$$x + y \geq 14$$

where the symbol "$\geq$" means "greater than or equal to." We will not consider inequality constraints in this chapter, but we will introduce inequalities in the next chapter when we discuss linear programming.

Right now, we must find values of x and y that solve both of these equations simultaneously:

$$x + 2y = 20$$

$$x + y = 14$$

This is called a *system of simultaneous linear equations with two equations and two variables*. We can solve the system by drawing a graph. The equation $x + y = 14$ can be written as $y = -x + 14$, which tells us that the equation represents a line with a slope of -1 and a vertical intercept of 14. This line is graphed in Figure 1-4.

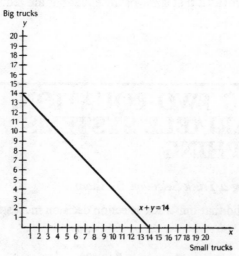

Figure 1-4

We need to find a solution for both equations, so we must look at a graph that contains both lines. (See Figure 1-5.) All points on one line represent points that solve the equation $x + 2y = 20$; all points on the other line represent points that solve the equation $x + y = 14$. We need a point that satisfies both equations, which means that we need a point on both of the lines. Therefore, the solution is the point where the two lines cross. By looking carefully at the diagram, we can see that this occurs where $x = 8$ and $y = 6$.

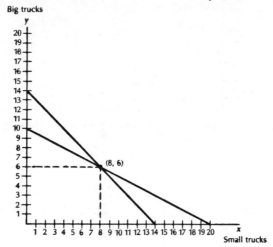

Figure 1-5

YOU SHOULD REMEMBER

To solve a system of simultaneous linear equations with two equations and two variables, draw a graph of the line representing each equation. The solution to the system occurs at the point where the two lines cross.

Example: Calculating the Equilibrium Price by Equating Supply and Demand

The demand for computer printer paper in Metropolis is given by the formula

$$Q = 152 - \frac{1}{2} P$$

where P represents the price of each box of paper, and Q represents the quantity demanded. Note that, as the price goes up, the quantity demanded goes down. Fewer people will buy at higher prices. Figure 1-6 shows a graph of the demand line. The equation can also be written in the form

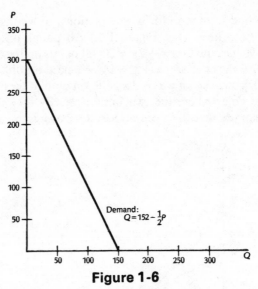

Figure 1-6

$$P = 304 - 2Q$$

which tells us that the slope is equal to -2 and the vertical intercept is 304.

The supply of boxes of paper is given by the formula

$$Q = 5P - 35$$

Note that, as the price goes up, the quantity supplied increases. More sellers will be willing to supply the good at a higher price. Figure 1-7 shows the graph of the supply line. The equation can also be written as

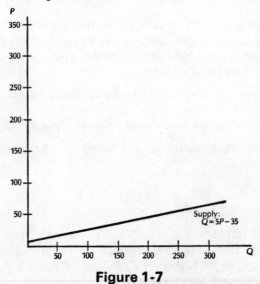

Figure 1-7

$$P = \frac{1}{5}Q + 7$$

which tells us that the slope is 1/5 and the vertical intercept is 7.

The equilibrium price for a good occurs at the quantity such that the quantity demanded equals the quantity supplied. We can solve for the equilibrium price by graphing the demand line and the supply line. (See Figure 1-8.) The equilibrium price is 34, which occurs where the quantity is 135.

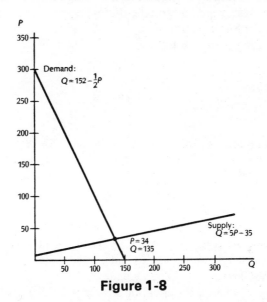

Figure 1-8

The graphical method is particularly helpful because it illustrates the nature of an equation system. However, to find exact answers it is necessary to draw the diagrams precisely. It is often easier to solve a system with an algebraic method. There are two different algebraic methods, which we will discuss next.

SOLVING TWO-EQUATION, TWO-VARIABLE SYSTEMS BY SUBSTITUTION

We will call the first method the **substitution method**. Suppose that we need to solve this equation system:

$$x + 2y = 20$$
$$x + y = 14$$

First, let's look only at the second equation, $x + y = 14$. We'll pretend that we are looking at a one-equation system and then solve for y:

$$x + y = 14$$
$$\rightarrow \quad y = 14 - x$$

This is not an acceptable solution for y, because x represents a quantity that is not known. However, we can take this expression for y and substitute it in place of y in the first equation.

First equation before substitution:

$$x + 2y = 20$$

First equation after substituting $14 - x$ in the place of y:

$$x + 2(14 - x) = 20$$

Now we have an equation with one variable, which we can solve to find $x = 8$. Once we have found x, we can find y by substituting the known value of x into either the first or the second equation.

Substituting $x = 8$ into the equation $x + 2y = 20$ gives

$$8 + 2y = 20$$
$$\rightarrow \quad y = 6$$

Substituting $x = 8$ into the equation $x + y = 14$ gives

$$8 + y = 14$$
$$\rightarrow \quad y = 6$$

Fortunately for us, both methods give the same value for y. (But this was not luck. If they had not given the same value for y, it would mean that we had made a mistake at some point.)

YOU SHOULD REMEMBER

To solve a two-equation, two-variable system by substitution, first solve one of the equations for one variable. Then substitute the resulting expression in place of that variable in the other equation, and proceed to solve the single-variable equation that is obtained. Once the value of one variable has been found, substitute that value into either one of the equations and then solve for the other variable.

Here is the general form of a simultaneous linear equation system with two equations and two variables:

$$a_1x + b_1y = c_1$$
$$a_2x + b_2y = c_2$$

The a's, b's and c's represent known quantities. (Assume that $b_2 \neq 0$.) First, use the second equation to solve for y in terms of x:

$$y = \frac{c_2 - a_2x}{b_2}$$

Now substitute this expression for y into the first equation:

$$a_1x + b_1\left(\frac{c_2 - a_2x}{b_2}\right) = c_1$$

This equation can be solved for x:

$$x\left(a_1 - \frac{b_1a_2}{b_2}\right) = c_1 - \frac{b_1c_2}{b_2}$$

$$x = \frac{c_1b_2 - b_1c_2}{a_1b_2 - b_1a_2}$$

(If $a_1b_2 - b_1a_2 = 0$, then this formula doesn't work; we'll cover that case later.)

Example: Solving a Macroeconomic Model of National Income

PROBLEM   Here is a macroeconomic model of a simple economy. The national income (Y) consists of two parts: consumption spending (C) and investment spending (I):

$$Y = C + I$$

The level of consumption spending depends on the level of national income according to this formula, which is called a **consumption function:**

$$C = 10 + \frac{4}{5} Y$$

The formula says that consumers will spend more if income increases.

The value of investment remains constant at 50:

$$I = 50$$

[Note that a realistic value of I would be closer to 500,000,000,000 (500 billion). It is very inconvenient to deal with such large numbers. We can change the units of the problem so that we can measure each quantity in units of 10 billion dollars, instead of individual dollars. Therefore, 500,000,000,000 dollars is equal to 50, measured in units of 10-billion dollars. Whenever you are dealing with a problem that involves large numbers, see whether it is possible to change the units you are using in order to make the numbers smaller without changing the meaning of the problem.]

What is the value of national income?

SOLUTION   If we replace the I in the first equation by its value of 50, then we can write the model as a two-equation, two-variable system:

$$Y = C + 50$$

$$C = 10 + \frac{4}{5} Y$$

This type of system can best be solved by substitution. We can substitute the expression for C from the second equation into the first equation:

$$Y = \left(10 + \frac{4}{5} Y \right) + 50$$

Now we have converted the system into a one-equation, one-variable system, so we can solve for the value for Y:

$$Y = 60 + \frac{4}{5}Y$$

$$\frac{1}{5}Y = 60$$

$$Y = 300$$

Inserting this value for Y into the equation for C, we find that $C = 250$.

Here is the general form of this model:

$$Y = C + I$$

$$C = a + bY$$

In this model I, a, and b represent known quantities. The solution (assume that $0 < b < 1$) is

$$Y = \frac{a + I}{1 - b}$$

$$C = \frac{a + bI}{1 - b}$$

SOLVING TWO-EQUATION, TWO-VARIABLE SYSTEMS BY ELIMINATION

The goal of the second method for solving a two-equation, two-unknown system is to convert the system into an equivalent system that is easier to solve. Look at the system for the truck problem:

$$\frac{x + 2y = 20}{x + y = 14}$$

Remember that the Golden Rule of Equations says that we can perform any operation on an equation as long as we perform the same operation on both sides. In particular, we can subtract 14 from both sides of the first equation if we want to. Why would we want to? Note that the second equation says that

$x + y$ is the same as 14. Therefore, if we subtract $x + y$ from the left-hand side of the first equation, it will be the same as subtracting 14. Therefore, we subtract $x + y$ from the left-hand side of the first equation, and subtract 14 from the right-hand side. This is permissible according to the Golden Rule of Equations.

We can think of it this way: we will subtract the second equation from the first equation. The advantage of performing this subtraction is that the x disappears from the new equation:

$$
\begin{array}{r}
x + 2y = 20 \\
-(x + y) = -(14) \\
\hline
0 + y = 6
\end{array}
$$

We are now left with one equation in one variable, which we can easily solve: $y = 6$. (Once we have found the value for y, we can find the value for x as we did in the preceding case by substituting the known value for y into either the first or the second equation.)

We will call this the **elimination method** since its goal is to eliminate one of the variables from one of the equations.

Example: Solving a Two-equation, Two-variable System by Elimination

PROBLEM
$$
\begin{aligned}
4x + 6y &= 148 \\
10x + 2y &= 136
\end{aligned}
$$

What is the value of x and of y?

SOLUTION   This time it is not immediately obvious what we should do. If we subtract the second equation from the first equation, we will not eliminate either of the variables. However, the Golden Rule of Equations says that we can perform the same operation on both sides of an equation. Let's multiply both sides of the second equation by 3:

$$
\begin{aligned}
3 \times 10x + 3 \times 2y &= 3 \times 136 \\
\rightarrow \qquad 30x + 6y &= 408
\end{aligned}
$$

The new equation system is:

$$
\begin{aligned}
4x + 6y &= 148 \\
30x + 6y &= 408
\end{aligned}
$$

Note that y is multiplied by 6 in both equations. Therefore, 6 is said to be the **coefficient** of y. The term *coefficient* refers to a quantity that is multiplied by another quantity. For example, 4 is the coefficient of x in the first equation, and 30 is the coefficient of x in the second equation.

Now we can subtract the second equation from the first equation:

$$(4x + 6y) - (30x + 6y) = 148 - 408$$

We have eliminated y from the new first equation:

$$-26x = -260$$

Therefore, $x = 10$. The value for y turns out to be 18. We have solved the system by using the elimination method.

YOU SHOULD REMEMBER

Elimination Method for Solving Two-Equation, Two-Variable Systems

1. Multiply both sides of the second equation by a number chosen so that the coefficient of one of the variables will become the same as the coefficient of that variable in the other equation.

2. Subtract the second equation from the first equation.

3. As a result of step 2, one of the variables will have vanished. Now solve the system as a one-equation, one-variable system.

4. Once the value for one variable has been found, substitute that known value into one of the original equations and then solve for the other variable.

In general, suppose that we need to solve the system

$$a_1x + b_1y = c_1$$
$$a_2x + b_2y = c_2$$

where the a's, b's, and c's represent known quantities. Multiply the second equation by b_1/b_2 (assume that $b_2 \neq 0$):

$$a_1 x + b_1 y = c_1$$

$$\left(\frac{b_1 a_2}{b_2}\right) x + b_1 y = \frac{c_2 b_1}{b_2}$$

Now subtract the second equation from the first equation:

$$a_1 x - \left(\frac{b_1 a_2}{b_2}\right) x = c_1 - \frac{c_2 b_1}{b_2}$$

Solve this equation for x:

$$x = \frac{c_1 b_2 - b_1 c_2}{a_1 b_2 - b_1 a_2}$$

(If $a_1 b_2 - b_1 a_2 = 0$, then this formula doesn't work; we'll cover that case later.)

CONTRADICTORY EQUATION SYSTEMS

Example: Truck Selection

PROBLEM   Start with the constraint that the total capacity of the trucks must be 20:

$$x + 2y = 20$$

where x = number of small trucks and y = number of big trucks.

For the moment suppose that we no longer have the constraint $x + y = 14$. Each large truck contains a 50-gallon fuel tank, and each small truck contains a 25-gallon fuel tank. The trucks are filled from a storage tank with a total capacity of 400 gallons. The fueling manager decides that we should arrange our truck purchase so that the total capacity of the fuel tanks in the trucks is equal to the storage capacity:

$$25x + 50y = 400$$

How many trucks of each type should be purchased?

SOLUTION   Now we have this two-equation, two-variable system to solve:

$$x + 2y = 20$$
$$25x + 50y = 400$$

The graph of these two equations is shown in Figure 1-9. We know that the solution occurs at the point where the two lines cross, but we can see that these two lines don't ever cross. They are parallel. There is no pair of values for x and y that will satisfy both equations simultaneously.

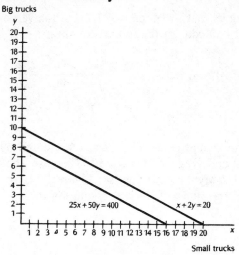

Figure 1-9

We saw that, if an equation system contains more equations than variables, it is quite likely that a contradiction will arise, meaning that there is no solution for the system. Now we see that a contradiction can arise even if the number of equations is equal to the number of variables. (Later we will discuss a more general method to determine whether a contradiction will arise in a set of equations.) If you try to solve a contradictory equation system by elimination, you will eventually run into a situation with a false equation, such as $0 = 100$.

If you are faced with a real problem where a contradiction arises, then one of the constraints has to be dropped. There is no way to meet all of the constraints, no matter how hard you try.

REDUNDANT EQUATION SYSTEMS

Example: Truck Selection

PROBLEM   After being frustrated by the preceding problem, suppose that the fueling manager replaces the old storage tank with a new storage tank having a capacity of 500 gallons.

Now we will try to solve this system:

$$x + 2y = 20$$
$$25x + 50y = 500$$

SOLUTION   The first equation can be converted into the form

$$y = 10 - \frac{1}{2}x$$

telling us that the slope is $-1/2$ and the vertical intercept is 10. We can convert the second equation:

$$y = \frac{500}{50} - \frac{25x}{50}$$

$$\rightarrow \qquad y = 10 - \frac{1}{2}x$$

The second equation is also represented by a line with slope $-1/2$ and vertical intercept 10. Therefore, both equations represent exactly the same line (see Figure 1-10). In this case any point along this line will work as a solution to both equations.

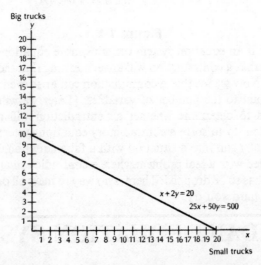

Figure 1-10

Earlier we found that a system with more variables than equations will quite likely have many solutions. Now we see that many solutions are possible even if there are exactly as many equations as variables. This situation arises if two of the equations are equivalent, meaning that they actually represent the same equation. For example, consider this system:

$$x + y = 30$$
$$x + y = 30$$

At first glance it looks like a two-equation, two-unknown system. However, if you look at it closely, you will see that both equations are the same. You cannot convert a one-equation, two-variable system into a two-equation, two-variable system simply by writing the same equation twice. This gives the same result as the situation in which two equations in the system are equivalent. If you try to solve a redundant system by elimination, you will sooner or later end up with a true but useless equation, such as $0 = 0$.

YOU SHOULD REMEMBER

For a system of simultaneous linear equations with two equations and two variables:

1. If the two equations contradict each other, then there will be no solution to the system. The two lines representing the equations will be parallel.

2. If the two equations are equivalent, then the system is redundant and there will be many solutions. Any solution to one of the equations will also be a solution for the other one. The two lines representing the equations will coincide.

THREE-EQUATION, THREE-VARIABLE SYSTEMS

Suppose that the Helpful Delivery trucking business suddenly expands. Now we, as advisers, need to consider buying some giant trucks. Each giant truck has a capacity of four containers. As before, each small truck has a capacity of one container and each big truck has a capacity of two containers. Now that the business has expanded, we need a total capacity of 36 containers:

$$x + 2y + 4z = 36$$

We will use z to represent the quantity of giant trucks purchased. Again x represents the quantity of small trucks, and y represents the quantity of big trucks.

In the new situation we must have the total number of trucks equal to 20:

$$x + y + z = 20$$

If these are the only equations to be considered, we have a two-equation, three-variable system. Since there are more variables than there are equations, we would expect there to be many solutions. For example, $(4, 16, 0)$, $(6, 13, 1)$, and $(8, 10, 2)$ are all solutions. (In each ordered pair, the value of x is written first, y is second, and z is third, as is traditional.)

However, our financial adviser informs us of another constraint: the total expenditure on the trucks must be \$325,000. Each small truck costs \$10,000; each big truck, \$18,000; and each giant truck, \$33,000. We will measure all dollar amounts in units of \$1,000, so we can write this equation:

$$10x + 18y + 33z = 325$$

Now we have a three-equation, three-variable system:

$$
\begin{aligned}
x + 2y + 4z &= 36 \\
x + y + z &= 20 \\
10x + 18y + 33z &= 325
\end{aligned}
$$

Our job is to find a solution. Unfortunately, the graphing method is very difficult since we now have three variables. It takes a three-dimensional diagram to represent a situation with three variables. (If there are four or more variables, it is impossible to draw a graph.) The substitution method is cumbersome in this case, so we will turn to a version of the elimination method. It would help if we could eliminate x from the last equation. To do that, we multiply both sides of the first equation by 10, and then subtract the result from the last equation:

$$
\begin{array}{rl}
10x + 18y + 33z = \quad 325 & \leftarrow \text{old last equation} \\
-10x + 20y + 40z) \quad -360 & \leftarrow \text{minus 10 times old first equation} \\
\hline
-2y - 7z = \; -35 & \leftarrow \text{new last equation}
\end{array}
$$

Now the system is

$$
\begin{aligned}
x + 2y + 4z &= 36 \\
x + y + z &= 20 \\
-2y - 7z &= -35
\end{aligned}
$$

Next, it would also help to eliminate x from the middle equation. To do that, we can subtract the first equation from the middle equation:

$$\begin{array}{rl} x + y + z = & 20 \quad \leftarrow \text{old middle equation} \\ \underline{-(x + 2y + 4z) \quad -36} & \quad \leftarrow \text{minus old first equation} \\ -y - 3z = -16 & \quad \leftarrow \text{new middle equation} \end{array}$$

Now the system is

$$\begin{array}{rl} x + 2y + 4z = & 36 \\ -y - 3z = & -16 \\ -2y - 7z = & -35 \end{array}$$

The elimination method has helped to simplify the system considerably. Note that the last two equations form a two-equation, two-variable system. To solve this system, we eliminate y from the last equation by multiplying the middle equation by 2 and then subtracting it from the last equation:

$$\begin{array}{rl} -2y - 7z = & -35 \quad \leftarrow \text{old last equation} \\ \underline{-(-2y - 6z) \quad -(-32)} & \quad \leftarrow \text{minus 2 times old middle equation} \\ -z = & -3 \quad \leftarrow \text{new last equation} \end{array}$$

The new version of the complete system is:

$$\begin{array}{rl} x + 2y + 4z = & 36 \\ -y - 3z = & -16 \\ -z = & -3 \end{array}$$

This equation system can be solved without difficulty. Note that the last equation contains only z and the middle equation contains only y and z. Only the first equation contains all three variables. We will say that this is a triangular system, since it looks a bit like a triangle.

We solve the last equation first, since it involves only z. Then we can substitute the known value for z into the middle equation to solve for y. Finally, we will substitute the known values for y and z into the first equation to solve for x.

From the last equation it is clear that $z = 3$. We substitute this into the middle equation:

$$\begin{array}{rl} & -y - 3 \times 3 = -16 \\ \rightarrow & y = 16 - 9 \\ \rightarrow & y = 7 \end{array}$$

Substituting $y = 7$ and $z = 3$ into the first equation gives

$$x + 2 \times 7 + 4 \times 3 = 36$$
$$\rightarrow \qquad x = 36 - 14 - 2$$
$$\rightarrow \qquad x = 10$$

Therefore the solution is $x = 10$, $y = 7$, $z = 3$.

After solving a system such as this, it is a good idea to verify your solution by checking to make sure that it does indeed satisfy all of the equations and that the values are appropriate. In some cases some of the values in the solution will be negative numbers, which may be inappropriate for a practical problem.

GRAPHICAL REPRESENTATION OF 3 BY 3 SYSTEMS

An equation in three variables, such as $ax + by + cz = d$, can be represented as a plane in three-dimensional space. (The coefficients a, b, c, and d represent known quantites. Assume that a, b, and c are not all zero. A plane is a flat two-dimensional surface, like a table top, that extends off to infinity.) If you have two equations with three variables, the solutions to the system will consist of all points where the two planes intersect. Two planes can intersect to form a line. However, the two planes could coincide (meaning that the two equations are equivalent), or they could be parallel (meaning that the two equations are contradictory, so there are no solutions to the system). See Figure 1-11.

A system of three equations in three variables can be represented by three planes. There are several possibilities for the solutions:

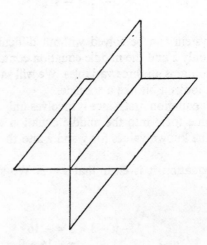

Figure 1-11

1. The three planes may intersect at one point. Then there is a unique solution for the system.

2. The three planes may intersect to form a line. Then there are an infnite number of solutions, all along that line.

3. The three planes may coincide. In this case the three equations are equivalent; any solution to one of the equations will also be a solution to the other two equations. There will be an infinite number of solutions for the system, all along that plane.

4. At least two of the three planes may be parallel to each other; which means the equations represented by those planes contradict each other so there is no solution to the system.

5. The intersections of the three planes may form three parallel lines. In this case there is no solution to the system, although no two equations contradict each other.

   See Figure 1-12.

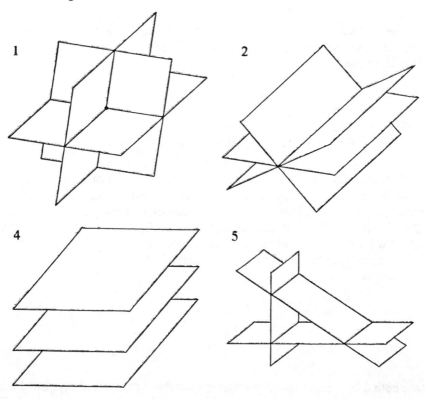

Figure 1-12

MATRIX MULTIPLICATION

Consider again the 3 by 3 equation system for the truck problem:

$$
\begin{aligned}
x + 2y + 4z &= 36 \\
x + y + z &= 20 \\
10x + 18y + 33z &= 325
\end{aligned}
$$

After writing this system several times, you are probably thinking, "There must be an easier way to write it." It shouldn't be necessary to write every letter in every equation. Let's write the system like this:

$$
\begin{pmatrix} 1 & 2 & 4 \\ 1 & 1 & 1 \\ 10 & 18 & 33 \end{pmatrix}
\begin{pmatrix} x \\ y \\ z \end{pmatrix}
=
\begin{pmatrix} 36 \\ 20 \\ 325 \end{pmatrix}
$$

The new way of writing the system contains exactly the same information as the old, long way. Note that all of the coefficients have been grouped together into this table:

$$
\begin{pmatrix} 1 & 2 & 4 \\ 1 & 1 & 1 \\ 10 & 18 & 33 \end{pmatrix}
$$

A rectangular table of numbers or variables like this is called a **matrix**. Each number is called an **element** of the matrix. A matrix may be classified by specifying its dimensions, meaning the number of rows and the number of columns it contains. Our coefficient matrix has three rows and three columns, so we will call it a 3 by 3 matrix. If the number of rows is equal to the number of columns, then the matrix is called a **square matrix**.

These two:

$$
\begin{pmatrix} x \\ y \\ z \end{pmatrix}
\begin{pmatrix} 36 \\ 20 \\ 325 \end{pmatrix}
$$

are both 3 by 1 matrices. (Note that the number of rows is always listed first.) A matrix with one column is also called a **column vector**, because it looks like one column of a matrix. A matrix with only one row is called a **row vector**.

The expression

$$\begin{pmatrix} 1 & 2 & 4 \\ 1 & 1 & 1 \\ 10 & 18 & 33 \end{pmatrix}\begin{pmatrix} x \\ y \\ z \end{pmatrix}$$

means that these two matrices are multiplied together. What does it mean to multiply two matrices? How do you do it? We need to develop some rules that determine how to multiply matrices. These rules will seem complicated at first, but we will find that the matrix multiplication procedure is designed to make it possible to express equation systems in a concise fashion.

The matrix that results from multiplying two other matrices will be called the **product matrix**. We know that we want to have the product of these two matrices equal to the left-hand side of the equation system:

$$\begin{pmatrix} 1 & 2 & 4 \\ 1 & 1 & 1 \\ 10 & 18 & 33 \end{pmatrix}\begin{pmatrix} x \\ y \\ z \end{pmatrix} \quad \text{should equal} \quad \begin{array}{l} x + 2y + 4z \\ x + y + z \\ 10x + 18y + 33z \end{array}$$

Therefore, to get the first element in the product matrix we take the first row of the left-hand matrix (1 2 4) and combine it with the first (in this case, only) column of the second matrix:

$$\begin{pmatrix} x \\ y \\ z \end{pmatrix}$$

Here is how we combine them. We multiply the two first elements (1 times x), multiply the two second elements (2 times y), multiply the two third elements (4 times z), and then add together these three products to get the result:

$$1 \times x + 2 \times y + 4 \times z$$

When a row vector is multiplied by a column vector like this, the result is called the **dot product**, or the **scalar product**, of the two vectors.

To find the second element in the product matrix, we take the dot product of the second row of the coefficient matrix and the xyz column vector. The third element of the product matrix is the dot product of the third row of the coefficient matrix and the xyz column vector.

If we give a name to each matrix, it is possible to represent the equation system in a very concise form. We will use **A** to represent the coefficient matrix:

$$\mathbf{A} = \begin{pmatrix} 1 & 2 & 4 \\ 1 & 1 & 1 \\ 10 & 18 & 33 \end{pmatrix}$$

Let **x** represent the column vector of variables:

$$\mathbf{x} = \begin{pmatrix} x \\ y \\ z \end{pmatrix}$$

Let **b** represent the column vector of right-hand-side constants:

$$\mathbf{b} = \begin{pmatrix} 36 \\ 20 \\ 325 \end{pmatrix}$$

Note that it is customary in books to print the names of vectors and matrices in boldface, such as **A**, **x**, or **b**. A name printed in italics, such as x, y, or z, is a variable name that represents a number.

The equation system can now be written in very concise form:

$$\mathbf{Ax} = \mathbf{b}$$

where **Ax** means the matrix product of **A** times **x**.

Now we can give the formal procedure for multiplying two matrices. First, we need to define the dot product.

Let **a** be a 1 by n row vector $(a_1, a_2, a_3, \ldots, a_n)$. Let **b** be an n by 1 column vector:

$$\begin{pmatrix} b_1 \\ b_2 \\ b_3 \\ \cdot \\ \cdot \\ \cdot \\ b_n \end{pmatrix}$$

Then the dot product of **a** and **b** (written as **a** · **b**) is the number found by multiplying together the corresponding elements in each of the two vectors, and then adding together all of those products:

$$\mathbf{a} \cdot \mathbf{b} = a_1 b_1 + a_2 b_2 + a_3 b_3 + \cdots + a_n b_n$$

Note that the dot product is a number, not a vector.

YOU SHOULD REMEMBER

Definition of Matrix Multiplication —
Let **A** be a matrix with m rows and n columns:

$$\mathbf{A} = \begin{pmatrix} a_{11} & a_{12} & \cdots & a_{1n} \\ a_{21} & a_{22} & \cdots & a_{2n} \\ \cdots & \cdots & \cdots & \cdots \\ a_{m1} & a_{m2} & \cdots & a_{mn} \end{pmatrix}$$

Let **B** be a matrix with n rows and p columns:

$$\mathbf{B} = \begin{pmatrix} b_{11} & b_{12} & \cdots & b_{1p} \\ b_{21} & b_{22} & \cdots & b_{2p} \\ \cdots & \cdots & \cdots & \cdots \\ b_{n1} & b_{n2} & \cdots & b_{np} \end{pmatrix}$$

Then the matrix product of **A** and **B** (written as **AB**) is a matrix with m rows and p columns. (The matrix product **AB** does not exist unless the number of *columns* in **A** is the same as the number of *rows* in **B**.)

Let $\mathbf{a}_{ri}$ represent the 1 by n row vector consisting of row i in the matrix **A**:

$$\mathbf{a}_{ri} = (a_{i1} \quad a_{i2} \quad \cdots \quad a_{in})$$

Let $\mathbf{b}_{cj}$ represent the n by 1 column vector consisting of column j in the matrix **B**:

$$\mathbf{b}_{cj} = \begin{pmatrix} b_{1j} \\ b_{2j} \\ \cdot \\ \cdot \\ \cdot \\ b_{nj} \end{pmatrix}$$

Then the element in row i, column j of the matrix product **AB** consists of the dot product $\mathbf{a}_{ri} \cdot \mathbf{b}_{cj}$:

$$\mathbf{AB} = \begin{pmatrix} \mathbf{a}_{r1} \cdot \mathbf{b}_{c1} & \mathbf{a}_{r1} \cdot \mathbf{b}_{c2} & \cdots & \mathbf{a}_{r1} \cdot \mathbf{b}_{cp} \\ \mathbf{a}_{r2} \cdot \mathbf{b}_{c1} & \mathbf{a}_{r2} \cdot \mathbf{b}_{c2} & \cdots & \mathbf{a}_{r2} \cdot \mathbf{b}_{cp} \\ \cdots & \cdots & \cdots & \cdots \\ \mathbf{a}_{rm} \cdot \mathbf{b}_{c1} & \mathbf{a}_{rm} \cdot \mathbf{b}_{c2} & \cdots & \mathbf{a}_{rm} \cdot \mathbf{b}_{cp} \end{pmatrix}$$

Writing this out the long way, without using the dot product notation, gives

$$\mathbf{AB} = \begin{pmatrix} [a_{11}b_{11} + a_{12}b_{21} + \cdots + a_{1n}b_{n1}] & \cdots & [a_{11}b_{1p} + a_{12}b_{2p} + \cdots + a_{1n}b_{np}] \\ [a_{21}b_{11} + a_{22}b_{21} + \cdots + a_{2n}b_{n2}] & \cdots & [a_{21}b_{1p} + a_{22}b_{2p} + \cdots + a_{2n}b_{np}] \\ & \cdots & \\ [a_{m1}b_{11} + a_{m2}b_{21} + \cdots + a_{mn}b_{n1}] & \cdots & [a_{m1}b_{1p} + a_{m2}b_{2p} + \cdots + a_{mn}b_{np}] \end{pmatrix}$$

This can also be written using *summation notation*:

$$\mathbf{AB} = \begin{pmatrix} \sum_{i=1}^{n} a_{1i}b_{i1} & \sum_{i=1}^{n} a_{1i}b_{i2} & \cdots & \sum_{i=1}^{n} a_{1i}b_{ip} \\ \sum_{i=1}^{n} a_{2i}b_{i1} & \sum_{i=1}^{n} a_{2i}b_{i2} & \cdots & \sum_{i=1}^{n} a_{2i}b_{ip} \\ \sum_{i=1}^{n} a_{mi}b_{i1} & \sum_{i=1}^{n} a_{mi}b_{i2} & \cdots & \sum_{i=1}^{n} a_{mi}b_{ip} \end{pmatrix}$$

The symbol Σ is the Greek capital letter sigma, which stands for summation. In summation notation, the expression below the sigma tells where to start (in this case, $i = 1$) and the symbol at the top tells where to stop (in this case, where $i = n$). The expression at the side tells what to add up (in this case, a_{mi} times b_{ip}). Therefore,

$$\sum_{i=1}^{n} a_{mi}b_{ip} \quad \text{means} \quad a_{m1}b_{1p} + a_{m2}b_{2p} + a_{m3}b_{3p} + \cdots + a_{mn}b_{np}$$

Here is an example of multiplying two 2 by 2 matrices:

$$\begin{pmatrix} 6 & 10 \\ 12 & 7 \end{pmatrix} \begin{pmatrix} 18 & 20 \\ 8 & 5 \end{pmatrix} = \begin{pmatrix} [\ 6 \times 18 + 10 \times 8] & [\ 6 \times 20 + 10 \times 5] \\ [12 \times 18 + \ 7 \times 8] & [12 \times 20 + \ 7 \times 5] \end{pmatrix}$$

$$= \begin{pmatrix} 188 & 170 \\ 272 & 275 \end{pmatrix}$$

Here is the general form for multiplying two 2 by 2 matrices:

$$\begin{pmatrix} a_{11} & a_{12} \\ a_{21} & a_{22} \end{pmatrix} \begin{pmatrix} b_{11} & b_{12} \\ b_{21} & b_{22} \end{pmatrix} = \begin{pmatrix} [a_{11}b_{11} + a_{12}b_{21}] & [a_{11}b_{12} + a_{12}b_{22}] \\ [a_{21}b_{11} + a_{22}b_{21}] & [a_{21}b_{12} + a_{22}b_{22}] \end{pmatrix}$$

Here is an example of multiplying two 3 by 3 matrices:

$$A = \begin{pmatrix} 10 & 7 & 12 \\ 11 & 6 & 3 \\ 5 & 1 & 2 \end{pmatrix}, \quad B = \begin{pmatrix} 4 & 17 & 15 \\ 29 & 21 & 25 \\ 9 & 19 & 8 \end{pmatrix}$$

$$AB = \begin{pmatrix} [10 \times 4 + 7 \times 29 + 12 \times 9] & [10 \times 17 + 7 \times 21 + 12 \times 19] & [10 \times 15 + 7 \times 25 + 12 \times 8] \\ [11 \times 4 + 6 \times 29 + 3 \times 9] & [11 \times 17 + 6 \times 21 + 3 \times 19] & [11 \times 15 + 6 \times 25 + 3 \times 8] \\ [5 \times 4 + 1 \times 29 + 2 \times 9] & [5 \times 17 + 1 \times 21 + 2 \times 19] & [5 \times 15 + 1 \times 25 + 2 \times 8] \end{pmatrix}$$

$$= \begin{pmatrix} 351 & 545 & 421 \\ 245 & 370 & 339 \\ 67 & 144 & 116 \end{pmatrix}$$

Here is the general form for multiplying two 3 by 3 matrices:

$$A = \begin{pmatrix} a_{11} & a_{12} & a_{13} \\ a_{21} & a_{22} & a_{23} \\ a_{31} & a_{32} & a_{33} \end{pmatrix}, \quad B = \begin{pmatrix} b_{11} & b_{12} & b_{13} \\ b_{21} & b_{22} & b_{23} \\ b_{31} & b_{32} & b_{33} \end{pmatrix}$$

$$AB = \begin{pmatrix} [a_{11}b_{11} + a_{12}b_{21} + a_{13}b_{31}] & [a_{11}b_{12} + a_{12}b_{22} + a_{13}b_{32}] & [a_{11}b_{13} + a_{12}b_{23} + a_{13}b_{33}] \\ [a_{21}b_{11} + a_{22}b_{21} + a_{23}b_{31}] & [a_{21}b_{12} + a_{22}b_{22} + a_{23}b_{32}] & [a_{21}b_{13} + a_{22}b_{23} + a_{23}b_{33}] \\ [a_{31}b_{11} + a_{32}b_{21} + a_{33}b_{31}] & [a_{31}b_{12} + a_{32}b_{22} + a_{33}b_{32}] & [a_{31}b_{13} + a_{32}b_{23} + a_{33}b_{33}] \end{pmatrix}$$

Matrix multiplication is unlike ordinary multiplication in one important respect: the order makes a difference. In ordinary multiplication the order does not make a difference. For example, $6 \times 7 = 7 \times 6$. (This is called the *commutative property* for ordinary multiplication.) The matrix product **AB** exists only if the number of columns in matrix **A** is the same as the number of rows in matrix **B**. For example, if **A** is an *m* by *n* matrix and **B** is an *n* by *p* matrix, then **AB** is an *m* by *p* matrix. The product **BA** does not even exist if the number of columns in **B** is not the same as the number of rows in **A**. Even if **AB** and **BA** both exist, they are not necessarily the same. For example:

$$\begin{pmatrix} 6 & 10 \\ 12 & 7 \end{pmatrix}\begin{pmatrix} 18 & 20 \\ 8 & 5 \end{pmatrix} = \begin{pmatrix} 188 & 170 \\ 272 & 275 \end{pmatrix}$$

$$\begin{pmatrix} 18 & 20 \\ 8 & 5 \end{pmatrix}\begin{pmatrix} 6 & 10 \\ 12 & 7 \end{pmatrix} = \begin{pmatrix} 348 & 320 \\ 108 & 115 \end{pmatrix}$$

SOLVING EQUATION SYSTEMS BY MATRIX TRIANGULARIZATION

Now we can use matrices to concisely solve the equation system for the truck problem:

$$\begin{pmatrix} 1 & 2 & 4 \\ 1 & 1 & 1 \\ 10 & 18 & 33 \end{pmatrix} \begin{pmatrix} x \\ y \\ z \end{pmatrix} = \begin{pmatrix} 36 \\ 20 \\ 325 \end{pmatrix}$$

We can express the system as a 3 by 4 matrix consisting of the 3 by 3 coefficient matrix adjacent to the 3 by 1 matrix of right-hand-side constants:

$$\begin{pmatrix} 1 & 2 & 4 & 36 \\ 1 & 1 & 1 & 20 \\ 10 & 18 & 33 & 325 \end{pmatrix}$$

Now we can perform operations on this matrix. Our goal is to triangularize the matrix; this means that all of the elements in the lower triangular-shaped part of the matrix will be zero. Then the matrix will have this form:

$$\begin{pmatrix} \# & \# & \# & \# \\ 0 & \# & \# & \# \\ 0 & 0 & \# & \# \end{pmatrix}$$

where the symbol " # " represents any number. We can perform the same moves that we performed when we simplified the 3 by 3 equation system on page 24, only now we will be working with the matrix that represents the equations instead of equations themselves.

The allowable moves are as follows:

1. We can multiply all of the elements in a single row by the same number.

2. We can add one row to (or subtract one row from) another row.

3. We can perform a combination move: multiply all elements in one row by another, and then add or subtract that row from another row.

These moves are allowable because they will not change the solution to the equation system that the matrix represents.

Move 1: Subtract 10 times the top row from the bottom row. The new matrix is

$$\begin{pmatrix} 1 & 2 & 4 & 36 \\ 1 & 1 & 1 & 20 \\ 0 & -2 & -7 & -35 \end{pmatrix}$$

(Compare the equation system on page 24.)

Move 2: Subtract the top row from the middle row. The new matrix is

$$\begin{pmatrix} 1 & 2 & 4 & 36 \\ 0 & -1 & -3 & -16 \\ 0 & -2 & -7 & -35 \end{pmatrix}$$

(Compare the equation system on page 25.)

Move 3: Subtract twice the middle row from the bottom row. The new matrix is

$$\begin{pmatrix} 1 & 2 & 4 & 36 \\ 0 & -1 & -3 & -16 \\ 0 & 0 & -1 & -3 \end{pmatrix}$$

Now we have turned the matrix into a triangularized matrix. Compare the equation system on page 25:

$$x + 2y + 4z = 36$$
$$-y - 3z = -16$$
$$- z = -3$$

This system can now be solved for z, then y, and finally x.

YOU SHOULD REMEMBER

A system of equations can be solved by setting up a combined matrix, consisting of the matrix of coefficients adjacent to the matrix of the right-hand-side constants. You can perform these operations on the matrix without changing the solution to the equation system it represents:

1. Multiply all elements in a row by a number.

2. Add one row to another row.

3. Add a multiple of one row to another row.

Perform operations on the matrix until it is in triangular form. Then the last row of the matrix represents a one-variable equation, which can be solved. You can then use this value to solve the two-variable equation that is represented by the second to the last row, and so on until all of the values have been found.

MATRIX ADDITION, SCALAR MULTIPLICATION, AND THE TRANSPOSE OF A MATRIX

Two matrices of the same dimensions can be added by adding each corresponding element. For example,

if **A** is the matrix $\begin{pmatrix} a_{11} & a_{12} \\ a_{21} & a_{22} \end{pmatrix}$ and **B** is the matrix $\begin{pmatrix} b_{11} & b_{12} \\ b_{21} & b_{22} \end{pmatrix}$

then

$$\mathbf{A} + \mathbf{B} \text{ is the matrix } \begin{pmatrix} [a_{11} + b_{11}] & [a_{12} + b_{12}] \\ [a_{21} + b_{21}] & [a_{22} + b_{22}] \end{pmatrix}$$

Note that matrix addition *does* follow the commutative property: **A** + **B** is the same as **B** + **A**.

A matrix consisting of all zeros is called a *zero matrix* (written as **0**). If it is added to another matrix of the same size, the original matrix stays the same:

$$\mathbf{A} + \mathbf{0} = \mathbf{A}$$

as long as **A** and **0** have the same dimensions.

It is possible to multiply a matrix by a single number (called a *scalar*). To do this, simply multiply every element of the matrix by that scalar. For example, 2**A** is the matrix

$$\begin{pmatrix} 2a_{11} & 2a_{12} \\ 2a_{21} & 2a_{22} \end{pmatrix}$$

It is possible also to flip a matrix over so that all of its rows become columns and all of its columns become rows. The resulting matrix is called the **transpose** of the original matrix. The transpose of matrix **A** is written as **A**′ (read as "A-prime" or "A transpose") or else as $\mathbf{A}^{\text{Tr}}$. If **A** has m rows and n columns, then **A**′ has n rows and m columns. For example, if **A** is the 3 by 4 matrix

$$\begin{pmatrix} 10 & 11 & 20 & 30 \\ 4 & 7 & 8 & 9 \\ 111 & 130 & 140 & 162 \end{pmatrix}$$

then **A′** is the 4 by 3 matrix

$$\begin{pmatrix} 10 & 4 & 111 \\ 11 & 7 & 130 \\ 20 & 8 & 140 \\ 30 & 9 & 162 \end{pmatrix}$$

IDENTITY MATRICES AND INVERSE MATRICES

A square matrix that has 0's everywhere except along the diagonal (all of the elements from the upper left-hand corner in a straight line down to the lower right-hand corner are 1's) is called an **identity matrix**.

$$\begin{pmatrix} 1 & 0 \\ 0 & 1 \end{pmatrix} \qquad \begin{pmatrix} 1 & 0 & 0 \\ 0 & 1 & 0 \\ 0 & 0 & 1 \end{pmatrix} \qquad \begin{pmatrix} 1 & 0 & 0 & 0 \\ 0 & 1 & 0 & 0 \\ 0 & 0 & 1 & 0 \\ 0 & 0 & 0 & 1 \end{pmatrix}$$

2 by 2 identity matrix   3 by 3 identity matrix   4 by 4 identity matrix

An identity matrix is symbolized by **I**. Identity matrices have the special property that another matrix remains unchanged when it is multiplied by an identity matrix: **IA = A** (provided that the product matrix **IA** exists). This also works the other way: **AI = A** (provided that the product matrix **AI** exists). In short, an identity matrix acts like the number 1 in ordinary multiplication. For example:

$$\begin{pmatrix} 1 & 0 & 0 \\ 0 & 1 & 0 \\ 0 & 0 & 1 \end{pmatrix} \begin{pmatrix} a_{11} & a_{12} \\ a_{21} & a_{22} \\ a_{31} & a_{32} \end{pmatrix}$$

$$= \begin{pmatrix} [1 \times a_{11} + 0 \times a_{21} + 0 \times a_{31}] & [1 \times a_{12} + 0 \times a_{22} + 0 \times a_{32}] \\ [0 \times a_{11} + 1 \times a_{21} + 0 \times a_{31}] & [0 \times a_{12} + 1 \times a_{22} + 0 \times a_{32}] \\ [0 \times a_{11} + 0 \times a_{21} + 1 \times a_{31}] & [0 \times a_{12} + 0 \times a_{22} + 1 \times a_{32}] \end{pmatrix}$$

$$= \begin{pmatrix} a_{11} & a_{12} \\ a_{21} & a_{22} \\ a_{31} & a_{32} \end{pmatrix}$$

Since there is matrix multiplication, you may be wondering whether there is such a thing as matrix division. No, there is not, but there is a related concept. For every real number (except 0) it is possible to calculate its inverse. For example, the inverse of 7 is 1/7 (also written as 7^{-1}). If you multiply a number by its inverse, then the result is 1, which is the identity element for ordinary multiplication:

$$7 \times 7^{-1} = 1$$

Now we will see whether we can find an **inverse matrix** for a particular matrix. If we start with a matrix **A**, we will represent the inverse matrix as $\mathbf{A}^{-1}$. The inverse matrix has the property that $\mathbf{AA}^{-1} = \mathbf{I}$.

In words, the product of the original matrix and its inverse matrix is an identity matrix. This also works the other way: $\mathbf{A}^{-1}\mathbf{A} = \mathbf{I}$.

For example, suppose that **A** is the 2 by 2 matrix

$$\begin{pmatrix} 1 & 2 \\ 1 & 1 \end{pmatrix}$$

It turns out that $\mathbf{A}^{-1}$ is the matrix

$$\begin{pmatrix} -1 & 2 \\ 1 & -1 \end{pmatrix}$$

(The appendix to Chapter 1 explains how matrix inverses can be calculated.) If we calculate the matrix product, we find that the result is the 2 by 2 identity matrix

$$\begin{pmatrix} 1 & 2 \\ 1 & 1 \end{pmatrix}\begin{pmatrix} -1 & 2 \\ 1 & -1 \end{pmatrix} = \begin{pmatrix} [1 \times (-1) + 2 \times 1] & [1 \times 2 + 2 \times (-1)] \\ [1 \times (-1) + 1 \times 1] & [1 \times 2 + 1 \times (-1)] \end{pmatrix}$$

$$= \begin{pmatrix} 1 & 0 \\ 0 & 1 \end{pmatrix}$$

Matrix inverses provide another method for solving systems of simultaneous linear equations. Suppose that we have the system

$$\mathbf{Ax = b}$$

We use matrix multiplication to multiply both sides by the matrix inverse $\mathbf{A}^{-1}$:

$$\mathbf{A}^{-1}\mathbf{Ax} = \mathbf{A}^{-1}\mathbf{b}$$

Since $\mathbf{A}^{-1}\mathbf{A} = \mathbf{I}$, this means

$$\mathbf{Ix} = \mathbf{A}^{-1}\mathbf{b}$$

Since $\mathbf{Ix = x}$, we have the solution:

$$\mathbf{x} = \mathbf{A}^{-1}\mathbf{b}$$

Therefore, if we know the matrix inverse $\mathbf{A}^{-1}$, all we have to do is multiply $\mathbf{A}^{-1}$ by the column vector of right-hand-side values, and we will find the solution for $\mathbf{x}$. For example, consider the two-equation, two-variable system for the truck problem on page 10, written in matrix notation:

$$\begin{pmatrix} 1 & 2 \\ 1 & 1 \end{pmatrix}\begin{pmatrix} x \\ y \end{pmatrix} = \begin{pmatrix} 20 \\ 14 \end{pmatrix}$$

The solution for x and y can be found by multiplying the inverse of the coefficient matrix by the column vector of right-hand-side constants:

$$\begin{pmatrix} x \\ y \end{pmatrix} = \begin{pmatrix} -1 & 2 \\ 1 & -1 \end{pmatrix}\begin{pmatrix} 20 \\ 14 \end{pmatrix} = \begin{pmatrix} -20+28 \\ 20-14 \end{pmatrix} = \begin{pmatrix} 8 \\ 6 \end{pmatrix}$$

YOU SHOULD REMEMBER

An identity matrix, symbolized by **I**, is a square matrix with 0's everywhere except along the diagonal, where there are 1's. Any matrix remains unchanged when it is multiplied by an identity matrix: **AI = I**. Also, **IA = A**.

The inverse of the matrix **A** is symbolized by $\mathbf{A}^{-1}$ (if it exists). The product of a matrix and its inverse is equal to the identity matrix: $\mathbf{A}\mathbf{A}^{-1} = \mathbf{I}$.

The solution to the equation system

Ax = b

can be found if the matrix inverse is known:

$\mathbf{x} = \mathbf{A}^{-1}\mathbf{b}$

THE DETERMINANT OF A MATRIX

We cannot find an inverse for every matrix. Only square matrices have inverses, but there are many square matrices that do not have inverses.

Here is a general formula for the inverse of a 2 by 2 matrix:

$$\begin{pmatrix} a_{11} & a_{12} \\ a_{21} & a_{22} \end{pmatrix}^{-1} = \begin{pmatrix} a_{22}/D & -a_{12}/D \\ -a_{21}/D & a_{11}/D \end{pmatrix}$$

where $D = a_{11}a_{22} - a_{21}a_{12}$.

Consider the equation system from page 21, written with matrix notation:

$$\begin{pmatrix} 1 & 2 \\ 25 & 50 \end{pmatrix} \begin{pmatrix} x \\ y \end{pmatrix} = \begin{pmatrix} 20 \\ 400 \end{pmatrix}$$

To calculate the matrix inverse for the matrix of coefficients $\begin{pmatrix} 1 & 2 \\ 25 & 50 \end{pmatrix}$, we need to first calculate D:

$$D = 1 \times 50 - 25 \times 2 = 0$$

Now we have a real problem, since the formula for the inverse of the matrix requires that we divide by D. Since we cannot divide by zero, we cannot calculate an inverse for this matrix. This makes sense, if you recall that we found that there was no solution for this equation system.

For any 2 by 2 matrix where $a_{11}a_{22} - a_{21}a_{12}$ is equal to zero, it will not be possible to find an inverse. Because the quantity $a_{11}a_{22} - a_{21}a_{12}$ determines the properties of the matrix, it is called the **determinant** of the matrix. If the determinant of a matrix is zero, then it does not have an inverse matrix.

We will write vertical lines on both sides of a matrix to indicate that the determinant is to be taken:

$$\begin{vmatrix} a_{11} & a_{12} \\ a_{21} & a_{22} \end{vmatrix} = a_{11}a_{22} - a_{21}a_{12}$$

We will also use "det" as an abbreviation for "determinant." For example, det **A** means to calculate the determinant of the matrix **A**.

YOU SHOULD REMEMBER

The determinant for a 2 by 2 matrix is found from this formula:

$$\begin{vmatrix} a_{11} & a_{12} \\ a_{21} & a_{22} \end{vmatrix} = a_{11}a_{22} - a_{21}a_{12}$$

If the determinant is zero, then the matrix does not have an inverse.

The concept of the determinant can also be applied to any square matrix. The determinant of a 3 by 3 matrix:

$$\begin{vmatrix} a_{11} & a_{12} & a_{13} \\ a_{21} & a_{22} & a_{23} \\ a_{31} & a_{32} & a_{33} \end{vmatrix}$$

is found from this formula:

$$a_{11}a_{22}a_{33} + a_{12}a_{23}a_{31} + a_{13}a_{32}a_{21} - a_{31}a_{22}a_{13} - a_{21}a_{12}a_{33} - a_{11}a_{23}a_{32}$$

The lines below show which elements are multiplied together to form the first three products in the formula:

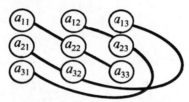

These lines show which elements are multipled together to form the last three products:

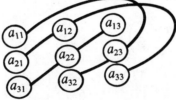

For example, this determinant:

$$\begin{vmatrix} 5 & 3 & 8 \\ 1 & 4 & 2 \\ 7 & 3 & 1 \end{vmatrix}$$

is found from the formula:

$$5 \times 4 \times 1 + 3 \times 2 \times 7 + 8 \times 3 \times 1 - 7 \times 4 \times 8 - 1 \times 3 \times 1 - 5 \times 2 \times 3 = -171$$

Section B of the appendix to Chapter 1 describes how to calculate determinants for matrices larger than 3 by 3. However, in those cases the calculation process becomes very tedious and is best left to a computer.

Here are some general properties of determinants:

1. If det **A** = 0, then **A** does not have an inverse matrix.

2. $\det \mathbf{I} = 1$.
   The determinant of any identity matrix is equal to 1.

3. $\det(\mathbf{AB}) = (\det \mathbf{A})(\det \mathbf{B})$
   The determinant of the product of two matrices is equal to the product of the individual determinants.

4. $\det(\mathbf{A}^{-1}) = 1/\det \mathbf{A}$.
   The determinant of a matrix is 1 over the determinant of its inverse matrix. For example, the inverse of the matrix

$$\begin{pmatrix} 5 & 3 & 8 \\ 1 & 4 & 2 \\ 7 & 3 & 1 \end{pmatrix}$$

is the matrix

$$\begin{pmatrix} 2/171 & -7/57 & 26/171 \\ -13/171 & 17/57 & 2/171 \\ 25/171 & -2/57 & -17/171 \end{pmatrix}$$

which has the determinant

$$\frac{2}{171} \times \frac{17}{57} \times \left(-\frac{17}{171}\right) + \left(-\frac{7}{57}\right) \times \frac{2}{171} \times \frac{25}{171} + \frac{26}{171} \times \left(-\frac{2}{57}\right) \times \left(-\frac{13}{171}\right)$$

$$-\frac{25}{171} \times \frac{17}{57} \times \frac{26}{171} - \left(-\frac{13}{171}\right) \times \left(-\frac{7}{57}\right) \times \left(-\frac{17}{171}\right) - \frac{2}{171} \times \frac{2}{171} \times \left(-\frac{2}{57}\right)$$

$$= -\frac{1}{171}$$

SOLVING EQUATION SYSTEMS WITH DETERMINANTS

Determinants provide an important clue for determining the nature of an equation system. Here is the general form for a two-equation, two-variable system:

$$\begin{pmatrix} a_1 & b_1 \\ a_2 & b_2 \end{pmatrix}\begin{pmatrix} x \\ y \end{pmatrix} = \begin{pmatrix} c_1 \\ c_2 \end{pmatrix}$$

We found a formula for the solution to this system:

$$x = \frac{c_1 b_2 - b_1 c_2}{a_1 b_2 - b_1 a_2}$$

$$y = \frac{a_1 c_2 - c_1 a_2}{a_1 b_2 - b_1 a_2}$$

(We found the formula for x in two ways: first by substitution and then by elimination; see pages 15 and 19. The formula for y can be found by substitution, once the formula for x has been found.)

These formulas can be expressed with determinants:

$$x = \frac{\begin{vmatrix} c_1 & b_1 \\ c_2 & b_2 \end{vmatrix}}{\begin{vmatrix} a_1 & b_1 \\ a_2 & b_2 \end{vmatrix}}, \qquad y = \frac{\begin{vmatrix} a_1 & c_1 \\ a_2 & c_2 \end{vmatrix}}{\begin{vmatrix} a_1 & b_1 \\ a_2 & b_2 \end{vmatrix}}$$

Now consider the general form for a 3 by 3 equation system:

$$\begin{pmatrix} a_1 & b_1 & c_1 \\ a_2 & b_2 & c_2 \\ a_3 & b_3 & c_3 \end{pmatrix} \begin{pmatrix} x \\ y \\ z \end{pmatrix} = \begin{pmatrix} d_1 \\ d_2 \\ d_3 \end{pmatrix}$$

The solution to this system can also be expressed with determinants:

$$x = \frac{\begin{vmatrix} d_1 & b_1 & c_1 \\ d_2 & b_2 & c_2 \\ d_3 & b_3 & c_3 \end{vmatrix}}{\begin{vmatrix} a_1 & b_1 & c_1 \\ a_2 & b_2 & c_2 \\ a_3 & b_3 & c_3 \end{vmatrix}}, \quad y = \frac{\begin{vmatrix} a_1 & d_1 & c_1 \\ a_2 & d_2 & c_2 \\ a_3 & d_3 & c_3 \end{vmatrix}}{\begin{vmatrix} a_1 & b_1 & c_1 \\ a_2 & b_2 & c_2 \\ a_3 & b_3 & c_3 \end{vmatrix}}, \quad z = \frac{\begin{vmatrix} a_1 & b_1 & d_1 \\ a_2 & b_2 & d_2 \\ a_3 & b_3 & d_3 \end{vmatrix}}{\begin{vmatrix} a_1 & b_1 & c_1 \\ a_2 & b_2 & c_2 \\ a_3 & b_3 & c_3 \end{vmatrix}}$$

We will not derive these formulas in this book; you will have to take our word for them.

Note that the form of the solution follows the same form as it did in the 2 by 2 case. For each variable, the denominator of the solution consists of the determinant of the matrix of coefficients for the equation system. The numerator for the solution for x consists of the determinant of the coefficient matrix, except that the column of coefficients of x has been replaced by the column of right-hand-side constants. Likewise, the numerators in the solutions for y and z consist of the determinant of the coefficient matrix, except that the column of coefficients for that variable has been replaced by the column of right-hand-side constants. The same pattern works for equation systems of any size. These formulas provide another method for solving systems of linear equations. The method is known as *Cramer's rule*.

Suppose that we try to solve this equation system:

$$\begin{pmatrix} 1 & 2 & 3 \\ 2 & 4 & 6 \\ 7 & 8 & 9 \end{pmatrix} \begin{pmatrix} x \\ y \\ z \end{pmatrix} = \begin{pmatrix} 14 \\ 28 \\ 40 \end{pmatrix}$$

We can use the formulas from Cramer's rule:

$$x = \frac{\begin{vmatrix} 14 & 2 & 3 \\ 28 & 4 & 6 \\ 40 & 8 & 9 \end{vmatrix}}{\begin{vmatrix} 1 & 2 & 3 \\ 2 & 4 & 6 \\ 7 & 8 & 9 \end{vmatrix}}, \quad y = \frac{\begin{vmatrix} 1 & 14 & 3 \\ 2 & 28 & 6 \\ 7 & 40 & 9 \end{vmatrix}}{\begin{vmatrix} 1 & 2 & 3 \\ 2 & 4 & 6 \\ 7 & 8 & 9 \end{vmatrix}}, \quad z = \frac{\begin{vmatrix} 1 & 2 & 14 \\ 2 & 4 & 28 \\ 7 & 8 & 40 \end{vmatrix}}{\begin{vmatrix} 1 & 2 & 3 \\ 2 & 4 & 6 \\ 7 & 8 & 9 \end{vmatrix}}$$

Unfortunately, when we calculate the determinants, we end up with

$$x = \frac{0}{0}, \quad y = \frac{0}{0}, \quad z = \frac{0}{0} \qquad 3$$

Since we know that we cannot divide by zero, these formulas do not do any good. When we look at the equation system, we can see why:

$$x + 2y + 3z = 14$$
$$2x + 4y + 6z = 28$$
$$7x + 8y + 9z = 40$$

The second equation can be obtained by multiplying both sides of the first equation by 2. Therefore, the first equation and the second equation are equivalent equations, which means that we really have only a two-equation, three-unknown system. There will be many solutions to this system. There will be many solutions to an equation system any time the Cramer's rule formulas give the result 0/0. This is consistent with what we found earlier: if the determinant of the matrix of coefficients is zero, then that matrix does not have an inverse and we cannot find a unique solution to the equation system.

Now consider this equation system:

$$x + 2y + 3z = 14$$
$$2x + 4y + 6z = 27$$
$$7x + 8y + 9z = 40$$

If we try to solve this system with Cramer's rule, we end up with

$$x = -\frac{6}{0}, \quad y = \frac{12}{0}, \quad z = -\frac{6}{0}$$

Again, we know that the formulas do not work because of the division by zero. This system is exactly the same as the first system, except that the right-hand-side constant for the second equation is 27 instead of 28. Now the first and second equations are not equivalent; instead they are contradictory. Since the system contains two equations that contradict each other, there is no solution for the system. This result will occur whenever the Cramer's rule formulas give results such as $a/0$, where a is some number other than zero.

These results also illustrate another general property of determinants: if one row of a matrix is a multiple of another row, then the determinant of that matrix will be zero. In this matrix:

$$\begin{pmatrix} 1 & 2 & 3 \\ 2 & 4 & 6 \\ 7 & 8 & 9 \end{pmatrix}$$

the second row can be found by multiplying each element in the first row by 2. Therefore, the determinant of the matrix is zero.

It is possible for a 3 by 3 system to be arranged so that no two equations are contradictory, but the system as a whole is contradictory. Consider this equation system:

$$\begin{pmatrix} 3 & 9 & 4 \\ 7 & 5 & 8 \\ 13 & 23 & 16 \end{pmatrix} \begin{pmatrix} x \\ y \\ z \end{pmatrix} = \begin{pmatrix} 10 \\ 20 \\ 30 \end{pmatrix}$$

If we calculate the determinant of the matrix of coefficients, we end up with zero. The Cramer's rule formulas give these results:

$$x = -\frac{520}{0}, \quad y = -\frac{40}{0}, \quad z = \frac{480}{0}$$

Therefore, there is no solution to this system. Look closely at the matrix of coefficients. There is a pattern:

$$13 = 2 \times 3 + 7$$
$$23 = 2 \times 9 + 5$$
$$16 = 2 \times 4 + 8$$

The third row can be found by multiplying the first row by 2 and then adding the second row. Any time it is possible to express one of the rows of a matrix as the sum of the other rows multiplied by some numbers, the determinant of the matrix is zero. The appendix to the chapter contains the technical definition for this situation.

Note that 30 does not equal $2 \times 10 + 20$. However, if we replaced the value 30 in the right-hand-side column vector by 40, then we could convert the system into a system with many solutions.

YOU SHOULD REMEMBER

Consider the equation system $\mathbf{Ax} = \mathbf{b}$, where $\mathbf{A}$ is a square matrix.

If the determinant of $\mathbf{A}$ is not zero, then there is a unique solution for the system.

If the determinant of $\mathbf{A}$ is zero, then either there are no solutions or there are many solutions.

Here is one final point to consider in solving systems of equations. Mathematically, a solution that involves negative numbers will be just as good as a solution with all nonnegative numbers. However, in many practical situations negative numbers have no meaning (for example, it does not mean anything for the Helpful Delivery Company to own -3 trucks). In the next chapter we will add the constraint that the variables must have nonnegative values.

Some of the material near the end of this chapter has become complicated. The calculations involved with matrices and determinants are quite tedious. In practice, you will usually be able to use a computer to perform the numerical calculations. The important part of the chapter is to learn the concepts involved with solving equation systems, and to develop an intuition for contradictory systems and redundant systems. Matrices and determinants provide powerful tools for understanding the nature of equation systems. The exercises provide more practice with these concepts. The appendix to the chapter contains additional details of the mathematics.

In Chapter 2, we take into account the fact that in reality many business problems involve constraints that are expressed as inequalities, instead of equations.

APPENDIX TO CHAPTER 1

A. GENERAL METHOD FOR CALCULATING A MATRIX INVERSE

Start with an *n* by *n* square matrix **A**. Create a new matrix with 2*n* rows and *n* columns, consisting of **A** stacked on top of an identity matrix. Then perform operations on this combined matrix to turn the top half into an identity matrix. The allowable operations are as follows:

1. Multiply one column of the matrix by a number.

2. Add one column to another column.

3. Perform a combination move: add a multiple of one column to another column.

Once the top half of the combined matrix has been turned into an identity matrix, the bottom half of the combined matrix will be the inverse matrix for the original matrix.

Here is an example of the procedure.

Find the inverse for the matrix:

$$\begin{pmatrix} 1 & 2 \\ 1 & 1 \end{pmatrix}$$

Set up the combined matrix:

$$\begin{pmatrix} 1 & 2 \\ 1 & 1 \\ 1 & 0 \\ 0 & 1 \end{pmatrix}$$

Subtract twice the first column from the second column:

$$\begin{pmatrix} 1 & 0 \\ 1 & -1 \\ 1 & -2 \\ 0 & 1 \end{pmatrix}$$

Add the second column to the first column, and multiply the second column by -1:

$$\begin{pmatrix} 1 & 0 \\ 0 & 1 \\ -1 & 2 \\ 1 & -1 \end{pmatrix}$$

The top half has been converted into an identity matrix, so the bottom half now is the inverse of the original matrix:

$$\begin{pmatrix} -1 & 2 \\ 1 & -1 \end{pmatrix}$$

B. GENERAL PROCEDURE FOR CALCULATING DETERMINANTS

The *minor* of a matrix element a_{ij} is the matrix consisting of all of the elements in the original matrix except for the elements in row i and column j. For example, the minor of the element 12 in the 3 by 3 matrix

$$\begin{pmatrix} 11 & 12 & 13 \\ 21 & 22 & 23 \\ 31 & 32 & 33 \end{pmatrix}$$

is the matrix

$$\begin{pmatrix} 21 & 23 \\ 31 & 33 \end{pmatrix}$$

To calculate the determinant of the matrix, start with the first element in the first row. Multiply this element by the determinant of its minor. Next, subtract the product of the second element in the first row and the determinant of its minor. Then add the product of the third element and its minor. Keep going in the same way, alternating between negative and positive signs, until you have reached the end of the first row.

For example, a 3 by 3 determinant can be found from the expression

$$\begin{vmatrix} a_1 & b_1 & c_1 \\ a_2 & b_2 & c_2 \\ a_3 & b_3 & c_3 \end{vmatrix} = a_1 \begin{vmatrix} b_2 & c_2 \\ b_3 & c_3 \end{vmatrix} - b_1 \begin{vmatrix} a_2 & c_2 \\ a_3 & c_3 \end{vmatrix} + c_1 \begin{vmatrix} a_2 & b_2 \\ a_3 & b_3 \end{vmatrix}$$

This method will work for a matrix of any size. However, note that you will need to calculate four 3 by 3 determinants in order to calculate a 4 by 4 determinant. The number of calculations becomes very large as the size of the determinants increases. You don't have to use the first row for this process, though; you can use any row or column. For example, if a row or column contains a lot of zeros, it is easiest to work along that one.   However, for any matrix larger than 3 by 3 it is best to have a computer do the work.

C. LINEAR INDEPENDENCE

A *linear combination* of a set of vectors consists of a sum of the vectors where each vector is multiplied by a number (called a *scalar*). For example, consider this matrix:

$$\begin{pmatrix} 3 & 9 & 4 \\ 7 & 5 & 8 \\ 13 & 23 & 16 \end{pmatrix}$$

Each row can be thought of as a row vector. Therefore, "2 times the first row plus the second row" is a linear combination of the first and second rows. Since the third row of the matrix is equal to 2 times the first row plus the second row, we can say that the third row is a linear combination of the first and second rows.

The second row is equal to the third row minus twice the first row, so the second row is a linear combination of the first and third rows. Likewise, the first row is a linear combination of the second and third rows.

Consider the matrix:

$$\begin{pmatrix} 1 & 0 & 1 \\ 0 & 1 & 0 \\ 1 & 0 & 3 \end{pmatrix}$$

Here it is not possible to express any of the rows as a linear combination of the other rows. In such cases the rows are said to be *linearly independent*.

Usually it is not obvious whether the rows are linearly independent. However, we can make use of an important theorem:

THEOREM. *If the rows of a matrix are linearly independent, then the determinant of the matrix is not zero. Conversely, if the rows of the matrix are not linearly independent, then the determinant is zero.*

Interestingly enough, if the rows of a square matrix are linearly independent, then the columns of the matrix are also linearly independent. If the rows are not linearly independent, then neither are the columns. For example, in this matrix:

$$\begin{pmatrix} 3 & 9 & 4 \\ 7 & 5 & 8 \\ 13 & 23 & 16 \end{pmatrix}$$

the third column is equal to 13/12 times the first column plus 1/12 times the second column.

KNOW THE CONCEPTS

DO YOU KNOW THE BASICS?

Test your understanding of Chapter 1 by answering the following questions:

1. How can you tell whether an equation is a linear equation?
2. Do the matrix methods discussed in this chapter work for linear equation systems or nonlinear systems?
3. As long as you perform the same arithmetical operation on both sides, you may perform any operation you like on an equation. What is the one exception to this statement?
4. When will an equation system have no solution?
5. When will an equation system have many solutions?
6. When can an equation system be solved by graphing? How do you do so?
7. What operations can be performed on an equation system without changing the solutions to that system?
8. Is it acceptable to multiply both sides of an equation by zero?
9. If a linear equation system has the same number of equations as variables, is it possible to find a unique solution to the system?
10. How can you tell whether a matrix has an inverse?

TERMS FOR STUDY

coefficient	marginal cost
column vector	matrix
consumption function	row vector
determinant	scalar product

dot product	slope
element	square matrix
elimination method	substitution method
identity matrix	transpose
inverse matrix	vertical intercept
linear equation	

PRACTICAL APPLICATION

COMPUTATIONAL PROBLEMS

For Exercises 1–10, use elimination or substitution to solve the equation systems for x and y. If you do not find a unique solution, describe the nature of the equation system.

1. $3x + 5y = 18$
$6x + 10y = 36$

2. $3x + 5y = 18$
$6x + 10y = 32$

3. $x + y = 10$
$2x + y = 16$

4. $2x + 3y = 28$
$5x - 3y = 7$

5. $10x + 14y = 444$
$8x + 7y = 267$

6. $8x + 20y = 16$
$14x + 35y = 28$

7. $x + 2y = 3$
$2x + 3y = 6$

8. $2.5x + 4.8y = 16.93$
$1.8x + 9.6y = 22.02$

9. $7.82x - 4.36y = 11.94$
$-14.59x + 8.63y = 23.85$

10. $11.840x + 19.620y = 131.65$
$15.984x + 26.487y = 171.15$

11–20. Express each of the equation systems in Exercises 1–10 in matrix notation. Calculate the determinant and the inverse matrix (if possible) for the matrix of coefficients.

21. Determine the value that k must have if the following system is to have a solution:

$$10x + 6y = 30$$
$$20x + 12y = k$$

22. Determine the value that k must have if the following system is to have an infinite number of solutions:

$$8x + 12y = 2$$
$$12x + ky = 3$$

23. Determine the value that k must *not* have if the following system is to have a solution:

$$6x + 9y = 15$$
$$8x + ky = 18$$

For Exercises 24–30, determine the unique solution to each equation system, if possible. If there is a contradiction, describe the contradiction. If there are an infinite number of solutions, then give formulas that either
  (a) express x and y in terms of z or constants, or
  (b) express x in terms of y and z or constants.

24. $x + y + z = 14$
$12x - 3y + 9z = 18$
$4x - y + 3z = 12$

25. $x + y + z = 165$
$2x + y + z = 190$
$x + 2y + z = 240$

26. $x + y + z = 14$
$2x + y - 2z = 8$
$3x + 2y - z = 12$

27. $x + 2y + z = 14$
$x - y + z = 8$
$2x + y + 2z = 22$

28. $3x + 12y - 6z = 3$
$x + 4y - 2z = 1$
$5x + 20y - 10z = 5$

29. $x + 2y + z = 36$
$5x - y - 2z = 8$
$13x + y - z = 92$

30. $x + 2y + z = 14$
$x - y + 2z = 16$
$2x + y + 3z = 30$

31. A factory produces three products (radios, tape recorders, and stereos) and operates with three capacity limits (assembly, storage, and inspection). The three constraints can be represented by these equations:

assembly constraint: $2x + 4y + 10z = 2{,}540$
storage constraint: $x + 2y + 15z = 2{,}170$
inspection constraint: $x + y + 3z = 830$

where $x =$ number of radios, $y =$ number of tape recorders, and $z =$ number of stereos. How many of each product can be produced?

32. Consider an economy that can be described by these equations:

$Y = C + 1 + G$ ($Y =$ national income,
      $G =$ government spending).

$C = 10 + \dfrac{4}{5}(Y - T)$ ($C =$ consumption spending, $T =$ taxes)

$T = \dfrac{Y}{4}$

$I = 60 - 100r$ ($r =$ interest rate)

$$G = 30$$
$$L = \frac{Y}{4} - 100r \qquad (L = \text{money demand})$$
$$M = 57 \qquad (M = \text{money supply})$$
$$L = M$$

Solve for the values of Y and r.

33. Write the equation system from Exercise 32 in matrix notation.

34. Find a general formula for Y for this system:

$$Y = C + I + G$$
$$C = a + b(Y - T)$$
$$T = t_0 Y$$
$$I = I_0 - hr$$
$$M = kY - nr$$

Express the formula for Y in terms of G, a, b, t_0, I_0, h, k, n, and M.

35. Input/output analysis, pioneered by economist Wassily Leontief, can be used to analyze the allocation of products among different industries. Consider an economy with n industries. Each industry needs to use the products of the other industries (for example, the electricity industry needs to use the products of the coal industry). Let a_{ij} represent the amount of product i that is needed for each unit of production of product j. Let k_i represent the amount of final product desired for product i. (The final product amount is the amount that is available for consumers to use after the demands of all of the other industries have been satisfied.) For each product i, the following equation must be satisfied:

$$a_{i1}x_1 + a_{i2}x_2 + \cdots + a_{in}x_n + k_i = x_i$$

where x_j is the amount of product j that is produced in total, and $a_{ij}x_j$ is the amount of product j that is used in industry i.

Use matrix notation to express the solution for x_1 to x_n.

36. Consider an economy with just three industries (steel, coal, and electricity). The matrix of requirements of each industry is as follows:

	steel	coal	electricity
steel	0.05	0.10	0.20
coal	0.40	0.15	0.60
electricity	0.25	0.30	0.20

To produce 1 unit of the product designated at the top of the column, it is necessary to use the indicated amounts of the other products in each row. For example, each unit of coal production requires 0.10 unit of steel.

The final demands are as follows: 200 units steel, 150 units coal, 180 units electricity. How much of each good needs to be produced? Use the result from Exercise 35.

ANSWERS

KNOW THE CONCEPTS

1. In a linear equation, there is no variable raised to any power other than 1, and no variables are multiplied together.

2. Linear equation systems.

3. You cannot divide by zero.

4. If there are more independent equations than variables, or if at least two of the equations contradict each other.

5. If there are more variables than equations, or if some of the equations in the system are redundant.

6. When there are two linear equations with two variables, each equation can be graphed as a line. The solution to the system occurs where the two lines cross.

7. (a) Multiply both sides of an equation by a constant; (b) add one equation to another equation; (c) add a multiple of one equation to another equation.

8. It is acceptable, but it doesn't accomplish anything. The resulting equation is $0 = 0$, which does not give you any information about the solution to the original equation.

9. There will not be a solution if two of the equations contradict each other. There will be more than one solution if two of the equations are redundant, or if one of the equations can be expressed as a linear combination of the other equations. Otherwise, there will be a unique solution if the number of equations matches the number of variables.

10. Only square matrices have inverses. If the determinant of the matrix is nonzero, then the matrix has an inverse.

PRACTICAL APPLICATION

1. The second equation can be formed by multiplying both sides of the top equation by 2. Therefore, the system is redundant, and there are an infinite number of solutions.

2. No solutions

3. $x = 6, y = 4$

4. $x = 5, y = 6$

5. $x = 15, y = 21$

6. Redundant equations; infinite number of solutions

7. $x = 3, y = 0$

8. $x = 3.7, y = 1.6$

9. $x = 53.44, y = 93.11$

10. No solutions

11. Equation system written in matrix notation:

$$\begin{pmatrix} 3 & 5 \\ 6 & 10 \end{pmatrix} \begin{pmatrix} x \\ y \end{pmatrix} = \begin{pmatrix} 18 \\ 36 \end{pmatrix}$$

	Determinant	Inverse
11.	0	—
12.	0	—
13.	-1	$\begin{pmatrix} -1 & 1 \\ 2 & -1 \end{pmatrix}$
14.	-21	$\begin{pmatrix} 0.143 & 0.143 \\ 0.238 & -0.095 \end{pmatrix}$
15.	-42	$\begin{pmatrix} -0.167 & 0.333 \\ 0.190 & -0.238 \end{pmatrix}$
16.	0	—
17.	-1	$\begin{pmatrix} -3 & 2 \\ 2 & -1 \end{pmatrix}$
18.	15.360	$\begin{pmatrix} 0.625 & -0.312 \\ -0.177 & 0.163 \end{pmatrix}$
19.	3.874	$\begin{pmatrix} 2.228 & 1.125 \\ 3.766 & 2.018 \end{pmatrix}$
20.	0	—

21. 60

22. 18

23. 12

24. The last two equations contradict each other, so there is no solution.

25. $x = 25, y = 75, z = 65$

26. There are an infinite number of solutions for each pair of equations, but there is no solution to the entire system. To see this, add the second equation to the first equation, and then subtract the third equation. The result is the equation $0 = 10$.

27. There are an infinite number of solutions on one line. The variable y must have the value 2. For a given value of z, x is equal to $10 - z$.

28. The three equations are equivalent. Any solution to one of the equations is also a solution to the other two. If you choose the values for y and z, then the value of x can be found from the formula $x = 1 + 2z - 4y$.

29. $x = 6.857$, $y = 10.667$, $z = 7.81$

30. There are an infinite number of solutions along one line. If you choose the value of z, then the values for x and y can be found from these formulas:

$$y = (z - 2)/3, \quad x = (46 - 5z)/3.$$

31. $x = 300$, $y = 260$, $z = 90$

    (You might think that the constraints should be written as inequalities, rather than equalities, since you are not forced to use all of the available capacity. This issue will be discussed in the next chapter.)

32. $Y = 241.5$, $r = 0.034$. (This equation system has eight equations, but it can be solved readily by substitution since most of the equations contain only two or three of the variables.)

33.
$$\begin{pmatrix} 1 & -1 & -1 & -1 & 0 & 0 & 0 & 0 \\ -0.8 & 1 & 0 & 0 & 0.8 & 0 & 0 & 0 \\ 0.25 & 0 & 0 & 0 & -1 & 0 & 0 & 0 \\ 0 & 0 & 1 & 0 & 0 & 100 & 0 & 0 \\ 0 & 0 & 0 & 1 & 0 & 0 & 0 & 0 \\ -0.25 & 0 & 0 & 0 & 0 & 100 & 1 & 0 \\ 0 & 0 & 0 & 0 & 0 & 0 & 0 & 1 \\ 0 & 0 & 0 & 0 & 0 & 0 & 1 & -1 \end{pmatrix} \begin{pmatrix} Y \\ C \\ I \\ G \\ T \\ r \\ L \\ M \end{pmatrix} = \begin{pmatrix} 0 \\ 10 \\ 0 \\ 60 \\ 30 \\ 0 \\ 57 \\ 0 \end{pmatrix}$$

34. $Y = \dfrac{n(a + I_0 + G) + hM}{n[1 - b(1 - t_0)] + hk}$

35. Let $\mathbf{A}$ be the n by n matrix with a_{ij} equal to the element in row i and column j, $\mathbf{k}$ be the n by 1 matrix of final demands, and $\mathbf{x}$ be the n by 1 matrix giving the amount produced of each good. The equation system can be written as follows:

$$\mathbf{Ax} + \mathbf{k} = \mathbf{x} \quad \text{or} \quad (\mathbf{I} - \mathbf{A})\mathbf{x} = \mathbf{k}$$

The solution is

$$\mathbf{x} = (\mathbf{I} - \mathbf{A})^{-1}\mathbf{k}$$

36. The matrix $(\mathbf{I} - \mathbf{A})^{-1}$ is

$$\begin{pmatrix} 1.383 & 0.387 & 0.636 \\ 1.300 & 1.964 & 1.798 \\ 0.920 & 0.858 & 2.123 \end{pmatrix}$$

and the amounts that must be produced are as follows: steel = 449.24, coal = 878.28, electricity = 694.74.

2

LINEAR PROGRAMMING PROBLEMS WITH TWO VARIABLES

KEY TERMS

feasible region   a set of points that satisfy all of the constraints in a linear programming problem

linear programming   the study of problems where the goal is to maximize (or minimize) a particular linear function, called the *objective function*, subject to a set of constraints that are expressed as linear equations or inequalities

objective function   a function of several variables in a situation where the goal is to determine values of these variables that maximize or minimize the value of the objective function, subject to meeting a set of constraints

---

THE FURNITURE PRODUCTION PROBLEM

The Good'n'Solid Woodworks Company has asked us for advice in planning its production schedule. The company makes two products: chairs and tables. Machines perform each of the crucial steps in the production process. In the short run there is no possibility of expanding the factory or obtaining more machines, so we must base our decision on the existing capacity. (The question of whether to expand the facilities is an important long-run question. We will consider it later.)

The process for producing the chairs and tables consists of three steps. First, the main body of each item is cut by a table saw. The table body consists of one large sheet; the chair body consists of two smaller sheets. Second, another saw cuts the boards that are used for the legs. Each table has three legs, and each chair has one leg, which is attached to a flared base. Third, after the pieces have been cut, the items are assembled. There are two assembly machines, one for tables and one for chairs.

Each of these machines has a limited capacity, so four constraints limit the amount of furniture that can be produced:

1. Table assembly: The table assembly machine can produce a maximum of 50 tables per day.

2. Chair assembly: The chair assembly machine can produce a maximum of 60 chairs per day.

3. Leg production: The saw that cuts the legs can produce 170 legs per day.

4. Cutting machine: It takes 3.43 minutes to cut the wood for each table, and twice as long (6.86 minutes) to cut the two smaller pieces of wood needed for each chair. The factory operates 8 hours (480 minutes) each day. (At present we are assuming that it is not possible to operate the factory overtime.)

The goal of the factory is to maximize the total profit. The profit for each piece of furniture is the selling price minus the cost of the wood and other production costs. The profit for each table is \$7; the profit for each chair is \$2.

Suppose that we tried to produce 50 tables and 60 chairs, which would earn a total revenue of $7 \times 50 + 2 \times 60 = \$470$. However, we cannot produce that many tables and chairs because of the limited capacity of the machines. If we produced 50 tables and 60 chairs, we would use $3 \times 50 + 1 \times 60 = 210$ legs, and the cutting machine would need to operate $3.43 \times 50 + 6.86 \times 60 = 583$ minutes. However, our leg machine can produce only 170 legs per day, and the factory is open only 480 minutes per day. Therefore, the 50-table, 60-chair combination is out of reach, given our current capacity limitations.

MATHEMATICAL STATEMENT OF LINEAR PROGRAMMING PROBLEMS

We must choose the production plan that maximizes the total profit yet meets all four constraints. This problem is an example of a **linear programming** problem. In a linear programming problem there is an **objective function**, whose value we are trying to maximize or minimize. In this case our objective function is the profit, which we are trying to maximize. The problem contains two choice variables: the quantity of tables and the quantity of chairs produced. The problem also contains four constraints.

Now we will state the problem mathematically. Let x represent the quantity of tables produced, and let y represent the quantity of chairs. The objective function is as follows:

$$\text{profit} = 7x + 2y$$

Here are the four constraints:

table assembly constraint:	$x \leq 50$
leg production constraint:	$3x + y \leq 170$
cutting constraint:	$3.43x + 6.86y \leq 480$
chair assembly constraint:	$y \leq 60$

Note that the constraints are written as inequalities. The symbol "$\leq$" means "less than or equal to." In economic terms, it is obvious why the constraints are written as inequalities, rather than as equalities. There is no requirement that all machines be used at their full capacity. For example, we could produce only 30 tables per day if we wanted to. In that case the table assembly machine would be idle part of the time, since it has a capacity of 50 tables.

It is a shame to waste capacity, so we might wish to use each machine at its full capacity. However, that doesn't work. Suppose that the four constraints were as follows:

$$x = 50$$
$$3x + y = 170$$
$$3.43x + 6.86y = 480$$
$$y = 60$$

This is a four-equation system with two unknowns. As we found in Chapter 1, there is usually no way to find a solution to a simultaneous equation system that has more equations than unknowns. Looking at the problem mathematically, we are very fortunate that the four constraints contain inequalities, instead of equalities.

When we state the problem mathematically, there is one more type of constraint we must add: the values of the variables must be positive. It is perfectly obvious to you and me that there is no such thing as -2 chairs, but that fact is not obvious in our system of mathematical inequalities. Therefore, we must include two additional constraints:

$$x \geq 0, \qquad y \geq 0$$

These two constraints are called, quite logically, **nonnegativity constraints.** Notice that they are written with a "greater than or equal to" sign, since zero is a permissible value for either variable.

Here is one helpful simplification. It is possible to divide both sides of an inequality by a positive number to produce a new inequality that is equivalent to the original one. We divide both sides of the cutting constraint by 3.43:

$$\frac{3.43x}{3.43} + \frac{6.86y}{3.43} \leq \frac{480}{3.43}$$

The result is easier to deal with:

$$x + 2y \leq 140$$

Here is the complete mathematical statement of our linear programming problem:

$x =$ quantity of tables produced $y =$ quantity of chairs produced

Maximize $7x + 2y$
subject to:
$$x \leq 50$$
$$3x + y \leq 170$$
$$x + 2y \leq 140$$
$$y \leq 60$$
$$x \geq 0$$
$$y \geq 0$$

There is another type of constraint you might think we should add. Since it is not practicable to produce half of a table, perhaps we should add a constraint requiring that x and y be whole numbers. In practice this constraint is often not needed; the cases where it is are covered in Chapter 8.

We can save writing if we express the problem using matrix notation, explained in Chapter 1:

Max $7x + 2y$
subject to:

$$\begin{pmatrix} 1 & 0 \\ 3 & 1 \\ 1 & 2 \\ 0 & 1 \end{pmatrix} \begin{pmatrix} x \\ y \end{pmatrix} \leq \begin{pmatrix} 50 \\ 170 \\ 140 \\ 60 \end{pmatrix}$$

GRAPHING THE FEASIBLE SOLUTIONS

Now we have to solve the problem. In the next three chapters we will develop a general solution procedure (called the *simplex algorithm*). Now, though, we can solve the problem by drawing a graph of the situation.

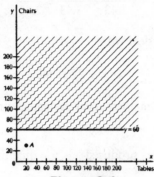

Figure 2-1

Figure 2-1 shows a graph where the quantity of chairs produced (y) is measured along the vertical axis, and the quantity of tables produced (x) is measured along the horizontal axis. Any combination of chairs and tables can be represented as a point on this diagram. For example, point A shows 20 tables and 30 chairs. Note that our graph shows only nonnegative values of x and y, which are just what we need because we will be looking only at nonnegative values for the numbers of tables and chairs. From now on we will use the term *point* to mean a pair of values that make up a possible production plan.

Now we need to start indicating the constraints on the graph. First, we look at the constraint $y \leq 60$. If we draw a graph of the equation $y = 60$, the result is a horizontal line that crosses all of the points whose y-coordinate is 60. (See Figure 2-1.) This line divides the plane into two regions: points where $y < 60$ (which are below the line), and points where $y > 60$ (which are above the line). We can eliminate all points above the line because they don't meet the chair assembly constraint. The points that are eliminated are shaded in the figure.

Figure 2-2 illustrates the table assembly constraint ($x \leq 50$). The graph of the equation $x = 50$ is a vertical line. All points to the left of the line satisfy the constraint; all points to the right of the line can be eliminated from consideration.

The inequality for the leg production constraint is $3x + y \leq 170$. We draw a graph of the equation $3x + y = 170$. This graph will also be a line, but it will not be horizontal or vertical. (See Figure 2-3.) We can rewrite the equation as

$$y = -3x + 170$$

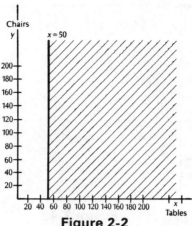

Figure 2-2

which tells us that the slope of the line is -3. The region on one side of the line satisfies the inequality $3x + y < 170$, and the region on the other side of the line does not satisfy it. You should be able to convince yourself that all points below and to the left of the line meet the constraint. All points above and to the right of the line (the region that is shaded) do not meet the constraint, so we can eliminate them from consideration.

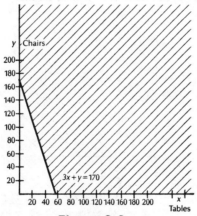

Figure 2-3

Figure 2-4 shows the graph of the cutting constraint: $x + 2y \le 140$. We graph the line $x + 2y = 140$. All points below the line satisfy the constraint, and all points above the line do not. The equation of the line can be rewritten as

$$y = -\frac{1}{2}x + 70$$

which tells us that the slope is $-1/2$.

To solve our problem we need to identify the points that satisfy *all* of the four constraints. It would help to draw graphs of all the constraints on the same

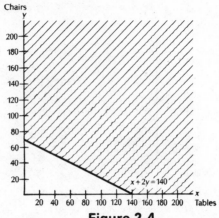

Figure 2-4

diagram. We will imagine that each of the four preceding diagrams was drawn on transparent plastic, and we will put the four diagrams one on top of another. (See Figure 2-5.) Any point that is shaded in the new diagram can be eliminated because it fails to meet at least one of the constraints. The six-sided region that is not shaded consists of the points that satisfy all of the constraints. A point satisfying the constraints is called a *feasible* point. Therefore, we will call the region satisfying all constraints the **feasible region.**

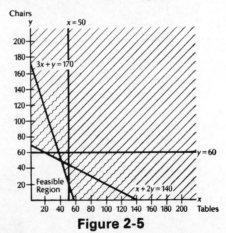

Figure 2-5

In our case the feasible region has six corners. One corner is at $(0, 0)$; another is at $(0, 60)$; and another is at $(50, 0)$. It would help to identify the locations of the other three corners. By looking carefully at the graph, we can read the locations of the corners, but it is best to use algebra to find the exact locations of the points. Each corner point occurs at the intersection of two lines representing constraints. For example, corner point A in Figure 2-6 represents the point that exactly meets the leg production constraint with no excess capacity ($3x + y = 170$) and that meets the cutting constraint with no excess capacity

$(x + 2y = 140)$. Therefore, to find the coordinates of the corner point, we need to solve a simultaneous equation system with two equations and two unknowns:

$$3x + y = 170$$
$$x + 2y = 140$$

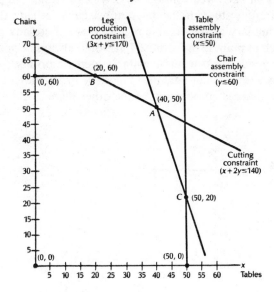

Figure 2-6

To solve this system, we multiply both sides of the first equation by 2, and then subtract the second equation from the first one. The value of x is 40. Substituting this value back into the equation $x + 2y = 140$ gives us the equation

$$40 + 2y = 140 \quad \text{or} \quad 2y = 100 \quad \text{or} \quad y = 50$$

Therefore, the corner point has coordinates (40, 50). (See Figure 2-6.)

Corner point B [coordinates (20, 60)] exactly satisfies the chair assembly constraint and the cutting constraint. Corner point C [coordinates (50, 20)] satisfies the table assembly constraint and the leg production constraint.

YOU SHOULD REMEMBER

Each constraint in a linear programming problem with two variables can be represented as a line. All points on one side of the line satisfy the constraint; the points on the other side of the line do not. The feasible region consists of the points that satisfy all of the constraints.

FINDING THE OPTIMAL POINT

Now that we have identified the feasible region, our search for the optimal solution has been narrowed considerably. We can reduce the possibilities even further. By carefully studying the diagram, we can eliminate all points that are not on the boundary of the feasible region. If we chose any point not on the boundary, such as point Q in Figure 2-7, it would always be possible to produce more of both goods. That would inevitably increase profits. At a point on the boundary, however, it is not possible to increase production of one of the items unless we also decrease production of the other item.

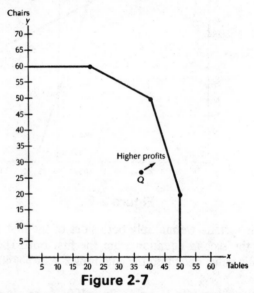

Figure 2-7

Now we need a way to search through the boundary points until we find the optimum point. Suppose we guess that the optimum is at point ($x = 50, y = 9$). This point would earn a total profit of $7 \times 50 + 2 \times 9 = 368$. We need to know whether there are other points on the boundary of the feasible region that would earn greater profits. We can say this much about any other possible point: the profit must be greater than 368, or equal to 368, or less than 368. (Logically, these are the only possibilities.) Let's look for all other points with profits equal to 368. Those points are given by the solutions to this equation:

$$7x + 2y = 368$$

which defines a line. The equation can be written in the form

$$y = -\frac{7}{2}x + \frac{368}{2}$$

which tells us that the slope of the line is $-7/2$. The graph of the line is shown in Figure 2-8. This line is called an **isoprofit line**, since all points on the line have the same profit. [The prefix *iso-* means "same"; it is used in words such as *isobar* ("same pressure") and *isotope* ("same number of protons").] For example, point (38, 51) is also on the line, and sure enough the profit is also equal to 368:

$$7 \times 38 + 2 \times 51 = 368$$

All points that are below the isoprofit line will have lower profits than points on the line. For example, point (0, 0) is below the line, and it has a profit of zero. All points that are above the isoprofit line will have greater profits than the points on the line. We can see from Figure 2-8 that there are many points in the feasible region that are above the line, so clearly point (50, 9) is not the optimum.

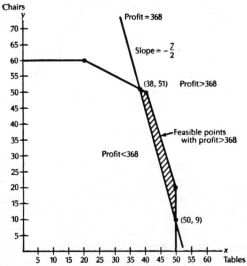

Figure 2-8

We can draw more isoprofit lines, and we can use these lines to help us find the optimal point. Each value of the profit will correspond to a different isoprofit line. Let P represent the level of the profit, c_x equal the profit from good x (which is 7 in our example), and c_y equal the profit from good y (2 in our example). Then the general equation for an isoprofit line can be written:

$$c_x x + c_y y = P$$

This can be rewritten as

$$y = -\frac{c_x}{c_y} x + \frac{P}{c_y}$$

Therefore, the slope of each line is $-c_x/c_y$. All of the isoprofit lines will be parallel. The intercept for each line will be different because the value of P (the profit) will be different.

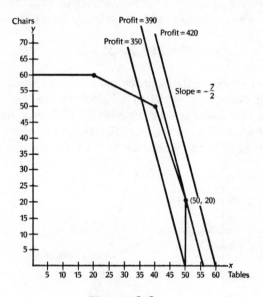

Figure 2-9

Figure 2-9 shows three different isoprofit lines for our example. Each line is labeled by indicating the amount of profit earned by the points on the line. None of the points on the line earning profits of 420 is in the feasible region. We would be glad to earn a profit of 420 if we could, but that amount is out of reach. Therefore, we will need to restrict our attention to the remaining two isoprofit lines. Many points along the line representing profits of 350 are feasible, but many points in the feasible region are above this line. Any time an isoprofit line cuts across the feasible region in such a manner that some points in the feasible region are above the line, the optimum cannot be on that line. There will be other feasible points that have higher profits. Therefore, the optimum must occur where an isoprofit line just touches the feasible region at one point.

The middle isoprofit line in Figure 2-9, representing a profit of 390, looks just right. It touches the boundary of the feasible region at point (50, 20), so it is a feasible point. Any point that is above the isoprofit line is outside the feasible region. Therefore, there is no way to do better. We have found the solution: produce 50 tables and 20 chairs, earning a profit of 390. The table assembly machine will be used at its full capacity (50 tables). The leg production machine will also be used at full capacity ($3 \times 50 + 1 \times 20 = 170$ legs). However, we will not use the full capacity of the chair assembly machine or the cutting machine.

Jubilantly we take our results to the managers of the furniture factory. They are very pleased, but they tell us one sobering fact: the prices of tables and chairs frequently change, as does the price of the wood used to make the furniture. As a result, the profit per unit for each piece of furniture changes. We need to think of a general procedure that will allow us to directly solve any linear programming problem, so we will not need to repeat the laborious analysis that led us to the optimum in this case.

The diagram showing the feasible region and the isoprofit lines provides an important clue. We need to find a point where an isoprofit line just touches the boundary of the feasible region at one point. The slope of the isoprofit lines depends on the per-unit profit for tables and chairs, so the slope will change if the per-unit profits change. For example, suppose that the per-unit profit for tables changes to $c_x = 2$, and the per-unit profit for chairs changes to $c_y = 10$. The slope of the isoprofit lines (equal to $-c_x/c_y$) then becomes $-1/5$. (See Figure 2-10.) The line representing a profit of 640 touches the boundary at the point where $x = 20$, $y = 60$, so this is the new optimum. Note that we will be producing more chairs and fewer tables than we did when c_x equaled 7 and c_y equaled 2. There is a very logical reason for this. Since chairs have now become more profitable in relation to tables, we will naturally want to produce more chairs than we did originally. Also, since we have to stay on the boundary of the feasible region, producing more chairs will inevitably mean producing fewer tables.

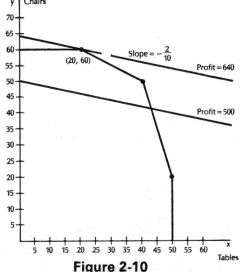

Figure 2-10

There is a pattern to these results. Note that the optimum always occurs at a corner point of the feasible region—a point where two of the lines representing the constraints intersect. This fact is the key to developing a solution method for linear programming problems: we can restrict our attention to corner points. The slope of the isoprofit lines determines which corner point will be optimum.

YOU SHOULD REMEMBER

An isoprofit line consists of all points that have the same value for the profit. All points above the isoprofit line will have greater profit; all points below the line will have less profit.

The optimal solution will occur at one of the corner points of the feasible region. The isoprofit line that passes through the optimum will not cross any other point inside the feasible region.

MINIMIZING PROBLEMS

Linear programming problems have a wide variety of applications. Here is an example of the opposite type of linear programming problem, where the objective function represents a value we are trying to minimize. Suppose that we are trying to choose an optimal diet involving two foods: rice and oat cereal. The diet must meet minimum requirements for three nutrients: protein, iron, and thiamine. The optimal diet will meet all of the nutrient requirements at the lowest possible cost. (A realistic diet problem would involve a large number of foods and nutrients, but linear programming could still be used to find optimum.)

We need a table showing the requirement for each nutrient, and the amount of each nutrient contained in each food:

| Nutrient | Requirement | Contained in: | |
		Cereal (1 ounce)	Rice (1 cup)
Protein	21 g	6 g	6 g
Thiamine	1 mg	0.30 mg	0.24 mg
Iron	12 mg	5 mg	1.5 mg

g = grams; mg = milligrams.

The cereal costs 20 cents per ounce, and the rice costs 15 cents per cup. Let x represent the amount of cereal, and y represent the amount of rice. Then the linear programming problem can be written as follows:

Minimize $20x + 15y$
subject to:

    protein constraint: $6x + 6y \geq 21$
    thiamine constraint: $0.3x + 0.24y \geq 1$
    iron constraint: $5x + 1.5y \geq 12$

Note that the constraints are written with inequality signs ("$\geq$" means "greater than or equal to"), since it is permissible to include more than the required amount of any nutrient.

Figure 2-11 shows a graph of the feasible region. Again each equation can be represented as a line, with the points on one side of the line satisfying the constraint. The shaded region indicates the points that are not feasible. In minimization problems the feasible region has no upper boundary.

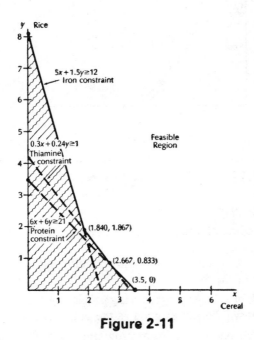

Figure 2-11

The solution will again occur at a corner point on the boundary of the feasible region. Figure 2-12 shows an **isocost line**. Isocost lines are very similar to the isoprofit lines we discussed earlier. *Isocost* means "same cost," so all of the points along an isocost line represent diet combinations with the same cost. The slope of the isocost lines will be $-c_x/c_y$, where $c_x = 20$ is the cost of good x (cereal) and $c_y = 15$ is the cost of good y (rice). Therefore, the optimal diet occurs at the point where $x = 1.84$, $y = 1.867$, which represents a cost of 64.8 cents.

In Chapter 3 we begin to develop a more general method for solving linear programming problems.

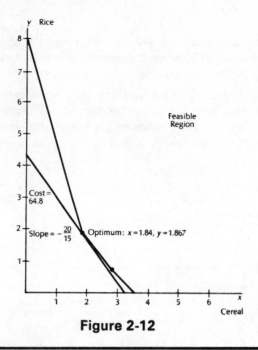

Figure 2-12

KNOW THE CONCEPTS

DO YOU KNOW THE BASICS?

Test your understanding of Chapter 2 by answering the following questions:

1. Give an intuitive explanation why the optimum point must be one of the corner points of the feasible region.

2. Can you think of a linear programming problem where a point that is not a corner point will be just as good as the optimal corner point?

3. Can the feasible region in a linear programming problem have a dent in it, as shown in Figure 2-13? Why or why not?

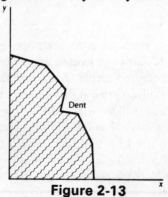

Figure 2-13

4. List two differences between a linear programming problem and a problem requiring the solution to a system of simultaneous linear equations.

5. Can the variables in a linear programming problem be zero at the optimum?

6. Can the variables in a linear programming problem be negative at the optimum?

7. How does the isoprofit line change if the profits for the two goods change? Give an intuitive explanation.

8. How many isoprofit lines can you draw?

TERMS FOR STUDY

feasible region	linear programming
isocost line	nonnegativity constraints
isoprofit line	objective function

PRACTICAL APPLICATION

COMPUTATIONAL PROBLEMS

For Exercises 1–5, consider the furniture production problem presented in the chapter.

1. In each of the following cases, what quantity of chairs and of tables will be produced if the profits from the two products are as given?
   (a) tables: 8; chairs: 2
   (b) tables: 6; chairs: 6
   (c) tables: 4; chairs: 9
   (d) tables: 9; chairs: 3

2. Suppose that the profit for each chair remained constant at 2.
   (a) What range of values for the profit per table would cause you to produce 50 tables?
   (b) What range of values for the profit per table would cause you to produce 40 tables?
   (c) What range of values for the profit per table would cause you to produce 20 tables?

3. Given the four capacity constraints, would a situation ever arise where the optimum would involve the production of no chairs?

For Exercises 4 and 5, suppose that the profit per table remains constant at 7 and the profit per chair remains constant at 2.

4. Suppose that leg production capacity has expanded so much that the leg production constraint can be ignored. The other three constraints remain unchanged. What is the optimal level of production?

5. Suppose that table assembly capacity has expanded so much that the table assembly constraint can be ignored. The other three constraints, including the leg production constraint, remain as given in the chapter. What is the optimal level of production?

Solve Exercises 6–11 by graphing the feasible region in each case.

6. A factory produces plates and bowls, subject to the following constraints:

- The number of plates produced must be less than or equal to 30.

- The number of bowls produced must be less than or equal to 36.

- Each plate requires 6 ounces of clay, each bowl requires 18 ounces of clay, and the total amount of clay must be less than or equal to 684.

Each bowl can be sold for a profit of $6, and each plate for a profit of $3. How much of each good should be produced to maximize the profit? (Put the number of plates on the horizontal axis.)

7. Suppose you have enrolled at a university that offers two kinds of courses: hard courses and easy courses. Hard courses are worth 2 credits each, and easy courses are worth 1 credit. Here are the requirements to graduate:

- You must earn at least 36 total credits.

- You must take at least 12 easy courses.

- You must take at least six hard courses.

Each hard course costs $300, and each easy course costs $100. (Put the number of easy courses on horizontal axis.)

(a) How many hard courses and how many easy courses should you take if you want to graduate at the lowest possible cost?

(b) Suppose the requirement that you take at least 12 easy courses is abolished (the other two requirements stay the same). How will that change your answer for the optimal number of courses to take?

(c) Suppose the requirement that you take at least six hard courses is abolished [the other two requirements stay the same as they are in part (a)]. How will that change your answer for the optimal number of courses to take?

8. A business needs to buy some trucks. It must choose between small trucks (which have a capacity of one container) and big trucks (which have a capacity of two containers). The following three constraints must be satisfied:

- Purchase a total of at least 12 trucks.

- Purchase at least two big trucks.

- Purchase trucks that have a total capacity of at least 18 containers.

   Each small truck costs $6,000, and each big truck costs $9,000. (Put the number of big trucks on the horizontal axis.)
   (a) What is the optimal number of small trucks and big trucks to purchase?
   (b) By how much would the price of big trucks have to increase to cause you to decrease the number of big trucks that you purchase at the optimal solution?

9. You are comparing two brands of cereal to determine the cost-minimizing diet, subject to constraints for three nutrients:

Cereal Brand	Nutrient 1	Nutrient 2	Nutrient 3	Price of Cereal
	Amount of Nutrient for Each Cereal			
X	2	1	1	3
Y	1	2	1	2
Requirement for each nutrient:	12	10	9	

How much of each type of cereal should be included in the diet?

10. A computer company produces two types of computers: model 1, with floppy disks, and model 2, with a hard disk. There are five capacity limitations:

Resource	Amount Used for Each Model 1 Machine	Amount Used for Each Model 2 Machine	Capacity Limit
Floppy disk production	1	0	30
Hard disk production	0	1	60

Resource	Amount Used for Each Model 1 Machine	Amount Used for Each Model 2 Machine	Capacity Limit
Controller circuits	20	2	620
Assembling machine	2	4	260
Testing station	1	1	58

Each model 1 machine sells for $1,500, and each model 2 machine sells for $3,000. (Put the number of model 1 machines on the horizontal axis.)
(a) How much of each machine should be produced to earn the maximum revenue?
(b) How much could the revenue be increased if the capacity of the assembling machine could be raised by 10 percent?

11. A company faces the following linear programming problem:

Maximize $18x + 30y$
subject to:
    sales constraint: $12x + 18y \leq 108$
    storage constraint: $5x + 3y \leq 75$
    production constraint: $10x + 20y \leq 300$
    shipping constraint: $3x + 15y \leq 180$

Determine the optimal values for x and y.

ANSWERS

KNOW THE CONCEPTS

1. All of the points above an isoprofit line have higher values for the profit. If some points above the isoprofit line are in the feasible region, then you cannot be at the optimum. The isoprofit line must pass through one of the corner points of the feasible region if there are to be no feasible points above the line.

2. This situation will occur if the isoprofit lines happen to be parallel to one of the line segments comprising the boundary of the feasible region. (See Figure 2-14.) However, in a linear programming problem it is not possible for a noncorner point to have a better value of the objective function than the optimal corner point.

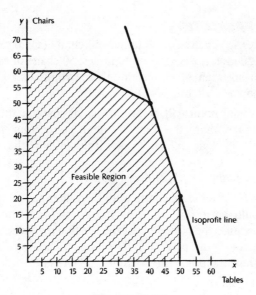

Figure 2-14

3. No. Each constraint in a linear programming problem can be represented as a line, and the points that satisfy the constraint are on one side of the line. If the feasible region had a dent, then you could find at least one constraint such that some feasible region points were on one side of the line representing that constraint, and some feasible region points were on the other side. It would not be possible for all of these points to meet that constraint.

4. (1) A linear programming problem usually involves inequality constraints, instead of equations. (2) In a system of simultaneous equations, there will often be only one solution that satisfies all of the equations. In a linear programming problem, there will generally be many solutions that satisfy all of the constraints. The goal is to find the one solution that achieves the best value for the objective function.

5. Yes.

6. No. A linear programming problem is set up with the assumption that the variables are required to be nonnegative.

7. If the profit of the good on the horizontal axis increases in relation to the good on the vertical axis, then the isoprofit lines become steeper. This means that you no longer need as large a quantity for the horizontal-axis good to achieve a given level of profit.

8. As many as you like. Each isoprofit line corresponds to a different value of the profit.

PRACTICAL APPLICATION

1. (a) 50 tables, 20 chairs (b) 40 tables, 50 chairs (c) 20 tables, 60 chairs
    (d) Either 50 tables, 20 chairs or 40 tables, 50 chairs or any point on the straight-line segment connecting these two points. (This is the situation shown in Figure 2-14.)

2. (a) The optimal point will be 50 tables, 20 chairs if the isoprofit lines are steeper than the line segment connecting points $(50, 20)$ and $(40, 50)$. This will be the case if the price of the tables is greater than 6.
    (b) Between 6 and 1   (c) Less than 1

3. If the profit for producing chairs were zero, then the point for 50 tables, 0 chair would be just as good as the point for 50 tables, 20 chairs. However, because the boundary of the feasible region between these two points is vertical, the point for 50 tables, 0 chair will never be more profitable than the point for 50 tables, 20 chairs.

4. 50 tables, 45 chairs

5. 56.67 tables, 0 chair

6. 30 plates, 28 bowls. See Figure 2-15, which shows the objective function value at each corner point so that you can see which is the optimum.

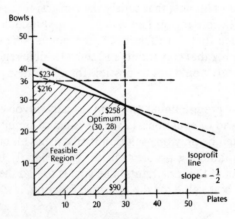

Figure 2-15

7. (a) 6 hard, 24 easy. See Figure 2-16.
    (b) In part (a), you are taking more than 12 easy courses. Therefore, the requirement that you must take 12 easy courses has no effect, so its removal will not change the optimum.
    (c) The requirement that you take six hard courses did make a difference in part (a). If that requirement is removed, then the optimum plan is to take 36 easy courses.

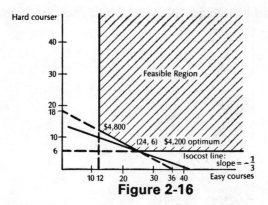

Figure 2-16

8. (a) 6 big trucks, 6 small trucks. See Figure 2-17.
   (b) The price would have to increase by at least $3,000.

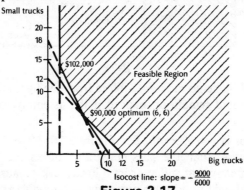

Figure 2-17

9. $X = 3$, $Y = 6$. See Figure 2-18.

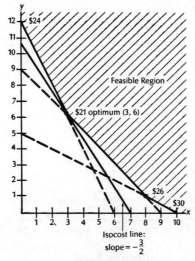

Figure 2-18

10. (a) 28 model 1 machines, 30 model 2 machines. See Figure 2-19.

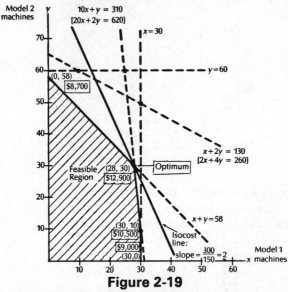

Figure 2-19

(b) It would make no difference. Note from the figure that the feasible region would remain unchanged if the assembly constraint disappeared.

11. The optimum is $y = 6$, $x = 0$. See Figure 2-20. Note that none of the constraints other than the sales constraint affects the feasible region. This is a company that suffers from a bottleneck because its sales force is too small. It will not do this company any good to expand any other capacity unless it also expands its sales force. Chapter 6 contains further discussion of this issue.

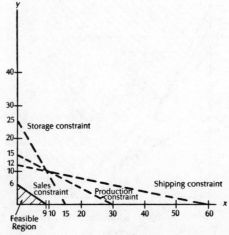

Figure 2-20

3

SEARCHING FOR THE OPTIMAL BASIC FEASIBLE SOLUTION

KEY TERMS

basic feasible solution   a basic solution that is also feasible (that is, all variables are nonnegative); the basic feasible solutions correspond to the corner points of the feasible region

basic solution   a solution to the Constraint Simultaneous Equation (CSE) system for a linear programming problem where the number of nonzero variables is the same as (or, in exceptional cases, less than) the number of constraints

slack variable   a variable included in a linear programming problem that measures the excess capacity associated with a particular constraint; the inclusion of slack variables converts inequality constraints into equations

Now we will develop a mathematical method for solving linear programming problems. The graphical method we used in Chapter 2 has one advantage: the diagram illustrates clearly the nature of the constraints of the problem, and the procedure needed to find the optimum point. However, there are two big disadvantages to the graphical solution method. First, it is a lot of work to draw graphs accurately. We want a method that involves a step-by-step arithmetic procedure, which we will then turn over to a computer to perform the actual process of calculation. Second, the graphical method does not work if there are more than two choice variables. Since paper has only two dimensions, you cannot draw diagrams in more than two dimensions.

We will return to the Good'n'Solid Woodworks Company discussed in Chapter 2. At the moment, the profit for tables is 4 and the profit for chairs is 5. Here is the problem:

x = quantity of tables produced y = quantity of chairs produced

Maximize $4x + 5y$
subject to:
      table assembly constraint: $x \quad \leq 50$
      leg production constraint: $3x + y \leq 170$
      cutting constraint: $x + 2y \leq 140$
      chair assembly constraint: $y \leq 60$
      nonnegativity constraints: $x \geq 0$
                                      $y \geq 0$

SLACK VARIABLES

The first step in our mathematical solution method will be to add some new variables called **slack variables**. At first this seems to make matters more complicated, but in reality it helps because it allows us to replace the inequalities with equations. One slack variable is added for each constraint. In our case, we will have four slack variables. Each slack variable measures the amount of unused capacity, or slack, for its corresponding constraint.

For example, consider the leg production constraint:

$$3x + y \leq 170$$

We rewrite this constraint as follows:

$$3x + y + s_2 = 170$$

The slack variable s_2 measures the difference between the maximum number of legs we could be producing (170) and the number of legs we are actually using ($3x + y$). If we were using the leg production machine at full capacity, then s_2 would be equal to zero. If we were producing 20 tables and 60 chairs, then we would be using 120 legs, and s_2 would equal 50.

There is one other constraint we need to add: the value of s_2 cannot be negative. Letting a slack variable become negative is a sneaky way to get around a constraint mathematically, but of course this would not work in the real world. For example, we could not let $x = 50$, $y = 60$ (thus using 210 legs) and then set s_2 equal to -40 to account for the fact that we are using more legs than we are capable of producing.

We will call the slack variables s_1, s_2, s_3, s_4. After adding the slack variables, the constraints look like this:

$$
\begin{array}{llll}
\text{table assembly:} & x & + s_1 & = 50 \\
\text{leg production:} & 3x + y & + s_2 & = 170 \\
\text{cutting:} & x + 2y & + s_3 & = 140 \\
\text{chair assembly:} & y & + s_4 = 60
\end{array}
$$

We will refer to these four equations as the **CSE system,** short for *Constraint Simultaneous Equation system.*

The CSE system can be written in matrix notation:

$$
\begin{pmatrix}
1 & 0 & 1 & 0 & 0 & 0 \\
3 & 1 & 0 & 1 & 0 & 0 \\
1 & 2 & 0 & 0 & 1 & 0 \\
0 & 1 & 0 & 0 & 0 & 1
\end{pmatrix}
\begin{pmatrix}
x \\ y \\ s_1 \\ s_2 \\ s_3 \\ s_4
\end{pmatrix}
=
\begin{pmatrix}
50 \\ 170 \\ 140 \\ 60
\end{pmatrix}
$$

We now have six variables: the two choice variables (x, y) and the four slack variables (s_1, s_2, s_3, s_4). There are only four equations. For a simultaneous equation system with more variables than equations, there are many solutions. We can immediately discard many of the solutions to the CSE system, since many solutions correspond to points that are not feasible. How will we recognize a nonfeasible solution? If the value of x or y is negative, we know immediately that we are not looking at a point that represents a solution to our problem in the real world. If one of the slack variables is negative, we have violated the constraint corresponding to this variable (see above). Therefore, a **feasible solution** is a set of values for $(x, y, s_1, s_2, s_3, s_4)$ that solves the CSE system, with all values for $(x, y, s_1, s_2, s_3, s_4)$ nonnegative. In general, the CSE system has many feasible solutions.

YOU SHOULD REMEMBER

Slack variables are included in a linear programming problem to measure the excess capacity associated with each constraint. The inclusion of slack variables makes it possible to write each constraint as an equation, instead of an inequality.

BASIC SOLUTIONS

Here is one way we could find a solution: choose any nonnegative values we like for any two of six variables and plug those values into the CSE system, creating a four-equation, four-unknown system. It is convenient to set two of the variables equal to zero and then solve for the remaining four variables. This type of solution is called a **basic solution**. It sounds as if we have pulled the term *basic solution* out of thin air. In fact, however, there is a logical mathematical reason for the use of this term, which we will explain later.

Here is the general definition of a basic solution: Suppose that we have a linear programming problem with m constraints and n total variables (including both choice variables and slack variables). In our case $m = 4$ and $n = 6$. A solution to the *CSE* system in which exactly $n - m$ variables are equal to zero is called a *basic solution*. It is also correct to say that the number of nonzero variables in a basic solution is equal to the number of constraints (m). According to this definition, a basic solution need not be a feasible solution to the linear programming problem. If a basic solution is indeed feasible (in other words, all of the n variables have nonnegative values), then the solution is called, logically enough, a **basic feasible solution**. (It is possible in exceptional cases for a basic solution to have more than $n - m$ variables equal to zero. This complication will be considered in Chapter 5.) We will soon see why basic solutions are important.

For our problem there are three types of basic solutions:

1. Both x and y are zero; all of the slack variables are nonzero. This is feasible, but it is a rather silly solution because it involves doing nothing.

2. Either x or y is zero, and one of the slack variables is zero.

3. Both x and y are nonzero; two of the slack variables are nonzero, and the other two slack variables are zero.

We found in Chapter 2 that three of the feasible-region corner points [(20, 60), (40, 50), and (50, 20)] occur where two constraints are met exactly (in other words, the corresponding slack variables are zero), while the other two constraints have excess capacity (in other words, the corresponding slack variables are positive). These three corner points are basic feasible solutions of the third type. (See Figure 3-1.) Point (0, 0), also a corner point, is a basic feasible solution of the first type. The other two corner points [(0, 60) and (50, 0)] are basic feasible solutions of the second type. Therefore, the basic feasible solutions correspond to the corner points of the feasible region. Suddenly we realize why basic feasible solutions are important. In Chapter 2 we found that the optimal solution to the linear programming problem under discussion was at a corner point. Therefore, we have discovered a result that is a fundamental theorem of linear programming:

THEOREM. *The optimal solution to a linear programming problem will be a basic feasible solution.*

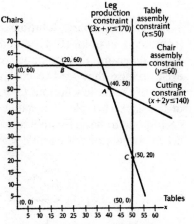

Figure 3-1

(There are some complications that will be considered in Chapter 5. We need to consider the possibility that there may not be any feasible solutions. Also, in some cases some nonbasic feasible solutions may be just as good as the optimal basic solution, but there is no way for a nonbasic feasible solution to be better than the optimal basic solution.)

This result gives us an idea for how to track down the optimal solution: we need to start checking the basic feasible solutions until we find the optimal solution. One possibility is to check the value of the objective function for each of the basic feasible solutions.

In our case there are six variables, and there will be 15 basic solutions. (The general formula for the number of basic solutions is $n!/[m!(n-m)!]$. See Chapter 12.) This number is small enough that we can list them all:

Variables That Have Zero Values		Values of the Variables at Each Basic Solution					
		x	y	s_1	s_2	s_3	s_4
a.	x, y	0	0	50	170	140	60
b.	x, s_4	0	60	50	110	20	0
c.	x, s_3	0	70	50	100	0	−10
d.	x, s_2	0	170	50	0	−200	−110
e.	s_3, s_4	20	60	30	50	0	0
f.	s_2, s_3	40	50	10	0	0	10
g.	s_2, s_4	36.7	60	13.3	0	−16.7	0
h.	s_1, s_4	50	60	0	−40	−30	0
i.	s_1, s_3	50	45	0	−25	0	15
j.	s_1, s_2	50	20	0	0	50	40
k.	y, s_1	50	0	0	20	90	60
l.	y, s_2	56.7	0	−6.7	0	83.3	60
m.	y, s_3	140	0	−90	−250	0	60
n.	y, s_4			—			
o.	x, s_1			—			

Eleven of the basic solutions are shown in Figure 3-2. Two basic solutions [solution d, at point $(0, 170)$, and solution m, at point $(140, 0)$] are off the scale of the diagram. Two potential basic solutions (labeled n and o above) do not exist because they lead to contradictory equations, such as $0 = 50$ or $0 = 60$. Seven of the basic solutions (c, d, g, h, i, l, m) are not feasible, since at least one of the slack variables is negative. There are only six points (a, b, e, f, j, k) that correspond to basic feasible solutions; and, just as we suspected, all these points are at corners of the feasible region.

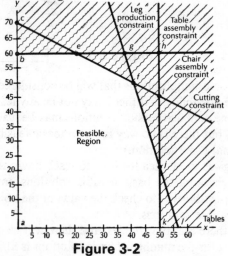

Figure 3-2

In most practical problems there are far too many basic solutions to list. For example, if there are six choice variables and five constraints, there will be 462 basic solutions. What we need is a method that works like this:

Step 1. Start at one of the basic feasible solutions. Check to see whether it is the optimum. If it is the optimum, stop. If not, go to step 2.

Step 2. Move to a different basic feasible solution that has a higher value for the objective function. Then go back to step 1 and repeat the process until the optimum is found.

In order to perform this process, we need two things:

1. We need a way to determine whether a particular basic feasible solution is in fact the optimum.

2. We need a method that takes us from one basic feasible solution to a new basic feasible solution that is guaranteed to have a higher value for the objective function.

In addition, we will need an organized method for keeping track of the work that will be involved. All of these elements are part of the linear programming solution method known as the **simplex method**. In the next chapter we will illustrate how to perform the simplex method in a practical problem. In this chapter we will illustrate how the method is able to search through the basic feasible solutions until it finds the optimum. The simplex method is an **iterative procedure**, which means that, when following it, we will keep repeating a particular sequence of steps until the optimal solution is found.

YOU SHOULD REMEMBER

Consider a linear programming problem with m constraints and n total variables (including slack variables). A solution to the Constraint Simultaneous Equation (CSE) system with $n - m$ variables equal to zero is called a *basic solution*. The number of nonzero variables in a basic solution will be the same as the number of constraints (although in some special cases it may be less than the number of constraints). If all of the variables in the basic solution are nonnegative, then the solution satisfies the constraints of the linear programming problem and is called a *basic feasible solution*.

The basic feasible solutions are represented by the corner points of the feasible region. The optimum solution to the linear programming problem will be at one of the basic feasible solutions.

The simplex method is a procedure for solving a linear programming problem by first identifying an initial basic feasible solution. At each stage of the process, the method provides a way of checking to see whether the optimum has been reached. If the optimum has not been reached, the method provides a way of moving to a new basic feasible solution that will have a better value of the objective function.

THE INITIAL BASIC FEASIBLE SOLUTION

To start the simplex method, we need to find a basic feasible solution. If we are dealing with a problem where the origin (the point $x = 0$, $y = 0$) is a feasible solution, we can use that as the first basic solution. The origin will be a feasible solution in a linear programming problem that involves maximizing an objective function, subject to "less than or equal to" constraints. As we will see later, the origin is not a feasible solution for the opposite type of linear programming problem, which involves minimizing an objective function subject to "greater than or equal to" constraints.

The four slack variables (s_1, s_2, s_3, s_4) will have nonzero values in our initial solution. We will say that these four variables are "in the basis," or "in the solution." When we write the CSE system, we will put asterisks over the variables that are in the basis, and print the variables that are not in the basis on a gray background.

$$
\begin{array}{rcl}
\overset{***}{x} & +s_1 & = 50 \\
3x + y & +s_2 & = 170 \\
x + 2y & +s_3 & = 140 \\
y & +s_4 & = 60
\end{array}
$$

Now we set the values of the nonbasis variables (x and y) equal to zero and solve for the variables that are in the basis. We are left with a four-equation, four-unknown system, which is trivial to solve. We can read the values for the four variables directly from the last column:

$$s_1 = 50, \qquad s_2 = 170, \qquad s_3 = 140, \qquad s_4 = 60, \qquad x = 0, \qquad y = 0$$

A simultaneous equation system is easy to solve if each variable appears in one, but only one, of the equations, and if the coefficient equals 1 for the variable that does appear in this equation. We will say that an equation system in this form is in *Standard Easily Solvable form* (**SES form**).

The initial solution leads to zero profits, so we need to look for a better point. Here is how we move to a new basic feasible solution: We choose one variable that is currently in the basis (either s_1, s_2, s_3, or s_4) and take it out. (Taking a variable out of the basis means that its value will be set to zero.) Then we place in the basis one of the variables that is currently out of it (x or y). The question is: Which variable should we take out, and which should we put in?

Adding either x or y to the basis will improve the situation (by making the objective function larger). We will choose the one that will help to the greater extent. Since increasing the value of x by 1 will increase the objective function by 4, whereas increasing y by 1 will increase it by 5, we will add y to the basis. Here is a definition: the **marginal net gain** for a variable is the amount by which the objective function will rise if this variable is increased by 1. Therefore, x has a marginal net gain of 4 and y has a marginal net gain of 5. Calculating the net gain was simple in this case; we shall see that the process becomes more complicated in other situations.

Now we have to decide which variable to take out of the basis. We must be careful when we make this decision; otherwise we might end up with a basic solution that is not a feasible solution. Here are the equations in the CSE system:

*** *** *** ***

$$
\begin{aligned}
x \quad + s_1 \qquad\qquad\qquad &= 50 \\
3x + y \qquad + s_2 \qquad\qquad &= 170 \\
x + 2y \qquad\qquad + s_3 \quad\ &= 140 \\
y \qquad\qquad\qquad + s_4 &= 60
\end{aligned}
$$

Look what happens if we make y bigger: the slack variables must become smaller. There is one exception: since y does not appear in the equation containing s_1, it is possible for the value of y to increase without making the value of s_1 decrease. We can ignore x, since it is currently out of the basis and we intend to keep it there for the present.

Suppose that we look at the second equation and reason as follows: "Let's take s_2 out of the basis. Taking it out of the basis means that its value will become zero. If the value of s_2 becomes zero, then the value of y becomes 170."

This reasoning works fine for the second constraint. However, look at the third and fourth constraint equations. If the value of y became 170, then the values of both s_3 and s_4 would be forced to become negative—in other words, we would end up at a nonfeasible point. Therefore, we cannot let y become that big.

We need to look at each constraint in turn. The first equation ($x + s_1 = 50$), representing the table assembly constraint, imposes no limitation on y at all. If this was the only constraint, we could make y as large as we wanted. However, the other constraints impose strict limits. The second constraint equation ($3x + y + s_2 = 170$) tells us that the largest value y can have is 170. The third constraint ($x + 2y + s_3 = 140$) tells us that the largest value y can have is $140/2 = 70$. The fourth constraint ($y + s_4 = 60$) imposes an upper limit on y of 60. Therefore, the fourth constraint imposes the tightest squeeze on y. If we let y take on the value 60, then we will be sure of meeting all of the other constraints. This means that the value of s_4 becomes zero (that is, s_4 will be taken out of the basis).

We have made our decision: y will enter the basis, and s_4 will leave it. Now, how do we implement the decision? The CSE system now looks like this:

*** *** *** ***

$$
\begin{aligned}
(1) \quad & x \qquad\ + s_2 \qquad\qquad\qquad\ = 50 \\
(2) \quad & 3x + y \qquad + s_2 \qquad\qquad = 170 \\
(3) \quad & x + 2y \qquad\quad + s_3 \qquad\ = 140 \\
(4) \quad & y \qquad\qquad\qquad + s_4 = 60
\end{aligned}
$$

where $x = 0$ and $s_4 = 0$; the values of y, s_1, s_2, and s_3 need to be determined.

In order to solve the system, we would like to transform it into SES form:

$$
\begin{array}{lcccc}
*** & *** & *** & *** \\
?x & +s_1 & & +?s_4 = ? \\
?x & & +s^2 & +?s_4 = ? \\
?x & & & +s^3 & +?s_4 = ? \\
?x+y & & & & +?s_4 = ?
\end{array}
$$

The values on the right-hand side and the coefficients of x and s_4 can be any values. We would like each basis variable to appear in one and only one equation, and we would like each basis variable to have its coefficient equal to 1 in the equation in which it does appear. We need to transform the system without doing violence to it—in other words, turn it into an equivalent equation system that has the same solutions as the original. As we saw in Chapter 1, there are two operations we can perform on equation systems:

- Multiply (or divide) both sides of an equation by a constant.

- Add one equation to (or subtract one equation from) another equation.

We can also perform a combination of these two operations:

- Multiply both sides of one equation by a constant, and then add the resulting equation to one of the other equations.

Here are the steps:
Step 1. Convert equation (4) so that the coefficient of y is 1. We can do this by dividing both sides of the equation by the current coefficient of y. In our case, y already has a coefficient of 1, so this step has been done for us.

$$
\begin{array}{lllll}
*** & *** & *** & *** \\
(1) & x & +s_1 & & = 50 \\
(2) & 3x+ y & +s_2 & & = 170 \\
(3) & x+2y & & +s_3 & = 140 \\
(4) & y & & +s_4 & = 60
\end{array}
$$

Step 2. Convert equation (1) so that the coefficient of y is zero. Again, this has already been done.
Step 3. Convert equation (2) so that the coefficient of y is zero. We can do this by subtracting the fourth equation from the old second equation, giving a new second equation:

$$\begin{aligned}
&[3x + y + s_2 && = 170] && \leftarrow \text{old second equation} \\
-&[y && + s_4 = 60] && \leftarrow \text{minus fourth equation} \\
=&[3x && + s_2 - s_4 = 110] && \leftarrow \text{new second equation}
\end{aligned}$$

Step 4. Convert equation (3) so that the coefficient of y is zero. We can do this by subtracting 2 times the fourth equation from the old third equation, giving a new third equation:

$$\begin{aligned}
&[x + 2y + s_3 && = 140] && \leftarrow \text{old third equation} \\
-&[2y && + 2s_4 = 120] && \leftarrow \text{minus 2 times fourth equation} \\
=&[x && + s_3 - 2s_4 = 20] && \leftarrow \text{new third equation}
\end{aligned}$$

The transformed CSE system looks like this:

$$\begin{array}{llllll}
& *** & *** & *** & *** & \\
x & + s_1 & & & = & 50 \\
3x & & + s_2 & & - s_4 = & 110 \\
x & & & + s_3 & - 2s_4 = & 20 \\
& y & & & + s_4 = & 60
\end{array}$$

The system is now in SES form. Here is the solution:

$$s_1 = 50, \qquad s_2 = 110, \qquad s_3 = 20, \qquad y = 60, \qquad x = 0, \qquad s_4 = 0$$

We have moved from our original point $(0, 0)$ to the new point $(0, 60)$. At this point the chair assembly machine is used at full capacity ($s_4 = 0$), but the other three machines are used below their capacities (the three other slack variables are positive). The profits are $5 \times 60 = 300$, which is a big improvement over a profit of zero at our initial point.

THE SECOND ITERATION

Now we have to repeat the entire process: check to see whether 300 is the optimum value for the profit; if it is not, move to a new basic feasible point. It will be a lot of work, but we don't despair. We are moving through this problem very slowly to make it possible to understand what is going on. For a practical problem a computer will do the tedious work.

There are two variables currently outside the basis: x and s_4. If we are not at the optimum, then one of these variables needs to be added to the basis, and one of the variables currently in the basis must be taken out.

The marginal net gain for x is still 4. Since s_4 does not appear in the objective function, there is no direct gain from adding this variable to the basis. However, we also need to consider the fact that adding s_4 to the basis will affect some of the other variables; this could help us or hurt us. We look at the fourth equation:

$$y + s_4 = 60$$

This equation says that, if s_4 goes up by 1, then y must go down by 1, thereby causing the objective function to decrease by 5. In this case our choice is clear: x has a marginal net gain of 4 and s_4 has a marginal net gain of -5, so clearly we will want to choose x as the variable to be added to the basis. (You might think it is not necessary to check s_4 to see whether it should be put back in the basis, since we took this variable out of the basis in the last step. However, a variable that has been taken out of the basis may need to be returned to it during some future step.)

You may wonder what would happen if the marginal net gain for both of the variables had been negative. That would mean that the objective function would go down if we added either of these two variables to the basis. Therefore, we would have reached the long-sought optimum point.

In our situation we will add x to the basis, and now we need to decide which variable to take out. For each of the four equations, we calculate this ratio:

$$(\text{right-hand-side number})/(\text{coefficient of } x)$$

which we will call the **constraint ratio**.

Equation					Constraint Ratio
***	***	***	***		
x	$+ s_1$			$= 50$	$50/1 = 50$
$3x$		$+ s_2$		$- s_4 = 110$	$110/3 = 36\frac{2}{3}$
x			$+ s_3$	$- 2s_4 = 20$	$20/1 = 20$
	y			$+ s_4 = 60$	$60/0 = \text{infinity}$

As we did in the preceding iteration, we need to choose the smallest value of the constraint ratio (in this case, the value 20 from the third equation). The third equation contains the basis variable s_3, so it is s_3 that we will want to take out of the basis.

Now we need to transform the CSE system to be in Standard Easily Solvable form:

***	***	***	***	
x	$+ s_1$			$= 50$
$3x$		$+ s_2$		$- s_4 = 110$
x			$+ s_3 - 2s_4 =$	20
	y		$+ s_4 =$	60

The steps are as follows:

1. The coefficient of x in the third equation is already 1. We do not need to transform the third equation.

2. We subtract the third equation from the old first equation, giving the new first equation:
$$s_1 - s_3 + 2s_4 = 30$$
(This is done to eliminate x from the first equation.)

3. We subtract 3 times the third equation from the old second equation, giving the new second equation:
$$s_2 - 3s_3 + 5s_4 = 50$$
(This is done to eliminate x from the second equation.)

4. Since x has already been eliminated from the fourth equation, we can leave that equation alone.

The transformed system is as follows:

	***	***	***	***
(1)		s_1		$- s_3 + 2s_4 = 30$
(2)			s_2	$- 3s_3 + 5s_4 = 50$
(3)	x			$+ s_3 - 2s_4 = 20$
(4)		y		$+ s_4 = 60$

Now we can read off the solution:

$$s_1 = 30, \quad s_2 = 50, \quad x = 20, \quad y = 60, \quad s_3 = 0, \quad s_4 = 0$$

We have moved to the point with 20 tables and 60 chairs. The chair assembly machine and the cutting machine are used at full capacity (since s_4 and s_3 are equal to zero). The profits at this point are $4 \times 20 + 5 \times 60 = 380$.

YOU SHOULD REMEMBER

The variable with the largest marginal net gain will be added to the basis (that is, its value can become nonzero). If all of the marginal net gains are negative, then the optimum has been found.

Once it has been determined which variable will be added to the basis, calculate the constraint ratio for each equation. Choose the smallest positive value for this ratio. The variable currently in the basis that corresponds to the equation with the smallest positive constraint ratio is the variable that will be taken out of the basis (that is, its value will be set to zero).

THE THIRD ITERATION

Here we go again. We need to check the marginal net gains for s_3 and s_4 to see whether either of these variables should be added to the basis. If s_3 goes up by 1, then x must go down by 1, thereby lowering the objective function by 4. Therefore, the marginal net gain of s_3 is -4. This tells us that we don't want to add s_3 to the basis.

If s_4 goes up by 1, then y must go down by 1 [see equation (4)], but x must go up by 2 [see equation (3)]. We lose 5 because y goes down by 1, but we gain $2 \times 4 = 8$ because x goes up by 2. Therefore, the marginal net gain from adding s_4 to the basis is $8 - 5 = 3$. Since this is positive, we are not at the optimum; we can improve our situation by adding s_4 to the basis. (If both s_3 and s_4 had had positive net gains, we would choose the one with the larger net gain.)

Now the question is: Which of the variables currently in the basis (x, y, s_1, s_2) do we take out? Again we calculate the constraint ratios:

(right-hand-side number)/(coefficient of s_4)

		Equation	Constraint Ratio		
s_1		$- s_3 + 2s_4 = 30$	$30/2$	$=$	15
	s_2	$-3s_3 + 5s_4 = 50$	$50/5$	$=$	10
x		$+ s_3 - 2s_4 = 20$	$20/(-2)$	$=$	-10
y		$+ s_4 = 60$	$60/1$	$=$	60

In this case the smallest value is -10 for the third equation. What does it mean if the constraint ratio is negative? Look at the third equation:

$$x + s_3 - 2s_4 = 20$$

Since s_3 is out of the basis, it is equal to zero. If we set x equal to zero, then s_4 will become negative. We cannot allow a variable to become negative. Therefore, we do not consider an equation where the constraint ratio is negative.

We choose the smallest positive value of the constraint ratio (in this case, the value 10 from the second equation). The second equation contains the basis variable s_2, so we will remove s_2 from the basis.

$$*** \quad *** \quad *** \qquad ***$$

s_1	$- s_3$	$+ 2s_4 = 30$
s_2	$- 3s_3$	$+ 5s_4 = 50$
x	$+ s_3$	$- 2s_4 = 20$
y		$+ s_4 = 60$

Now we convert to SES form by following these steps:

1. Divide both sides of the second equation by 5 (to make the coefficient of s_4 in the second equation equal to 1):

$$\frac{s_2 - 3s_3 + 5s_4}{5} = \frac{50}{5}$$

new second equation: $\quad \frac{1}{5}s_2 - \frac{3}{5}s_3 + s_4 = 10$

Now perform the following three steps to eliminate s_4 from the first, third, and fourth equations:

2. Subtract twice the new second equation from the old first equation, giving the new first equation:

$$s_1 - \frac{2}{5}s_2 + \frac{1}{5}s_3 = 10$$

3. Add twice the new second equation to the old third equation, giving the new third equation:

$$x + \frac{2}{5}s_2 - \frac{1}{5}s_3 = 40$$

4. Subtract the new second equation from the old fourth equation, giving the new fourth equation:

$$y - \frac{1}{5}s_2 + \frac{3}{5}s_3 = 50$$

The transformed CSE system is

		*** *** ***	***	
(1)	s_1	$-\frac{2}{5}s_2 + \frac{1}{5}s_3$		$= 10$
(2)		$\frac{1}{5}s_2 - \frac{3}{5}s_3$	$+ s_4$	$= 10$
(3)	x	$+\frac{2}{5}s_2 - \frac{1}{5}s_3$		$= 40$
(4)	y	$-\frac{1}{5}s_2 + \frac{3}{5}s_3$		$= 50$

We read off the solution:

$$s_1 = 10, \qquad s_4 = 10, \qquad x = 40, \qquad y = 50, \qquad s_2 = 0, \qquad s_3 = 0.$$

We have moved to the point with 40 tables and 50 chairs. Figure 3-3 illustrates how we have moved from one corner point to another. The big question is: Have we finished? No, we need to calculate the marginal net gains for s_2 and s_3.

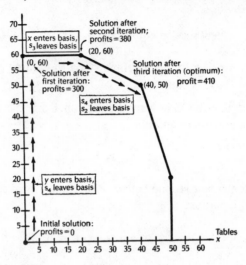

Figure 3-3

If s_2 goes up by 1, then x goes down by 2/5 [see equation (3)], costing $2/5 \times 4$ dollars; also y goes up by 1/5 [see equation (4)], gaining $1/5 \times 5$ dollars. The marginal net gain for s_2 can be found from the formula

$$0 - \left(\frac{2}{5}\right)(4) - \left(\frac{-1}{5}\right)(5) = -0.6$$

If s_3 goes up by 1, then x goes up by 1/5 [see equation (3)], gaining $1/5 \times 4$ dollars; also y goes down by 3/5 [see equation (4)], costing $3/5 \times 5$ dollars. Therefore, the marginal net gain for s_3 is

$$0 - (-0.2)(4) - (0.6)(5) = -2.2$$

Just what we wanted to see—both of the net gains are negative! Therefore, we don't want to add either s_2 or s_3 to the basis. We will stay right where we are—at the optimum.

We have learned the principles behind the simplex method. In the next chapter we will develope the mechanism for implementing the method.

KNOW THE CONCEPTS

DO YOU KNOW THE BASICS?

Test your understanding of Chapter 3 by answering the following questions:

1. What is the difference between a basic feasible solution and a basic solution?

2. On a graph, where are the points that correspond to the basic feasible solutions?

3. Why are the slack variables required to be nonnegative?

4. Is it possible to find a solution to a linear programming problem where all of the constraints are satisfied with no excess capacity?

5. What will be true about the solution to a two-variable, three-constraint linear programming problem if the optimal isoprofit line passes through the point where the three lines representing the constraints intersect?

6. At the optimum, what is true about the marginal net gains? Why?

7. Why is it permissible to add a multiple of one equation to another, as is done in this chapter?

TERMS FOR STUDY

basic feasible solution
basic solution
constraint ratio
CSE system
feasible solution

iterative procedure
marginal net gain
SES form
simplex method
slack variable

ANSWERS

KNOW THE CONCEPTS

1. A basic solution is a solution to the constraint simultaneous equation (CSE) system where the number of nonzero variables equals the number of constraints. A basic feasible solution is a basic solution that satisfies all of the constraints (meaning that the choice variables and slack variables all have nonnegative values).

2. The corner points (also called *vertices*) of the feasible region.

3. If a slack variable was negative, then the constraint corresponding to that variable would be violated.

4. This is not possible if the number of constraints is greater than the number of choice variables (not including the slack variables), provided that none of the constraints is redundant. If the number of constraints is less than or equal to the number of choice variables, then it might be possible that all constraints could be satisfied exactly with no excess capacity. However, even if this was possible it might not be the optimum.

5. All three of the slack variables will be zero. This is an example of a special situation (called *degeneracy*) where it is possible for the number of nonzero variables to be less than the number of constraints. This situation is discussed in Chapter 5.

6. The marginal net gain for each variable not in the basis must be negative. If one of these marginal net gains was positive, the objective function could be increased by adding that variable to the basis, so you could not have been at the optimum.

7. These operations do not change the solutions to the equation system. See Chapter 1.

4

THE SIMPLEX LINEAR PROGRAMMING ALGORITHM: INTRODUCTION

KEY TERMS

pivoting the process of adjusting the simplex tableau to remove one variable from the basis and add another variable to the basis

simplex tableau a table used to arrange the data utilized in the simplex linear programming algorithm

THE SIMPLEX TABLEAU

In Chapter 3 we illustrated how the simplex method works to solve a linear programming problem. In order for the method to have more practical value, however, we need a better way to organize our work. We shall do that by working with a special matrix called the **simplex tableau**. The simplex method was developed by mathematician George Dantzig. The name of the method comes from a mathematical figure known as a *simplex*, which can be thought of as a generalization of a triangle to *n* dimensions. The feasible region for a linear programming problem consists of a set of simplexes.

Let's return to the furniture problem discussed in Chapter 3:

Maximize $4x + 5y$
subject to:

table assembly:	x	$+s_1$		$= 50$
leg production:	$3x + y$	$+s_2$		$= 170$
cutting:	$x + 2y$	$+s_3$		$= 140$
chair assembly:	y		$+s_4$	$= 60$

To construct the simplex tableau, we put the matrix of coefficients next to a column containing the right-hand-side values. To help keep track of the variables, we put the name of each variable above the column representing its coefficients, and put the objective function coefficient (Ob. Fn. Coeff.) for each variable above the variable name. In writing tableaus, we will use roman capital letters with lining numbers, not subscripts, for variables: X, S1, etc.

4	5	**** 0	**** 0	**** 0	**** 0	≪ Obj. Fn. Coeff.
X	Y	S1	S2	S3	S4	RHS
1	0	1	0	0	0	50
3	1	0	1	0	0	170
1	2	0	0	1	0	140
0	1	0	0	0	1	60

Here "RHS" stands for "Right-Hand Side." The objective function coefficients for the slack variables are zero. Again, we will use asterisks to indicate which variables are currently in the basis. As you recall, initially the four slack variables are in the basis.

Each of the basis variables has a coefficient equal to 1 in only one of the equations. On the right-hand side of the tableau, we will list the basis variable that appears in the equation represented by that row. In a column headed "CBV," we will list the objective function coefficient next to the name of the basis variable. Note that the variable names in the column headings do not change, but the variable names in the column labeled "BASIS VRS" will change as we change the basis.

4	5	**** 0	**** 0	**** 0	**** 0	≪ Obj. Fn. Coeff.		
X	Y	S1	S2	S3	S4	RHS	BASIS VRS	CBV
1	0	1	0	0	0	50	S1	0
3	1	0	1	0	0	170	S2	0
1	2	0	0	1	0	140	S3	0
0	1	0	0	0	1	60	S4	0

The lines indicate how to make sure that the entries in the "BASIS VRS" column are put in the correct place. For each column in the basis, read down until you find the value 1. Then read across to make sure that the variable name in the "BASIS VRS" column is the same as the variable name at the top of the column containing the 1 in that row.

The heading "CBV" stands for "Coefficients of the Basis Variables"; that column contains the objective function coefficient for the basis variable in that row. Initially, all of the CBV values happen to be zero; this is so because the basis initially contains only the four slack variables.

At the bottom of the tableau we will list the marginal net gains. For the four variables already in the basis, the net gain is zero. In Chapter 3 we found that initially the net gain of x is 4 and the net gain of y is 5. Later we will give the general formula for calculating the net gain.

****	****	****	****					
4	5	0	0	0	0	≪ Obj. Fn. Coeff.		
X	Y	(S1)	(S2)	(S3)	(S4)	RHS	BASIS VRS	CBV
1	0	(1)	0	0	0	50	(S1)	0
3	1	0	(1)	0	0	170	(S2)	0
1	2	0	0	(1)	0	140	(S3)	0
0	1	0	0	0	(1)	60	(S4)	0
4	5	0	0	0	0	≪ Marginal Net Gain		

(Note: Different books may use slightly different forms for writing the simplex tableau.)

As we found in Chapter 3, the simplex method works by moving from one basic feasible solution to a new basic feasible solution that has a higher value of the objective function. We do this by removing one variable from the basis and replacing it with one of the other variables. This process is known as **pivoting**. The variable with the largest marginal net gain is the variable that enters the basis. The column in the tableau corresponding to this variable is called the *pivot column*.

To determine which variable comes out of the basis, we need to calculate the constraint ratio for each equation. This ratio is equal to the RHS element in each row divided by the element in the pivot column in that row. Will will list the ratio at the right edge of the tableau. The smallest positive value of this ratio determines the *pivot row*; the basis variable corresponding to this row is the one that leaves the basis. The element in the pivot row and the pivot column is called the *pivot element*; in our case it is the number 1 in row 4, column 2. (Note: We start numbering the rows with the first row below the line. For example, in the tableau below, the first row is the one containing "1 0 1 0 0 0 50.")

Here is the complete simplex tableau for the initial situation:

****	****	****	****						
4	5	0	0	0	0	≪ Obj. Fn. Coeff.			
X	Y	S1	S2	S3	S4	RHS	BASIS VRS	CBV	RATIO
1	0	1	0	0	0	50	S1	0	—
3	1	0	1	0	0	170	S2	0	170
1	2	0	0	1	0	140	S3	0	70
0	1	0	0	0	1	60	S4	0	60 ≪
4	5̂	0	0	0	0	≪ Marginal Net Gain			

Pivot element: row 4, column 2

The symbol "$\hat{}$" indicates the pivot column, and the symbol "≪" indicates the pivot row. The dash ("—") indicates that the constraint ratio involves dividing by zero.

Two steps are needed to perform the pivot process:

1. Divide each element of the pivot row by the pivot element, so as to make the element in the pivot position equal to 1. In our initial tableau the pivot element is already equal to 1.

2. Convert all other elements of the pivot column to zero by adding (or subtracting) a multiple of the pivot row to (or from) each of the other rows. In our case here is what we need to do:
    Row 1: The element in the pivot column already is zero, so we don't do anything.
    Row 2: We subtract row 4 from row 2.
    Row 3: We subtract 2 times row 4 from row 3.

Here is the new tableau:

****	****	****	****					
4	5	0	0	0	0	≪ Obj. Fn. Coeff.		
X	Y	S1	S2	S3	S4	RHS	BASIS VRS	CBV
1	0	1	0	0	0	50	S1	0
3	0	0	1	0	−1	110	S2	0
1	0	0	0	1	−2	20	S3	0
0	1	0	0	0	1	60	Y	5

(Compare with the CSE system on page 91.)

The marginal net gain for x is

$$4 - (1 \times 0) - (3 \times 0) - (1 \times 0) - (0 \times 5) = 4$$

The marginal net gain for s_4 is

$$0 - (0 \times 0) - (-1 \times 0) - (-2 \times 0) - (1 \times 5) = -5$$

The first term in the marginal net gain is the objective function coefficient for that variable. Each of the remaining four terms consists of an element in the column corresponding to that variable multiplied by the objective function coefficient of the basis variable corresponding to that row. For example, the column corresponding to x contains four elements: 1, 3, 1, and 0. The corresponding basis variables are s_1, s_2, s_3, and y; the corresponding objective function coefficients are 0, 0, 0, and 5.

Simplex Tableau, Second Stage

	****	****	****	****						
4	5	0	0	0	0	≪ Obj. Fn. Coeff.				
X	Y	S1	S2	S3	S4	RHS	BASIS VRS	CBV	RATIO	
1	0	1	0	0	0	50	S1	0	50	
3	0	0	1	0	-1	110	S2	0	36.667	
1	0	0	0	1	-2	20	S3	0	20	≪
0	1	0	0	0	1	60	Y	5	—	
4.	0	0	0	0	-5	≪ Marginal Net Gain				

Pivot element: row 3, column 1

To carry out the pivot operation, proceed as follows:

1. Divide each element in row 3 by 1 (in other words, leave the elements alone).
2. Subtract row 3 from row 1 (the result is the new row 1).
3. Subtract 3 times row 3 from row 2 (the result is the new row 2).
4. Leave row 4 alone (since the value in the pivot column is already equal to zero).

Simplex Tableau, Third Stage

****	****	****	****						
4	5	0	0	0	0	≪ Obj. Fn. Coeff.			
X	Y	S1	S2	S3	S4	RHS	BASIS VRS	CBV	RATIO
0	0	1	0	−1	2	30	S1	0	15
0	0	0	1	−3	5	50	S2	0	10≪
1	0	0	0	1	−2	20	X	4	−10
0	1	0	0	0	1	60	Y	5	60
0	0	0	0	−4	$\hat{3}$		≪ Marginal Net Gains		

(Compare with the CSE system on page 93 .)

The marginal net gain for s_3 is found from the formula

$$0 - (-1 \times 0) - (-3 \times 0) - (1 \times 4) - (0 \times 5) = -4$$

The marginal net gain for s_4 is given by

$$0 - (2 \times 0) - (5 \times 0) - (-2 \times 4) - (1 \times 5) = 3$$

Therefore, s_4 will enter the basis. After calculating the values in the ratio column, we can see that s_2 is the variable that leaves the basis. Therefore, the pivot element is in row 2, column 6. To perform the pivot:

1. Divide each element in row 2 by 5. The new row 2 is

X	Y	S1	S2	S3	S4	RHS
0	0	0	0.2	−0.6	1	10

2. Subtract twice the new row 2 from row 1 (the result is the new row 1).

3. Add twice the new row 2 to row 3 (the result is the new row 3).

4. Subtract the new row 2 from row 4 (the result is the new row 4).

Simplex Tableau, Fourth Stage

****	****	****			****			
4	5	0	0	0	0	≪ Obj. Fn. Coeff.		
X	Y	S1	S2	S3	S4	RHS	BASIS VRS	CBV
0	0	1	−0.4	0.2	0	10	S1	0
0	0	0	0.2	−0.6	1	10	S4	0
1	0	0	0.4	−0.2	0	40	X	4
0	1	0	−0.2	0.6	0	50	Y	5
0	0	0	−0.6	−2.2	0	≪ Marginal Net Gain		

(Compare with the CSE system on page 95 .)

To find the marginal net gain for s_2, proceed as follows:

$$0 - (-0.4 \times 0) - (0.2 \times 0) - (0.4 \times 4) - (-0.2 \times 5) = -0.6$$

For s_3:

$$0 - (0.2 \times 0) - (-0.6 \times 0) - (-0.2 \times 4) - (0.6 \times 5) = -2.2$$

Since the marginal net gains are both negative, we have found the optimum solution. The value for the solution for each basis variable is given in the RHS column: $s_1 = 10$, $s_4 = 10$, $x = 40$, $y = 50$. (The values of s_2 and s_3 are zero, of course, since they are not in the basis.)

If you compare the steps we just performed with the steps we performed in Chapter 3, you will find that everything we did is the same. The only difference is that the use of the simplex tableau makes it much easier to keep track of our work.

OUTLINE OF THE SIMPLEX METHOD

Now we can describe the general form of the simplex procedure for maximization problems with two variables and four constraints. (In the next chapter we will also look at the simplex procedure for problems of any size, and we will also look at minimization problems. Also, we will consider at that time some complications that can arise.)

Step 0. Arrange the problem as follows:

Maximize $c_1x_1 + c_2x_2$
subject to:

$$\begin{pmatrix} a_{11} & a_{12} & 1 & 0 & 0 & 0 \\ a_{21} & a_{22} & 0 & 1 & 0 & 0 \\ a_{31} & a_{32} & 0 & 0 & 1 & 0 \\ a_{41} & a_{42} & 0 & 0 & 0 & 1 \end{pmatrix} \begin{pmatrix} x_1 \\ x_2 \\ s_1 \\ s_2 \\ s_3 \\ s_4 \end{pmatrix} = \begin{pmatrix} r_1 \\ r_2 \\ r_3 \\ r_4 \end{pmatrix}$$

Here x_1 and x_2 are the two choice variables; s_1, s_2, s_3, and s_4 are the four slack variables. All six variables—x_1, x_2, s_1, s_2, s_3, s_4—must be nonnegative at a feasible solution. It is possible to arrange the problem so that r_1, r_2, r_3, and r_4 are all positive; we will discuss this in the next chapter.

Step 1. Set up the initial simplex tableau:

| c_1 | c_2 | 0 | 0 | 0 | 0 | ≪ "Objective Fn. Coeff" | | |
"x_1"	"x_2"	"s_1"	"s_2"	"s_3"	"s_4"	"RHS"	"BASIS VRS"	"CBV"
a_{11}	a_{12}	1	0	0	0	r_1	"s_1"	0
a_{21}	a_{22}	0	1	0	0	r_2	"s_2"	0
a_{31}	a_{32}	0	0	1	0	r_3	"s_3"	0
a_{41}	a_{42}	0	0	0	1	r_4	"s_4"	0
c_1	c_2	0	0	0	0	≪ "Marginal Net Gain"		

The quotation marks mean that you write that exact letter, or those exact letters, at that position. When a letter appears without quotation marks, you write the numerical value of that variable in that position.

Step 2. Use this form to represent the tableau at any particular stage of the process:

| c_1 | c_2 | 0 | 0 | 0 | 0 | ≪ "Objective Fn. Coeff" | | |
"x_1"	"x_2"	"s_1"	"s_2"	"s_3"	"s_4"	"RHS"	"BASIS VRS"	"CBV"
A11	A12	A13	A14	A15	A16	R1	first b.v.	CBV1
A21	A22	A23	A24	A25	A26	R2	second b.v.	CBV2
A31	A32	A33	A34	A26	A36	R3	third b.v.	CBV3
A41	A42	A34	A44	A27	A46	R4	fourth b.v.	CBV4

Here "first b.v." represents the name of the first basis variable, and so on.

(What is the difference between the lowercase letters that appeared in the tableau of step 1, and the capital letters that appear here? The lowercase letters in step 1 represent the initial values that come with the problem, as specified in step 0. The capital letters represent the entries in the tableau at any particular stage. For example, in the first stage, A32 (the tableau element in row 3, column 2) will be equal to a_{32}. We have seen that the values in the tableau change as we move through the process, so after the second stage A32 will probably take on a different value.)

Here is how to determine the basis variable corresponding to each row. The *column* corresponding to each basis variable should contain all zeros, except for one row that has the value 1. The row containing the 1 is the row corresponding to that basis variable. The value CBV_i is equal to the objective function coefficient for the variable that corresponds to row i.

Calculate the net gain for the variable in column j from this formula:

$$NG_j = c_j - A1_j \times CBV_1 - A2_j \times CBV_2 - A3_j \times CBV_3 - A4_j \times CBV_4$$

Step 3. Look at the net gain for each variable not in the basis. If all of the net gains are negative, then you have found the optimum; go to step 7. If not, then determine which column has the largest net gain. This will determine the pivot column, that is, the variable that will enter the basis.

Step 4. Calculate the constraint ratio for each row. Suppose that k is the pivot column. Then the constraint ratio for row i is given by the formula

$$CR_i = \frac{R_i}{A_{ik}}$$

Here is the tableau with the net gains and constraint ratios added:

c_1	c_2	0	0	0	0	≪ "Objective Fn. Coeff"			
"x_1"	"x_2"	"s_1"	"s_2"	"s_3"	"s_4"	"RHS"	"BASIS VRS"	"CBV"	"RATIO"
A11	A12	A13	A14	A15	A16	R1	first b.v.	CBV1	CR1
A21	A22	A23	A24	A25	A26	R2	second b.v.	CBV2	CR2
A31	A32	A33	A34	A26	A36	R3	third b.v.	CBV3	CR3
A41	A42	A34	A44	A27	A46	R4	fourth b.v.	CBV4	CR4
NG1	NG2	NG3	NG4	NG5	NG6		≪ "Marginal Net Gain"		

Choose the smallest positive value for the constraint ratio. This will determine the pivot row (that is, which variable will leave the basis).

Step 5. Carry out the pivot process. Suppose that h is the pivot row and k is the pivot column. Therefore, $\mathrm{A}hk$ is the pivot element. For the pivot row, the new value in row h, column j is given by

$$\mathrm{A}hj_{\mathrm{new}} = \frac{\mathrm{A}hj}{\mathrm{A}hk}$$

For the other rows, the new value in row i, column j is given by

$$\mathrm{A}ij_{\mathrm{new}} = \mathrm{A}ij - \mathrm{A}ik\left(\frac{\mathrm{A}hj}{\mathrm{A}hk}\right)$$

($\mathrm{A}ij$ represents the old value in row i, column j.)

Step 6. Return to step 2. Keep returning to step 2 until the optimum has been found.

Step 7. The optimum has been found! The solution value for each basis variable can be found by reading the corresponding value from the RHS column. The value for each nonbasis variable is zero.

The simplex procedure can be outlined in a flowchart (see Figure 4-1). Appendix 2 at the end of the book contains a computer program written in the BASIC programming language that performs the simplex procedure.

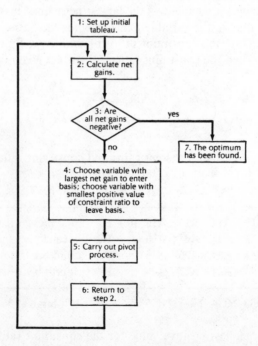

Figure 4-1. Simplex Procedure for Maximization Problem

YOU SHOULD REMEMBER

The simplex procedure leads you from one basic feasible solution to another until the optimum is found. The simplex tableau is a table for arranging the work.

The process of moving from one basic feasible solution to another is called *pivoting*. The pivot column corresponds to the variable with the largest marginal net gain, which will enter the basis. The pivot row is the row with the smallest positive value of the constraint ratio. The basis variable corresponding to that row is the variable that will leave the basis. The element in the pivot row and the pivot column is called the *pivot element*.

To carry out the pivoting process, multiply rows by constants or add multiples of one row to another row until the pivot element has been transformed to have the value 1 and all other elements in the pivot column have been transformed to have the value 0.

THE SIMPLEX METHOD WITH THREE VARIABLES

Here is an example of a linear programming problem with three variables:

Maximize $20x + 30y + 22z$
subject to:
$$6x + 3y + 4z \le 120$$
$$20x + 12y + 8z \le 420$$
$$5x + 12y + 8z \le 240$$

Since paper has only two dimensions, we cannot make a graph of the feasible region when there are three variables. However, we can draw a perspective diagram that looks three dimensional. This is not particularly easy to do, so this method is not recommended as a way to solve three-variable linear programming problems. However, it is helpful to see one example showing the geometry of a three-variable problem.

The graph of a three-variable equation such as

$$6x + 3y + 4z = 120$$

will be a plane. For this problem there are six constraints (the three constraints given above and the three nonnegativity constraints), so the feasible region will be bounded by six planes. Figure 4-2 illustrates the feasible region. The z-axis is oriented upward. The coordinates of the seven corner points are as follows:

		x	y	z
a:	(	0,	0	0)
b:	(	20,	0	0)
c:	(	15,	10,	0)
d:	(	12,	14,	1.5)
e:	(	12,	15,	0)
f:	(	0,	20	0)
g:	(	0,	0,	30)

Figure 4-2

Figure 4-2

Points *b*, *c*, *d*, and *g* are on the plane representing the equation

$$6x + 3y + 4z = 120$$

Points *c*, *d*, and *e* are on the plane representing the equation

$$20x + 12y + 8z = 420$$

Points *d*, *e*, *f*, and *g* are on the plane representing the equation

$$5x + 12y + 8z = 240$$

Points a, b, c, e, and f are on the plane representing the equation $z = 0$.
Points a, b, and g are on the plane representing the equation $y = 0$.
Points a, f, and g are on the plane representing the equation $x = 0$.

Just as in the two-variable situation, the optimal solution will be at a corner point of the feasible region, which will represent a basic feasible solution. We write the problem in matrix notation, with the slack variables included:

Maximize $20x + 30y + 22z$
subject to:

$$
\begin{pmatrix}
6 & 3 & 4 & 1 & 0 & 0 \\
20 & 12 & 8 & 0 & 1 & 0 \\
5 & 12 & 8 & 0 & 0 & 1
\end{pmatrix}
\begin{pmatrix}
x \\ y \\ z \\ s_1 \\ s_2 \\ s_3
\end{pmatrix}
=
\begin{pmatrix}
120 \\ 420 \\ 240
\end{pmatrix}
$$

In this case there are three slack variables, since there are three constraints. A basic solution will occur where three variables are positive and three variables are zero. The initial basis will contain the three slack variables. Here is the initial tableau:

20	30	22	***** 0	***** 0	***** 0	≪ Obj. Fn. Coeff.			
X	Y	Z	S1	S2	S3	RHS	BASIS VRS	CBV	RATIO
6	3	4	1	0	0	120	S1	0	40
20	12	8	0	1	0	420	S2	0	35
5	12	8	0	0	1	240	S3	0	20 ≪
20	30̂	22	0	0	0	≪ Marginal Net Gain			

The initial basic feasible solution corresponds to point a in Figure 4-2, with x, y, and z all equal to zero. The pivot element is in row 3, column 2, meaning that y will be added to the basis and s_3 will be removed. The second tableau is as follows:

20	***** 30	22	***** 0	***** 0	0	≪Obj. Fn. Coeff.			
X	Y	Z	S1	S2	S3	RHS	BASIS VRS	CBV	RATIO
4.75	0	2	1	0	−0.25	60	S1	0	12.632
15	0	0	0	1	−1	180	S2	0	12 ≪
0.417	1	0.667	0	0	0.083	20	Y	30	48
7.5̂	0	2	0	0	−2.5	≪ Marginal Net Gain			

This tableau represents point f in Figure 4-2, with coordinates (0, 20, 0.) The pivot element is in row 2, column 1, meaning that x will be added to the basis and s_2 will be removed. Here is the third tableau:

*****	*****		*****						
20	30	22	0	0	0	≪Obj. Fn. Coeff.			
X	Y	Z	S1	S2	S3	RHS	BASIS VRS	CBV	RATIO
0	0	2	1	−0.317	0.067	3	S1	0	1.5≪
1	0	0	0	0.067	−0.067	12	X	20	—
0	1	0.667	0	−0.028	0.111	15	Y	30	22.5

This tableau represents point e in Figure 4-2, with coordinates (12, 15, 0). The pivot element is row 1, column 3, meaning that z will be added to the basis and s_1 will be removed. The fourth tableau is as follows:

*****	*****	*****						
20	30	22	0	0	0	≪ Obj. Fn. Coeff.		
X	Y	Z	S1	S2	S3	RHS	BASIS VRS	CBV
0	0	1	0.5	−0.158	0.033	1.5	Z	22
1	0	0	0	0.067	−0.067	12	X	20
0	1	0	−0.333	0.078	0.089	14	Y	30
0	0	0	−1	−0.183	−2.067	≪ Marginal Net Gain		

All of the net gains are negative, so we have reached the optimal solution. The solution values are $x = 12$, $y = 14$, and $z = 1.5$, so the optimal solution corresponds to point d in Figure 4-2.

If there are more than three variables, then we cannot draw a diagram. We will see in the next chapter, however, that the principle of the simplex method remains the same: keep moving from one basic feasible solution to another until the optimum is reached.

KNOW THE CONCEPTS

DO YOU KNOW THE BASICS?

Test your understanding of Chapter 4 by answering the following questions:

1. Why is the simplex method better than simply checking all of the basic feasible solutions to determine which has the best value for the objective function?

2. How can you tell if a basic solution is not feasible?

3. How do you tell which variable to add to the basis?

4. How do you tell which variable to remove?

5. What happens if the wrong variable is brought into the basis?

6. Why does the objective function value always increase as you use the simplex method to move from one basic feasible solution to another?

7. What is the difference between working with the simplex tableau and working with the CSE system directly, as was done in Chapter 3?

8. Why isn't the marginal net gain for a variable simply equal to the objective function coefficient for that variable?

9. If there are three variables, what geometric shape corresponds to all points that have the same profit?

10. If there are three variables, how many feasible region corner points are adjacent to a particular corner point? (Two corner points are adjacent if they are connected by one of the straight line segments marking the edges of the feasible region.) What is the significance of this answer for the simplex method?

TERMS FOR STUDY

pivoting   simplex tableau

PRACTICAL APPLICATION

COMPUTATIONAL PROBLEMS

Use the simplex method to solve each of the following problems, which were solved graphically in Chapter 2:

1. Chapter 2, Exercise 6   3. Chapter 2, Exercise 11

2. Chapter 2, Exercise 10

4. Use the simplex method to solve the furniture problem discussed in Chapter 2, with the profit from each table equal to 9 and the profit from each chair equal to 3:

Maximize $9x + 3y$
subject to:

table assembly constraint:	$x \quad\quad \leq 50$
leg production constraint:	$3x + y \leq 170$
cutting constraint:	$x + 2y \leq 140$
chair assembly constraint:	$y \leq 60$

What is unusual about the graph of the solution for this problem?

5. Use the simplex method to solve the furniture problem in Exercise 4, with these changes: (1) the profit from each table is now 7; (2) the profit from each chair is now 2; (3) the capacity of the leg production constraint has been expanded from 170 to 195 (the other three constraints remain the same as in Exercise 4).

What is unusual about the graph of the solution for this problem?

6. (a) Here is the initial simplex tableau for a linear programming problem. State the problem corresponding to this tableau, without using matrix notation.

3	4	0	0	0	0	0	0	0	≪ Obj. Fn. Coeff.	
X1	X2	S1	S2	S3	S4	S5	S6	S7	RHS	BASIS VRS
1	4	1	0	0	0	0	0	0	81	S1
1	3	0	1	0	0	0	0	0	62	S2
1	2	0	0	1	0	0	0	0	44	S3
1	1	0	0	0	1	0	0	0	24	S4
2	1	0	0	0	0	1	0	0	38	S5
3	1	0	0	0	0	0	1	0	47	S6
5	1	0	0	0	0	0	0	1	75	S7

(b) Calculate the marginal net gains and the constraint ratios for the tableau from part (a).

(c) Here is the second stage of the tableau. Fill in the right-hand-side values, basing your calculations on the initial tableau. Also fill in the entries in the CBV and BASIS VRS column.

3	4	0	0	0	0	0	0	0	≪ Obj. Fn. Coeff.			
X1	X2	−0.75	S2	S3	S4	S5	S6	S7	RHS	BASIS VRS	CBV	RATIO
0.25	1	0.25	0	0	0	0	0	0				81
0.25	0	−0.75	1	0	0	0	0	0				5
0.50	0	−0.5	0	1	0	0	0	0				7
0.75	0	−0.25	0	0	1	0	0	0				5
1.75	0	−0.25	0	0	0	1	0	0				10.143
2.75	0	−0.25	0	0	0	0	1	0				9.727
4.75	0	−0.25	0	0	0	0	0	1				11.526
3	0	−1	0	0	0	0	0	0	≪ Marginal Net Gain			

(d) Which is the pivot element for the tableau in part (c)?

(e) Here is the third-stage tableau for this problem. On the basis of the second-stage tableau, fill in the values in column S2.

3	4	0	0	0	0	0	0	0	« Obj. Fn Coeff.			
X1	X2	S1	S2	S3	S4	S5	S6	S7	RHS	BASIS VRS	CBV	RATIO
0	1	1		0	0	0	0	0	19	X2	4	
1	0	-3		0	0	0	0	0	5	X1	3	
0	0	1		1	0	0	0	0	1	S3	0	
0	0	2		0	1	0	0	0	0	S4	0	
0	0	5		0	0	1	0	0	9	S5	0	
0	0	8		0	0	0	1	0	13	S6	0	
0	0	14		0	0	0	0	1	31	S7	0	

0	0	5	-8	0	0	0	0	0	« Marginal Net Gain

(f) Here is the fourth-stage tableau. Calculate the marginal net gains.

3	4	0	0	0	0	0	0	0	« Obj. Fn. Coeff.		
X1	X2	S1	S2	S3	S4	S5	S6	S7	RHS	BASIS VRS	CBV
0	1	0	0.5	0	-0.5	0	0	0	19	X2	4
1	0	0	-0.5	0	1.5	0	0	0	5	X1	3
0	0	0	-0.5	1	-0.5	0	0	0	1	S3	0
0	0	1	-1.5	0	0.5	0	0	0	0	S1	0
0	0	0	0.5	0	-2.5	1	0	0	9	S5	0
0	0	0	1	0	-4	0	1	0	13	S6	0
0	0	0	2	0	-7	0	0	1	31	S7	0

(g) What is the solution to the linear programming problem?

7. (a) Here are several stages of the tableau for a linear programming problem. In each case calculate the marginal net gains and the constraint ratios, and determine the pivot element.

		*****	*****	*****	*****	*****			
110	240	0	0	0	0	0	« Obj. Fn. Coeff.		
X1	X2	S1	S2	S3	S4	S5	RHS	BASIS VRS	CBV
5	9	1	0	0	0	0	7	S1	0
10	4	0	1	0	0	0	9	S2	0
7	18	0	0	1	0	0	5	S3	0
11	7	0	0	0	1	0	10	S4	0
2	9	0	0	0	0	1	12	S5	0

*****	****	*****			*****	*****			
110	240	0	0	0	0	0	≪ Obj. Fn. Coeff.		
X1	X2	S1	S2	S3	S4	S5	RHS	BASIS VRS	CBV
1.5	0	1	0	−0.5	0	0	4.5	S1	0
8.444	0	0	1	−0.222	0	0	7.889	S2	0
0.389	1	0	0	0.056	0	0	0.278	X2	240
8.278	0	0	0	−0.389	1	0	8.056	S4	0
−1.5	0	0	0	−0.5	0	1	9.5	S5	0

***		****	****		***	***			
110	240	0	0	0	0	0	≪ Obj. Fn. Coeff.		
X1	X2	S1	S2	S3	S4	S5	RHS	BASIS VRS	CBV
0	−3.857	1	0	−0.714	0	0	3.429	S1	0
0	−21.714	0	1	−1.429	0	0	1.857	S2	0
1	2.571	0	0	0.143	0	0	0.714	X1	110
0	−21.286	0	0	−1.571	1	0	2.143	S4	0
0	3.857	0	0	−0.286	0	1	10.571	S5	0

(b) What is the solution to the linear programming problem?

8. You are managing a portfolio and have to choose how much to invest in each of three stocks. Here is the information on each stock:

	Stock X	Stock Y	Stock Z
Expected return	0.03	0.05	0.08
Variance	1	2	5

Stock X is a safe stock with a low return; stock Z has a higher expected return but is much riskier. (Both the expected return and the variance are subjective estimates.) All three stocks are independent. (Chapter 12 discusses why this is important.) You must choose what fraction of the portfolio to put in each stock, trying to maximize the expected return while keeping the risk (variance) within acceptable limits:

Maximize $0.03x + 0.05y + 0.08z$
subject to: $x + 2y + 5z \le 2.4$

You also face the constraint that the shares cannot sum to more than 1:

$$x + y + z \le 1$$

and you are subject to constraints that prevent you from investing more than 40 percent of the portfolio in a single stock. What is the optimal share to invest in each stock?

ANSWERS

KNOW THE CONCEPTS

1. For many practical problems there will be so many basic feasible solutions that it will be impracticable to check them all. At each stage of the simplex process you are guaranteed to move to a new point with a higher value for the objective function, so you will reach the optimum more quickly than you would if you had to check all of the possibilities.

2. If one of the variables (either a choice variable or a slack variable) is negative, then you are not at a feasible point.

3. Add the variable with the largest marginal net gain.

4. Remove the variable corresponding to the row with the smallest positive value of the constraint ratio.

5. The result could be a point outside the feasible region.

6. At any stage of the simplex method, a new variable is brought into the basis only if its marginal net gain is positive. Therefore, the objective function must increase.

7. The simplex tableau is more convenient to work with. The information content is exactly the same as if the equations were written explicitly.

8. If one variable is brought into the basis, then the values of the other variables will be affected; this could affect the value of the objective function.

9. A plane, since a linear equation with three variables can be represented as a plane. See Chapter 1.

10. Three corner points will be adjacent to a given corner point. For example, see Figure 4-2. If there are m constraints and three choice variables for a linear programming problem, then a basic feasible solution will have m nonzero variables. There will be three variables outside the basis at a given stage of the simplex method. Moving one of these variables into the basis can be represented geometrically as moving to one of the three adjacent corner points.

PRACTICAL APPLICATION

1. $X1$ = plates, $X2$ = bowls

	*****	*****	*****					
6	3	0	0	0	≪ Obj. Fn. Coeff.			
X1	X2	S1	S2	S3	RHS	BASIS VRS	CBV	RATIO
1	0	1	0	0	30	S1	0	30 ≪
0	1	0	1	0	36	S2	0	
6	18	0	0	1	684	S3	0	114
6	3	0	0	0	≪ Marginal Net Gain			

Pivot element: row 1, column 1

	*****		*****	*****				
6	3	0	0	0	≪ Obj. Fn. Coeff.			
X1	X2	S1	S2	S3	RHS	BASIS VRS	CBV	RATIO
1	0	1	0	0	30	X1	6	
0	1	0	1	0	36	S2	0	36
0	18	−6	0	1	504	S3	0	28 ≪
0	3	−6	0	0	≪ Marginal Net Gain			

Pivot element: row 3, column 2

*****	*****			*****			
6	3	0	0	0	≪ Obj. Fn. Coeff.		
X1	X2	S1	S2	S3	RHS	BASIS VRS	CBV
1	0	1	0	0	30	X1	6
0	0	0.333	1	−0.056	8	S2	0
0	1	−0.333	0	0.056	28	X2	3
0	0	−5	0	−0.167	≪ Marginal Net Gain		

Solution: $x_1 = 30$, $x_2 = 28$, $s_2 = 8$; objective function value: 264.

2.

Final Tableau

| **** | ***** | | ***** | | ***** | ***** | | | |
| 1500 | 3000 | 0 | 0 | 0 | 0 | 0 | ≪ Obj. Fn. Coeff. | | |
X1	X2	S1	S2	S3	S4	S5	RHS	BASIS VRS	CBV
1	0	1	0	0	0	0	30	X1	1500
0	0	0.1	1	−0.05	0	0	32	S2	0
0	1	−0.1	0	0.05	0	0	28	X2	3000
0	0	−3.8	0	−0.1	1	0	84	S4	0
0	0	−0.9	0	−0.05	0	1	0	S5	0
0	0	−1200	0	−150	0	0	≪ Marginal Net Gain		

Solution: $x_1 = 30$, $x_2 = 28$, $s_2 = 32$, $s_4 = 84$, $s_5 = 0$; objective function value: 129,000.

3.

Final Tableau

| | ***** | | ***** | ***** | ***** | | | |
| 18 | 30 | 0 | 0 | 0 | 0 | ≪ Obj. Fn. Coeff. | | |
X	Y	S1	S2	S3	S4	RHS	BASIS VRS	CBV
0.667	1	0.056	0	0	0	6	Y	30
3	0	−0.167	1	0	0	57	S2	0
−3.333	0	−1.111	0	1	0	180	S3	0
−7	0	−0.833	0	0	1	90	S4	0
−2	0	−1.667	0	0	0	≪ Marginal Net Gain		

Solution: $x = 0$, $y = 6$; objective function value: 180.

4.

Final Tableau

| ***** | ***** | | | ***** | ***** | | | |
| 9 | 3 | 0 | 0 | 0 | 0 | ≪ Obj. Fn. Coeff. | | |
X1	X2	S1	S2	S3	S4	RHS	BASIS VRS	CBV
1	0	1	0	0	0	50	X1	9
0	1	−3	1	0	0	20	X2	3
0	0	5	−2	1	0	50	S3	0
0	0	3	−1	0	1	40	S4	0
0	0	0	−3	0	0	≪ Marginal Net Gain		

Solution: $x_1 = 50$, $x_2 = 20$, $s_3 = 50$, $s_4 = 40$; objective function value: 510.

Note that the net gain for S1 is zero. This means that the objective function would not change if S1 was added to the basis. Adding S1 to the basis means that you would move from point (50, 20) to point (40, 50). (See Figure 2-14). This situation occurs when the slope of the isoprofit line is the same as the slope of one of the line segments on the boundary of the feasible region. In this case two corner points, and all points on the segment between them, are tied for the optimum.

5.

Final Tableau

***	*****			*****	*****			
7	2	0	0	0	0	≪ Obj. Fn. Coeff.		
X1	X2	S1	S2	S3	S4	RHS	BASIS VRS	CBV
1	0	1	0	0	0	50	X1	7
0	1	−3	1	0	0	45	X2	2
0	0	5	−2	1	0	0	S3	0
0	0	3	−1	0	1	15	S4	0
0	0	−1	−2	0	0	≪ Marginal Net Gain		

Solution: $x_1 = 50$, $x_2 = 45$, $s_3 = 0$, $s_4 = 15$; objective function value: 440.

Note that S3 has the value zero, even though it is in the basis. This is an example of the special situation that arises when the number of nonzero variables in a basic feasible solution is less than the number of constraints. This situation (called *degeneracy*) will be discussed in more detail in the next chapter. The graph of the feasible region (Figure 4-3) shows that three of the constraints intersect at one point, which happens to be the optimum. Therefore, three of the slack variables have zero value at the optimum.

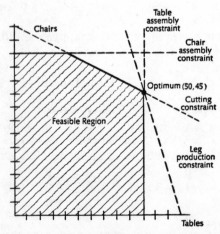

Figure 4-3

6. (a) Maximize $3x_1 + 4x_2$
subject to:
$$x_1 + 4x_2 \leq 81$$
$$x_1 + 3x_2 \leq 62$$
$$x_1 + 2x_2 \leq 44$$
$$x_1 + x_2 \leq 24$$
$$2x_1 + x_2 \leq 38$$
$$3x_1 + x_2 \leq 47$$
$$5x_1 + x_2 \leq 75$$

(b) Marginal net gains: for $x_1 = 3$, for $x_2 = 4$; constraint ratio values: 20.25, 20.667, 22, 24, 38, 47, 75

(c)

RHS	BASIS VRS	CBV
20.25	X2	4
1.25	S2	0
3.50	S3	0
3.75	S4	0
17.75	S5	0
26.75	S6	0
54.75	S7	0

(d) Row 2, column 1 (Note that there is a tie for the lowest value of the constraint ratio. This situation will be discussed further in the next chapter.)

(e) $-1, 4, -2, -3, -7, -11, -19$

(f) Marginal net gains: for $s_2 = -0.5$, for $s_4 = -2.5$

(g) $x_1 = 5$, $x_2 = 19$

7. (a) First stage–marginal net gains: for $x_1 = 110$, for $x_2 = 240$; constraint ratio values: 0.778, 2.25, 0.278, 1.429, 1.333; pivot element: row 3, column 2

Second stage—marginal net gains: for $x_1 = 16.667$, for $s_3 = -13.333$; constraint ratio values: 3, 0.934, 0.714, 0.973, -6.333; pivot element: row 3, column 1

Third stage—marginal net gains: for $x_2 = -42.857$, for $s_3 = -15.714$. The marginal net gains are both negative, so this is the optimum.

(b) Solution: $x_1 = 0.714$, $s_1 = 3.429$, $s_2 = 1.857$, $s_4 = 2.143$, $s_5 = 10.571$; objective function value: 78.571.

8. $X = 0.35$, $Y = 0.40$, $Z = 0.25$.

5

USING THE
SIMPLEX METHOD

KEY TERMS

degeneracy a situation that arises in a linear programming problem when more than one row of the simplex tableau gives the same constraint ratio, or the constraint ratio is zero

normal form a linear programming problem has been converted into normal form when it can be expressed as follows: maximize cx, subject to $Ax = R$, where all of the elements of R are nonnegative and all of the variables in x are required to be nonnegative

phase I the first phase of the simplex method, which consists of finding an initial basic feasible solution

phase II the second phase of the simplex method, which consists of moving from the initial basic feasible solution to the optimal basic feasible solution

redundancy a situation that arises in a linear programming problem when some of the constraint equations can be derived from other constraint equations

In this chapter we provide a more detailed treatment of the simplex method for solving linear programming problems. We will do the following:

- Develop a standard way of representing all linear programming problems (called the *normal form*).

- Establish mathematically that the optimum solution will occur at a basic feasible solution. (In the preceding chapters we demonstrated for two- or three-dimensional problems that the optimum will occur at one of the corner points of the feasible region, which will be one of the basic feasible solutions. In this chapter we will prove that this result is true for any number of dimensions.)

- Provide a procedure to use the simplex method when it is difficult to determine the initial basic feasible solution. (In Chapters 3 and 4 we could use the origin as the first basic feasible solution, but this is not always possible.)

- Consider two of the special types of difficulties that can arise when applying the simplex method: degeneracy (which arises when more than one row of the simplex tableau gives the same constraint ratio, or the constraint ratio is zero), and redundancy (which arises when some of the constraint equations can be derived from other constraint equations).

THE NORMAL FORM OF A LINEAR PROGRAMMING PROBLEM

First, we want to make sure that we have the problem well defined. We'd like it to be of as general a form as possible, but still of a fixed form and structure.

We saw in Chapter 2 that we start out with conditions, or constraints, on our variables. In most applications, we also want our variables to be greater than or equal to zero. If we have a variable x_i that is free to take any value (positive, zero, or negative), we can replace it everywhere that it appears with $u_i - v_i$, where u_i and v_i are nonnegative. Then we can change the original problem to one with nonnegative variables. Sums of multiples of the variables have to be less than or equal to, greater than or equal to, or just equal to given numbers. Right off the bat, we'd like to pin down which of these three cases exists for each of the constraints. We do this by using slack variables to turn any inequalities into equalities.

Then we have the following:

$$a_{11}x_1 + a_{12}x_2 + \cdots + a_{1n}x_n = R_1$$
$$a_{21}x_1 + a_{22}x_2 + \cdots + a_{2n}x_n = R_2$$
$$\cdots \cdots \cdots \cdots \cdots \cdots \cdots \cdots \cdots \cdots \cdots$$
$$a_{m1}x_1 + a_{m2}x_2 + \cdots + a_{mn}x_n = R_n$$

where a_{ij} is the coefficient of the jth variable in the ith row, and R_i is the constant term on the right-hand side of the ith equation. For reasons that we'll talk about later, we require all of the R_i's to be nonnegative. We can always eliminate a negative R_i by multiplying the ith equation by -1.

Then we have our CSE in the following matrix form: $\mathbf{Ax} = \mathbf{R}$, where $\mathbf{A}$ is our coefficient matrix with m rows and n columns, $\mathbf{x}$ is a column vector made up of our n nonnegative variables, including the original variables and the slack variables that we added, and $\mathbf{R}$ is a column vector made up of the m nonnegative constant terms in our set of constraints.

Mind you, we might be stopped at this point if there are no feasible solutions. For example, if we have the one constraint $-x_1 = 1$, it is impossible to find any feasible solutions. Later on, we'll show how to determine whether there are no feasible solutions.

If there are feasible solutions, then it makes sense to talk about the best one. We are given an objective function of the form

$$c_1 x_1 + c_2 x_2 + \cdots + c_n x_n$$

which we would like to make either as big (for example, a profit function) or as small (for example, a cost function) as possible.

Again, we use matrix terminology to write this more concisely. Let $\mathbf{c}$ be a one-row matrix, consisting of the coefficients of the variables; $\mathbf{c} = (c_1, c_2, \ldots, c_n)$. Then the objective function can be written as the matrix product $\mathbf{cx}$ ($\mathbf{c}$ has one row and n columns, and $\mathbf{x}$ has n rows and one column; therefore, $\mathbf{cx}$ has one row and one column—in other words, it is a scalar).

It would help if we could always express the objective function in a form that we want to maximize. If the goal is to minimize $\mathbf{cx}$, we can accomplish the same thing by maximizing $(-\mathbf{c})\mathbf{x}$. Therefore, if we have a minimization problem, by negating the coefficients in the objective function, we change the problem to a maximization problem with the same solution (if any).

Here is a linear programming problem in **normal form**: Find nonnegative variables $x_1, x_2, \ldots, x_n$ such that $\mathbf{Ax} = \mathbf{R}$ (where the entries of $\mathbf{R}$ are nonnegative), and $\mathbf{cx}$ is at a maximum.

To transform an arbitrary linear programming problem to normal form, proceed as follows:

1. If there is any variable x_i that is not required to be nonnegative, replace it by $u_i - v_i$, where u_i and v_i are required to be nonnegative.

2. If any of the constraints are inequalities, use slack variables to change them to equalities.

3. Relabel the variables if necessary.

4. If any constant term is negative, multiply that equation by -1.

5. If the problem seeks to minimize an objective function, negate the objective function, and look for its maximum.

If you have solved a problem in normal form, discard the values of the slack variables and calculate $x_i = u_i - v_i$ where necessary. Then you have an optimal solution for your original problem.

Example: Transforming a Problem to Normal Form

Suppose that you want to minimize $4x_1 - x_2 + 2x_3$, where x_2 and x_3 are nonnegative, and

$$\begin{aligned} x_1 + x_2 + x_3 &\geq 1 \\ 2x_1 - 3x_2 &= -5 \end{aligned}$$

To transform this problem to normal form, since x_1 isn't necessarily non-negative, start by letting $x_1 = u_1 - v_1$. Now you want to minimize $4u_1 - 4v_1 - x_2 + 2x_3$, where u_1, v_1, x_2, and x_3 are nonnegative, and

$$\begin{aligned} u_1 - v_1 + x_2 + x_3 &\geq 1 \\ 2u_1 - 2v_1 - 3x_2 &= -5 \end{aligned}$$

To change the first inequality to an equality, introduce a slack variable s_1. Minimize $4u_1 - 4v_1 - x_2 + 2x_3$, where u_1, v_1, x_2, x_3, and s_1 are nonnegative, and

$$\begin{aligned} u_1 - v_1 + x_2 + x_3 - s_1 &= 1 \\ 2u_1 - 2v_1 - 3x_2 &= -5 \end{aligned}$$

Let

$$x_1' = u_1, \qquad x_2' = v_1, \qquad x_3' = x_2, \qquad x_4' = x_3, \qquad \text{and} \qquad x_5' = s_1$$

Then minimize $4x_1' - 4x_2' - x_3' + 2x_4'$, where $x_i' \geq 0$ for $1 \leq i \leq 5$, and

$$\begin{aligned} x_1' - x_2' + x_3' + x_4' - x_5' &= 1 \\ 2x_1' - 2x_2' - 3x_3' &= -5 \end{aligned}$$

Since -5 is negative, multiply the second equation by -1. Minimize $4x_1' - 4x_2' - x_3' + 2x_4'$, where $x_i' \geq 0$ for $1 \leq i \leq 5$, and

$$\begin{aligned} x_1' - x_2' + x_3' + x_4' - x_5' &= 1 \\ -2x_1' + 2x_2' + 3x_3' &= 5 \end{aligned}$$

To make this a maximization problem, negate the objective function. Maximize $-4x_1' + 4x_2' + x_3' - 2x_4'$, where $x_i' \geq 0$ for $1 \leq i \leq 5$, and

$$\begin{aligned} x_1' - x_2' + x_3' + x_4' - x_5' &= 1 \\ -2x_1' + 2x_2' + 3x_3' &= 5 \end{aligned}$$

This is now in normal form, where

$$\mathbf{A} = \begin{pmatrix} 1 & -1 & 1 & 1 & -1 \\ -2 & 2 & 3 & 0 & 0 \end{pmatrix}, \quad \mathbf{R} = \begin{pmatrix} 1 \\ 5 \end{pmatrix}, \quad \text{and } \mathbf{c} = (-4 \quad 4 \quad 1 \quad -2 \quad 0)$$

Note that for the slack variable, x_5, we have $c_5 = 0$.

From now on, we will assume that all problems are in normal form.

SOLUTIONS

Now that we have the problem well defined, is there a solution? We've already seen that there may not be any feasible solutions. Even if feasible solutions exist, there may not be an optimal feasible solution if the objective function can become arbitrarily large, that is, go off to infinity. This happens, for example, if $c = (1 \quad 0)$, $A = (1 \quad -1)$, and $R = (1)$. Then we are trying to maximize x_1, where x_1 and x_2 are nonnegative and $x_1 - x_2 = 1$. If we let $x_2 = x_1 - 1$, where $x_1 \geq 1$, then x is a feasible solution, and x_1 can be made as large as we like.

If we are fortunate, there is an optimal feasible solution. It may or may not be unique. Our algorithm will find only one solution even if there are several. Presumably all these solutions would be of equal value to us, since the objective function gives us the same maximal value at each.

For the time being, we assume that there are at least as many variables (n) as constraints (m), that is, that $m \leq n$. (This is certainly true if we have to add a slack variable for each equation. Later we will show how to deal with the case where $m > n$.)

YOU SHOULD REMEMBER

A linear programming problem has been converted into normal form when it can be expressed as follows: Maximize **cx**, subject to **Ax = R**, where all of the entries of **R** are nonnegative, and all of the variables in **x** are required to be nonnegative.

A constraint that is written as an inequality can be turned into an equation by including a slack variable.

A minimization problem can be turned into a maximization problem by reversing the signs of all of the coefficients in the objective function (that is, turning all the positive coefficients to negative, and all the negative coefficients to positive).

If the right-hand-side constant is negative for a constraint equation, multiply both sides of the equation by −1.

If any variable is not constrained to be nonnegative, replace it by the difference of two variables, both of which are constrained to be nonnegative.

BASIC SOLUTIONS

On the face of it, we seem to be confronted with a problem having an infinite number of possible solutions to check. Fortunately, we need examine only the basic solutions. (Remember that a solution is basic if it has no more than m of the variables different from zero.) For each subset of m variables that are nonzero, with the other $n - m$ set to zero, there is at most one feasible solution. Thus there are only a finite number of basic solutions that we will have to check.

An important theorem in linear programming states why we need only to concentrate on the basic feasible solutions:

THEOREM. *If there is a feasible solution, there is a basic feasible solution, and if there is an optimal feasible solution, there is a basic optimal feasible solution.*

Since there are only a finite number of basic solutions, we need only to check a finite number of possible solutions. If there are no basic feasible solutions, there are no feasible solutions at all, and we have finished. If there are basic feasible solutions, but none is optimal, then we know that there are no optimal feasible solutions, and that we can make the objective function go off to infinity.

Proof. Now let's prove the theorem. We'll play the role of the devil's advocate, and suppose that the theorem is false. We assume that there is at least one feasible solution, but no basic feasible solutions, to the problem. We pick a feasible solution $\mathbf{x}^*$ with the largest possible number of zeros in it, and let s represent the number of nonzero entries in $\mathbf{x}^*$. Since we are assuming that there are no basic feasible solutions, it must be true that $s > m$. We relabel the variables so that $x_1^*, x_2^*, \ldots, x_s^*$ are these nonzero entries (we relabel $\mathbf{A}$ and $\mathbf{c}$ also, so that we still have the problem in normal form).

Then

$$x_1^* \mathbf{A}_1 + x_2^* \mathbf{A}_2 + \cdots + x_s^* \mathbf{A}_s = \mathbf{R}$$

where $\mathbf{A}_i$ is the ith column of $\mathbf{A}$ (since the rest of the x_j^*'s are zero), and thus has m entries.

We have a linear algebra theorem that says the following:

Given any s *vectors, each with* m *entries, where* s > m, *there is a linear combination of them (that is, a sum of multiples of them) that is the zero vector, where not all of the coefficients are zero.* (We say that the vectors are **linearly dependent.** See Section C of the appendix to Chapter 1.)

Now we know that there are numbers $d_1, d_2, \ldots, d_s$, not all zero, such that

$$d_1 A_1 + d_2 A_2 + \cdots + d_s A_s = 0$$

(where 0 is the column vector made up of m zeros). If none of the d_i is positive, we multiply the equation by -1. (Since the d_i's aren't all zero, this turns the negative d_i's into positive numbers.) Therefore, we can assume that at least one of the d_i's is positive. We let d_j be a positive d_i with x_i^*/d_i as small as possible (among all the positive d_i's). Then, if $d_i > 0$, we have $(x_i^*/d_i) \geq (x_j^*/d_j)$.

Let Y be the column vector with n entries, where $Y_i = x_i^* - (d_i/d_j)x_j^*$ for $1 \leq i \leq s$, and $Y_i = 0$ for $i > s$. We claim that Y is a feasible solution.

First, we need to show that each Y_i is nonnegative. This is true by definition for $i > s$. If $1 \leq i \leq s$, then we have two cases for each i. If $d_i > 0$, then $(x_i^*/d_i) \geq (x_j^*/d_j)$, and

$$x_i^* - \left(\frac{d_i}{d_j}\right)x_j^* = d_i\left(\frac{x_i^*}{d_i} - \frac{x_j^*}{d_j}\right) \geq 0$$

If $d_i \leq 0$, then $(d_i/d_j)x_j^* \leq 0$, and

$$x_i^* - \left(\frac{d_i}{d_j}\right)x_j^* \geq x_i^* \geq 0$$

Next, we need to show that $AY = R$. As before,

$$AY = Y_1 A_1 + Y_2 A_2 + \cdots + Y_s A_s$$

$$= \left[x_1^* - \left(\frac{d_i}{d_j}\right)x_j^*\right]A_1 + \left[x_2^* - \left(\frac{d_2}{d_j}\right)x_j^*\right]A_2 + \cdots + \left[x_s^* - \left(\frac{d_s}{d_j}\right)x_j^*\right]A_s$$

$$= (x_1^* A_1 + x_2^* A_2 + \cdots + x_s^* A_s) - \left(\frac{x_j^*}{d_j}\right)(d_1 A_1 + d_2 A_2 + \cdots + d_s A_s)$$

$$= x_1^* A_1 + x_2^* A_2 + \cdots + x_s^* A_s - \left(\frac{x_j^*}{d_j}\right)0$$

$$= x_1^* A_1 + x_2^* A_2 + \cdots + x_s^* A_s$$

$$= Ax = R$$

Thus, by assuming that our feasible solution, with the largest possible number of zero entries, could not be a basic feasible solution, we were able to construct our feasible solution $\mathbf{Y}$. However, $x_j^* \neq 0$ while $Y_j = x_j^* - (d_i/d_j)x_j^* = 0$. Therefore, $\mathbf{Y}$ has more zero entries than $\mathbf{x}$; this is a contradiction. Thus there must be a basic feasible solution.

The proof of the second part of the theorem is similar. Assume now that there is at least one optimal feasible solution. This means that the objective function has a maximum; call it M. Assume also that there is no basic optimal solution. We'll then show that this leads to a contradiction.

Let $\mathbf{x}^*$ be an optimal feasible solution with the largest possible number of zero entries. Since there are no basic optimal solutions, if s is the number of nonzero entries in $\mathbf{x}^*$, $s > m$. Again, we relabel the variables in $\mathbf{x}^*$ (and thus relabel the entries in A and $\mathbf{c}$) so that $x_1^*, x_2^*, \ldots, x_s^*$ are the nonzero entries. Then

$$x_1^* \mathbf{A}_1 + x_2^* \mathbf{A}_2 + \cdots + x_s^* \mathbf{A}_s = \mathbf{R} \quad \text{and} \quad c_1 x_1^* + c_2 x_2^* + \cdots + c_s x_s^* = M$$

Again, since $s > m$, $\mathbf{A}_1, \mathbf{A}_2, \ldots, \mathbf{A}_s$ are linearly dependent, and we have

$$d_1 \mathbf{A}_1 + d_2 \mathbf{A}_2 + \cdots + d_s \mathbf{A}_s = \mathbf{0}.$$

where not all of the d_i's are zero, and, by multiplying by -1 if necessary, at least one of the d_i's is positive.

Let μ be any number such that $|\mu| \leq |x_i^*/d_i|$ for all the i between 1 and s such that $d_i \neq 0$. Since $x_i^* > 0$ for each such i, μ can be nonzero, either positive or negative. Then, if $z_i = x_i^* + \mu d_i$ for $1 \leq i \leq s$ and $z_i = 0$ for $i > s$, the column vector $\mathbf{z}$, consisting of the z_i's, is a feasible solution: by the restriction on μ, $z_i \geq 0$ for all i.

$$
\begin{aligned}
\mathbf{Az} &= z_1 \mathbf{A}_1 + z_2 \mathbf{A}_2 + \cdots + z_s \mathbf{A}_s \\
&= (x_1^* + \mu d_1)\mathbf{A}_1 + (x_2^* + \mu d_2)\mathbf{A}_2 + \cdots + (x_s^* + \mu d_s)\mathbf{A}_s \\
&= (x_1^* \mathbf{A}_1 + x_2^* \mathbf{A}_2 + \cdots + x_s^* \mathbf{A}_s) + \mu(d_1 \mathbf{A}_1 + d_2 \mathbf{A}_2 + \cdots + d_s \mathbf{A}_s) \\
&= x_1^* \mathbf{A}_1 + x_2^* \mathbf{A}_2 + \cdots + x_s^* \mathbf{A}_s \\
&= \mathbf{Ax}^* = \mathbf{R}
\end{aligned}
$$

Then

$$
\begin{aligned}
M = \mathbf{cx}^* &\geq \mathbf{cz} \\
&= c_1(x_1^* + \mu d_1) + c_2(x_2^* + \mu d_2) + \cdots + c_s(x_s^* + \mu d_s) \\
&= (c_1 x_1^* + c_2 x_2^* + \cdots + c_s x_s^*) + \mu(c_1 d_1 + c_2 d_2 + \cdots + c_s d_s) \\
&= M + \mu(c_1 d_1 + c_2 d_2 + \cdots + c_s d_s)
\end{aligned}
$$

Since μ can be chosen to be negative or positive, we must have

$$c_1 d_1 + c_2 d_2 + \cdots + c_s d_s = 0$$

Let **Y** be defined as in the first part of this proof. **Y** is again a feasible solution:

$$
\begin{aligned}
\mathbf{cY} &= c_1\left[x_1^* - \left(\frac{d_i}{d_j}\right) x_j^* \right] + c_2\left[x_2^* - \left(\frac{d_2}{d_j}\right) x_j^* \right] + \cdots + c_2\left[x_s^* - \left(\frac{d_s}{d_j}\right) x_j^* \right] \\
&= (c_1 x_1^* + c_2 x_2^* + \cdots + c_s x_s^*) - \left(\frac{x_j^*}{d_j}\right)(c_1 d_1 + c_2 d_2 + \cdots + c_s d_s) \\
&= c_1 x_1^* + c_2 x_2^* + \cdots + c_s x_s^* = \mathbf{cx}
\end{aligned}
$$

and **Y** is also an optimal feasible solution, again with more zeros than **x***, a contradiction. Thus, if there is an optimal feasible solution, there must be a basic optimal feasible solution.

LOOKING FOR BASIC FEASIBLE SOLUTIONS

To start, we need to find any basic feasible solution. This process is called the **phase I** calculation. From there we can move from basic feasible solution to basic feasible solution, looking for an optimal one (this being the **phase II** calculation). For the time being, therefore, we'll ignore **c** and its objective function, and concentrate on finding a basic feasible solution.

If our original problem consisted of "less than or equal to" inequalities that looked like this:

$$
\begin{aligned}
a_{11}x_1 + a_{12}x_2 + \cdots + a_{1n}x_n &\leq R_1 \\
a_{21}x_1 + a_{22}x_2 + \cdots + a_{2n}x_n &\leq R_2 \\
&\cdots\cdots\cdots\cdots\cdots\cdots\cdots \\
a_{m1}x_1 + a_{m2}x_2 + \cdots + a_{mn}x_n &\leq R_m
\end{aligned}
$$

where each $R_i \geq 0$, we obtained our normal form by adding slack variables $s_1, s_2, \ldots, s_m$ to obtain equalities that looked like this:

$$
\begin{aligned}
a_{11}x_1 + a_{12}x_2 + \cdots + a_{1n}x_n + s_1 &= R_1 \\
a_{21}x_1 + a_{22}x_2 + \cdots + a_{2n}x_n + s_2 &= R_2 \\
&\cdots\cdots\cdots\cdots\cdots\cdots\cdots\cdots\cdots \\
a_{m1}x_1 + a_{m2}x_2 + \cdots + a_{mn}x_n + s_m &= R_m
\end{aligned}
$$

We can easily find one basic feasible solution: $s_i = R_i$ for each i, and $x_j = 0$ for each j. (This is why it's helpful to require that each $R_i \geq 0$.) This was the situation in Chapters 3 and 4.

Sad to say, not every linear programming problem starts out this way. Sometimes the inequalities go the other way, and sometimes there are equalities instead of inequalities. However, we can still use slack variables to start our algorithm.

Let's take our normal form: $\mathbf{A}\mathbf{x} = \mathbf{R}$, and introduce m new slack variables $s_1, s_2, \ldots, s_m$ (all nonnegative) in the following way. Now we require that $\mathbf{A}\mathbf{x} + \mathbf{s} = \mathbf{R}$, where $\mathbf{s}$ is the column vector consisting of the s_i's. This can be written out as follows:

$$\begin{pmatrix} a_{11} & a_{12} & \cdots & a_{1n} \\ a_{21} & a_{22} & \cdots & a_{2n} \\ \cdots & \cdots & \cdots & \cdots \\ a_{m1} & a_{m2} & \cdots & a_{mn} \end{pmatrix} \begin{pmatrix} x_1 \\ x_2 \\ \cdot \\ x_n \end{pmatrix} + \begin{pmatrix} s_1 \\ s_2 \\ \cdot \\ s_m \end{pmatrix} = \begin{pmatrix} R_1 \\ R_2 \\ \cdot \\ R_m \end{pmatrix}$$

This is still a normal form, if we relabel all the terms. Let $\mathbf{A}^1$ be the m by $(m + n)$ matrix whose first n columns are those of $\mathbf{A}$, and whose last m columns form the m by m identity matrix (that is, a matrix with 1's along the diagonal and 0's elsewhere). Then

$$\mathbf{A}^1 = \begin{pmatrix} a_{11} & a_{12} & \cdots & a_{1n} & 1 & 0 & \cdots & 0 \\ a_{21} & a_{22} & \cdots & a_{2n} & 0 & 1 & \cdots & 0 \\ \cdots & \cdots & \cdots & \cdots & \cdots & \cdots & \cdots & \cdots \\ a_{m1} & a_{m2} & \cdots & a_{mn} & 0 & 0 & \cdots & 1 \end{pmatrix}$$

Let $\mathbf{x}^1 =$ the column vector of length $m + n$, whose first n components are those of $\mathbf{x}$ and whose last m components are those of $\mathbf{s}$. Then

$$\mathbf{x}^1 = \begin{pmatrix} x_1 \\ x_2 \\ \cdot \\ x_n \\ s_1 \\ s_2 \\ \cdot \\ s_m \end{pmatrix}$$

You should verify for yourself that $\mathbf{A}^1\mathbf{x}^1 = \mathbf{A}\mathbf{x} + \mathbf{s}$. Therefore, we have a new linear programming problem in normal form: Maximize $\mathbf{c}^1\mathbf{x}^1$ subject to

$A^1 x^1 = R$. This problem has an easy basic solution corresponding to $s = R$ and $x = 0$ (where 0 is the column vector consisting of n zeros).

So what, you may well say. Indeed, s has nothing to do with the original problem.

If, however, we could move to a different basic feasible solution for the new problem, where all of the new slack variables are equal to zero, then we would have a basic feasible solution for the original problem. Then

$$R = A^1 x^1 = Ax + s = Ax$$

each x_i would be nonnegative, and at most m would be nonzero, making x the sought-after basic feasible solution.

Now we have to do a bit of foreshadowing. Suppose we knew how to go from a basic feasible solution to an optimal basic feasible solution, that is, we already knew how to do a phase II calculation. Could we then move to a basic feasible solution x^1 for the new problem with $s = 0$?

To answer that question, we need to use a different objective function for the phase I calculation. The phase I objective function must be designed so that the optimum will occur when all of the slack variables are zero. To do that, let c^1 be a row vector of length $m + n$, whose first n components are 0, and whose last m components are -1. Then $c^1 x^1$ is equal to

$$(0, 0, \ldots, -1, -1, \ldots, -1) \begin{pmatrix} x_1 \\ x_2 \\ \cdot \\ x_n \\ s_1 \\ s_2 \\ \cdot \\ s_m \end{pmatrix} = -s_1 - s_2 - \cdots - s_m$$

Note that $c^1 x^1 \leq 0$. What happens if we try to maximize $c^1 x^1$, using the phase II calculation? If the maximal value, zero, is achieved, then $s = 0$ and x is our basic feasible solution for the original problem. If $c^1 x^1$ is still negative at its maximum, then we can never have $s = 0$, and there is no basic feasible solution, and thus no feasible solution.

Phase I calculations, therefore, are the same as phase II calculations, with A^1, x^1, and c^1 substituted for A, x, and c, respectively.

YOU SHOULD REMEMBER

Phase I of the simplex method is the procedure for finding an initial basic feasible solution. In maximization problems, the origin can often be used as the initial basic feasible solution, so the phase I calculation is not necessary. However, in minimization problems the origin is usually not feasible, and therefore the phase I process is needed.

For phase I, introduce a new slack variable for each constraint. It is possible to start with a basic feasible solution such that all of these slack variables are in the basis. Set up the objective function for phase I so that all of the original variables have coefficients of 0 and the new slack variables have coefficients of -1. Then proceed to use the simplex method. The maximum possible value for this objective function will be 0, which can occur only if all of the new slack variables have been removed from the basis (that is, their values have been set to 0). Once this occurs, the values for the remaining variables can be used as an initial basic feasible solution for the original problem, and it becomes possible to proceed with the phase II calculations.

Example: Calculating the Minimum-Cost Diet

PROBLEM In Chapter 2 we found the diet with the minimum cost by graphing the feasible region and checking the corner points. We will consider the same problem, with two changes: (1) we will now use x_1 to represent the amount of cereal, and x_2 to represent the amount of rice; and (2) the prices have changed so that cereal now costs 12 cents per ounce and rice costs 11 cents per cup.

Here is the problem:

Minimize $12x_1 + 11x_2$
subject to:
protein constraint: $6x_1 +   6x_2 \geq 21$
thiamine constraint: $0.3x_1 + 0.24x_2 \geq 1$
iron constraint: $5x_1 +   1.5x_2 \geq 12$

SOLUTION To convert the problem into a maximizing problem, we need merely to reverse the sign of the objective function coefficients: maximize $-12x_1 - 11x_2$.

We convert the inequalities into equations by adding three slack variables, which measure the amount of surplus for each nutrient: x_3 will measure the amount of surplus protein; x_4 will measure the amount of surplus thiamine; and x_5 will measure the amount of surplus iron. The problem becomes

Maximize $-12x_1 - 11x_2$
subject to:

protein constraint:	$6x_1 + 6x_2 - x_3$	$= 21$
thiamine constraint:	$0.3x_1 + 0.24x_2 - x_4$	$= 1$
iron constraint:	$5x_1 + 1.5x_2 - x_5$	$= 12$

Note that the coefficients for the slack variables are negative, because the original constraints contained "greater than or equal to" signs. Remember that the slack variables had positive coefficients when the original constraints contained "less than or equal to" signs. Sometimes these variables are called *surplus variables* when the original constraints involve "greater than or equal to" signs.

To conduct the phase I calculation, we need to add three new slack variables, s_1, s_2, and s_3:

$$6x_1 + 6x_2 - x_3 \qquad\qquad + s_1 \qquad\qquad = 21$$
$$0.3x_1 + 0.24x_2 \qquad - x_4 \qquad\quad + s_2 \qquad = 1$$
$$5x_1 + 1.5x_2 \qquad\qquad - x_5 \qquad\qquad + s_3 = 12$$

The initial basic feasible solution for phase I will be

$$s_1 = 21, \qquad s_2 = 1, \qquad s_3 = 12, \qquad x_1 = 0,$$
$$x_2 = 0, \qquad x_3 = 0, \qquad x_4 = 0, \qquad x_5 = 0$$

For the phase I calculation, we will use this objective function:

Maximize $0 \times x_1 + 0 \times x_2 + 0 \times x_3 + 0 \times x_4 + 0 \times x_5 - s_1 - s_2 - s_3$

Remember that the point of the phase I calculation is to make sure that the solution at the end of phase I does not contain s_1, s_2, or s_3.

Initial Tableau

0	0	0	0	0	−1	−1	−1	≪ Obj. Fn. Coeff.			
X1	X2	X3	X4	X5	S1	S2	S3	RHS	BASIS VRS	CBV	RATIO
6	6	−1	0	0	1	0	0	21	S1	−1	3.50
0.30	0.24	0	−1	0	0	1	0	1	S2	−1	3.33
5	1.50	0	0	−1	0	0	1	12	S3	−1	2.40 ≪
11.30	7.74	−1	−1	−1	0	0	0	≪ Marginal Net Gain			

Pivot element: row 3, column 1

After pivoting, x_1 is added to the basis and s_3 is removed.

Second Tableau

0	0	0	0	0	−1	−1	−1	≪ Obj. Fn. Coeff.			
X1	X2	X3	X4	X5	S1	S2	S3	RHS	BASIS VRS	CBV	RATIO
0	4.20	−1	0	1.20	1	0	−1.20	6.60	S1	−1	1.57 ≪
0	0.15	0	−1	0.06	0	1	−0.06	0.28	S2	−1	1.87
1	0.30	0	0	−0.20	0	0	0.20	2.40	X1	0	8
0	4.35	−1	−1	1.26	0	0	−2.26	≪ Marginal Net Gain			

Pivot element: row 1, column 2

Here x_2 is added to the basis and s_1 is removed.

Third Tableau

0	0	0	0	0	−1	−1	−1	≪ Obj. Fn. Coeff.			
X1	X2	X3	X4	X5	S1	S2	S3	RHS	BASIS VRS	CBV	RATIO
0	1	−0.24	0	0.29	0.24	0	−0.29	1.57	X2	0	−6.60
0	0	0.04	−1	0.02	−0.04	1	−0.02	0.04	S2	−1	1.24 ≪
1	0	0.07	0	−0.29	−0.07	0	0.29	1.93	X1	0	27.00
0	0	0.04	−1	0.02	−1.04	0	0	−1.02	≪ Marginal Net Gain		

Pivot element: row 2, column 3

Here x_3 is added to the basis and s_2 is removed.

Fourth Tableau

0	0	0	0	0	−1	−1	−1	≪ Obj. Fn. Coeff.		
X1	X2	X3	X4	X5	S1	S2	S3	RHS	BASIS VRS	CBV
0	1	0	−6.67	0.40	0	6.67	−0.40	1.867	X2	0
0	0	1	−28.00	0.48	−1	28.00	−0.48	1.24	X3	0
1	0	0	2.00	−0.32	0	−2.00	0.32	1.84	X1	0
0	0	0	0	0	−1	−1	−1	≪ Marginal Net Gain		

All of the marginal net gains are negative, so we have reached the optimum. Just as we hoped, s_1, s_2, and s_3 have all been removed from the basis. The solution is as follows:

cereal:	$x_1 = 1.84$
rice:	$x_2 = 1.867$
surplus protein:	$x_3 = 1.24$
surplus thiamine:	$x_4 = 0$
surplus iron:	$x_5 = 0$

This is a basic solution, since the number of nonzero variables (three) is the same as the number of constraints. We can check each of the constraints to verify that the solution is also feasible. Here is the initial tableau for phase II:

**** −12 X1	**** −11 X2	**** 0 X3	0 X4	0 X5	RHS	≪ Obj. Fn. Coeff. BASIS VRS	CBV	RATIO
0	1	0	−6.67	0.40	1.87	X2	−11	4.67
0	0	1	−28	0.48	1.24	X3	0	2.58 ≪
1	0	0	2	−0.32	1.84	X1	−12	−5.75
0	0	0	−49.33	0.56ˆ		≪ Marginal Net Gain		

Pivot element: row 2, column 5

Note that this tableau is the same as the final tableau for phase I, except for two differences: (1) s_1, s_2, and s_3 have been removed, and (2) the objective function now corresponds to the objective function for our actual problem, instead of the artificial objective function used in phase I. Of course, changing the objective function changes the "CBV" column and the marginal net gains. The marginal net gain for x_5 is positive, so x_5 will be added to the basis; x_3 will be removed. Here is the new tableau:

**** −12 X1	**** −11 X2	0 X3	0 X4	**** 0 X5	RHS	≪ Obj. Fn. Coeff. BASIS VRS	CBV
0	1	−0.83	16.67	0	0.83	X2	−11
0	0	2.08	−58.33	1	2.58	X5	0
1	0	0.67	−16.67	0	2.67	X1	−12
0	0	−1.17	−16.67	0		≪ Marginal Net Gain	

The marginal net gain is negative for both of the variables outside the basis, so we have reached the optimum:

cereal:	$x_1 = 2.67$
rice:	$x_2 = 0.83$
surplus protein:	$x_3 = 0$
surplus thiamine:	$x_4 = 0$
surplus iron:	$x_5 = 2.58$

The total cost of the diet is $12 \times 2.67 + 11 \times 0.83 = 41.17$.

Now we will cover the formal explanation as to why the pivoting process of the simplex method works. Be warned: the following sections become more intensely mathematical; less mathematically inclined readers may wish to skip to the end of the chapter.

LOOKING FOR OPTIMAL BASIC FEASIBLE SOLUTIONS

Assume now that we are in a phase II calculation, and that we have a basic feasible solution x, with $Ax = R$. If possible, we'd like to find a new basic feasible solution x', with a higher value for the objective function, that is, $cx < cx'$. If there is none, x is the optimal basic feasible solution. If there is one, then we've eliminated x as a candidate for the optimal basic feasible solution; and since there are only a finite number of basic feasible solutions, we are well on our way.

Since x is a *basic* feasible solution, it has no more than m of its components different from zero. If we ignore for the time being $n - m$ of the entries that are set equal to zero, and concentrate on the m remaining ones (including all of the nonzero ones), then, temporarily, we are dealing with a set of m equations in m variables. This is simpler to handle, so we single out a set of m entries of x that include all of the nonzero x_i's, and call it the **basis set**. We label these components $x_{1B}, x_{2B}, \ldots, x_{mB}$, where the B in the index tells us that we are dealing with the components in the basis set. (Thus x_{2B} is not necessarily x_2, but is just the second component of x in the basis set.) Likewise, let $A_{1B}, A_{2B}, \ldots, A_{mB}$ be the columns of A corresponding to our basis set. Then, since all of the other components are zero,

$$Ax = x_{1B}A_{1B} + x_{2B}A_{2B} + \cdots + x_{mB}A_{mB} = R$$

$A_{1B}, A_{2B}, \ldots, A_{mB}$ are called **basis vectors**, and R is a linear combination of them. The simplest way to go from one basic solution to another is to delete one basis vector A_{iB} (that is, set x_{iB} equal to zero), and bring in another column of A, A_L, to be A'_{iB}, the new ith basis vector. We have to be careful how we do this to ensure that we don't make any of our new basis set negative.

How do we bring A_L in? It turns out that, at any step in the algorithm, our basis vectors will span our space of vectors of length m. This means that every such vector can be expressed as a linear combination of the basis vectors (in fact, we will be able to read off the coefficients from our simplex tableau whenever we need them). This is certainly true at the start of phase I calculations, where the basis vectors (corresponding to the basis set, $s_1, s_2, \ldots, s_m$) are the unit column vectors of length m (A^1_{iB} has 1 for its ith component, and 0's elsewhere).

Thus, for each L, we have

$$A_L = d_1 A_{1B} + d_2 A_{2B} + \cdots + d_m A_{mB}$$

where the coefficients $d_1, d_2, \ldots, d_m$ are determined by A_L. Another way of writing this is

$$A_L - d_1 A_{1B} - d_2 A_{2B} - \cdots - d_m A_{mB} = 0$$

If we multiply this by μ, and add it to

$$x_{1B} A_{1B} + x_{2B} A_{2B} + \cdots + x_{mB} A_{mB} = R$$

we get

$$\mu A_L + (x_{1B} - \mu d_1) A_{1B} + (x_{2B} - \mu d_2) A_{2B} + \cdots + (x_{mB} - \mu d_m) A_{mB} = R$$

This will be a new feasible solution x' with $x'_L = \mu$, and $x'_{jB} = x_{jB} - \mu d_j$ for each j, if $\mu > 0$ and $x_{jB} \geq \mu d_j$ for each j. (If $\mu = 0$, it is the same solution, with a different basis set.) This will be a new basic solution if, for at least one j, $x_{jB} = \mu d_j$. This is impossible if $d_j < 0$. Thus it is necessary and sufficient to have $\mu \leq x_{jB}/d_j$ for each positive d_j (assuming there is at least one), with equality for at least one such j. Thus we want μ to be the smallest x_{jB}/d_j, where $d_j > 0$. For such a j, $x_{jB} - \mu d_j = 0$, and we delete A_{jB} from the basis and replace it with A_L. (For the present, assume that only one j gives us this value. Otherwise, the problem is *degenerate*, a situation that we will deal with later.)

Now we know how to bring A_L into the basis, deleting A_{jB}. But do we want to? What does this do to the objective function?

For x,

$$cx = c_{1B} x_{1B} + c_{2B} x_{2B} + \cdots + c_{mB} x_{mB}$$

(where c_{iB} is the coefficient of the objective function corresponding to x_{iB}), since all of the other components of $\mathbf{x}$ are zero. For $\mathbf{x}'$,

$$\mathbf{cx}' = c_L x'_L + c_{1B} x'_{1B} + c_{2B} x'_{2B} + \cdots + c_{mB} x'_{mB}$$
$$= c_L \mu + c_{1B}(x_{1B} - \mu d_1) + c_{2B}(x_{2B} - \mu d_2) + \cdots + (x_{mB} - \mu d_m)$$

Also

$$\mathbf{cx}' - \mathbf{cx} = c_L \mu - \mu c_{1B} d_1 - c_{2B} d_2 - \cdots - c_{mB} d_m$$
$$= \mu(c_L - c_{1B} d_1 - c_{2B} d_2 - \cdots - c_{mB} d_m)$$

If μ is positive, the objective function will increase, stay the same, or decrease if the last term is positive, zero, or negative, respectively. It will be in our best interest to move to $\mathbf{x}'$ from $\mathbf{x}$ if this term, called the **marginal net gain** for x_L and denoted by MNG_L, is positive.

PIVOTING

All of this may seem rather complicated—and so it is. Fortunately, the simplex algorithm does all of the work for us.

Given our simplex tableau, we need to be able to do two things to perform the algorithm. First, we need to find where to pivot, and, second, we need to pivot.

Let's look at our very first tableau, from the phase I calculation:

0	0	...	0	−1	−1	...	−1	≪ Obj. Fn. Coeff.		
X1	X2	...	Xn	S1	S2	...	Sm	RHS	BASIS VRS	CBV
a_{11}	a_{12}	...	a_{1n}	1	0	...	0	R_1	s_1	−1
a_{21}	a_{22}	...	a_{2n}	0	1	...	0	R_2	s_2	−1
...	...									
a_{m1}	a_{m2}	...	a_{mn}	0	0	...	1	R_m	s_m	−1
$\Sigma_k a_{k1}$	$\Sigma_k a_{k2}$	...	$\Sigma_k a_{kn}$	0	0	...	0	≪ Marginal Net Gain		

Notice three things:

1. Setting the variables listed in the "BASIS VRS" column equal to the adjacent numbers in the "RHS" column yields a basic feasible solution.

2. Under each variable is a column consisting of the coefficients $d_1, d_2, \ldots, d_m$ expressing the corresponding column of $\mathbf{A}$ as a linear combination of the basis vectors.

3. The last row in the tableau contains the marginal net gain for each column as we've defined these gains.

These three things will remain true about our tableau after every pivot that we do. Then μ will just be the constraint ratio defined in Chapter 4.

Assume, now, that we are at an arbitrary stage in the algorithm, where the three things listed above are true.

c_1	c_2	...	c_n	$\ll$ Obj. Fn. Coeff.		
X1	X2	...	Xn	RHS	BASIS VRS	CBV
A_{11}	A_{12}	...	A_{1n}	R_1	x_{1B}	C_{1B}
A_{21}	A_{22}	...	A_{2n}	R_2	x_{2B}	C_{2B}
A_{m1}	A_{m2}	...	A_{mn}	R_m	x_{mB}	c_{mB}

MNG_1 MNG_2 ... MNG_n $\ll$ Marginal Net Gain

Think of the tableau as representing the following set of equations:

$$A_{11}x_1 + A_{12}x_2 + \cdots + A_{1n}x_n = R_1$$
$$A_{21}x_1 + A_{22}x_2 + \cdots + A_{2n}x_n = R_2$$
$$\cdots\cdots\cdots\cdots\cdots\cdots\cdots\cdots\cdots\cdots$$
$$A_{m1}x_1 + A_{m2}x_2 + \cdots + A_{mn}x_n = R_m$$

as it does. Once we have found where to pivot, say at the ith row and the jth column, we divide the jth equation by A_{ij} (which is positive), and subtract multiples of this equation from the other equations in such a way as to leave the coefficients of x_j in the other equations equal to zero:

$$A'_{11}x_1 + A'_{12}x_2 + \cdots + (0)x_j + \cdots + A'_{1n}x_n = R'_1$$
$$A'_{21}x_1 + A'_{22}x_2 + \cdots + (0)x_j + \cdots + A'_{2n}x_n = R'_2$$
$$\cdots\cdots\cdots\cdots\cdots\cdots\cdots\cdots\cdots\cdots\cdots\cdots\cdots$$
$$A'_{i1}x_1 + A'_{i2}x_2 + \cdots + (1)x_j + \cdots + A'_{in}x_n = R'_i$$
$$\cdots\cdots\cdots\cdots\cdots\cdots\cdots\cdots\cdots\cdots\cdots\cdots\cdots$$
$$A'_{m1}x_1 + A'_{m2}x_2 + \cdots + (0)x_j + \cdots + A'_{mn}x_n = R'_m$$

For the coefficients corresponding to the columns of the basis vectors (which have one 1 and $m - 1$ 0's), nothing will change except for the ith basis vector, since the coefficients of x_j will be 0, except in the ith row. Thus we will again end up after the pivot with m columns of coefficients with 1's in distinct rows and 0's elsewhere. A basic feasible solution for the set of new equations is to set all of the other variables equal to 0, and the new basis set of variables equal to the constants on the right-hand side. But this is just what item 1 in our list requires.

Let A'_{kB} be the new kth basis vector.

$$\mathbf{A}'_{kB} = \mathbf{A}_j \quad \text{if } k = j, \quad \text{and} \quad \mathbf{A}'_{kB} = \mathbf{A}_{kB} \quad \text{if } k \neq j$$

Let A'_{kL} be the element in the new tableau in the kth row and Lth column.

$$A'_{kL} = \frac{A_{iL}}{A_{ij}} \text{ if } k = i, \quad \text{and} \quad A_{kL} - \left(\frac{A_{kj}}{A_{ij}}\right)A_{iL} \text{ if } k \neq i$$

Then

$$\sum_k A'_{kL}\mathbf{A}_{kB} = A'_{iL}\mathbf{A}'_{iB} + \sum_{k \neq i} A'_{kL}\mathbf{A}'_{kB} = \left(\frac{A_{iL}}{A_{ij}}\right)\mathbf{A}_i + \sum_{k \neq i}\left[A_{kL} - \left(\frac{A_{kj}}{A_{ij}}\right)A_{iL}\right](\mathbf{A}_{kB})$$

$$= \left(\frac{A_{iL}}{A_{ij}}\right)\mathbf{A}_i + \sum_{k \neq i} A_{kL}\mathbf{A}_{kB} - \left(\frac{A_{iL}}{A_{ij}}\right)\sum_{k \neq i} A_{kj}\mathbf{A}_{kB}$$

$$= \left(\frac{A_{iL}}{A_{ij}}\right)\mathbf{A}_i + \sum_k A_{kL}\mathbf{A}_{kB} - A_{iL}\mathbf{A}_{iB} - \left(\frac{A_{iL}}{A_{ij}}\right)\sum_k A_{kj}\mathbf{A}_{kB} + \left(\frac{A_{iL}}{A_{ij}}\right)A_{ij}\mathbf{A}_{iB}$$

$$= \left(\frac{A_{iL}}{A_{ij}}\right)\mathbf{A}_j + \mathbf{A}_L - \left(\frac{A_{iL}}{A_{ij}}\right)\mathbf{A}_j = \mathbf{A}_L$$

The (A'_{kL})'s are still the coefficients of $\mathbf{A}_L$ in the new basis, and requirement 2 in our list is still satisfied.

Now let c'_{kB} be the coefficient of x'_{kB}.

$$c'_{kB} = c_j \text{ if } k = i, \quad \text{and} \quad c'_{kB} = c_{kB} \text{ if } k \neq i$$

The new last row has in the Lth column

$$\text{MNG}_L - \left(\frac{\text{MNG}_i}{A_{ij}}\right)A_{iL} = c_L - \sum_k A_{kL}c_{kB} - \left(\frac{A_{il}}{A_{ij}}\right)\left(c_j - \sum_k A_{kj}c_{kB}\right)$$

$$= c_L - \sum_k A_{kL}c_{kB} - \left(\frac{A_{iL}}{A_{ij}}\right)c_j + \left(\frac{A_{iL}}{A_{ij}}\right)\sum_k A_{kj}c_{kB}$$

Now

$$\text{MNG}'_L = c_L - \sum_k A'_{kL}c'_{kB} = c_L - \sum_{k \neq i}\left[A_{kL} - \left(\frac{A_{kj}}{A_{ij}}\right)A_{iL}\right]c'_{kB} - \left(\frac{A_{iL}}{A_{ij}}\right)c'_{kB}$$

$$= c_L - \sum_{k \neq i} A_{kL}c'_{kB} + \sum_{k \neq i}\left(\frac{A_{ij}}{A_{ij}}\right)A_{iL}c'_{kB} - \left(\frac{A_{iL}}{A_{ij}}\right)c'_{iB}$$

$$= c_L - \sum_{k \neq i} A_{kL}c_{kB} + \sum_{k \neq i}\left(\frac{A_{kj}}{A_{ij}}\right)A_{iL}c_{kB} - \left(\frac{A_{iL}}{A_{ij}}\right)c_j$$

$$= c_L - \sum_k A_{kL}c_{kB} + A_{iL}c_{iB} + \sum_k\left(\frac{A_{ij}}{A_{ij}}\right)A_{iL}c_{kB} - \left(\frac{A_{ij}}{A_{ij}}\right)A_{iL}c_{iB} - \left(\frac{A_{iL}}{A_{ij}}\right)c_j$$

$$= c_L - \sum_k A_{kL}c_{kB} - \left(\frac{A_{iL}}{A_{ij}}\right)c_j + \left(\frac{A_{iL}}{A_{ij}}\right)\sum_k A_{kj}c_{kB}$$

and item 3 in our list is satisfied.

Since items 1, 2, and 3 are true at the beginning of the simplex method, and remain true after each pivot, they are true at every stage of the algorithm. Thus, in terms of the work we need to do for the simplex method, pivoting the tableau does it all for us; it automatically finds our new basic solution with a higher value for the objective function, and new marginal net gains for the new basic feasible solution.

DEGENERACY

It is possible that μ (the constraint ratio) can acquire the value zero at some stage of the process. This will really mess up our algorithm if we're not careful, because then, even if the MNG for our new basis vector is positive, our objective function value will stay the same for our new basic feasible solution. In theory, the algorithm could enter into an infinite loop, going back and forth between two basic feasible solutions. Fortunately, because of round-off errors, it is unlikely in practice that μ will become zero.

The problem can start, however, before $\mu = 0$. Suppose that we are pivoting on column k. If the constraint ratio μ is attained at two rows i and j, so that $\mu = R_i/A_{ik} = R_j/A_{jk}$, and we choose row i to pivot on,

$$R'_j = R_j - \left(\frac{A_{jk}}{A_{ik}}\right)R_i = R_j - \left(\frac{R_j}{R_i}\right)R_i = 0$$

Then, if $A'_{jk} > 0$, our new constraint ratio will be at $\mu' = 0 = R'_j/d'_j$. Unless we start out at the beginning with some $R_i = 0$, this is the only way we will ever end with some $R_i = 0$, and thus $\mu = 0$.

Example: An Ambiguous Pivot

Suppose that we want to solve for nonnegative x_1 and x_2 such that

$$x_1 + 2x_2 = 5$$
$$3x_1 + 4x_2 = 10$$

and $x_1 + x_2$ is as large as possible. Then

$$\mathbf{A} = \begin{pmatrix} 1 & 2 \\ 3 & 4 \end{pmatrix}, \qquad \mathbf{R} = \begin{pmatrix} 5 \\ 10 \end{pmatrix}, \qquad \mathbf{c} = (1 \quad 1)$$

Phase I: $\mathbf{A}^1 = \begin{pmatrix} 1 & 2 & 1 & 0 \\ 3 & 4 & 0 & 1 \end{pmatrix}, \qquad \mathbf{R} = \begin{pmatrix} 5 \\ 10 \end{pmatrix}, \qquad \mathbf{c}^1 = (0 \quad 0 \quad -1 \quad -1)$

0	0	−1	−1	≪ Obj. Fn. Coeff.			
X1	X2	S1	S2	RHS	BASIS VRS	CBV	RATIO
1	2	1	0	5	s_1	−1	5/2
3	4	0	1	10	s_2	−1	5/2
4	6	0	0	≪ Marginal Net Gain			

We want to pivot on the second column, but which row do we choose to pivot on? The constraint ratios are the same.

This situation is called **degeneracy** (a value judgment, perhaps, but the situation certainly complicates things).

We would like to be able to ensure that we do not cycle between basic feasible solutions with the same objective function value. One way is to find some other measuring numbers that we can require to increase as we go from one solution to the next. Then we could never cycle back to a previous solution—its measurements would be smaller.

This can be done, but it is complicated (the preceding stuff was easy!), and requires some knowledge of linear algebra. If you trust in round-off errors to prevent this problem, skip the next section.

THE AUXILIARY TABLEAU

We want to adjust our algorithm so that, given a constraint ratio attained by more than one row, our algorithm will pick one row unambiguously, in a way that will prevent cycling. To do this we need to construct an **auxiliary tableau**. Assume that we're pivoting on the jth column:

$$
\begin{array}{ll|llll}
A_{1j} & R_1 & u_{11} & u_{12} & \cdots & u_{1m} \\
A_{2j} & R_2 & u_{21} & u_{22} & \cdots & u_{2m} \\
\multicolumn{6}{c}{\dotfill} \\
A_{mj} & R_m & u_{m1} & u_{m2} & \cdots & u_{mm}
\end{array}
$$

The first column is the jth column from our simplex tableau, the one with positive MNG that we are pivoting on. The second column is the RHS column, with the value of the objective function at its base.

The next m columns make up an m by m matrix that we will call **U**. **U** is the inverse matrix of the matrix $(\mathbf{A}_{1B}, \mathbf{A}_{2B}, \ldots, \mathbf{A}_{mB})$ (that is, the matrix whose first column is $\mathbf{A}_{1B}$, whose second column is $\mathbf{A}_{2B}$, and so on; this matrix is invertible since the basis vectors span the set of vectors of length m).

Now, a fact of life from linear algebra is that, if we pivot our auxiliary tableau as if it were tacked onto the right of our regular simplex tableau, we will end up with a new auxiliary tableau corresponding to the new tableau. (You think of it as being part of our simplex tableau, to be looked at only when needed.)

The way we use the auxiliary tableau is to take the ratios of each column (starting with the second) to the first-column positive entries. Since the second column is the "RHS" column, this involves merely looking for a minimal constraint ratio. If two or more of these ratios tie for minimum, we examine the ratios for the third column (only for the rows that tied) and look for a minimal ratio. If there are still ties, we go to the fourth column for a tie breaker, and so on. Eventually we will find a column that breaks all the ties; otherwise, two or more rows of U would be multiples of each other, which is impossible since U is invertible.

Why does this work? If we wanted to, we could add another row at the bottom of our auxiliary tableau, corresponding to the marginal net gains:

A_{1j}	R_1	u_{11}	u_{12}	$\cdots$	u_{1m}
A_{2j}	R_2	u_{21}	u_{22}	$\cdots$	u_{2m}
. . . .					
A_{mj}	R_m	u_{m1}	u_{m2}	$\cdots$	u_{mm}
MNG_L	$-\Sigma_i c_{iB} R_i$	$-\Sigma_i c_{iB} u_{i1}$	$-\Sigma_i c_{iB} u_{i2}$	$\cdots$	$-\Sigma_i c_{iB} u_{im}$

By choosing the row to pivot on the way we do, we ensure that we increase $\Sigma_i c_{iB} R_i$ or leave it the same. If we leave it the same, we increase $\Sigma_i c_{iB} u_{i1}$ or leave it the same. If we leave it the same, we increase $\Sigma_i c_{iB} u_{i2}$, or leave it the same, and so on, until we increase at least one of the sums. This way, even if

$$\sum_i c_{iB} R_i = \sum_i c_{iB} x_{iB} = \mathbf{cx}$$

stays the same, we are changing the sums $\Sigma_i c_{iB} u_{ik}$ in such a way that we can never cycle. Thus the algorithm must come to an end.

YOU SHOULD REMEMBER

Degeneracy occurs if, at some stage of the simplex process, the constraint ratio becomes zero. The auxiliary tableau is set up to prevent this situation from causing the algorithm to cycle endlessly back and forth between two basic feasible solutions.

STOPPING POINTS

The important thing about the simplex method is that the problem becomes a finite one. Therefore, it should end sometime. How?

Let's stick with the phase II calculations for the time being. What if we can't find a positive marginal net gain? Then we can't increase the objective function by bringing in a new basis vector. A priori, there might be a basic feasible solution with a higher value for the objective function, that differed from the current one by more than one basis vector. But since the objective function is a linear function, it can't get smaller before it gets bigger, so if all of the marginal net gains are nonpositive, we've found an optimal feasible solution. (See Figure 5-1.)

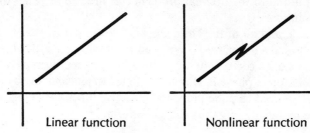

Linear function   Nonlinear function

Figure 5-1

Suppose that we have a positive marginal net gain, $\text{MNG}_L > 0$, but $A_{kL} \leq 0$ for each k. Then we can't pivot and we're stuck.

Let's go back to the change of basis vectors. We have

$$\mathbf{A}_L = \sum_k A_{kL}\mathbf{A}_{kB}, \qquad \mathbf{A}_L - \sum_k A_{kL}\mathbf{A}_{kB} = 0, \qquad \sum_k x_{kB}\mathbf{A}_{kB} = \mathbf{R}$$

and, if $\mu \geq 0$,

$$\mathbf{R} = \mu\left(\mathbf{A}_L - \sum_k A_{kL}\mathbf{A}_{kB}\right) + \sum_k x_{kB}\mathbf{A}_{kB}$$

$$= \mu\mathbf{A}_L + \sum_k (x_{kB} - \mu A_{kL})\mathbf{A}_{kB}$$

Since $A_{kL} \leq 0$ for each k, $x_{kB} - \mu A_{kL} \geq 0$, and if

$$x'_{kB} = x_{kB} - \mu A_{kL}, \qquad x'_L = \mu, \qquad x'_j = 0 \qquad \text{for all other } j$$

then $\mathbf{x}'$ is a nonbasic feasible solution.

$$\mathbf{cx}' = c_L x'_L + \sum_k c_{kB} x'_{kB}$$

$$= c_L\mu + \sum_k c_{kB}(x_{kB} - \mu A_{kL})$$

$$= \sum_k c_{kB}x_{kB} + \mu\left(c_L - \sum_k A_{kL}c_{kB}\right)$$

$$= \mathbf{cx} + \mu\text{MNG}_L$$

Since MNG_L is positive, by choosing μ large enough, we can make the value of the objective function as large as we want, and there is no optimal solution.

Now let's return to the phase I calculation. Since $\mathbf{c}^1\mathbf{x}^1 = \Sigma_i(-s_i) \le 0$, $\mathbf{c}^1\mathbf{x}^1$ has a maximum, and the latter case above will never happen. We will find at some point that all of the marginal net gains are nonpositive, and we have our phase I optimal basic feasible solution. At that point, if $\mathbf{c}^1\mathbf{x}^1 < 0$, there is no basic feasible solution to the original problem (we need to have $\mathbf{s} = \mathbf{0}$), and thus no feasible solution.

If $\mathbf{c}^1\mathbf{x}^1 = \mathbf{0}$, and all of the basic vectors correspond to x_i's (and not s_j's), we are ready to move to phase II. We need to simplify the tableau first by getting rid of the columns corresponding to the s_i's—we used them only to find a basic feasible solution in phase I. This corresponds to replacing $\mathbf{A}^1$ by $\mathbf{A}$ and $\mathbf{x}^1$ by $\mathbf{x}$.

Finally, we need to put $\mathbf{c}$ in for the objective function coefficients, and recalculate the marginal net gains, using the formula

$$\text{MNG}_L = c_L - \sum_k A_{kL}c_{kB}$$

Example: Another Phase I Calculation

Let

$$\mathbf{A} = \begin{pmatrix} 1 & -1 & 1 & 1 & -1 \\ -2 & 2 & 3 & 0 & 0 \end{pmatrix}, \quad \mathbf{R} = \begin{pmatrix} 1 \\ 5 \end{pmatrix}, \quad \mathbf{c} = (-4 \quad 4 \quad 1 \quad -2 \quad 0)$$

(This is the example that we put into normal form earlier.)

$$\text{Phase I: } \mathbf{A}^1 = \begin{pmatrix} 1 & -1 & 1 & 1 & -1 & 1 & 0 \\ -2 & 2 & 3 & 0 & 0 & 0 & 1 \end{pmatrix}, \quad \mathbf{R} = \begin{pmatrix} 1 \\ 5 \end{pmatrix},$$

$$\mathbf{c}^1 = (0 \quad 0 \quad 0 \quad 0 \quad 0 \quad -1 \quad -1)$$

0	0	0	0	0	-1	-1	≪ Obj. Fn. Coeff.			
X1′	X2′	X3′	X4′	X5′	S1′	S2′	RHS	BASIS VRS	CBV	RATIO
1	-1	1	1	-1	1	0	1	s_1'	-1	1
-2	2	3	0	0	0	1	5	s_2'	-1	5/3
-1	1	4	1	-1	0	0	≪ Marginal Net Gain			

We will pivot on the third column and the first row.

0	0	0	0	0	−1	−1	≪ Obj. Fn. Coeff.			
X1′	X2′	X3′	X4′	X5′	S1′	S2′	RHS	BASIS VRS	CBV	RATIO
1	−1	1	1	−1	1	0	1	x_3'	−1	
−5	5	0	−3	3	−3	1	2	s_2'	−1	2/5
−5	5	0	−3	3	−4	0	≪ Marginal Net Gain			

We will pivot on the second column and the second row.

0	0	0	0	0	−1	−1	≪ Obj. Fn. Coeff.		
X1′	X2′	X3′	X4′	X5′	S1′	S2′	RHS	BASIS VRS	CBV RATIO
0	0	1	2/5	−2/5	2/5	1/5	7/5	x_3'	0
−1	1	0	−3/5	3/5	−3/5	1/5	2/5	x_2'	0
0	0	0	0	0	−1	−1	≪ Marginal Net Gain		

We are done with phase I (successfully).

Phase II

−4	4	1	−2	0	≪ Obj. Fn. Coeff.		
X1′	X2′	X3′	X4′	X5′	RHS	BASIS VRS	CBV
0	0	1	2/5	−2/5	7/5	x_3'	0
−1	1	0	−3/5	3/5	2/5	x_2'	0
0	0	0	−12/5	−2	≪ Marginal Net Gain		

and we have finished: **x** is our optimal solution, where

$$x_1' = 0, \qquad x_2' = \frac{2}{5}, \qquad x_3' = \frac{7}{5}, \qquad \text{and} \qquad x_4' = 0$$

in terms of our original problem,

$$x_1 = u_1 - v_1 = x_1' - x_2' = -\frac{2}{5}, \qquad x_2 = x_3' = \frac{7}{5}, \qquad x_3 = x_4' = 0$$

and

$$x_1 + x_2 + x_3 = 1 \qquad \geq \quad 1$$
$$2x_1 - 3x_2 \quad = -\frac{4}{5} - \frac{21}{3} = -5$$

REDUNDANCY

We may, sad to say, find that $\mathbf{c}^1\mathbf{x}^1 = 0$ but that some of the s_1's are still in the basis set (the adjacent numbers in the RHS column would then have to be zero). We have our basic feasible solution, but the tableau is not ready for the phase II calculations.

Let's look at the marginal net gains. For x_L,

$$\text{MNG}_L = c_L - \sum_k A_{kL}c_{kB} = 0 + \text{the sum of the } A_{kL}$$

where $\mathbf{x}_{kB}^1$ is a slack variable. This is nonpositive, since the marginal net gains are nonpositive.

Suppose that $\mathbf{x}_{kB}^1$ is a slack variable, and thus $R_k = 0$. The kth row of our tableau corresponds to the equation

$$A_{k1}x_1 + A_{k2}x_2 + \cdots + A_{kn}x_n = R_k = 0$$

If we add up all the equations corresponding to slack variables in the basis set, we get

$$\left(\sum_{\text{such } k} A_{k1} \right)x_1 + \left(\sum_{\text{such } k} A_{k2} \right)x_2 + \cdots + \left(\sum_{\text{such } k} A_{kn} \right)x_n = 0$$

By the above,

$$\sum_{\text{such } k} A_{kL} = \text{MNG}_L$$

Thus we obtain

$$\text{MNG}_1 x_1 + \text{MNG}_2 x_2 + \cdots + \text{MNG}_n x_n = 0$$

We will call this equation the **redundancy equation**, and the situation it represents **redundancy**, for the following reasons.

If any of the coefficients in this equation are negative, the corresponding x_i's must be zero, for *every* feasible solution, since all of the terms are nonpositive (the coefficients are nonpositive and the x_i's are nonnegative). Then we may as well set these x_i's equal to zero, and strike out the columns of A and the components of c that correspond to them.

Once we've done that, we have determined that the sum of these equations (corresponding to the x_{kB}^1's that are slack variables) is just $0 = 0$. This means that one of these equations, say the one corresponding to the ith row of the tableau, gives us no new information, since it is the sum of a group of constraint equations that we already have. If this equation gives us no new information, neither does the original ith one, corresponding to the ith row of A, and we can eliminate it.

Thus we have reduced the number of rows of A (and thus the length of R) by 1, and possibly reduced the number of columns (and thus the length of c). We can start over again with the phase I calculations with a simpler problem.

This can happen only a finite number of times, since A has only a finite number of rows. By the nature of the reduction, we can never eliminate the last row. If we set all of the x_i's equal to zero, we are done—this is the only feasible solution.

Note that this procedure allows us to deal with a matrix A with $m > n$: eventually, we will end up with a new A with $m \leq n$, or we will have 0 as the only feasible solution, or we will show that there is no feasible solution.

Example: Redundancy

Let

$$A = \begin{pmatrix} 1 & 2 & 1 \\ 2 & 1 & 1 \\ -1 & 2 & 1 \end{pmatrix}, \quad R = \begin{pmatrix} 4 \\ 2 \\ 4 \end{pmatrix}, \quad c = (1 \ \ 1 \ \ 1)$$

Phase I: $A^1 = \begin{pmatrix} 1 & 2 & 1 & 1 & 0 & 0 \\ 2 & 1 & 1 & 0 & 1 & 0 \\ -1 & 2 & 1 & 0 & 0 & 1 \end{pmatrix}, \quad c^1 = (0 \ \ 0 \ \ 0 \ \ 0\!-\!1 \ \ -1 \ \ -1)$

0	0	0	−1	−1	−1	« Obj. Fn. Coeff.			
X1	X2	X3	S1	S2	S3	RHS	BASIS VRS	CBV	RATIO
1	2	1	1	0	0	4	s_1	−1	2
2	1	1	0	1	0	2	s_2	−1	2
−1	2	1	0	0	1	4	s_3	−1	2
2	5	3	0	0	0	« Marginal Net Gain			

We would like to pivot on the second column. In order to do so, since we are in a degenerate case, we will have to appeal to the auxiliary tableau:

$$(A_{1B}, A_{2B}, A_{3B}) = \begin{pmatrix} 1 & 0 & 0 \\ 0 & 1 & 0 \\ 0 & 0 & 1 \end{pmatrix}$$

and our auxiliary tableau is

$$2|4|1 \quad 0 \quad 0$$
$$1|2|0 \quad 1 \quad 0$$
$$2|4|0 \quad 0 \quad 1$$

From the third column, both 0/1 and 0/2 are less than 1/2, so we know not to pivot on the first row. From the fourth column, 0/2 is less than 1/1, so we want to pivot on the third row.

0	0	0	-1	-1	-1				
X1	X2	X3	S1	S2	S3	RHS	BASIS VRS	CBV	RATIO
2	0	0	1	0	-1	0	s_1	-1	0
5/2	0	1/2	0	1	$-1/2$	0	s_2	-1	0
$-1/2$	1	1/2	0	0	1/2	2	x_2	0	
9/2	0	1/2	0	0	$-5/2$				

$\ll$ Obj. Fn. Coeff. (top row)

$\ll$ Marginal Net Gain (bottom row)

We would like to pivot on the first column. Our auxiliary tableau

$$(A_{1B}, A_{2B}, A_{3B}) = \begin{pmatrix} 1 & 0 & 2 \\ 0 & 1 & 1 \\ 0 & 0 & 2 \end{pmatrix}$$

and our auxiliary tableau is

$$2|0|1 \quad 0 \quad -1$$
$$5/2|0|0 \quad 1 \quad -1/2$$
$$-1/2|2|0 \quad 0 \quad 1/2$$

From the third column, 0/(5/2) is less than 1/2, and we want to pivot on the second row.

0	0	0	-1	-1	-1			
X1	X2	X3	S1	S2	S3	RHS	BASIS VRS	CBV
0	0	$-2/5$	1	$-4/5$	$-3/5$	0	s_1	-1
1	0	1/5	0	2/5	$-1/5$	0	x_1	0
0	0	3/5	0	1/5	2/5	2	x_2	0
0	0	$-2/5$	0	$-9/5$	$-8/5$			

$\ll$ Obj. Fn. Coeff. (top row)

$\ll$ Marginal Net Gain (bottom row)

We have finished with phase I, but unsuccessfully, since s_1 is still in the basis. Our redundancy equation is

$$(0)x_1 + (0)x_2 + \left(-\frac{2}{5}\right)x_3 = 0$$

We know that $x_3 = 0$ for all feasible solutions, and we can eliminate the first row of A and entry of R, and the third column of A and entry of c.

$$A' = \begin{pmatrix} 2 & 1 \\ -1 & 2 \end{pmatrix}, \qquad R' = \begin{pmatrix} 2 \\ 4 \end{pmatrix}, \qquad c' = (1 \quad 1)$$

Phase I: $A^{1'} = \begin{pmatrix} 2 & 1 & 1 & 0 \\ -1 & 2 & 0 & 1 \end{pmatrix}, \qquad c^{1'} = (0 \quad 0 \quad -1 \quad -1)$

| 0 | 0 | −1 | −1 | ≪ Obj. Fn. Coeff. | | | |
X1	X2	S1′	S2′	RHS	BASIS VRS	CBV	RATIO
2	1	1	0	2	s_1'	−1	2
−1	2	0	1	4	s_2'	−1	2
1	3	0	0	≪ Marginal Net Gain			

We need the auxiliary tableau, to pivot on the second column.

$$(A_{1B}, A_{2B}) = \begin{pmatrix} 1 & 0 \\ 0 & 1 \end{pmatrix}$$

and the auxiliary tableau is

$$1|2|1 \quad 0$$
$$2|4|0 \quad 1$$

Since 0/2 is less than 1/1, looking at the third column, we want to pivot on the second row.

| 0 | 0 | −1 | −1 | ≪ Obj. Fn. Coeff. | | | |
X1	X2	S1′	S2′	RHS	BASIS VRS	CBV	RATIO
5/2	0	1	−1/2	0	s_1'	−1	0
−1/2	1	0	1/2	2	x_2	0	
5/2	0	0	−3/2	≪ Marginal Net Gain			

We want to pivot on the first column and the first row.

0	0	−1	−1	≪ Obj. Fn. Coeff.		
X1	X2	S1′	S2′	RHS	BASIS VRS	CBV
1	0	2/5	−1/5	0	x_1	0
0	1	1/5	2/5	2	x_2	0
0	0	−1	−1	≪ Marginal Net Gain		

and we are done with phase I (successfully).

Phase II

1	1	≪ Obj. Fn. Coeff.		
X1	X2	RHS	BASIS VRS	CBV
1	0	0	x_1	1
0	1	2	x_2	1
0	0	≪ Marginal Net Gain		

and our optimal solution is $x_1 = 0$, $x_2 = 2$, and $x_3 = 0$.

KNOW THE CONCEPTS

DO YOU KNOW THE BASICS?

Test your understanding of Chapter 5 by answering the following questions:

1. Can a linear programming problem have a nonbasic feasible solution? A nonbasic optimal solution?
2. Under what circumstances are phase I calculations unnecessary?
3. What does it mean when a linear programming problem is redundant?
4. What does it mean when a linear programming problem is inconsistent?
5. Why do we put linear programming problems into normal form?
6. What would happen if we pivoted on the wrong row of a simplex tableau?

TERMS FOR STUDY

auxiliary tableau	normal form
basis set	phase I
basis vectors	phase II
degeneracy	redundancy
linearly dependent	redundancy equation
marginal net gain	

PRACTICAL APPLICATION

COMPUTATIONAL PROBLEMS

Put the problems in Exercises 1–4 into normal form (that is, calculate **A**, **R**, *and* **c**).

1. $x_1 - 2x_2 \geq 0$
$x_2 - x_1 \leq -2$
$x_1 \geq 0$
Maximize x_2.

2. $x_1 - x_2 + x_3 = 5$
$2x_2 - 3x_3 \geq 2$
$x_1 \geq 0, x_2 \geq 0, x_3 \geq 0$
Minimize $x_1 + x_2 + x_3$.

3. $x_2 + 5x_3 \geq 5$
$x_1 - x_2 \leq -1$
$x_1 + 2x_2 + x_3 = 6$
$x_1 \geq 0, x_2 \geq 0, x_3 \geq 0$
Maximize x_3.

4. $x_1 - x_2 + 3x_3 \geq 1$
$x_1 + x_2 - x_3 \leq 2$
$x_1 \geq 0, x_2 \geq 0$
Maximize $x_2 + x_3$.

Use phase I calculations to find basic feasible solutions to Exercises 5–8.

5. $x_1 + 2x_2 + x_3 = 4$
$2x_1 - x_2 = -1/2$
$x_1 \geq 0, x_2 \geq 0, x_3 \geq 0$

6. $x_1 + x_2 \geq 5$
$2x_1 - x_2 \leq 4$
$x_1 \geq 0, x_2 \geq 0$

7. $2x_1 + 3x_2 = 13$
$3x_1 - 2x_2 \leq 0$
$x_1 \geq 0, x_2 \geq 0$

8. $2x_1 + x_2 - 3x_3 = 5$
$-2x_1 + 7x_2 + x_3 = 9$
$x_1 \geq 0, x_2 \geq 0$

Find the redundancy equations for Exercises 9 and 10.

9. $x_1 + x_2 + x_3 = 5$
$2x_1 - x_2 - 2x_3 = 7$
$3x_1 + x_2 + x_3 = 13$
$4x_1 - x_2 + 5x_3 = 15$

10. $2x_1 + x_2 + x_3 = 7$
$3x_1 + 2x_2 - x_3 = 3$
$4x_1 + 3x_2 + x_3 = 11$
$5x_1 + 4x_2 - x_3 = 7$

Solve the linear programming problems in Exercises 11–14 for the given **A**, **R**, *and* **c**.

11. $A = \begin{pmatrix} 1 & 2 & 3 \\ 1 & -2 & 6 \end{pmatrix}$, $R = \begin{pmatrix} 9 \\ 9 \end{pmatrix}$, $c = (1 \quad 0 \quad 1)$

12. $A = \begin{pmatrix} 1 & 2 & 3 & -4 \\ 4 & 3 & 2 & 1 \end{pmatrix}$, $R = \begin{pmatrix} 3 \\ 12 \end{pmatrix}$, $c = (1 \quad 1 \quad 1 \quad 1)$

13. $A = \begin{pmatrix} 1 & 0 & 1 & 0 \\ 1 & 2 & 0 & 3 \end{pmatrix}$, $R = \begin{pmatrix} 10 \\ 10 \end{pmatrix}$, $c = (-1 \quad 1 \quad -1 \quad 1)$

14. $A = \begin{pmatrix} 1 & -1 & 2 \\ 2 & 1 & 1 \end{pmatrix}$, $\quad R = \begin{pmatrix} 10 \\ 20 \end{pmatrix}$, $\quad c = (2 \quad 1 \quad 2)$

15. $A = \begin{pmatrix} 3 & 2 \\ 1 & -4 \\ 2 & -3 \end{pmatrix}$, $\quad R = \begin{pmatrix} 17 \\ 1 \\ 7 \end{pmatrix}$, $\quad c = (1 \quad 1)$

ANSWERS

KNOW THE CONCEPTS

1. The answer to both questions is yes. If there are feasible/optimal solutions, ther are basic feasible/optimal solutions, but not all such solutions need be basic.

2. Phase I calculations are unnecessary if you already have a basic feasible solution. An example is a problem involving inequalities, as in Chapter 2, where all nonslack variables are set to zero for the first basic solution.

3. Some of the constraint equations can be derived from the other constraint equations. These redundant constraints contribute no new information to the problem, and can be ignored.

4. The constraint equations contradict each other. If there were a feasible solution, the equations would cause a contradiction, for example, a negative number being greater than or equal to a positive number. Thus there are no feasible solutions to an inconsistent linear programming problem.

5. The normal form is a standard expression of the problem that makes it easy to use the simplex method. If we left problems in other forms, we would need to devise many kinds of simplex methods.

6. The pivot row is chosen, using the constraint ratio, to provide the new basic solution with nonnegative entries. If the wrong row were chosen, a variable in the new basic solution would be negative, making the solution infeasible.

PRACTICAL APPLICATION

1. $A = \begin{pmatrix} 1 & -2 & 2 & -1 & 0 \\ 1 & -1 & 1 & 0 & -1 \end{pmatrix}$, $\quad R = \begin{pmatrix} 0 \\ 2 \end{pmatrix}$, $\quad c = (0 \quad 1 \quad -1 \quad 0 \quad 0)$

2. $A = \begin{pmatrix} 1 & -1 & 1 & 0 \\ 0 & 2 & -3 & -1 \end{pmatrix}$, $\quad R = \begin{pmatrix} 5 \\ 2 \end{pmatrix}$, $\quad c = (-1 \quad -1 \quad -1)$

3. $A = \begin{pmatrix} 0 & 1 & 5 & -1 & 0 \\ -1 & 1 & 0 & 0 & -1 \\ 1 & 2 & 1 & 0 & 0 \end{pmatrix}$, $R = \begin{pmatrix} 5 \\ 1 \\ 6 \end{pmatrix}$, $c = (0 \ \ 0 \ \ 1 \ \ 0 \ \ 0)$

4. $A = \begin{pmatrix} 1 & -1 & 3 & -3 & -1 & 0 \\ 1 & 1 & -1 & 1 & 0 & 1 \end{pmatrix}$, $R = \begin{pmatrix} 1 \\ 2 \end{pmatrix}$,

$c = (0 \ \ 1 \ \ 1 \ \ -1 \ \ 0 \ \ 0)$

5. $x_1 = 3/5, x_2 = 17/10, x_3 = 0$

6. $x_1 = 3, x_2 = 2$

7. $x_1 = 2, x_2 = 3$

8. $x_1 = 13/8, x_2 = 7/4$

9. $(-25/7)x_3 = 0$, i.e., $x_3 = 0$

10. $(-8/9)x_2 = 0$, i.e., $x_2 = 0$

11. $x_1 = 9, x_2 = 0, x_3 = 0, cx = 9$

12. $x_1 = x_2 = 0, x_3 = 51/11,$
$x_4 = 30/11, cx = 81/11$

13. $x_1 = 0, x_2 = 5, x_3 = 10, x_4 = 0,$
$cx = -5$

14. $x_1 = 0, x_2 = x_3 = 10, cx = 30$

15. $x_1 = 5, x_2 = 1, cx = 6$

6

THE DUAL FOR A LINEAR PROGRAMMING PROBLEM

KEY TERMS

complementary slackness a set of conditions that assert that, if the optimal value of a variable for the dual to a linear programming problem is greater than zero, then the corresponding slack variable in the primal problem will be zero at the optimum

dual problem the dual problem for a linear programming problem is a new linear programming problem formed by interchanging the features of the original problem; each variable in the dual problem corresponds to one of the constraints in the original problem

primal problem the original problem in a linear programming situation; the term is used to distinguish this from the dual problem

shadow prices the shadow price associated with each constraint in a linear programming problem tells how much the value of the objective function would be improved if that constraint was relaxed by 1 unit; the shadow prices are equal to the optimal values of the variables for the dual to the original problem

THE VALUE OF INCREASING CAPACITY

Let's return to the furniture problem in Chapter 3:

x = quantity of tables produced y = quantity of chairs
Maximize $4x + 5y$
subject to:

table assembly constraint:	$x \leq 50$
leg production constraint:	$3x + y \leq 170$
cutting constraint:	$x + 2y \leq 140$
chair assembly constraint:	$y \leq 60$
nonnegativity constraints:	$x \geq 0$
	$y \geq 0$

We found that the optimum occurred where $x = 40$, $y = 50$. The value of the profit was 410. Note that the leg production machine and the cutting machine are used at their capacities, but the table assembly machine and the chair assembly machine are not used at full capacity (since x is less than 50 and y is less than 60). Suppose that a salesman came by and asked us whether we would be willing to pay to expand the capacity of the table assembly machine. Since we observe that we are not using all of the capacity we already have, it is not going to do us any good to expand that capacity. Therefore, we will decline the offer. Likewise, we would not pay to expand the capacity of the chair assembly machine, since we are not currently using the full capacity of that machine.

However, the leg production constraint does impose a limit on the numbers of chairs and tables we can produce. If that capacity could be increased, we could produce more products and increase profits. The big question is: How much would we be willing to pay for an increase in leg production capacity? We would not choose to increase the capacity if it would cost more to do so than this benefit would be worth. Let's find out how much the value of our output would increase if the capacity of the leg production machine could be increased by 1 (raising the capacity to 171). We need to solve this linear programming problem:

Maximize $4x + 5y$
subject to:

table assembly constraint:	$x \leq 50$
leg production constraint:	$3x + y \leq 171$
cutting constraint:	$x + 2y \leq 140$
chair assembly constraint:	$y \leq 60$
nonnegativity constraints:	$x \geq 0$
	$y \geq 0$

The optimum turns out to be $x = 40.4$, $y = 49.8$, giving a value of 410.6 for the total profit. (For the present we can ignore the fact that we end up with fractional values.) When the leg production capacity was 170, we found that the optimal solution was $x = 40$, $y = 50$, with a total profit of 410. Therefore, increasing the capacity of the leg production constraint by 1 unit would be worth 60 cents per day.

Likewise, we could find out how much we would be willing to pay if the cutting capacity could be increased. Current production consumes all of the available cutting capacity. Suppose that the cutting constraint became $x + 2y \leq 141$ (with the leg production capacity returning to its initial level of 170). Then we could solve this linear programming problem:

Maximize $4x + 5y$
subject to:

table assembly constraint:	$x \leq 50$
leg production constraint:	$3x + y \leq 170$
cutting constraint:	$x + 2y \leq 141$
chair assembly constraint:	$y \leq 60$
nonnegativity constraints:	$x \geq 0$
	$y \geq 0$

The optimum here turns out to be $x = 39.8$, $y = 50.6$, giving a total profit of 412.2. Therefore, increasing the cutting constraint by 1 unit would be worth $412.2 - 410 = 2.2$.

The numbers 0.6 and 2.2 ring a bell. Turning back to page 105, we note that these two numbers are exactly the negatives of the marginal net gains for the slack variables s_2 and s_3 at the optimal solution. The marginal net gain for the slack variable s_2 tells us how much the objective function would be increased if s_2 was increased by 1 unit. But s_2 can be increased 1 unit only by reducing our use of leg production capacity by 1 unit. If we could increase our use of the leg production constraint by 1 unit, then the change in the objective function should be the opposite: $+0.6$ instead of -0.6.

The values 0.6 and 2.2 are called the **shadow prices** associated with the leg production and cutting constraints, respectively. Each shadow price tells how much the objective function would be improved if the capacity limit associated with that constraint could be relaxed by 1 unit. In the next section we will see how the shadow prices are related to the solution of the linear programming problem.

THE DUAL FOR A LINEAR PROGRAMMING PROBLEM

Suppose now that we do not own the machines in the factory. Instead, we must rent each machine from its owner. The prices need to be determined by negotiation between us and the owners. The amount we have to pay is equal to the price for each machine times the capacity of that machine. For the moment, we will suppose that we do not have any costs other than those that must be paid to the machine owners. There are no workers or shareholders who need to be paid, but the machine owners have demanded that they receive the full amount of the profits.

Let t be the rental price of the table assembly machine, u be the price for the leg production machine, v be the price for the cutting machine, and w be the price for the chair assembly machine. Then the total amount we have to pay is

$$50t + 170u + 140v + 60w$$

Our goal will be to minimize this amount. However, we cannot set each price to zero, because the machine owners will not accept this.

Each table that is produced uses 1 unit of the table production capacity, 3 units of the leg production capacity, and 1 unit of the cutting capacity. The total amount that will be spent on machine rental for each table produced is

$$1 \times t + 3 \times u + 1 \times v$$

The machine owners will insist that they receive at least as much in payments as the table is worth. Since the per-unit profit of each table is 4, this means that the machine owners will insist that

$$t + 3u + v \geq 4$$

Likewise the total amount that will be spent on machine rental for each chair produced is $u + 2v + w$. The machine owners will insist that this payment be at least as great as the net profit for each chair, which is equal to 5. Therefore, the machine owners will insist that

$$u + 2v + w \geq 5$$

We now have this linear programming problem:

Minimize $50t + 170u + 140v + 60w$
subject to:

$$t + 3u + v \qquad \geq 4$$
$$u + 2v + w \geq 5$$
$$t \geq 0, u \geq 0, v \geq 0, w \geq 0$$

We write this problem using matrix notation:

$$\text{Minimize } (50 \quad 170 \quad 140 \quad 60) \begin{pmatrix} t \\ u \\ v \\ w \end{pmatrix}$$

subject to:

$$\begin{pmatrix} 1 & 3 & 1 & 0 \\ 0 & 1 & 2 & 1 \end{pmatrix} \begin{pmatrix} t \\ u \\ v \\ w \end{pmatrix} \geq \begin{pmatrix} 4 \\ 5 \end{pmatrix}$$

Compare this with our original linear programming problem:

$$\text{Maximize } (4 \quad 5) \begin{pmatrix} x \\ y \end{pmatrix}$$

subject to:

$$\begin{pmatrix} 1 & 0 \\ 3 & 1 \\ 1 & 2 \\ 0 & 1 \end{pmatrix} \begin{pmatrix} x \\ y \end{pmatrix} \leq \begin{pmatrix} 50 \\ 170 \\ 140 \\ 60 \end{pmatrix}$$

The original linear programming problem is called the **primal problem**; the new problem is called the **dual problem**. Note that the dual problem looks like the primal problem with everything interchanged. The primal problem is a maximizing problem; the dual problem is a minimizing problem. The number of variables in the primal problem is the same as the number of constraints in the dual problem; the number of constraints in the primal problem is the same as the number of variables in the dual problem. The objective function coefficients in the primal problem show up as the right-hand-side constants in the dual problem. The right-hand-side constants in the primal problem show up as the objective function coefficients in the dual problem. The coefficients of the constraints are twisted around so that each row of the coefficient matrix in the primal problem shows up as a column of the coefficient matrix for the dual problem.

Each variable in the dual problem corresponds to one of the constraints in the primal problem. Once you have found the optimal values for the dual variables, here is how to interpret them: the value of the dual variable tells by how much the objective function of the primal problem would be increased if you were able to increase the capacity limit for the constraint corresponding to that variable by 1 unit. In other words, the dual variables serve as the shadow prices for each constraint.

In general, suppose that you were given this linear programming problem (written in matrix notation):

Maximize **cx**
subject to $\mathbf{Ax} \leq \mathbf{r}$

Here **c** is a 1 by n row vector of objective function coefficients; **x** is an n by 1 column vector of choice variables; **A** is an m by n matrix of contraint coefficients; and **r** is an m by 1 column vector of right-hand-side variables (which serve as capacity limits).

The dual problem then is

Minimize **r′s**
subject to $\mathbf{A's} \geq \mathbf{c'}$

where **s** is an m by 1 column vector of the dual-problem choice variables. The prime ($'$) symbol stands for matrix transpose (see Chapter 1). For both the dual and primal problems the nonnegativity constraints are assumed to be present. Note that it is arbitrary which problem is called the primal problem, and which the dual problem. If you had started with a minimization problem as the primal, the dual would be a maximizing problem. If you looked at the dual problem for the dual problem itself, you would be looking at the primal problem.

Here are the simplex tableaus that show the calculations for the dual problem. We will use the two-phase method demonstrated in Chapter 5. We need to add two sets of slack variables: r_1 and r_2, which represent the surplus amount for each of the original constraints; and s_1 and s_2, which serve as the extra slack variables for the phase 1 calculations.

Phase 1 Calculations

| | | | | | | **** | **** | | | | |
| T | U | V | W | R1 | R2 | S1 | S2 | RHS | BASIS VRS | CBV | RATIO |
0	0	0	0	0	0	−1	−1	≪ Obj. Fn. Coeff.			
1	3	1	0	−1	0	1	0	4	S1	−1	1.33 ≪
0	1	2	1	0	−1	0	1	5	S2	−1	5
1	4	3	1	−1	−1	0	0	≪ Marginal Net Gain			

Pivot element: row 1, column 2

	****					****					
0	0	0	0	0	0	-1	-1	« Obj. Fn. Coeff.			
T	U	V	W	R1	R2	S1	S2	RHS	BASIS VRS	CBV	RATIO
0.33	1	0.33	0	-0.33	0	0.33	0	1.33	U	0	4
-0.33	0	1.67	1	0.33	-1	-0.33	1	3.67	S2	-1	2.20 «
-0.33	0	1.67ˉ	1	0.33	-1	-1.33	0	« Marginal Net Gains			

Pivot element: row 2, column 3

	****	****									
0	0	0	0	0	0	-1	-1	« Obj. Fn. Coeff.			
T	U	V	W	R1	R2	S1	S2	RHS	BASIS VRS	CBV	RATIO
0.40	1	0	-0.20	-0.40	0.20	0.40	-0.20	0.60	U	0	
-0.20	0	1	0.60	0.20	-0.60	-0.20	0.60	2.20	V	0	
0	0	0	0	0	0	-1	-1	« Marginal Net Gain			

Phase 1 Solution

$$u = 0.60$$
$$v = 2.20$$

Objective function value: 0

We set up the initial phase 2 tableau:

	****	****						
-50	-170	-140	-60	0	0	« Obj. Fn. Coeff.		
T	U	V	W	R1	R2	RHS	BASIS VRS	CBV
0.40	1	0	-0.20	-0.40	0.20	0.60	U	-170
-0.20	0	1	0.60	0.20	-0.60	2.20	V	-140
-10	0	0	-10	-40	-50	« Marginal Net Gain		

Since all of the marginal net gains are negative, in this case we have found the optimal solution by the end of phase 1: $u = 0.60$, $v = 2.20$. The other variables are zero: $t = 0$, $w = 0$, $r_1 = 0$, $r_2 = 0$. The objective function value is 410.

As we expected, the values of the solution variables are the negatives of the marginal net gains for the slack variables for the corresponding constraints. We also found that these values give the amount by which the objective function of the primal problem will increase if the capacity of the corresponding constraint is increased by 1. Note that the optimal value of the objective function for the dual problem (410) is the same as the optimal value of the objective function for the primal problem. This is a general property that will always be true for a linear programming problem. (See the appendix to the chapter.)

There are two other connections between primal and dual problems that match the intuition we had at the start of the chapter:

1. If a slack variable in the primal optimal solution is greater than zero, then the optimal value of the dual variable corresponding to the constraint represented by that slack variable will be zero. This means that, if you currently have some excess capacity for a particular constraint, then the shadow price associated with that constraint is zero. You won't be willing to pay to increase that capacity.

2. If the value of a dual variable at the optimum is greater than zero, then the corresponding slack variable will be zero at the optimum. This means that you will be willing to pay to expand the capacity of a constraint only if it is being used to its full capacity now.

These are called the **complementary slackness** conditions.

The dual also has another practical advantage: in some cases the dual problem is easier to solve than the primal problem. Since it is possible to obtain the solution to the primal problem by looking at the simplex tableau for the dual problem, it may sometimes be a good strategy to work on solving the dual problem instead. In particular, suppose that the primal problem is a minimizing problem. We found that it can be difficult to determine the initial basic feasible solution in that case. That is the reason why we developed the two-phase method in Chapter 5. However, if the dual problem is a maximization problem where the origin works as the initial basic feasible solution, then it will be easier to solve the dual problem.

The appendix to the chapter contains proofs of some of the properties of the dual problem for the mathematically inclined reader.

APPENDIX TO CHAPTER 6

We will prove the duality and equilibrium theorems, but a few comments are in order here.

First, will be taking the transpose of numerous matrices and will often use the following fact: if M is an m by n matrix, and N is an n by p matrix, so that the product MN is defined and is an m by p matrix, then

$$(MN)' = N'M'$$

(You should be able to prove this to yourself.)

If $m = p = 1$, then $\mathbf{MN}$ is a number, and

$$\mathbf{MN} = (\mathbf{MN})' = \mathbf{N'M'}$$

The second thing to note is that, if $\mathbf{x}$ is a feasible solution to the primal problem, and $\mathbf{s}$ is a feasible solution to the dual problem, then

$$\mathbf{Ax} \leq \mathbf{r}, \qquad \mathbf{s'} \geq \mathbf{0}, \qquad \mathbf{s'Ax} \leq \mathbf{s'r}, \qquad \mathbf{A's} \geq \mathbf{c'}$$

$$\mathbf{x'} \geq \mathbf{0}, \qquad \mathbf{x'A's} \geq \mathbf{x'c'}, \qquad \mathbf{s'Ax} \geq \mathbf{cx}, \qquad \mathbf{cx} \leq \mathbf{s'Ax} \leq \mathbf{s'r}$$

Therefore, any feasible solution for the primal problem gives a smaller value than any feasible solution for the dual problem.

Finally, we will have to use the following theorem (due to Farkas), which we will state without proof (and which should be intuitively obvious):

> THEOREM. *Let* **A** *be a* **p** *by* **q** *matrix,* **b** *a column vector of length* **q**, **x** *any column vector of length* **p**, *and* **y** *any column vector of length* **p**.
>
> *Then either* (i) *there is an* **x** *such that* **Ax** ≤ **b** *and* **x** ≥ **0**, *or* (ii) *there is a* **y** *such that* **y'A** ≥ **0** *but* **y'b** < **0**, *but both* (i) *and* (ii) *cannot occur. Otherwise,* 0 ≤ **y'Ax** ≤ **y'b** < **0**. *Thus, given any such* **A** *and* **b**, *the pair falls into either category* (i) *or category* (ii).
> (ii).

A. DUALITY THEOREM

We can now state the duality theorem. Recall that the primal problem is
Primal: Find $\mathbf{x} \geq \mathbf{0}$ such that $\mathbf{Ax} \leq \mathbf{r}$ and $\mathbf{cx}$ is maximized.

The dual problem is
Dual: Find $\mathbf{s} \geq \mathbf{0}$ such that $\mathbf{A's} \geq \mathbf{c'}$ and $\mathbf{r's}$ is minimized.

DUALITY THEOREM. *One of the following four cases occurs:*

1. *(Normal Case) Both the primal and dual problems have optimal solutions,* **x** *and* **s**, *and* **cx** = **r's**.

2. *The primal problem has a feasible solution, but the dual problem doesn't. Then* **cx** *can be made arbitrarily large.*

3. *The dual problem has a feasible solution, but the primal problem doesn't. Then* **r's** *can be made arbitrarily small.*

4. *Neither the primal nor the dual problem has a feasible solution.*

Note that, if there are feasible solutions for both the primal and dual problems, then we must be in the normal case.

Proof. We will use the earlier theorem to show that, if the normal case doesn't occur, one of the other three must.

Assume for the time being that we are in case 1. Then

$$\mathbf{x} \geq 0, \qquad \mathbf{Ax} \leq \mathbf{r}, \qquad \mathbf{s} \geq 0, \qquad \mathbf{A's} \geq \mathbf{c'}, \qquad \mathbf{cx} = \mathbf{r's} = \mathbf{s'r}$$

We can rewrite these inequalities and equation. Note that since, for any feasible $\mathbf{x}$ and $\mathbf{s}$, $\mathbf{cx} \leq \mathbf{s'r}$, it is enough to assume that $\mathbf{cx} \geq \mathbf{s'r}$; then we know that we are at optimal solutions.

Then we have

$$\mathbf{Ax} \leq \mathbf{r}, \qquad (-\mathbf{A'})\mathbf{s} \leq -\mathbf{c'}, \qquad -\mathbf{cx} + \mathbf{s'r} \leq 0, \qquad \mathbf{x} \geq 0, \qquad \mathbf{s} \geq 0$$

Let

$$\bar{\mathbf{A}} = \begin{pmatrix} \mathbf{A} & 0 \\ 0 & -\mathbf{A'} \\ -\mathbf{c} & \mathbf{r'} \end{pmatrix}, \quad \bar{\mathbf{x}} = \begin{pmatrix} \mathbf{x} \\ \mathbf{s} \end{pmatrix}, \quad \bar{\mathbf{b}} = \begin{pmatrix} \mathbf{r} \\ -\mathbf{c'} \\ 0 \end{pmatrix}$$

$\bar{\mathbf{A}}$ is an $(m+n)$ by $(m+n+1)$ matrix, $\bar{\mathbf{x}}$ is a column vector of length $m+n$, $\bar{\mathbf{b}}$ is a column vector of length $m+n+1$, $\bar{\mathbf{x}} \geq 0$, and $\bar{\mathbf{A}}\bar{\mathbf{x}} \leq \bar{\mathbf{b}}$.

This is case 1. If it can't happen (that is, there are no optimal solutions or $\mathbf{cx} = \mathbf{r's}$), then there is a $\bar{\mathbf{y}}$ (of length $m+n+1$) such that $\bar{\mathbf{y}} \geq 0$, $\bar{\mathbf{y}}'\bar{\mathbf{A}} \geq 0$, and $\bar{\mathbf{y}}'\bar{\mathbf{b}} < 0$.

We write

$$\bar{\mathbf{y}} = \begin{pmatrix} \mathbf{u} \\ \mathbf{v} \\ \lambda \end{pmatrix}$$

where $\mathbf{u}$ is a column vector of length m, $\mathbf{v}$ is a column vector of length n, and λ is a number. Since $\bar{\mathbf{y}} \geq 0$, $\mathbf{u} \geq 0$, $\mathbf{v} \geq 0$, and $\lambda \geq 0$.

$$\bar{\mathbf{y}}' = (\mathbf{u'}, \mathbf{v'}, \lambda), \qquad 0 \leq \bar{\mathbf{y}}'\bar{\mathbf{A}} = (\mathbf{u'A} - \lambda\mathbf{c'} - \mathbf{v'A'} + \lambda\mathbf{r'}), \qquad 0 > \bar{\mathbf{y}}'\bar{\mathbf{b}} = \mathbf{u'r} - \mathbf{v'c'}$$

Thus

$$\mathbf{u'A} \geq \lambda\mathbf{c}, \qquad \lambda\mathbf{r'} \geq \mathbf{v'A'}, \qquad \mathbf{u'r} < \mathbf{v'c'}$$

We assume for the time being that λ is positive. Dividing each line by λ, we have, with $(\mathbf{u}/\lambda) \geq 0$, $(\mathbf{v}/\lambda) \geq 0$,

$$\left(\frac{\mathbf{u}}{\lambda}\right)' \mathbf{A} \geq \mathbf{c} \qquad \text{or} \qquad \mathbf{A'}\left(\frac{\mathbf{u}}{\lambda}\right) \geq \mathbf{c'}$$

$$\mathbf{r'} \geq \left(\frac{\mathbf{v}}{\lambda}\right)' \mathbf{A'} \qquad \text{or} \qquad \mathbf{r} \geq \mathbf{A}\left(\frac{\mathbf{v}}{\lambda}\right)$$

$$\mathbf{r}'\left(\frac{\mathbf{u}}{\lambda}\right) < \mathbf{c}\left(\frac{\mathbf{v}}{\lambda}\right)$$

Thus $\mathbf{v}/\lambda$ is a feasible primal solution, and $\mathbf{u}/\lambda$ is a feasible dual solution. But we know that, for any such feasible solutions,

$$\mathbf{r}'\left(\frac{\mathbf{u}}{\lambda}\right) \geq \mathbf{c}\left(\frac{\mathbf{v}}{\lambda}\right)$$

a contradiction.

Thus, since $\lambda \geq 0$, λ must be 0. Then we have

$$\mathbf{u} \geq \mathbf{0}, \mathbf{v} \geq \mathbf{0}$$

$$\mathbf{u}'\mathbf{A} \geq \mathbf{0}, \text{ that is, } \mathbf{A}'\mathbf{u} \geq \mathbf{0}$$

$$\mathbf{0} \geq \mathbf{v}'\mathbf{A}', \text{ that is, } \mathbf{A}\mathbf{v} \leq \mathbf{0}$$

$$\mathbf{u}'\mathbf{r} < \mathbf{v}'\mathbf{c}', \text{ that is, } \mathbf{r}'\mathbf{u} < \mathbf{c}\mathbf{v}$$

Now, we examine $\mathbf{r}'\mathbf{u} < \mathbf{c}\mathbf{v}$. Either $\mathbf{r}'\mathbf{u}$ is negative, or $\mathbf{c}\mathbf{v}$ is positive; otherwise, a nonnegative number would be strictly less than a nonpositive number.

Now, if $\mathbf{r}'\mathbf{u} < 0$, then the primal problem has no feasible solution. Otherwise, if $\mathbf{x}$ were a feasible solution, we would have

$$\mathbf{x} \geq \mathbf{0}$$

$$\mathbf{A}\mathbf{x} \leq \mathbf{r}, \text{ that is, } \mathbf{x}'\mathbf{A}' \leq \mathbf{r}'$$

$$\mathbf{0} \leq \mathbf{A}'\mathbf{u}$$

$$\mathbf{0} \leq \mathbf{x}'\mathbf{A}'\mathbf{u} \leq \mathbf{r}'\mathbf{u} < 0$$

a contradiction.

If the dual problem doesn't have a feasible solution either, we're in case 4. If it has one, $\mathbf{s}$, then, for any number $\mu \geq 0$, $\mathbf{s} + \mu\mathbf{u} \geq \mathbf{0}$,

$$\mathbf{A}'(\mathbf{s} + \mu\mathbf{u}) = \mathbf{A}'\mathbf{s} + \mu\mathbf{A}'\mathbf{u} \geq \mathbf{A}'\mathbf{s} \geq \mathbf{c}'$$

and $\mathbf{s} + \mu\mathbf{u}$ is also feasible for the dual problem. But

$$\mathbf{r}'(\mathbf{s} + \mu\mathbf{u}) = \mathbf{r}'\mathbf{s} + \mu\mathbf{r}'\mathbf{u}$$

becomes arbitrarily small as μ grows larger, since $\mathbf{r}'\mathbf{u} < 0$. Then we're in case 3.

If, now, $\mathbf{cv} > 0$, then the dual problem has no feasible solution. Otherwise, if **s** were a feasible solution,

$$\mathbf{s} \geq 0$$
$$A'\mathbf{s} \geq \mathbf{c'}, \text{ that is, } \mathbf{s}'A \geq \mathbf{c}$$
$$0 \geq A\mathbf{v}$$
$$0 \geq \mathbf{s}'A\mathbf{v} \geq \mathbf{cv} > 0$$

a contradiction.

If the primal problem has no feasible solution, we're back in case 4 again.

If the primal problem has a feasible solution, **x**, then, for any number $\mu \geq 0$, $\mathbf{x} + \mu\mathbf{v} \geq 0$,

$$A(\mathbf{x} + \mu\mathbf{v}) = A\mathbf{x} + \mu A\mathbf{v} \leq A\mathbf{x} \leq \mathbf{r},$$

and $\mathbf{x} + \mu\mathbf{v}$ is a feasible solution for the primal problem. But

$$\mathbf{c}(\mathbf{x} + \mu\mathbf{v}) = \mathbf{cx} + \mu\mathbf{cv}$$

becomes arbitrarily large as μ grows larger, since $\mathbf{cv} > 0$. We're then in case 2. Thus, if we're not in case 1, we're in one of the other cases.

B. EQUILIBRIUM THEOREM

We can now prove the following:

COMPLEMENTARY SLACKNESS CONDITIONS (ALSO CALLED THE EQUILIBRIUM THEOREM). *In the normal case, if* $(A\mathbf{x})_j < \mathbf{r}_j$ *for some j, then* $s_j = 0$. *If* $s_j > 0$, *then* $(A\mathbf{x})_j = \mathbf{r}_j$.

Proof. If **x** and **s** are feasible solutions, then

$$\mathbf{cx} \leq \mathbf{s}'A\mathbf{x} \leq \mathbf{s}'\mathbf{r}$$

and, if they are also optimal, then $\mathbf{cx} = \mathbf{s}'\mathbf{r}$, so $\mathbf{s}'A\mathbf{x} = \mathbf{s}'\mathbf{r}$.

$$0 = \mathbf{s}'\mathbf{r} - \mathbf{s}'A\mathbf{x} = \mathbf{s}'(\mathbf{r} - A\mathbf{x}) = \sum_j s'_j(\mathbf{r} - A\mathbf{x})_j$$

Now, $s_j \geq 0$, and since $\mathbf{r} \geq A\mathbf{x}$,

$$(\mathbf{r} - A\mathbf{x})_j = r_j - (A\mathbf{x})_j \geq 0$$

so all of the terms in the sum are nonnegative, and each must be zero for the sum to be zero.

$$s_j[r_j - (A\mathbf{x})_j] = 0$$

and thus $s_j = 0$ or $r_j = (A\mathbf{x})_j$. If $r_j > (A\mathbf{x})_j$, $s_j = 0$; and if $s_j > r_j = (A\mathbf{x})_j$.

KNOW THE CONCEPTS

DO YOU KNOW THE BASICS?

Test your understanding of Chapter 6 by answering the following questions:

1. Is the dual problem easier to solve than the primal problem?
2. How do you tell which is the dual and which is the primal problem?
3. What is the dual of the dual problem?
4. Give an intuitive explanation of the relationship between the slack variables and the corresponding shadow prices.
5. What is the connection between the marginal net gains in the primal problem and the variables in the dual problem?
6. What is the relationship between the optimal value of the dual-problem objective function and the optimal value of the primal-problem objective function?
7. Suppose that you know the optimal values of the variables in the dual problem. What is the quickest way to solve for the optimal values of the primal problem?

TERMS FOR STUDY

complementary slackness   primal problem
dual problem   shadow prices

PRACTICAL APPLICATION

COMPUTATIONAL PROBLEMS

For Exercises 1–3, write the dual problem for the indicated minimization problem from Chapter 2, and then use the simplex method to solve the dual problem. Use your solution to the dual problem to determine the solution to the primal problem.

1. Chapter 2, Exercise 7   3. Chapter 2, Exercise 9
2. Chapter 2, Exercise 8

For Exercise 4–6, write the dual problem for the indicated maximization problem from Chapter 2, and then use the simplex method to solve the dual problem.

4. Chapter 2, Exercise 6   6. Chapter 2, Exercise 11
5. Chapter 2, Exercise 10

7. Consider this linear programming problem:

Maximize $10x_1 + 18x_2 + 24x_3$
subject to:

(1) $x_1 + 2x_2 \qquad \leq 30$
(2) $x_1 \qquad + 4x_3 \leq 42$
(3) $\qquad + 5x_2 + 6x_3 \leq 80$
(4) $10x_1 + 12x_2 + 9x_3 \leq 360$
(5) $28x_1 + 32x_2 + 24x_3 \leq 640$

Here is the optimal solution for the dual to this problem:

$$v_1 = 0, \quad v_2 = 1.67, \quad v_3 = 1.70, \quad v_4 = 0, \quad v_5 = 0.30$$

where v_i is the dual variable corresponding to constraint i. Use this information to find the optimal solution to the primal problem, without having to use the simplex method.

ANSWERS

KNOW THE CONCEPTS

1. The problem that is easier to solve is determined by other factors (such as how many choice variables there are, and whether there is an obvious choice for the initial basic feasible solution). Either the primal or the dual could be easier to solve.

2. The decision is arbitrary.

3. The primal problem.

4. If a constraint has excess capacity, the objective function would not be improved if you could expand the capacity of that constraint. Therefore, its shadow price is zero.

5. At the optimum, the marginal net gain for a variable is equal to the negative of the optimal value of the corresponding variable in the dual problem.

6. They are equal.

7. Determine which constraints in the primal problem correspond to the variables in the dual problem that have positive values at the optimum. These constraints must be satisfied exactly, with no excess capacity, so that you can set up an equation system and solve it.

PRACTICAL APPLICATION

1. Dual problem:

Maximize $36x_1 + 12x_2 + 6x_3$
subject to:
$$x_1 + x_2 \qquad \le 100$$
$$2x_1 \qquad + x_3 \le 300$$

Here is the simplex tableau:

			*****	*****				
36	12	6	0	0	≪ Obj. Fn. Coeff.			
X1	X2	X3	S1	S2	RHS	BASIS VRS	CBV	RATIO
1	1	0	1	0	100	S1	0	100 ≪
2	0	1	0	1	300	S2	0	150
36 ^	12	6	0	0	≪ Marginal Net Gain			

Pivot element: row 1, column 1

*****				*****				
36	12	6	0	0	≪ Obj. Fn. Coeff.			
X1	X2	X3	S1	S2	RHS	BASIS VRS	CBV	RATIO
1	1	0	1	0	100	X1	36	
0	−2	1	−2	1	100	S2	0	100 ≪
0	−24	6 ^	− 36 ^	0	≪ Marginal Net Gain			

Pivot element: row 2, column 3

	*****		*****				
36	12	6	0	0	≪ Obj. Fn. Coeff.		
X1	X2	X3	S1	S2	RHS	BASIS VRS	CBV
1	1	0	1	0	100	X1	36
0	−2	1	−2	1	100	X3	6
0	−12	0	−24	−6	≪ Marginal Net Gain		

Solution: $x_1 = 100$, $x_3 = 100$; objective function value: 4,200

From the marginal net gains for s_1 and s_2 we can find the solution to the primal problem: (24, 6).

2. Dual problem:

$$\text{Maximize } 12x_1 + 2x_2 + 18x_3$$
subject to:
$$x_1 + x_2 + 2x_3 \le 9{,}000$$
$$x_1 \quad\ + x_3 \le 6{,}000$$

Solution: $x_1 = 3{,}000$, $x_3 = 3{,}000$; objective function value: 90,000
From the marginal net gains for s_1 and s_2 we can find the solution to the primal problem: (6, 6).

3. Dual problem:

$$\text{Maximize } 12x_1 + 10x_2 + 9x_3$$
subject to:
$$2x_1 + \ x_2 + x_3 \le 3$$
$$x_1 + 2x_2 + x_3 \le 2$$

Solution: $x_1 = 1$, $x_3 = 1$; objective function value: 21
From the marginal net gains for s_1 and s_2 we can find the solution to the primal problem: (3, 6).

4. Here are the phase I calculations:

					****	********					
0	0	0	0	0	−1	−1	≪ Obj. Fn. Coeff.				
X1	X2	X3	X4	X5	S1	S2	RHS	BASIS VRS	CBV	RATIO	
1	0	6	−1	0	1	0	3	S1	−1	0.50	
0	1	18	0	−1	0	1	6	S2	−1	0.33 ≪	
1	1	24̂	−1	−1	0	0	≪ Marginal Net Gain				

Pivot element: row 2, column 3

0	0	0	0	0	−1	−1	≪ Obj. Fn. Coeff.				
X1	X2	X3	X4	X5	S1	S2	RHS	BASIS VRS	CBV	RATIO	
1	−0.33	0	−1	0.33	1	−0.33	1	S1	−1	1 ≪	
0	0.06	1	0	−0.06	0	0.06	0.33	X3	0		
1̂	−0.33	0	−1	0.33	0	−1.33	≪ Marginal Net Gain				

Pivot element: row 1, column 1

*** ****

0	0	0	0	0	−1	−1	≪ Obj. Fn. Coeff.		
X1	X2	X3	X4	X5	S1	S2	RHS	BASIS VRS	CBV

1	−0.33	0	−1	0.33	1	−0.33	1	X1	0
0	0.06	1	0	−0.06	0	0.06	0.33	X3	0

0	0	0	0	0	−1	−1	≪ Marginal Net Gain

Phase I solution: $x_1 = 1$, $x_3 = 0.33$; objective function value: 0

**** ****

−30	−36	−684	0	0	≪ Obj. Fn. Coeff.			
X1	X2	X3	X4	X5	RHS	BASIS VRS	CBV

1	−0.33	0	−1	0.33	1	X1	−30
0	0.06	1	0	−0.06	0.33	X3	−684

0	−8	0	−30	−28	≪ Marginal Net Gain

Since the marginal net gains are all negative, we have reached the optimal solution: $x_1 = 1$, $x_3 = 0.33$; objective function value: 258.

5. Phase I solution: $x_3 = 118.42$, $x_4 = 315.79$
Final solution: $x_1 = 1{,}200$, $x_3 = 150$; objective function value: 129,000

6. Phase I solution: $x_1 = 1.43$, $x_4 = 0.29$
Final solution: $x_1 = 1.67$, $x_5 = 2$; objective function value: 180

7. Since v_2, v_3, and v_5 are nonzero, we know that the corresponding slack variables must be zero; in other words, the corresponding constraints must be satisfied as equalities:

$$
\begin{aligned}
x_1 \quad\quad + 4x_3 &= 42 \\
5x_2 + 6x_3 &= 80 \\
28x_1 + 32x_2 + 24x_3 &= 640
\end{aligned}
$$

Now we have a three-equation, three-variable system, which can be solved:

$$x_1 = 8.835, \quad x_2 = 6.051, \quad x_3 = 8.291$$

7

TRANSPORTATION AND ASSIGNMENT PROBLEMS

KEY TERMS

assignment problem   a special kind of transportation problem in which all supplies and demands are equal to 1 (for example, where individuals are to be assigned different jobs)

northwest corner rule   a method for determining a basic feasible solution to a transportation problem

stepping-stone algorithm   a method for moving from one basic feasible solution of a transportation problem to another of lower cost, and determining whether a basic feasible solution is optimal

transportation problem   a problem that involves transporting goods from where they are stored to where they are needed in a way that minimizes cost

---

INTRODUCTION

The **transportation problem** is a special kind of linear programming problem with many applications.

Example 7-1: Formulating the Problem

PROBLEM   Suppose that we have 3,000 yo-yos stored in a warehouse in Axville and 4,000 yo-yos stored in Betatown. Suppose that our yo-yo outlets in Ceeburg, Deltana, and Epcity put in orders for 1,000, 4,000, and 2,000 yo-yos, respectively. Suppose that the transportation costs (in cents per yo-yo) are as follows:

$$c_{AC} = 2, \qquad c_{AD} = 3, \qquad c_{AE} = 4,$$
$$c_{BC} = 1, \qquad c_{BD} = 7, \qquad c_{BE} = 2$$

where c_{AE} is the cost of shipping from Axville to Epcity, etc.

What is the cheapest way of shipping the yo-yos from the warehouses to the outlets?

SOLUTION A solution to the problem would be a set of numbers $x_{AC}, x_{AD}, x_{AE}, x_{BC}, x_{BD}$, and x_{BE} that would tell us how many yo-yos to ship along each route. Such a solution would have to satisfy these demands:

$$x_{AC} + x_{BC} = 1,000, \quad x_{AD} + x_{BD} = 4,000, \quad x_{AE} + x_{BE} = 2,000$$

but not overtax our supplies:

$$x_{AC} + x_{AD} + x_{AE} = 3,000, \qquad x_{BC} + x_{BD} + x_{BE} = 4,000$$

We want each x to be nonnegative, since we cannot transport a negative number of yo-yos. We also require that each x be an integer, since we would not want to split yo-yos in half.

If such a solution existed, we would want it to minimize the transportation cost:

$$2x_{AC} + 3x_{AD} + 4x_{AE} + (1)x_{BC} + 7x_{BD} + 2x_{BE}$$

GENERAL PROBLEM

The general transportation problem consists of a set of supplies, $s_1, s_2, \ldots, s_m$; a set of demands, $d_1, d_2, \ldots, d_n$; and a set of transportation costs $\{c_{ij} = \text{cost per unit transported from supply } i \text{ to demand } j\}$.

Then we want the following:

(a) $\Sigma_i x_{ij} = d_j$

so that we can supply the demands;

(b) $\Sigma_j x_{ij} = s_i$

so that we don't overtax the supplies (note that $\Sigma_i s_i = \Sigma_{ij} x_{ij} = \Sigma_j d_j$);

(c) x_{ij} is a nonnegative integer for each route; and

(d) $\Sigma_{ij} c_{ij} x_{ij}$ is a minimum.

Example 7-2: Transporting Television Sets

Suppose that we have three warehouses storing television sets in Philadelphia, Los Angeles, and Dallas. These television sets are selling for the same price in New Orleans, New York, Chicago, and Seattle. There are 3,000 sets in Philadelphia, 2,000 in Los Angeles, and 10,000 in Dallas. Orders have been placed for 4,000 in New Orleans, 3,000 in New York, 3,000 in Chicago, and 4,000 in Seattle. Suppose that the transportation costs in dollars per set are as follows·

To:

From:	New Orleans	New York	Chicago	Seattle
Philadelphia	10	2	8	15
Los Angeles	17	12	7	4
Dallas	4	8	6	10

For example, the transportation cost from Los Angeles to New Orleans is $17.
Now, we have

$$3,000 + 2,000 + 10,000 = 15,000 \text{ sets}$$

in warehouses, with orders for

$$4,000 + 3,000 + 3,000 + 4,000 = 14,000 \text{ sets}$$

and demands are less than supplies.

We can still treat this as a general problem. (We will want to have all transportation problems in the same form, so that we can use one method to solve them all.)

If we are able to solve the problem, we will have 1,000 sets left in storage since the demand is 1,000 sets less than the supply. Let's treat the amount being left in storage as if it were another demand.

$$
\begin{array}{llr}
\text{Supplies:} & \text{Philadelphia} & = 3,000 \\
& \text{Los Angeles} & = 2,000 \\
& \text{Dallas} & = 10,000 \\
\\
\text{Demands:} & \text{New Orleans} & = 4,000 \\
& \text{New York} & = 3,000 \\
& \text{Chicago} & = 3,000 \\
& \text{Seattle} & = 4,000 \\
& \text{Storage} & = 1,000
\end{array}
$$

Our transportation costs are now as follows:

| | To: | | | | |
From:	New Orleans	New York	Chicago	Seattle	Storage
Philadelphia	10	2	8	15	0
Los Angeles	17	12	7	4	0
Dallas	4	8	6	10	0

Note that it costs nothing to transport television sets to storage.

LINEAR PROGRAMMING

Transportation problems are linear programming problems (ignoring for the present the fact that our solutions should be integers).

Example 7-1 can be written as

$$
\begin{aligned}
x_{AC} \quad\quad\quad + x_{BC} \quad\quad\quad &= 1{,}000 \\
x_{AD} \quad\quad\quad + x_{BD} \quad\quad &= 4{,}000 \\
x_{AE} \quad\quad\quad + x_{BE} &= 2{,}000 \\
x_{AC} + x_{AD} + x_{AE} \quad\quad\quad\quad\quad &= 3{,}000 \\
x_{BC} + x_{BD} + x_{BE} &= 4{,}000
\end{aligned}
$$

The variables x_{AC}, x_{AD}, x_{AE}, x_{BC}, x_{BD}, and x_{BE} are nonnegative, and

$$2x_{AC} + 3x_{AD} + 4x_{AE} + (1)x_{BC} + 7x_{BD} + 2x_{BE}$$

is to be minimized. In normal form, we would have

$$
\mathbf{A} = \begin{pmatrix}
1 & 0 & 0 & 1 & 0 & 0 \\
0 & 1 & 0 & 0 & 1 & 0 \\
0 & 0 & 1 & 0 & 0 & 1 \\
1 & 1 & 1 & 0 & 0 & 0 \\
0 & 0 & 0 & 1 & 1 & 1
\end{pmatrix}, \quad
\mathbf{R} = \begin{pmatrix}
1{,}000 \\
4{,}000 \\
2{,}000 \\
3{,}000 \\
4{,}000
\end{pmatrix},
$$

$$\mathbf{c} = (-2 \quad -3 \quad -4 \quad -1 \quad -7 \quad -2)$$

We could use the simplex method to solve this problem, and indeed our approach will apply the same principles. But at this very simple level (two factories, three demands), we already have a 5 by 6 constraint matrix. In real life, the constraint matrices could be much larger.

What we shall do is find simpler ways to determine the initial basic feasible solution and, once we have one solution, move to better ones.

NORTHWEST CORNER RULE

What is a basic feasible solution for the transportation problem? How many nonzero entries should it have?

In general, we start with m supply constraints and n demand constraints, so we might be tempted to say $m + n$. That's close—it's actually $m + n - 1$, and here's why: one of the constraints is redundant.

If we add all of the demand constraints:

$$\sum_{ij} x_{ij} = \sum_j d_j$$

and all of the supply constraints:

$$\sum_{ij} x_{ij} = \sum_i s_i$$

and subtract, we get

$$0 = 0 \quad \left(\text{since } \sum_j d_j = \sum_i s_i \right)$$

Thus one of the constraints can be obtained by adding and subtracting the others. In Example 7-1, we can get the first demand constraint:

$$x_{AC} \qquad\qquad + x_{BC} \qquad\qquad = \quad 1{,}000$$

by adding

$$
\begin{aligned}
-x_{AD} \qquad\qquad\quad -x_{BD} \qquad &= -4{,}000 \\
-x_{AE} \qquad\qquad -x_{BE} &= -2{,}000 \\
x_{AC} + x_{AD} + x_{AE} \qquad\qquad\qquad &= \quad 3{,}000 \\
x_{BC} + x_{BD} + x_{BE} &= \quad 4{,}000
\end{aligned}
$$

It can be shown that the remaining $m + n - 1$ constraints will always be independent. Thus a basic solution will have $m + n - 1$ positive entries.

Rather than go through the phase 1 calculations of the simplex method, we will use the **northwest corner rule** to get our first basic solution.

First, we draw the following diagram:

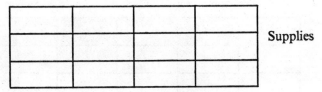

Demands

For example, Example 7-2 would be represented as follows:

	New Orleans	New York	Chicago	Seattle	Storage	
Philadelphia						3,000
Los Angeles						2,000
Dallas						10,000
	4,000	3,000	3,000	4,000	1,000	

The locations of the warehouses go on the left, the amounts of the supplies on the right, the names of the ordering cities on the top, and the sizes of the orders on the bottom.

Then, any solution to the transportation problem can be represented by a diagram such as this:

	New Orleans	New York	Chicago	Seattle	Storage	
Philadelphia	1,000	1,000	1,000	0	0	3,000
Los Angeles	1,000	1,000	0	0	0	2,000
Dallas	2,000	1,000	2,000	4,000	1,000	10,000
	4,000	3,000	3,000	4,000	1,000	

This is a feasible solution, since the sum of the entries in each column (the number of television sets being shipped to a given city) equals the order size for that column, and, likewise, the sum of the entries in each row equals the supply for that row.

This solution is not basic, since there are 10 positive entries, while $m + n - 1 = 3 + 5 - 1 = 7$.

Now we are ready for the northwest corner rule. We take an empty diagram, find the northwest corner, and write in the largest number that we can without violating either a supply or a demand constraint. Since the first-row constraint is 3,000, and the first-column constraint is 4,000, we write in 3,000. Since the first-row constraint is now full, we shade the other boxes in the first row, so that we will know not to put anything else in that row.

	New Orleans	New York	Chicago	Seattle	Storage	
Philadelphia	3,000					3,000
Los Angeles						2,000
Dallas						10,000
	4,000	3,000	3,000	4,000	1,000	

Now we do the same thing with the empty part of the diagram. The new northwest corner is Los Angeles to New Orleans, the row constraint is 2,000, and the first-column constraint has $4,000 - 3,000 = 1,000$ left, so we write in 1,000. Since the first-column constraint is now full, we shade in the rest of the column.

	New Orleans	New York	Chicago	Seattle	Storage	
Philadelphia	3,000					3,000
Los Angeles	1,000					2,000
Dallas						10,000
	4,000	3,000	3,000	4,000	1,000	

Now the northwest corner of the empty diagram is Los Angeles to New York. There are $2,000 - 1,000 = 1,000$ left in the second-row constraint, and 3,000 left in the second-column constraint, so we write in 1,000. Since the second-row constraint is now full, we shade in the rest of the second row.

	New Orleans	New York	Chicago	Seattle	Storage	
Philadelphia	3,000					3,000
Los Angeles	1,000	1,000				2,000
Dallas						10,000
	4,000	3,000	3,000	4,000	1,000	

We fill in the rest of the diagram quickly in the same way, and end up with this:

	New Orleans	New York	Chicago	Seattle	Storage	
Philadelphia	3,000					3,000
Los Angeles	1,000	1,000				2,000
Dallas		2,000	3,000	4,000	1,000	10,000
	4,000	3,000	3,000	4,000	1,000	

There are, in fact, seven positive entries, and this represents a basic solution. It is not by accident that this solution is basic. Every entry represents the filling of at least one constraint, and the last entry fills both a row and a column constraint. Since there are $m + n$ constraints, there are at most $m + n - 1$ positive entries. (If there are fewer than $m + n - 1$ entries, we have a degenerate case, which we will deal with later.)

The first basic solution for Example 7-1 would be found by the northwest corner rule as follows:

	C	D	E	
A	1,000			3,000
B				4,000
	1,000	4,000	2,000	

	C	D	E	
A	1,000	2,000		3,000
B				4,000
	1,000	4,000	2,000	

	C	D	E	
A	1,000	2,000		3,000
B		2,000	2,000	4,000
	1,000	4,000	2,000	

STEPPING-STONE ALGORITHM

In linear programming, once we have a basic solution, we look for negative marginal net gains (when seeking a minimum) before pivoting to a new basic solution. This pivoting involves expressing a new basis entry in terms of the old basis.

We shall do the same thing now, using the diagram for our given basic solution. We want to calculate the marginal net gain for each transportation route not used in the current basis.

Let's look at route x_{AE} in Example 7-1, with the basic solution we just found. We want to see how our old basis would be affected by shipping yo-yo along x_{AE}. If we shipped one yo-yo along x_{AE}, we would want to ship one yo-yo less along x_{BE}, so that Epcity would still get just 2,000 yo-yos. If we shipped one less yo-yo along x_{BE}, in order to still ship 4,000 from Betatown, we would have to increase x_{BD} by 1. We would then have to decrease x_{AD} by 1, which would leave our first-row constraint just filled.

	C	D	E
A		−1	1
B		1	−1

There is only one way to express x_{AE} in terms of the old basis, and we have just found it. In doing so, we have formed a closed path. We shipped one extra yo-yo along x_{AE}, and then found the expression for x_{AE} in terms of the old basis by alternating our fixing of the disturbed column and row constraints. We had to end up where we started in order to fix the first-row constraint. This method is called the **stepping-stone algorithm**.

If we had first tried fixing the disturbed first-row constraint, we would have had to choose between x_{AC} and x_{AD}. If we had chosen x_{AC}, there would have been no way to fix the first-column constraint. On the other hand, x_{AD} would have given us the same closed path.

What is the marginal net gain for x_{AE}? It is the extra cost per yo-yo to ship along x_{AE}. Since $c_{AE} = 4$, $c_{BE} = 2$, $c_{BD} = 7$, and $c_{AD} = 3$, the marginal net cost is

$$4(1) + 2(-1) + 7(1) + 3(-1) = 6$$

Since this is positive, we would not want to bring x_{AE} into our basis; it would increase the overall cost.

The marginal net gain for x_{BC}, using the following closed path;

	C	D	E
A	−1	1	
B	1	−1	

is

$$1(1) + 2(-1) + 3(1) + 7(-1) = -5$$

We write, in parentheses, the marginal net costs into our diagram:

	C	D	E
A	1,000	2,000	(6)
B	(−5)	2,000	2,000

Since the marginal net gain at x_{BC} is negative, we want to bring x_{BC} into the basis. (If there were more than one negative marginal net cost, we would choose the most negative one in order to lower the cost as much as possible.)

To bring in x_{BC}, we want to add as large a multiple of $BC - AC + AD - BD$ as possible. This means adding the largest multiple that won't make x_{AC} or x_{BD} negative. Since $x_{AC} = 1,000$ and $x_{BD} = 2,000$, 1,000 is the largest multiple possible. Then

$$x_{BC} = 1,000, \qquad x_{AC} = 1,000 + 1,000(-1) = 0,$$

$$x_{AD} = 2,000 + 1,000(1) = 3,000,$$

and

$$x_{BD} = 2,000 + 1,000(-1) = 1,000$$

	C	D	E
A	(5)	3,000	(6)
B	1,000	1,000	2,000

All the new marginal net gains are nonnegative, and we are done. This is an optimal solution, with cost = 21,000 cents = \$210.

The marginal net gains for the basic solution for Example 7-2 are calculated as follows (see Figure 7-1):

Philadelphia–New York

Los Angeles–Chicago

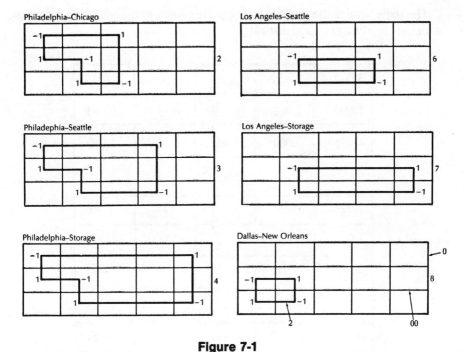

Figure 7-1

$$\text{MNG(Philadelphia–New York)} = 2(1) + 12(-1) + 17(1) + 10(-1) = -3$$
$$\begin{aligned}\text{MNG(Philadelphia–Chicago)} &= 8(1) + 10(-1) + 17(1) + 12(-1)\\ &\quad + 8(1) + 6(-1)\\ &= 5\end{aligned}$$
$$\begin{aligned}\text{MNG(Philadelphia–Seattle)} &= 15(1) + 10(-1) + 17(1) + 12(-1)\\ &\quad + 8(1) + 10(-1)\\ &= 8\end{aligned}$$
$$\begin{aligned}\text{MNG(Philadelphia–Storage)} &= 0(1) + 10(-1) + 17(1) + 12(-1)\\ &\quad + 8(1) + 0(-1)\\ &= 3\end{aligned}$$
$$\text{MNG(Los Angeles–Chicago)} = 7(1) + 12(-1) + 8(1) + 6(-1) = -3$$
$$\text{MNG(Los Angeles–Seattle)} = 4(1) + 12(-1) + 8(1) + 10(-1) = -10$$
$$\text{MNG(Los Angeles–Storage)} = 0(1) + 12(-1) + 8(1) + 0(-1) = -4$$
$$\text{MNG(Dallas–New Orleans)} = 4(1) + 17(-1) + 12(1) + 8(-1) = -9$$

The steps toward the optimal solution are shown in the following diagrams, with the pivot element underlined:

3,000	(−3)	(5)	(8)	(3)
1,000	1,000	(−3)	<u>(−10)</u>	(−4)
(−9)	2,000	3,000	4,000	1,000

3,000	(7)	(15)	(18)	(13)
1,000	(10)	(7)	1,000	(6)
<u>(−19)</u>	3,000	3,000	3,000	1,000

3,000	<u>(−12)</u>	(−4)	(−1)	(−6)
(19)	(10)	(7)	2,000	(6)
1,000	3,000	3,000	2,000	1,000

	3,000			
			2,000	
4,000		3,000	2,000	1,000

After the last pivot, we are left with only six positive entries. We are in a degenerate case.

DEGENERACY

One way of dealing with a degenerate diagram might be to ignore it. Unfortunately, with only six entries in the last diagram above, some marginal net gains can't be calculated.

Now, the empty boxes in a diagram represent zeros. If we write in small positive numbers for some of the zeros, we won't change the solution much. If s entries are lacking from our basic solution, we write in $\partial_1, \partial_2, \ldots, \partial_s$, and put these ∂'s anywhere in the diagram. When we're done, we will set them equal to zero to get the solution to our original problem.

In our television set example, we lack one entry, and we will put a ∂ in the first row and first column, since this was an entry before the last pivot:

∂	3,000	(-4)	(-1)	$\underline{(-6)}$
(19)	(22)	(7)	2,000	(6)
4,000	(12)	3,000	2,000	1,000

(6)	3,000	(2)	(5)	∂
(19)	(16)	(7)	2,000	(6)
$4,000 + \partial$	(6)	3,000	2,000	$1,000 - \partial$

and we have our optimal solution:

	3,000			
			2,000	
4,000		3,000	2,000	1,000

with cost

$$3,000(2) + 0(0) + 2,000(4) + 4,000(4) + 3,000(6) + 2,000(10) + 1,000(0)$$
$$= \$68,000$$

YOU SHOULD REMEMBER

If a marginal net gain is negative, we can lower our overall cost by bringing the corresponding variable into the basis. If no marginal net gain is negative, we have an optimal solution.

ASSIGNMENT PROBLEMS

Assignment problems are a special class of transportation problems in which supplies and demands are all equal to 1 (note that this means that there are as many supplies as demands).

The most common assignment problems concern job assignments.

Example 7-3: Assigning Jobs

PROBLEM   Suppose that we have four people and four jobs to be assigned. Each person has a different salary demanded (in thousands of dollars per year) for each job as follows:

Worker

		1	2	3	4
	1	23	30	40	19
	2	25	32	32	30
Job	3	22	17	18	20
	4	17	20	45	33

How can we minimize the salaries paid?

SOLUTION   The northwest corner rule gives us the following diagram, with the ∂'s added because of degeneracy (a basic solution should have $4 + 4 - 1 = 7$ positive entries).

1	∂_1	∂_2	∂_3
	1		
		1	
			1

There will always be degeneracy in an assignment problem, since a solution will have m positive entries, while a basic solution needs $m + n - 1 = m + m - 1 = 2m - 1$ positive entries.

Our solution follows from these diagrams:

1	∂_1	∂_2	∂_3
(0)	1	(−10)	(9)
(21)	(9)	1	(23)
(−20)	(−24)	(−9)	1

1	(24)	∂_2	$\partial_1 + \partial_3$
(−24)	1	(−34)	(−15)
(21)	(33)	1	(23)
(−20)	∂_1	(−9)	$1 - \partial_1$

1	(24)	(34)	$\partial_1 + \partial_2 + \partial_3$
(−24)	$1 - \partial_2$	∂_2	(−15)
(−13)	(−1)	1	(−11)
(−20)	$\partial_1 + \partial_2$	(25)	$1 - \partial_1 - \partial_2$

$\partial_1 + \partial_2$	(0)	(10)	$1 + \partial_3$
$1 - \partial_1 - \partial_2$	∂_1	∂_2	(9)
(11)	(−1)	1	(13)
(4)	1	(25)	(24)

$\partial_1 + \partial_2$	(1)	(10)	$1 + \partial_3$
$1 - \partial_1 - \partial_2$	(1)	$\partial_1 + \partial_2$	(9)
(11)	∂_1	$1 - \partial_1$	(13)
(3)	1	(24)	(23)

and our optimal solution is

Worker

	1	2	3	4
1				1
2	1			
3			1	
4		1		

Job

at cost $25 + 20 + 18 + 19 = \$82$.

INTEGRAL SOLUTIONS

You may have noticed by now that we haven't had to worry about our solutions being integers—they always were. There's a reason for this.

As long as our constraints are integers, our first basic solution, coming from the northwest corner rule, will always consist of integers. Our pivoting, starting with an integer basic solution, always yields us another integer basic solution, since it involves adding and subtracting the numbers in our diagram. Thus we always have integral solutions.

We can always find optimal solutions for transportation problems, since every pivot brings us to a new basic solution at lower cost. Eventually we will find the optimal basic solution. (This is in contrast with the general linear programming problem, where a pivot may be impossible to perform, and the cost may go off to negative infinity.)

UNUSABLE ROUTES

Sometimes there is no route connecting a given supply to a given demand. Likewise, a worker in a job assignment problem may not be qualified for a given job.

In such cases our problem becomes one of finding an optimal solution that does not include these unusable routes. (All options in a transportation problem are called *routes*. For example, assigning a particular worker to a particular job is a route.)

We don't want to just cross out these routes on our diagram. This would mess up our algorithms, and we would have to find a new way of solving the problem.

Rather, to each unusable route i, we assign a cost M_i that is a very large number (infinity, if you prefer). This will bias the algorithm against using this route if possible.

Example 7-4: A Problem with an Unusable Route

In our job assignment problem, assume that the first person is not qualified for the second or third job. The salaries are as follows:

		Worker			
		1	2	3	4
	1	23	30	40	19
	2	M_1	32	32	30
Job	3	M_2	17	18	20
	4	17	20	45	33

Our diagrams, en route to the solution, are these:

1	∂_1	∂_2	∂_3
$(M_1 - 25)$	1	(-10)	(9)
$(M_2 - 1)$	(9)	1	(23)
(-20)	$\underline{(-24)}$	(-9)	1

1	(24)	∂_2	$\partial_1 + \partial_3$
$(M_1 - 49)$	1	<u>(-34)</u>	(-15)
$(M_2 - 1)$	(33)	1	(23)
(-20)	∂_1	(-9)	$1 - \partial_1$

1	(24)	(34)	$\partial_1 + \partial_2 + \partial_3$
$(M - 49)$	$1 - \partial_2$	∂_2	(-15)
$(M - 35)$	(-1)	1	(-11)
<u>(-20)</u>	$1 + \partial_2$	(25)	$1 - \partial_1 - \partial_2$

$\partial_1 + \partial_2$	(4)	(14)	$1 + \partial_3$
$(M_1 - 29)$	$1 - \partial_2$	∂_2	(5)
$(M_2 - 15)$	<u>(-1)</u>	1	(9)
$1 - \partial_1 - \partial_2$	$\partial_1 + \partial_2$	(25)	(20)

$\partial_1 + \partial_2$	(4)	(13)	$1 + \partial_3$
$(M_1 - 28)$	(1)	1	(6)
$(M_2 - 14)$	$1 - \partial_2$	∂_2	(10)
$1 - \partial_1 - \partial_2$	$\partial_1 + \partial_2$	(24)	(20)

Our new solution is

Worker

	1	2	3	4
Job 1				1
2			1	
3		1		
4	1			

with cost $17 + 17 + 32 + 19 = \$89$.

If, after performing the algorithm, we still end up using an unusable route, the problem has no solution.

Example 7-5: Another Unusable Route Problem

Suppose that in Example 7-1 the route x_{BD} is closed (a bridge is out). Then our transportation costs would be as follows:

	C	D	E
A	2	3	4
B	1	M	2

Our solution would follow from these diagrams:

1,000	2,000	$(M-1)$
$\underline{(2-M)}$	2,000	2,000

$(M-2)$	3,000	$(M-1)$
1,000	1,000	2,000

and our solution:

	C	D	E
A		3,000	
B	1,000	1,000	2,000

is unacceptable. This solution would be optimal, no matter how expensive x_{BD} is; x_{BD} is essential for a solution to be feasible, and the problem has no solution without it.

YOU SHOULD REMEMBER

An unusable route is assigned a large, undetermined cost to keep if from being used in a solution. If the optimal solution still uses this route, the problem has no solution.

KNOW THE CONCEPTS

DO YOU KNOW THE BASICS?

Test your understanding of Chapter 7 by answering the following questions:

1. What is it about the constraints in a transportation problem that causes the solution to consist of integers?

2. Explain in general terms why there is always a feasible solution to a transportation problem.

3. In a degenerate transportation problem, what difference does it make where a ∂ is put in the diagram?

4. Show that, after eliminating one of the constraints in a transportation problem, the remaining $m + n - 1$ constraints are independent.

5. If, in an assignment problem, you had revenue (potential sales) figures for each individual rather than salaries, how would you set up the problem?

6. Why does degeneracy interfere with the stepping-stone algorithm?

7. If a constant per-item surcharge was added to the cost for each route, would this change the optimal solution to a transportation problem?

8. Will the solution to a transportation problem still consist of integers if the costs are nonintegers? What if the supply or demand constraints are nonintegers?

9. (a) With m supplies and n demands, what is the least number of unusable routes that will render a transportation problem infeasible?
   (b) What is the largest number of unusable routes that will permit a feasible solution?

10. There is nothing special about northwest as a direction. Formulate a southeast rule for finding a feasible basic solution to a transportation problem.

TERMS FOR STUDY

assignment problem   stepping-stone algorithm
northwest corner rule   transportation problem

PRACTICAL APPLICATION

COMPUTATIONAL PROBLEMS

Use the northwest corner rule to find feasible solutions for the transportation constraints given in Exercises 1–5. (Use storage demands where needed.)

1. $s_1 = 5$ $d_1 = 7$
   $s_2 = 4$ $d_2 = 3$
   $s_3 = 10$ $d_3 = 4$
             $d_4 = 5$

2. $s_1 = 5$ $d_1 = 20$
   $s_2 = 9$ $d_2 = 10$
   $s_3 = 11$
   $s_4 = 2$
   $s_5 = 13$

3. $s_1 = 1$ $d_1 = 9$
   $s_2 = 4$ $d_2 = 8$
   $s_3 = 9$ $d_3 = 7$
   $s_4 = 16$ $d_4 = 6$

4. $s_1 = 10$ $d_1 = 7$
   $s_2 = 10$ $d_2 = 6$
             $d_3 = 5$

5. $s_1 = 2$ $d_1 = 13$
   $s_2 = 3$ $d_2 = 15$
   $s_3 = 5$
   $s_4 = 7$
   $s_5 = 11$

*Solve for the optimal solutions of the transportation problems in Exercises 6–10, where **c** is the matrix of costs.*

6. $s_1 = 5$ $d_1 = 5$
   $s_2 = 4$ $d_2 = 5$ $\mathbf{c} = \begin{pmatrix} 2 & 5 \\ 6 & 3 \\ 4 & 2 \end{pmatrix}$
   $s_3 = 2$

7. $s_1 = 7$ $\quad d_1 = 4$
$\quad s_2 = 2$ $\quad d_2 = 6$ $\quad \mathbf{c} = \begin{pmatrix} 1 & 2 & 3 \\ 4 & 5 & 6 \\ 9 & 8 & 7 \end{pmatrix}$
$\quad s_3 = 5$ $\quad d_3 = 4$

8. $s_1 = 5$ $\quad d_1 = 10$
$\quad s_2 = 4$ $\quad d_2 = 6$ $\quad \mathbf{c} = \begin{pmatrix} 1 & 4 & 10 \\ 4 & 6 & 8 \\ 1 & 7 & 5 \\ 5 & 2 & 6 \end{pmatrix}$
$\quad s_3 = 3$ $\quad d_3 = 3$
$\quad s_4 = 7$

9. $s_1 = 3$ $\quad d_1 = 1$
$\quad s_2 = 10$ $\quad d_2 = 2$ $\quad \mathbf{c} = \begin{pmatrix} 1 & 5 & 2 & 7 \\ 6 & 1 & 4 & 2 \end{pmatrix}$
$\quad\quad\quad\quad d_3 = 3$
$\quad\quad\quad\quad d_4 = 7$

10. $s_1 = 10$ $\quad d_1 = 40$
$\quad s_2 = 20$ $\quad d_2 = 10$ $\quad \mathbf{c} = \begin{pmatrix} 5 & 8 & 2 \\ 12 & 20 & 7 \\ 8 & 5 & 30 \end{pmatrix}$
$\quad s_3 = 32$ $\quad d_3 = 12$

Solve transportation problems in Exercises 11–15, where a "U" in **c** *stands for an unusable route.*

11. $s_1 = 15$ $\quad d_1 = 5$
$\quad s_2 = 20$ $\quad d_2 = 15$ $\quad \mathbf{c} = \begin{pmatrix} 5 & U & 3 \\ 10 & 8 & U \end{pmatrix}$
$\quad\quad\quad\quad d_3 = 15$

12. $s_1 = 20$ $\quad d_1 = 10$
$\quad s_2 = 13$ $\quad d_2 = 20$ $\quad \mathbf{c} = \begin{pmatrix} 8 & U & 5 \\ U & 7 & 10 \\ 12 & 15 & 10 \end{pmatrix}$
$\quad s_3 = 17$ $\quad d_3 = 20$

13. $s_1 = 25$ $\quad d_1 = 40$
$\quad s_2 = 30$ $\quad d_2 = 30$ $\quad \mathbf{c} = \begin{pmatrix} 10 & 15 \\ U & 13 \\ 7 & 8 \end{pmatrix}$
$\quad s_3 = 15$

14. $s_1 = 50$ $\quad d_1 = 100$
$\quad s_2 = 40$ $\quad d_2 = 60$ $\quad \mathbf{c} = \begin{pmatrix} 10 & U \\ 15 & 13 \\ U & 8 \\ 20 & U \end{pmatrix}$
$\quad s_3 = 30$
$\quad s_4 = 40$

15. $s_1 = 50$ $\quad d_1 = 30$
$\quad s_2 = 40$ $\quad d_2 = 25$ $\quad \mathbf{c} = \begin{pmatrix} U & U & 8 & 7 \\ 13 & 15 & 20 & U \end{pmatrix}$
$\quad\quad\quad\quad d_3 = 20$
$\quad\quad\quad\quad d_4 = 15$

The matrices **c** *in Exercises 16–20 represent annual salaries (in thousands of dollars) for possible job assignments. In each case, find the optimal job assignment. (Again, "U" stand for an unusable job assignment.)*

16. $c = \begin{pmatrix} 100 & 15 & 20 \\ 90 & 30 & 25 \\ 70 & 20 & 23 \end{pmatrix}$

17. $c = \begin{pmatrix} 15 & 18 & 17 \\ 23 & 12 & 11 \\ 22 & 14 & 41 \\ 19 & 14 & 22 \end{pmatrix}$

18. $c = \begin{pmatrix} 21 & 17 \\ 19 & 13 \\ 42 & 32 \end{pmatrix}$

19. $c = \begin{pmatrix} 22 & 19 & 23 \\ 14 & U & 22 \\ 32 & 19 & 18 \end{pmatrix}$

20. $c = \begin{pmatrix} 19 & 23 & U \\ 35 & 42 & 40 \\ 18 & U & 20 \end{pmatrix}$

ANSWERS

KNOW THE CONCEPTS

1. Every pivot involved in the simplex algorithm has 1 for its pivot element, so that the numbers in the "RHS" column remain integers.

2. Since the supplies equal the demands, and there is a route connecting each supply to each demand, every demand can in turn satisfy its needs.

3. Since the ∂'s represent small positive numbers (for the duration of the algorithm), there are only certain optimal basic solutions. The placement of the ∂'s corresponds to a choice of basic solution, and some basic solutions are closer to the optimal basic solutions than others.

4. Suppose that the first supply constraint $\Sigma_j x_{1j} = s_1$ can be expressed in terms of the other constraints. Now, for each j, x_{1j} occurs in no other supply constraint, and in only one demand constraint, $\Sigma_i x_{ij} = d_j$. Thus we must have $\Sigma_j x_{1j} = s_1$ as the sum of each $\Sigma_i x_{ij} = d_j$ and some other terms. Now we have x_{2j}, x_{3j}, etc., appearing for each j. Therefore, we have to subtract $\Sigma_j x_{2j} = s_2$, $\Sigma_j x_{3j} = s_3$, etc., from the sum of each $\Sigma_i x_{ij} = d_j$ to get $\Sigma_j x_{1j} = s_1$. But now we've used all of the constraints, while we know that we've omitted one because of degeneracy—a contradiction. Similar reasoning applies to the other constraints.

5. Instead of looking for negative marginal net gains, you would look for positive ones.

6. With fewer than $m + n - 1$ positive entries, it is impossible to calculate some of the marginal net gains.

7. No, because the marginal net gains would not be affected by the surcharge.

8. The costs have no effect on whether or not the solution consists of integers, but the supplies and demands do, since they determine the values of the first basic solution.

9. (a) A transportation problem can be rendered infeasible by one unusable route.

   (b) Since each of the supplies and demands must have at least one unusable route, if M equals the larger of m and n, there can be at most $mn - M$ unusable routes.

10. At each stage, choose the lowest and rightmost corner of the empty part of the diagram to fill in next.

PRACTICAL APPLICATION

1.

5				5
2	2			4
	1	4	5	10
7	3	4	5	

2.

5			5
9			9
6	5		11
	2		2
	3		13
20	10	10	(storage)

3.

1				1
4				4
4	5			9
	3	7	6	16
9	8	7	6	

4.

7	3			10
	3	5	2	10
7	6	5	2	(storage)

5.

2		2
3		3
5		5
3	4	7
	11	11
13	15	

6.

5			s_1
	3	1	s_2
	2		s_3
d_1	d_2	storage	

cost $= 23$

7.

	d_1	d_2	d_3	
s_1	4	3		
s_2		2		
s_3		1	4	

cost = 56

8.

	d_1	d_2	d_3	
s_1	5			
s_2	2		2	
s_3	3			
s_4		6	1	

cost = 50

9.

	d_1	d_2	d_3	d_4	
s_1	1		2		
s_2		2	1	7	

cost = 25

10.

	d_1	d_2	d_3	
s_1	10			
s_2	8		12	
s_3	22	10		

cost = 456

11.

	d_1	d_2	d_3	
s_1			15	
s_2	5	15		

cost = 215

12.

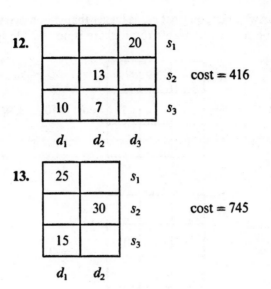

		20	s_1
	13		s_2
10	7		s_3
d_1	d_2	d_3	

cost = 416

13.

25		s_1
	30	s_2
15		s_3
d_1	d_2	

cost = 745

14.

50		s_1
10	30	s_2
	30	s_3
40		s_4
d_1	d_2	

cost = 2,080

15. The algorithm stops at either

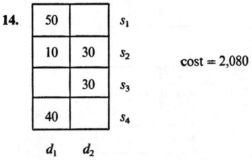

15		20	15
15	25		

or

	15	20	15
30	10		

depending on whether you treat c_{12} as bigger than c_{11} or vice versa. Since either solution uses an unusable route, there is no feasible solution.

16.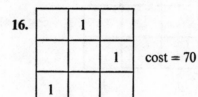

cost = 70

17.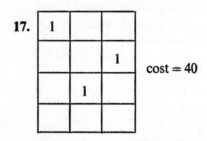

cost = 40

18.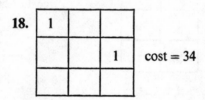

cost = 34

19.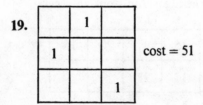

cost = 51

20.

cost = 78

8

INTEGER PROGRAMMING

KEY TERMS

branch-and-bound an algorithm for solving integer programming problems

integer programming the study of linear programming problems in which all numbers are required to be integers

---

INTRODUCTION

In Chapter 7, dealing with transportation problems, we had an extra constraint on our linear programming problems—the solutions had to be integers.

Often the solutions to practical linear programming problems are required to be integers. Although we can talk about ½ tons of coal, talking about half a yo-yo doesn't make much sense. If, as in Chapter 2, we are making furniture, we don't want to make two fifths of a chair.

In a transportation problem, for technical reasons having to do with the nature of the supply and demand constraints, our solutions (when they exist) will always consist of integers. In most other problems, however, this will not be true. The study of linear programming, with the added constraint that the solution also consist of integers, is called **integer programming.**
integer programming.

As in ordinary linear programming, there are three possible cases: (1) there may be no feasible integer solutions, (2) there may be feasible but no optimal integer solutions, or (3) there may well be an optimal integer solution. We will solve integer programming problems with an algorithm called **branch-and-bound**, which will take the set of feasible solutions to the corresponding linear programming problem, but add constraint equations that will eliminate non-integer solutions.

You might be tempted to solve an ordinary linear programming problem and then round the solution to the nearest feasible point with integer values. However, the result will not necessarily be the optimum to the integer programming problem. In some cases the optimal integer solution may be quite different from the solution to the ordinary linear programming problem.

Example 8-1: Locating Restaurants

PROBLEM A retail chain is planning to expand to a new region. The company will build a number of big stores (represented by x), each of which has an expected monthly profit of $123 thousand, and little stores (y), each of which has an expected profit of $20 thousand. Big stores cost $599 thousand, and little stores cost $95 thousand. The limited budget available for expansion imposes this constraint:

$$599x + 95y \leq 6,465.949$$

The limited capacities of the warehouse and distribution network impose this constraint:

$$20x + 4y \leq 225$$

As usual, the values for x and y must be nonnegative, and now they are also required to be integers. It would be meaningful to establish a fraction of a store.

SOLUTION Figure 8-1 illustrates the optimal solution to the linear programming problem if the solution values were not required to be integers:

$$x = 9.05, \ y = 11; \text{ objective function value: } 1,333.15$$

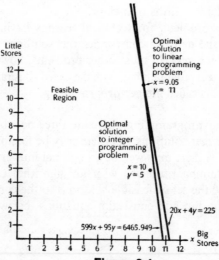

Figure 8-1

We might think that the solution to the integer programming problem could be found by rounding the solution to $x = 9$, $y = 11$. If we opened nine big stores and 11 little stores, we would have a total expected profit of \$1,327 thousand. (Check the constraints to verify that this solution is feasible.) However, suppose that we happened to try the solution $x = 10$, $y = 5$. This is a feasible solution with integer values. The total expected profit, \$1,330 thousand, is larger than what we had thought was the optimum. Clearly it makes a big difference if we build five little stores instead of 11 little stores.

Be warned, however, that the optimal solution to an integer programming problem is not necessarily obvious once the solution to the corresponding linear programming problem is known. Later in this chapter we will show that $x = 10$, $y = 5$ is in fact the optimum for this problem.

YOU SHOULD REMEMBER

An optimal integer solution is not always obtained by rounding off the solution to an ordinary linear program.

THE CORRESPONDING LINEAR PROGRAMMING PROBLEM

In an integer programming problem, we are given **A**, the matrix of constraint coefficients; **R**, the column vector of constraint constants; and **c**, the row vector of coefficients of the objective function. If we ignore the integer constraint, **A**, **R**, and **c** define a corresponding linear programming problem.

If there are no feasible solutions, then there are no feasible integer solutions.

If there is a feasible integer solution, with the value of its objective function equal to m, then we know that an optimal integer solution, if it exists, will have an objective function value greater than or equal to m. Thus any feasible integer solution give us a lower bound for the optimal objective function value.

On the other hand, if there is an optimal solution to the corresponding linear programming problem, with value M, then we know that the value of an optimal integer solution has to be less than or equal to M (since an optimal solution is optimal over all solutions, both integer and noninteger). Better yet, if we define $[M]$ to be the largest integer less than or equal to M, then $[M]$ will be an upper bound for our optimal value.

If the corresponding linear programming problem has feasible solutions but no optimal solutions, there are either no feasible integer solutions or no optimal integer solutions. In this case it is possible to construct a set of feasible solutions with arbitrarily large objective function values. This set may not include integer solutions if there are none; but if there is one, there will be an infinite number, also with arbitrarily large objective function values.

BRANCH-AND-BOUND

So much for the bound part of branch-and-bound. We know that any feasible integer solution gives us a lower bound for the optimal integer value. Given more than one, we choose the largest one to be MIN, our best lower bound, since the largest will be the closest to the real optimal value.

Given any optimal solution to the corresponding linear problem, we get for the integer programming problem an upper bound [M], which we call MAX.

In the following, since we are interested mainly in whether or not solutions consist of integers, all numbers will be rounded to the first nonzero decimal place.

Example 8-2: Finding the Solution by Branch and Bound
  Let

$$\mathbf{A} = \begin{pmatrix} 1 & -1 & 4 & 1 & -1 \\ 2 & 2 & -5 & 1 & 0 \\ 3 & -1 & 6 & 1 & 1 \end{pmatrix}, \qquad \mathbf{R} = \begin{pmatrix} 10 \\ 20 \\ 30 \end{pmatrix}, \qquad \mathbf{c} = (1 \quad 2 \quad -1 \quad 1 \quad -1)$$

Our simplex algorithm gives us the optimal solution

$$\mathbf{x} = \begin{pmatrix} 0 \\ 33.3 \\ 10 \\ 3.3 \\ 0 \end{pmatrix}$$

with $\mathbf{cx} = 60$. Now we know that an optimal integer solution will have an objective function value of 60 or less, and we set MAX = 60. Certainly $x_1 = 0$ is an integer, but $x_2 = 33.3$ isn't. In fact we know that either $x_2 \leq 33$ or $x_2 \geq 34$, but x_2 cannot be in between.

At this point we branch into two possibilities: case (1), where $x_2 \leq 33$, and case (2), where $x_2 \geq 34$ (see Figure 8-2). We know that any integer solution must satisfy one of these two constraints.

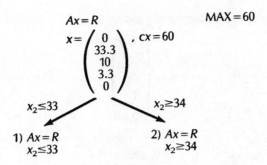

Figure 8-2

We run our simplex algorithm for our case (1) scenario, adding the constraint $x_2 \leq 33$. Our optimal solution is now

$$\mathbf{x} = \begin{pmatrix} 0.1 \\ 33 \\ 9.9 \\ 3.3 \\ 0 \end{pmatrix}$$

with $\mathbf{cx} = 59.5$. Now $x_1 = 0.1$ is not an integer, and we have two possibilities under case (1) to consider: case (3), where $x_2 \leq 33$ and $x_1 \leq 0$ (that is, $x_1 = 0$), and case (4), where $x_2 \leq 33$ and $x_1 \geq 1$ (see Figure 8-3).

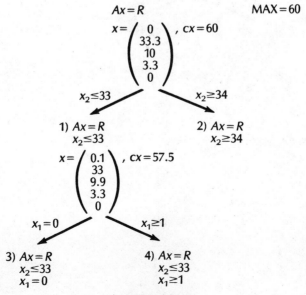

Figure 8-3

In case (3), our simplex algorithm yields

$$\mathbf{x} = \begin{pmatrix} 0 \\ 33 \\ 9.9 \\ 3.5 \\ 0.1 \end{pmatrix}$$

with $\mathbf{cx} = 59.5$. Now $x_3 = 9.9$ is the first noninteger variable, and we split into cases: case (5), where $x_2 \le 33$, $x_1 = 0$, and $x_3 \le 9$, and case (6), where $x_2 \le 33$, $x_1 = 0$, and $x_3 \ge 10$ (see Figure 8-4).

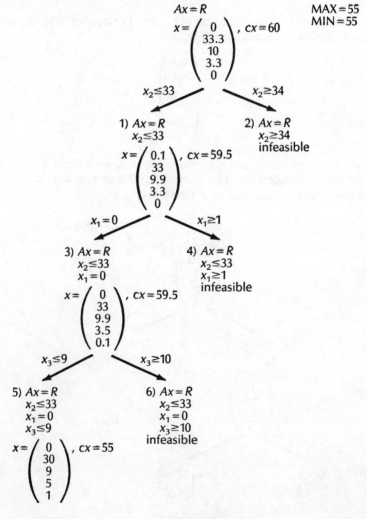

Figure 8-4

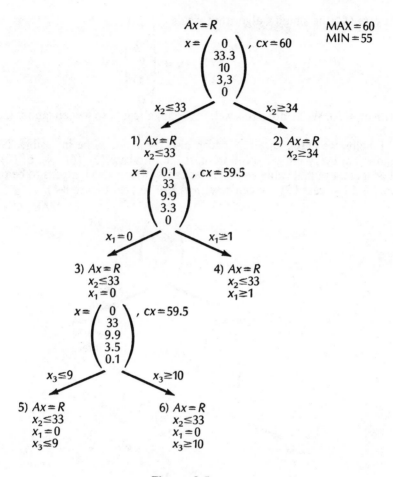

Figure 8-5

Now the simplex algorithm, in case (5), yields

$$\mathbf{x} = \begin{pmatrix} 0 \\ 30 \\ 9 \\ 5 \\ 1 \end{pmatrix}$$

with $\mathbf{cx} = 55$, which, finally, is an integer solution. It may not be the optimal integer solution, but we know that 55 is a lower bound for an optimal integer solution. Therefore, we set MIN = 55 (see Figure 8-5).

Now, returning to case (6), we find that the simplex algorithm tells us the extra constraints render the problem infeasible, and we can ignore this case.

At case (4), the simplex algorithm yields

$$\mathbf{x} = \begin{pmatrix} 1 \\ 30 \\ 9 \\ 3 \\ 0 \end{pmatrix}$$

with $\mathbf{cx} = 55$. We've done this well ($\mathbf{cx} = 55$) already, so we can ignore this case, too.

Finally, we check case (2), which also turns out to be infeasible. Now we know that every integer solution must fall into case (5), (6), (4), or (2). Since the biggest optimal value among these cases (which also happens to be the only one) is 55 at case (5), we can reset MAX = 55 (see Figure 8-6).

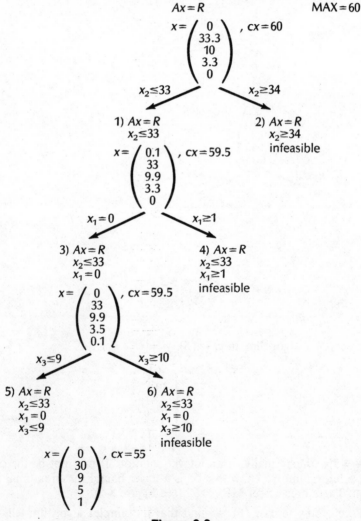

Figure 8-6

Now our upper bound, MAX, is equal to our lower bound, MIN, and the optimal integer value must be 55, which is attained at

Figure 8-7 shows the branching diagram for the retail problem discussed in Example 8-1:

$$\mathbf{A} = \begin{pmatrix} 599 & 95 \\ 20 & 4 \end{pmatrix}, \quad \mathbf{x} = \begin{pmatrix} x \\ y \end{pmatrix}, \quad \mathbf{R} = \begin{pmatrix} 6{,}465.949 \\ 225 \end{pmatrix}, \quad \mathbf{c} = (123 \quad 20)$$

Maximize **cx**
subject to:
   Ax ≤ **R**
   $x \geq 0, y \geq 0$
   x, y must be integers

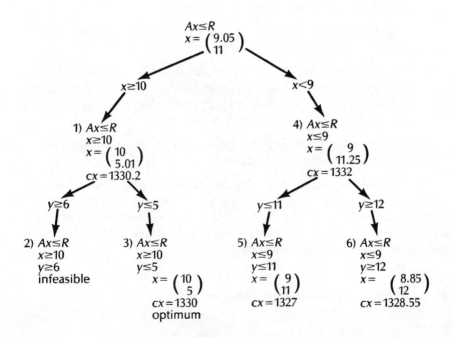

Figure 8-7

GENERAL METHOD

Given an arbitrary integer programming problem, you apply the branch-and-bound algorithm in the following way:

1. Solve the corresponding linear programming problem. If the solution is integer, you're done. Otherwise, set MAX equal to [**cx**] for that **x**.

2. Let x_i be the first noninteger entry of **x**. If $k < x_i < k + 1$ for some integer k, branch into the two cases $x_i \leq k$ and $x_i \geq k + 1$.

3. As you form your branching diagram (as was done in Example 8-2), solve the linear programming problem at each new case, adding the extra constraints.

4. If the solution is the first integer solution, set MIN = **cx**. If MIN has already been set and **cx** ≤ MIN, ignore this case (you've done at least as well elsewhere). If **cx** > MIN, reset MIN to be this higher **cx**, and **x** is your new best integer solution.

5. If the solution for the case is noninteger and **cx** < MIN, you can ignore it for the same reason.

6. If a case has no feasible solution, ignore it. If all subcases are infeasible, there is no feasible integer solution.

7. If, at any point, all subcases, such as cases (2), (4), (5), and (6) in Example 8-2, have been checked, reset MAX to be the maximal value of [**cx**] among these cases. This can only lower MAX, making it closer to the actual optimal value, or leave it unchanged.

8. If, at any point, MIN = MAX, stop—you have finished. The **x** that gave you MIN is the optimal integer solution.

The algorithm works by restricting the set of feasible solutions that the simplex algorithm examines, eliminating at each branching noninteger solutions. If the algorithm continued long enough, it would eliminate all noninteger solutions, and examine as subcases only the feasible integer solutions. Usually, though, the algorithm stops long before that.

Example 8-3: No Feasible Integer Solutions
    Let

$$\mathbf{A} = \begin{pmatrix} 3 & 1 & 1 & 0 & 0 \\ 1 & 2 & 0 & 1 & 0 \\ 6 & 6 & 0 & 0 & -1 \end{pmatrix}, \quad \mathbf{R} = \begin{pmatrix} 3 \\ 2 \\ 7 \end{pmatrix}, \quad \mathbf{c} = (2 \ 3 \ 0 \ 0 \ 0)$$

The full branching diagram is given in Figure 8-8. The corresponding linear programming problem yields

$$\mathbf{x} = \begin{pmatrix} 0.8 \\ 0.6 \\ 0 \\ 0 \\ 1.4 \end{pmatrix}$$

as its optimal solution, with $\mathbf{cx} = 3.4$. We set MAX $= [3.4] = 3$, and branch into two cases. In case (1), $x_1 = 0$; in case (2), $x_1 \geq 1$.

Both of these cases are infeasible, and there is no feasible integer solution.

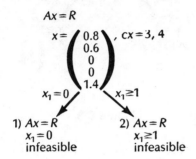

Figure 8-8

Example 8-4: Branch-and-Bound

Let

$$A = \begin{pmatrix} 1 & 2 & 3 \\ 4 & 2 & 1 \end{pmatrix}, \quad R = \begin{pmatrix} 10 \\ 11 \end{pmatrix}, \quad \mathbf{c} = (1 \quad 1 \quad 1)$$

The full diagram is shown in Figure 8-9. The solution to the corresponding linear programming problem is

$$\mathbf{x} = \begin{pmatrix} 0.3 \\ 4.8 \\ 0 \end{pmatrix}$$

with $\mathbf{cx} = 5.2$, so we set MAX $= [5.2] = 5$, and branch around x_1; case (1) has $x_1 = 0$, and case (2) has $x_1 \geq 1$.

Case (1) turns out to be infeasible. Case (2) has optimal solution

$$\mathbf{x} = \begin{pmatrix} 1 \\ 3 \\ 1 \end{pmatrix}$$

with $\mathbf{cx} = 5$. Thus we set $MIN = 5$. Since $MIN = MAX$, we stop, and our optimal integer solution is

$$\mathbf{x} = \begin{pmatrix} 1 \\ 3 \\ 1 \end{pmatrix}$$

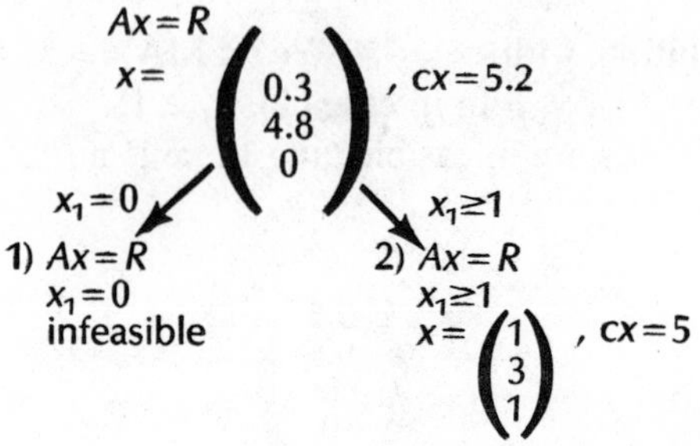

$$Ax = R$$
$$x = \begin{pmatrix} 0.3 \\ 4.8 \\ 0 \end{pmatrix}, \ cx = 5.2$$

$x_1 = 0$ $x_1 \geq 1$

1) $Ax = R$ 2) $Ax = R$
$x_1 = 0$ $x_1 \geq 1$
infeasible $x = \begin{pmatrix} 1 \\ 3 \\ 1 \end{pmatrix}, \ cx = 5$

Figure 8-9

YOU SHOULD REMEMBER

Integer programming problems can be solved using the simplex algorithm, adding additional constraints, and using the branch-and-bound algorithm.

KNOW THE CONCEPTS

DO YOU KNOW THE BASICS?

Test your understanding of Chapter 8 by answering the following questions:

1. Why can a linear programming problem, with **A**, **R**, and **c** consisting of integers, have a noninteger optimal solution?

2. (a) If a linear programming problem has a feasible integer solution for one vector, **c**, will it have one for another vector, **c′**?
   (b) If it has an optimal integer solution for **c**, will it have one for **c′**?
3. Do all branches always have to be checked in the branch-and-bound algorithm?
4. Why is the optimal value for integer solutions less than or equal to the optimal value over all possible solutions?
5. If you had an integer programming problem in which the variables represented dozens of eggs, and you wanted to transform the problem into one that dealt with individual eggs, what would you do the **A**, **R**, and **c**? Would you expect the optimal value of the objective function to change?

TERMS FOR STUDY

branch-and-bound   integer programming

PRACTICAL APPLICATION

COMPUTATIONAL PROBLEMS

Solve the integer programming problems in Exercises 1–10, where possible, for the given **A**, **R**, *and* **c**.

1. $A = \begin{pmatrix} 2 & 4 & 5 \\ 1 & 3 & 8 \end{pmatrix}$, $\quad R = \begin{pmatrix} 50 \\ 75 \end{pmatrix}$, $\quad c = (1 \quad -3 \quad 2)$

2. $A = \begin{pmatrix} 2 & 5 & 1 & 0 \\ 4 & 1 & 0 & 1 \end{pmatrix}$, $\quad R = \begin{pmatrix} 20 \\ 16 \end{pmatrix}$, $\quad c = (1 \quad 1 \quad 0 \quad 0)$

3. $A = \begin{pmatrix} 5 & 4 & 1 \\ 2 & -3 & 0 \\ -2 & 1 & 0 \end{pmatrix}$, $\quad R = \begin{pmatrix} 24 \\ 24 \\ 24 \end{pmatrix}$, $\quad c = (1 \quad 2 \quad 0)$

4. $A = \begin{pmatrix} -5 & 8 & 2 \\ 4 & 6 & 1 \end{pmatrix}$, $\quad R = \begin{pmatrix} 33 \\ 31 \end{pmatrix}$, $\quad c = (1 \quad -1 \quad -1)$

5. $A = \begin{pmatrix} 1 & 2 & 3 & 1 & 0 & 0 \\ 1 & -2 & 3 & 0 & 1 & 0 \\ 1 & 2 & -3 & 0 & 0 & 1 \end{pmatrix}$, $\quad R = \begin{pmatrix} 20 \\ 20 \\ 20 \end{pmatrix}$,

   $c = (5 \quad 2 \quad 1 \quad 0 \quad 0 \quad 0)$

6. $A = \begin{pmatrix} 6 & -5 & 1 & 0 \\ 1 & 2 & 0 & 1 \end{pmatrix}$, $\quad R = \begin{pmatrix} 20 \\ 30 \end{pmatrix}$, $\quad c = (2 \quad 3 \quad 0 \quad 0)$

7. $A = \begin{pmatrix} -1 & 1 & 1 & 0 \\ 1 & 0 & 1 & 0 \\ 1 & 1 & -1 & 1 \end{pmatrix}$, $\quad R = \begin{pmatrix} 15 \\ 20 \\ 25 \end{pmatrix}$ $\quad c = (1 \quad -1 \quad 1 \quad -1)$

8. $A = \begin{pmatrix} 2 & 6 & -1 & 0 \\ 3 & 1 & 0 & -1 \end{pmatrix}$, $\quad R = \begin{pmatrix} 50 \\ 60 \end{pmatrix}$, $\quad c = (5 \quad -4 \quad 0 \quad 0)$

9. $A = \begin{pmatrix} 1 & 2 & 6 & -1 & 0 & 0 \\ 4 & -3 & 2 & 0 & 1 & 0 \\ 1 & 5 & 4 & 0 & 0 & -1 \end{pmatrix}$, $\quad R = \begin{pmatrix} 35 \\ 30 \\ 20 \end{pmatrix}$,

$c = (-2 \quad -1 \quad -1 \quad 0 \quad 0 \quad 0)$

10. $A = \begin{pmatrix} 2 & 3 & 1 & 0 & 0 \\ 4 & 1 & 0 & 1 & 0 \\ 5 & 8 & 0 & 0 & 1 \end{pmatrix}$, $\quad R = \begin{pmatrix} 50 \\ 60 \\ 50 \end{pmatrix}$, $\quad c = (1 \quad -1 \quad 0 \quad 0 \quad 0)$

ANSWERS

KNOW THE CONCEPTS

1. The nonintegers can arise in the "RHS" column of the simplex tableau if the pivot element is not equal to 1, since the pivot row is divided by the pivot element, and multiples of the pivot row are added to the other rows.
2. (a) Yes, the feasibility of a solution does not depend on the objective function.
   (b) Not necessarily—the new problem with c' might have arbitrarily large values for $c'x$.
3. Not if MAX = MIN before the last branch is checked. If MAX = MIN, the algorithm stops.
4. The optimal value over all possible solutions is at least as big as the values for any other solutions, including the integer ones.
5. Let x' be the vector for the individual eggs. Then

$$x' = 12x, \quad Ax = R, \quad 12Ax = A(12x) = Ax' = 12R$$

Since c represents values per dozen, $(1/12)\,c$ represents values per egg. Thus you would set up the new problem as follows:

$$\text{Maximize } c'x', \text{ where } x' \geq 0, \ A'x' = R'$$

using

$$A' = A, \qquad R' = 12R, \quad c' = \frac{1}{12}c$$

Since

$$c'x' = \frac{1}{12}c(12)x = cx$$

the optimal value would not decrease, but might increase since solutions that involved numbers of eggs not divisible by 12 would now be possible.

PRACTICAL APPLICATION

1. Infeasible

2. $x = \begin{pmatrix} 3 \\ 2 \\ 4 \\ 2 \end{pmatrix}$, $\quad cx = 5$

3. Infeasible

4. $x = \begin{pmatrix} 1 \\ 4 \\ 3 \end{pmatrix}$, $\quad cx = -6$

5. $x = \begin{pmatrix} 20 \\ 0 \\ 0 \\ 0 \\ 0 \\ 0 \end{pmatrix}$, $\quad cx = 100$

6. $x = \begin{pmatrix} 10 \\ 10 \\ 10 \\ 0 \end{pmatrix}$, $\quad cx = 50$

7. $x = \begin{pmatrix} 12 \\ 19 \\ 8 \\ 2 \end{pmatrix}$, $\quad cx = -1$

8. $x = \begin{pmatrix} 19 \\ 3 \\ 6 \\ 0 \end{pmatrix}$, $\quad cx = -107$

9. $x = \begin{pmatrix} 0 \\ 0 \\ 6 \\ 1 \\ 18 \\ 4 \end{pmatrix}$, $\quad cx = -6$

10. $x = \begin{pmatrix} 10 \\ 0 \\ 30 \\ 20 \\ 0 \end{pmatrix}$, $\quad cx = 100$

9

OPTIMAL VALUES OF FUNCTIONS

KEY TERMS

critical points the points where the slope of a curve (that is, the derivative) is zero

derivative the derivative of a function $f(x)$ is a function $f'(x)$ whose value at a particular point is equal to the slope of the curve representing $f(x)$ at that point; it measures the rate of change of the dependent variable with respect to the independent variable

marginal cost the derivative of the total cost function with respect to the quantity produced; in some cases defined as the amount by which cost increases when 1 more unit is produced

marginal revenue the derivative of the total revenue function with respect to the quantitiy produced; in some cases defined as the amount that revenue increases when 1 more unit is produced

second derivative the derivative of the derivative

Now we turn to problems that involve choosing an optimal value in cases where we no longer have linear functions. A **function** is a rule that expresses the value of one quantity in terms of another quantity (or quantities). For example, the quantity demanded of a good is often expressed as a function of the price of the good. The quantity demanded is said to be the **dependent variable**, because the function is written so that the value of the quantity demanded depends on the value of the price. The price is said to be the **independent variable**. (Realistically, the quantity demanded will depend also on other factors. In this chapter we will consider only functions of one variable. In the next chapter we will introduce functions of more than one variable.)

THE SLOPE OF A CURVE

Example: Determining the Quantity That Maximizes Revenue

The WhizBang Computer Software Company has just introduced a new software package for improved business decision making. It is trying to decide how many packages to produce in order to earn the greatest possible total revenue. The revenue is equal to the price of each package sold, times the quantity sold. People will buy fewer packages if the price increases.

The WhizBang Company has obtained information that the demand function is given by this equation:

$$Q(P) = 12\frac{1}{7} - \frac{5}{7}P$$

The notation $Q(P)$ (read as "Q of P") indicates that the demand function expresses the quantity (Q) demanded (measured in thousands of packages per year) as a function of the price. In other words, if we know the value of the price, we can plug that value into the formula for the function and then calculate the quantity demanded. For example, the notation $Q(3)$ means that the demand function is to be evaluated for the particular case where $P = 3$:

$$Q(3) = 12\frac{1}{7} - \frac{5}{7} \times 3 = 10$$

In the real world it is difficult to determine demand functions. It is necessary to use techniques of statistical inference to estimate the nature of the demand. Statistical inference is described in the book *Business Statistics*, by Douglas Downing and Jeffrey Clark (Barron's Educational Series, Inc., 1985).

We can also calculate the *inverse* of the function above. The **inverse function** tells us what the price will be as a function of the quantity:

$$P(Q) = 17 - 1.4Q$$

This is how to think of the inverse function: Suppose we choose the quantity to produce. Then the formula above allows us to calculate the price that must be charged in order to sell that entire quantity. When we look at the inverse function, the quantity now is in the position of the independent variable and the price is the dependent variable. (Note that a business can choose either the price it wishes to charge for its product, or the quantity it wishes to sell, but it cannot choose both independently. Once it has chosen either the price or the quantity, the value of the other is determined by the demand in the market for the product.)

Since total revenue is equal to price times quantity, we can determine a function that gives the total revenue (TR) as a function of the quantity sold:

$$TR = PQ = (17 - 1.4Q)Q$$
$$= 17Q - 1.4Q^2$$

Figure 9-1 shows a graph of this function, with Q measured along the horizontal axis and TR measured along the vertical axis. Note that the function is represented by a curve, not a line, since the function $TR = 17Q - 1.4Q^2$ is not a linear function. A linear function contains no variables raised to any power other than 1. (See Chapter 1.) There is an intuitive explanation for the shape of the curve. If the quantity produced is zero, then the revenue is zero. Increasing the quantity above zero will increase the revenue. However, as the quantity is increased, the firm will have to decrease the price in order to sell the entire amount produced. Eventually the price will have to be lowered so much that each additional unit produced will actually cause a decline in total revenue.

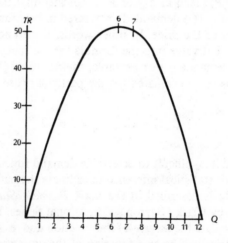

Figure 9-1

Figure 9-1 shows that the total revenue reaches a maximum at a quantity somewhere between 6 and 7. However, it is difficult to determine the precise amount from the diagram. We need a method that allows us to determine a formula for the maximum point of a curve.

Here is one clue. To the left of the maximum point, the curve slopes up as revenue is increasing; to the right of the maximum point, the curve slopes down as revenue is decreasing. (See Figure 9-2.) If we knew a formula for the slope of the curve at a particular quantity, we could determine where the curve stopped going up and started going down.

Recall how we found the slope of a line. We chose two points on the line, (x_1, y_1) and (x_2, y_2), and then calculated the ratio of the vertical distance divided

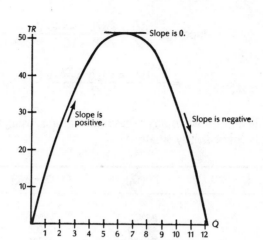

Figure 9-2

by the horizontal distance (giving the result a negative sign if the line was downward sloping):

$$\text{slope} = \frac{y_2 - y_1}{x_2 - x_1}$$

(See Chapter 1.)

When we calculate the slope of a line, it does not matter which two points we choose, since the slope is the same everywhere. However, the value of the slope of a curve will depend on which points are chosen. We choose two points that are very close together; and use Q_1 to represent the quantity at the first point, and $TR(Q_1)$ to represent the total revenue at that point. [The expression $TR(Q_1)$ is read as "TR of Q_1." It is written in this way to remind us that the total revenue depends on the quantity—in other words, total revenue is a function of quantity.] We will use $Q_1 + \Delta Q$ to represent the quantity at the second point. The little triangle, Δ, is the Greek capital letter **delta**, which is used to represent "change in." Therefore, the expression ΔQ means "the change in quantity." We will represent the quantity at the second point as $TR(Q_1 + \Delta Q)$. (See Figure 9-3.)

The slope between these two points can be found from the formula

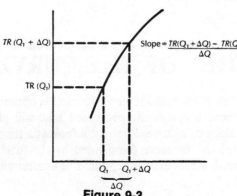

Figure 9-3

$$\text{slope} = \frac{TR(Q_1 + \Delta Q) - TR(Q_1)}{(Q_1 + \Delta Q) - (Q_1)}$$

$$= \frac{TR(Q_1 + \Delta Q) - TR(Q_1)}{\Delta Q}$$

Here is a table that shows some of these calculations, using the value 0.01 for ΔQ because it is conveniently small:

Q_1	$Q_1 + \Delta Q$	$TR(Q_1)$	$TR(Q_1 + \Delta Q)$	Slope
2	2.01	28.400	28.514	11.386
4	4.01	45.600	45.658	5.786
6	6.01	51.600	51.602	0.186
8	8.01	46.400	46.346	−5.414
10	10.01	30.000	29.890	−11.014
12	12.01	2.400	2.234	−16.613

Just as we suspected, the slope is positive when the quantity is less than 6. At some quantity above 6, the slope becomes negative as the curve turns down. Unfortunately, we would have to follow a tedious trial and error procedure to find the maximum point in this way. If we keep checking points, we will eventually find these two:

$$Q_1 = 6.07 \qquad\qquad Q_1 + \Delta Q = 6.08$$
$$TR(Q_1) = 51.60714 \qquad TR(Q_1 + \Delta Q) = 51.60704$$

$$\text{slope} = \frac{51.60704 - 51.60714}{6.08 - 6.07} = -0.01$$

This slope is very close to zero, so the point with zero slope must be near 6.07. Therefore, the WhizBang Company will maximize revenue if it produces a quantity of 6.07 thousand.

THE SLOPE OF THE CURVE $f(x) = x^2$

We will become extremely bored if we try to find the optimum by trial and error each time. We need a systematic procedure that will allow us to derive a formula for the slope of a curve. First, we'll look at a simpler example. Figure 9-4 shows a graph of the curve represented by the function $f(x) = x^2$. (The letter f is often used to represent functions. The expression $f(x)$ is read as "f of x.")

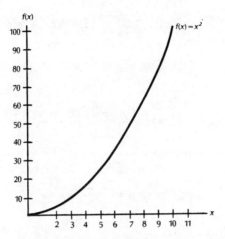

Figure 9-4

We can calculate the slope in the same way as we did in the preceding example. We choose two values to x that are very close to each other: x and $x + \Delta x$. Then we calculate the value of the function at each point: $f(x)$ and $f(x + \Delta x)$.

x	$x + \Delta x$	$f(x)$	$f(x + \Delta x)$	Slope
1	1.01	1	1.02	2.01
2	2.01	4	4.04	4.01
3	3.01	9	9.06	6.01
4	4.01	16	16.08	8.01
5	5.01	25	25.10	10.01
6	6.01	36	36.12	12.01
7	7.01	49	49.14	14.01

There seems to be a clear pattern. When $x = 1$, the slope is about 2; when $x = 2$, the slope is about 4; and so on. We are tempted to suppose that the slope at any point is $2x$.

Can we prove this property to be true in general? We need to examine this formula:

$$\text{slope function} = \frac{f(x + \Delta x) - f(x)}{\Delta x}$$

For the present, we will use the name *slope function*, since this function tells what the value of the slope will be for a given value of x.

Since $f(x) = x^2$, we can replace the f notation by writing the function explicitly:

$$\text{slope function} = \frac{(x + \Delta x)^2 - x^2}{\Delta x}$$

The expression $(x + \Delta x)^2$ is an algebraic expression that can be multiplied out:

$$\text{slope function} = \frac{x^2 + 2x \, \Delta x + \Delta x^2 - x^2}{\Delta x}$$

The x^2 and the $-x^2$ cancel out:

$$\text{slope function} = \frac{2x \, \Delta x + \Delta x^2}{\Delta x}$$

We factor a Δx in the numerator:

$$\text{slope function} = \frac{\Delta x(2x + \Delta x)}{\Delta x}$$

Two of the Δx's cancel out:

$$\text{slope function} = 2x + \Delta x$$

This formula agrees with our result from the preceding table.

As long as the two points are close together, the slope of the line between these points will be close to the slope of the curve. A line that crosses a curve at two points such as this is called a **secant line**. (See Figure 9-5.) However, the slope of the secant line is not exactly the same as the slope of the curve.

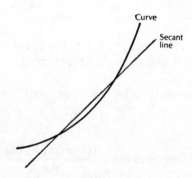

Curve

Secant line

Figure 9-5

We need to clarify what we mean by "the slope of a curve." By definition, we will say that the slope of a curve at a particular point is equal to the slope of the line that touches the curve at that point. A line that just touches a curve at one point without crossing it, as shown in Figure 9-6, is called a **tangent line**.

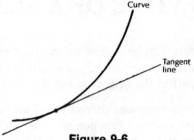

Figure 9-6

To find the slope of the tangent line, we need to let the two points move closer to each other until they merge into a single point. Mathematically, this means that Δx becomes zero. As Δx becomes smaller, the second point moves closer to the first point and the secant line moves closer to the tangent line. (See Figure 9-7.)

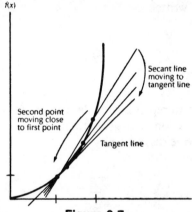

Figure 9-7

We cannot let Δx become zero in the original formula for the slope function:

$$\text{slope function} = \frac{f(x + \Delta x) - f(x)}{\Delta x}$$

because then we would end up with 0/0. However, now that we have transformed the slope function for the case $f(x) = x^2$, we *can* let Δx become zero:

$$\text{slope function} = 2x + \Delta x$$

After setting Δx to zero, we have

$$\text{slope function} = 2x$$

This confirms what we guessed after looking at the table of values for the slope.

THE DERIVATIVE OF A FUNCTION

Now we need a procedure that will allow us to calculate slope functions for different curves. The formal name for the slope function is the **derivative**. The study of derivatives is part of the subject of **calculus.**

We need a notation to represent derivatives. Two types of notation are commonly used. If $f(x)$ represents a function of x, then $f'(x)$ is used to represent the derivative of this function. The expression $f'(x)$ is read as "f-prime of x." Filling in a specific number, such as $f'(3)$, means that the derivative is to be evaluated at the point where the independent variable has the indicated value.

It is also helpful to have a notation that indicates both the independent variable and the dependent variable. If y represents the dependent variable and x represents the independent variable, the derivative of the function that gives y as a function of x is written as

$$\frac{dy}{dx}$$

In words, dy/dx is said to represent the derivative of y with respect to x.

When we have a function that gives total revenue (TR) as a function of quantity, we can write the derivative as

$$\frac{dTR}{dQ}$$

The derivative of a function tells how the value of the dependent variable changes when the independent variable changes. Suppose that x is the independent variable and y is the dependent variable. Let x initially have the value x_1. If x increases by Δx, where Δx is small, then the change in y (written as Δy) will be approximately

$$\Delta y = f'(x_1)\, \Delta x$$

Note that $f'(x_1)$ means to evaluate the derivative at the point where x is equal to x_1. (See Figure 9-8.) If $f'(x_1)$ is positive, then y will increase when x increases; if $f'(x_1)$ is negative, then y will decrease when x increases. Figure 9-8 shows by how much this approximation will be in error in relation to the true change in the value of y. The error will be small if Δx is small.

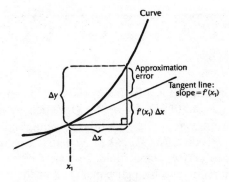

Figure 9-8

Derivatives have many applications, particularly in physics and other sciences. For example, if a function expresses the position of an object moving along one dimension as a function of time, then the derivative of the function gives the velocity of the object. In this book we will look at derivatives for one main reason: the location where the derivative is zero tells us where the slope is zero; this means that we have found the maximum or minimum point for a curve. (We looked at an example where the curve reached a maximum at the point where the slope was zero; we will soon see that the slope also becomes zero at the minimum point of a curve. However, matters do become slightly more complicated: we will learn that it is necessary to distinguish between absolute maximum points and relative maximum points.)

In the next section we present some rules for calculating derivatives, starting with the simplest cases first.

YOU SHOULD REMEMBER

The derivative of a function $f(x)$ is a function $f'(x)$ whose value at a particular point is equal to the slope of the curve representing $f(x)$ at that point. It measures the rate of change of the dependent variable with respect to the independent variable.

If y is expressed as a function of x, then the derivative of the function is written as dy/dx.

Relative maximum or minimum points will occur at points where the derivative is equal to zero.

THE DERIVATIVE OF A CONSTANT FUNCTION

The simplest type of function is a function whose value remains constant. For example, consider the Smith Pin Company (founded by distant relatives of economist Adam Smith, who wrote about the advantages of specialization in a pin factory in his 1776 book, *The Wealth of Nations*). The Smith company sells pins in a market with **perfect competition**. In a perfectly competitive market, each firm is so small relative to the entire market that the market price will not change if the firm changes the quantity that it produces. The Smith firm faces a constant market price of \$2 per case of pins. Then the function that expresses the price as a function of the quantity produced is

$$P = 2$$

This type of function is unusual because, unlike most functions, the value of the result does not depend on the value of the independent variable.

Figure 9-9 shows a graph of the demand function. This is simply a horizontal line that always has a slope of zero. Therefore, the derivative must be zero for this type of function. In general, if $f(x) = c$, where c is a constant that does not depend on x, then $f'(x) = 0$.

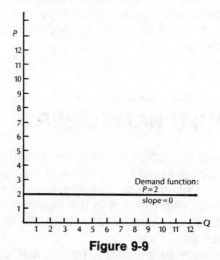

Figure 9-9

Note that this type of function does not have a maximum point. More precisely, we can say that every point is tied for the maximum point.

THE DERIVATIVE OF A LINEAR FUNCTION

Another simple type of function has the form $f(x) = cx$, where c is a constant that does not depend on x. For example, suppose that we graph the total revenue as a function of the quantity sold for the Smith Pin Company, discussed above. Since the price remains constant at 2, no matter what quantity the firm produces, the total revenue is found from the formula

$$TR = 2Q$$

(See Figure 9-10.)

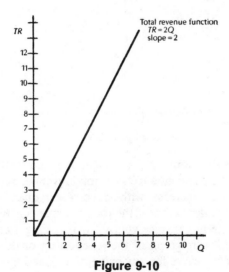

Figure 9-10

The graph is a straight line. We already know how to find the slope of such a line without using any calculus. In this case the slope is equal to 2. In general, if $f(x) = cx$, then $f'(x) = c$.

In this case there is no maximum point, because the total revenue will always become larger if Q becomes larger. Note that the slope will never become zero, as it does at a maximum point. In practice the firm will not expand its quantity of production to infinity. The firm is concerned about maximizing profits, rather than revenue; and it will find that for very large levels of production its cost of production increases enough that profits will eventually start to decline. Also, if a small firm expands its output by a large amount, it no longer will be a perfectly competitive firm because it cannot accurately be viewed as being too small to have a noticeable effect on market price. If the firm expands its output enough, eventually the price will start to decrease.

THE DERIVATIVE OF A SUM

Now suppose that the Smith Pin Company is the recipient of an inheritance payment of $5 per month that remains constant, no matter how many pins are produced. Then the total revenue as a function of quantity is given by this formula:

$$TR = 5 + 2Q$$

(See Figure 9-11.)

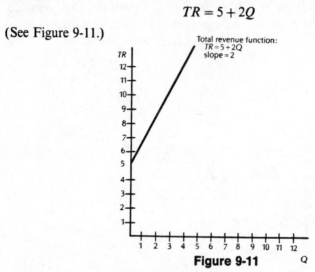

Total revenue function:
$TR = 5 + 2Q$
slope = 2

Figure 9-11

The total revenue function is still a straight line, and it still has a slope of 2. The addition of the $5 payment affects the total revenue, but it has no effect on the amount that revenue increases with an increase in quantity (in other words, it has no effect on the derivative of the total revenue function).

You should be able to convince yourself that adding a constant amount to any function will shift the graph of the function up or down, but it will not change the slope of the curve for any value of *x*. (See Figure 9-12.)

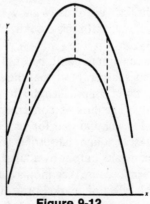

Figure 9-12

In general, if a constant is added to any function, the derivative remains unchanged. Mathematically, if $f(x)$ and $g(x)$ are two functions, and $g(x) = f(x) + c$, then

$$g'(x) = f'(x)$$

This rule can be stated in even more general terms: If two functions are added together, the derivative of their sum is equal to the sum of the two derivatives. Written mathematically, if $f(x)$ and $g(x)$ are two functions, and $h(x)$ is a new function defined as the sum of $f(x)$ and $g(x)$:

$$h(x) = f(x) + g(x).$$

then the derivative of $h(x)$ is equal to the derivative of $f(x)$ plus the derivative of $g(x)$:

$$h'(x) = f'(x) + g'(x)$$

For example, suppose that $h(x) = x^2 + 10x$. Let $f(x) = x^2$, and $g(x) = 10x$. Then

$$f'(x) = 2x, \qquad g'(x) = 10, \qquad \text{and} \qquad h'(x) = 2x + 10$$

We can extend the same rule to cases where three (or more) functions are added together:

$$h(x) = f(x) + g(x) + k(x)$$
$$h'(x) = f'(x) + g'(x) + k'(x)$$

Suppose that $h(x) = x^2 + 10x + 12$. Let $f(x) = x^2$, $g(x) = 10x$, and $k(x) = 12$. Then

$$f'(x) = 2x, \qquad g'(x) = 10, \qquad k'(x) = 0, \qquad \text{and} \qquad h'(x) = 2x + 10.$$

Here is another example. Suppose that

$$f(x) = x^2 + x^2 + x^2$$

We could also write this function as

$$f(x) = 3x^2$$

Then

$$f'(x) = 2x + 2x + 2x = 6x$$

In general, suppose that $f(x) = cx^2$. Then

$$f'(x) = 2cx$$

Even more generally, suppose that $g(x) = c f(x)$. Then

$$g'(x) = c f'(x)$$

In words, if a function is multiplied by a constant, then the derivative will also be multiplied by the same constant.

Example: Determining the Demand for WhizBang Decision-Making Software

Now we can find an exact value for the revenue-maximizing quantity for the example at the beginning of the chapter. The total revenue function was:

$$TR = 17Q - 1.4Q^2$$

The derivative of the first term is 17; the derivative of the second term is $1.4 \times 2Q = 2.8Q$. Therefore:

$$\frac{dTR}{dQ} = 17 - 2.8Q$$

We find the value of Q where the derivative is zero:

$$17 - 2.8Q = 0$$
$$Q = \frac{17}{2.8} = 6\frac{1}{14}$$

We can find the price that should be charged:

$$P = 17 - \frac{1}{4} \times 6\frac{1}{14} = 8.5$$

and the total revenue that will be earned:

$$TR = 17 \times 6\frac{1}{14} - 1.4 \times \left(6\frac{1}{14}\right)^2 = 51.6$$

Example: Maximizing Radio Station Revenue

PROBLEM   A radio station finds that it can charge higher prices for its advertisements if it has more listeners:

$$P = cL$$

where P = the price of advertisements, L = the estimated number of listeners, and c is a constant. The total revenue is equal to the price of the ads times the quantity:

$$TR = PQ$$

However, the radio station finds also that the number of listeners decreases if the number of ads increases, according to this function:

$$L = Lo - bQ$$

where Lo and b are constants. Therefore, the total revenue can be expressed as a function of the number of ads:

$$\begin{aligned} TR &= cLQ \\ &= c(Lo - bQ)Q \\ &= cLo\,Q - cbQ^2 \end{aligned}$$

What quantity of ads will lead to the maximum total revenue?

SOLUTION Let

$$f(Q) = cLo\,Q \qquad \text{and} \qquad g(Q) = -cbQ^2$$

Then the sum rule for derivatives tells us that:

$$\begin{aligned} \frac{dTR}{dQ} &= f'(Q) + g'(Q) \\ &= cLo - 2cbQ \end{aligned}$$

Now we need to find the value of Q where the derivative will be zero. We set up this equation:

$$0 = cLo - 2cbQ$$

and solve for Q:

$$Q = \frac{Lo}{2b}$$

In general, suppose that $y = ax^2 + bx + c$, where a, b, and c are known constants. Then $dy/dx = 2ax + b$. The derivative will be zero at the point where $x = -b/2a$. This point will be either a maximum point or a minimum point for the curve. Later in this chapter we will develop a method for distinguishing between the two.

POWER RULE

Suppose that we need to find the derivative of the function $f(x) = x^3$. The result turns out to be $f'(x) = 3x^2$. Here are the results if we make a table showing the derivatives of different functions that involve powers of x:

Function	Derivative
$f(x) = x^2$	$f'(x) = 2x$
$f(x) = x^3$	$f'(x) = 3x^2$
$f(x) = x^4$	$f'(x) = 4x^3$
$f(x) = x^5$	$f'(x) = 5x^4$

(In principle, we could find these results in the same way we found the result for $f(x) = x^2$. However, the algebra is complicated, so we will not present those calculations here.)

A pattern is apparent in the results shown in the table. It seems that, if $f(x) = x^n$, then $f'(x) = nx^{n-1}$. This result is true in general; it works even if the exponent n is a fraction or a negative number. (Recall from algebra that fractional exponents mean to take roots: $x^{1/n} = \sqrt[n]{x}$, and negative exponents mean to take reciprocals: $x^{-n} = 1/x^n$.)

We can state an even more general result, using the property about multiplication by a constant from the preceding section:

$$\text{If } f(x) = cx^n, \quad \text{then} \quad f'(x) = cnx^{n-1}$$

where c and n are constants that do not depend on x.

Example: Determining the Box with Minimum Surface Area

PROBLEM   A container company needs to design a small box that will have a square base and an open top. (See Figure 9-13.) The volume of the box must be 32 cubic inches. The box needs to be designed so that its surface area (not counting the open top) is at a minimum, so as to reduce the cost of materials.
What are the optimum dimensions for the box?

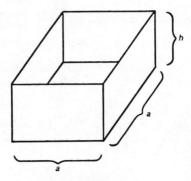

Figure 9-13

SOLUTION   Let $V = 32$ represent the volume of the box, a represent the length of one of the sides for the square base, and h represent the height of the box. Then the total surface area S is

$$S = a^2 + 4ah$$

The volume of the box is:

$$V = a^2 h$$

We rewrite the second equation as $h = V/a^2$, and then substitute this expression for h into the formula for the surface area:

$$S = a^2 + \frac{4aV}{a^2} = a^2 + 4Va^{-1}$$

The derivative of a function will be zero both at a maximum point and at a minimum point. (In the next section we will see how to tell which is which.) Therefore, we need to calculate the derivative of S with respect to a, and then find the value of a that makes the derivative equal to zero.

$$\frac{dS}{da} = 2a - 4Va^{-2}$$

We set the derivative equal to zero:

$$2a - 4Va^{-2} = 0$$
$$2a = 4Va^{-2}$$
$$= \frac{4V}{a^2}$$
$$a^3 = 2V$$
$$a = \sqrt[3]{2V}$$

Inserting the value $V = 32$ gives

$$a = \sqrt[3]{64}$$
$$= 4$$

We can also find that $h = 2$, so the optimum-size box will have dimensions 4 by 4 by 2, which will require 48 square inches of material.

Example: Determining the Optimal Number of Parking Spaces

PROBLEM   A small store finds that the number of customers depends on the number of parking places it provides. The relationship is given by this formula:

$$Q = Qo\, x^a$$

where Q is the quantity of customers, x is the number of parking spaces, and Qo and a are known constants. (The value of a is between 0 and 1, meaning that the increase in the number of customers is not proportional to the increase in the number of parking spaces. For example, if $a = 1/2$, then multiplying the number of parking spaces by 4 will only cause the number of customers to double.)

What formula should the store use to determine the optimal number of parking spaces?

SOLUTION   Let b represent the average amount spent by each customer, and c represent the cost of installing each parking space. Then bQ represents the total revenue, and cx represents the total cost of parking spaces. We can express the profit as a function of the number of parking spaces:

$$\text{profit} = P = bQ - cx$$
$$= bQo\, x^a - cx$$

We can calculate the derivative of the profit:

$$\frac{dP}{dx} = bQo\, ax^{a-1} - c$$

and find the value of x where the derivative is zero:

$$0 = bQo \, ax^{a-1} - c$$

$$x^{a-1} = \frac{c}{bQo \, a}$$

$$x = \left(\frac{c}{bQo \, a}\right)^{1/(a-1)}$$

This formula determines the optimal number of parking spaces.

YOU SHOULD REMEMBER

Here are rules for calculating derivatives. Assume that c and n represent constants.

Constant functions:

$$f(x) = c, \qquad f'(x) = 0$$

Linear functions:

$$f(x) = cx, \qquad f'(x) = c$$

Power rule:

$$f(x) = cx^n, \qquad f'(x) = cnx^{n-1}$$

Multiplication by a constant:

$$f(x) = c \, g(x), \qquad f'(x) = c \, g'(x)$$

Sum rule:

$$h(x) = f(x) + g(x), \qquad h'(x) = f'(x) + g'(x)$$

MARGINAL ANALYSIS

In economics the word *marginal* is used to express the same concept as the derivative: that is, the amount by which one variable changes when another variable changes. In particular, **marginal cost** is the derivative of the total cost with respect to the quantity produced, and **marginal revenue** is the derivative of the total revenue with respect to the quantity sold.

If a good, such as cars, can be produced only in whole-number quantities, instead of fractional quantities, then it is more appropriate to define the marginal cost in this way: marginal cost is the amount by which the cost goes up when 1 more unit of the good is produced. Likewise, marginal revenue is the amount by which revenue will go up if 1 more unit of the good is produced. If you don't know how much the cost will rise if 1 more unit is produced, but you do know that the cost will rise by ΔTC if production increases by ΔQ, then the marginal cost can be approximated as $\Delta TC/\Delta Q$.

Here is an example of the use of marginal analysis. The function giving profit as a function of quantity can be expressed as the difference between the total revenue function and the total cost function:

$$\text{profit}(Q) = TR(Q) - TC(Q)$$

We take the derivative of this function, using the sum rule:

$$\text{profit}'(Q) = TR'(Q) - TC'(Q)$$

To find the maximum, we set this equal to zero:

$$0 = TR'(Q) - TC'(Q)$$
$$TR'(Q) = TC'(Q)$$

Here $TR'(Q)$, the derivative of total revenue, is the marginal revenue, and $TC'(Q)$ is the marginal cost. Therefore, we have the following relationship, which must be true at the profit-maximizing optimum:

$$\text{marginal revenue} = \text{marginal cost}$$

Here is an intuitive explanation for this formula. If the marginal revenue was greater than marginal cost, you should increase production. Increasing production would increase revenue by more than it would increase cost, so the total profit would increase. You should keep expanding production as long as marginal revenue is greater than marginal cost. The optimum must occur at the point where they are equal.

For a perfectly competitive firm, the price for which it sells its output remains constant, regardless of the quantity produced. Therefore, we can write this formula for total revenue:

$$TR(Q) = PQ$$

Then $TR'(Q) = P$, so the marginal cost is equal to P. It makes sense that selling 1 more unit will cause the revenue to increase by the amount obtained by selling that unit, provided that the price remains constant. Therefore, this is the rule that applies for a perfectly competitive firm to determine how much output to produce:

$$price = marginal\ cost$$

The use of marginal analysis is fundamental to economic decision making. For any type of activity, the activity should be expanded if the marginal benefit from it is greater than the marginal cost. The optimum must occur where the marginal benefit is equal to the marginal cost.

THE SECOND DERIVATIVE

Now we turn to the problem of distinguishing maximum points from minimum points. Maximum and minimum points will occur at points, called **critical points**, where the first derivative is zero. If the derivative is zero at a particular point, then a maximum will occur if the curve opens downward, and a minimum will occur if the curve opens upward. (See Figure 9-14.) When a curve opens downward, we will say that it is oriented **concave downward**; when a curve opens upward, we will say that it is **concave upward**.

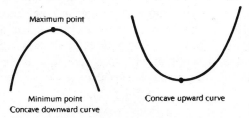

Figure 9-14

If the curve is concave downward, then the slope will be positive to the left of the maximum and negative to the right of the maximum. In other words, the slope will be decreasing as the quantity increases. Therefore, if we can determine whether the slope of a curve is increasing or decreasing, we can determine whether we are looking at a maximum or a minimum.

We have already found a way to determine whether a function is increasing or decreasing: calculate the derivative. If the derivative is positive, then the function is increasing; if the derivative is negative, then the function is decreasing. To determine whether the derivative itself is increasing or decreasing, we can calculate the derivative of the derivative. Remember that the result for the derivative is also a function, so we can calculate its derivative just the same as we can for any other function. The derivative of the derivative is called the

second derivative. (The derivative of the original function is sometimes called the **first derivative**.)

For example, for the total revenue function

$$TR = 17Q - 1.4Q^2$$

we found the derivative:

$$\frac{dTR}{dQ} = 17 - 2.8Q$$

The 17 is a constant, so its derivative is zero. The second term consists of a constant multiplied by the independent variable, so its derivative is -2.8. Therefore, in this case the second derivative is

$$\frac{d^2TR}{dQ^2} = -2.8$$

The notation d^2TR/dQ^2 represents the second derivative. The second derivative is also written with two prime symbols; $TR''(Q)$ (read as "TR-double prime of Q") stands for the second derivative of the total revenue with respect to quantity.

In this case the second derivative is negative, so the slope of the total revenue curve is decreasing. When the slope is decreasing, then the curve is concave downward, and the point with zero derivative is a maximum. On the other hand, if the second derivative is positive, then the slope is increasing, the curve is concave upward, and the point with zero derivative is a minimum.

In general, consider the curve given by the equation

$$y = ax^2 + bx + c$$

The derivative is $dy/dx = 2ax + b$, and the second derivative is $d^2y/dx^2 = 2a$. If a is positive, then the curve is concave upward and has a minimum at the point $x = -b/2a$. If a is negative, then the curve is concave downward and has a maximum at the point $x = -b/2a$.

Example: Choosing the Quantity Where Price = Marginal Cost

If we graph the total cost of producing a good as a function of the quantity produced, we will typically see a curve such as the one shown in Figure 9-15. Note that the total cost will be greater than zero even if the quantity is zero, because some costs, called **fixed costs**, must be paid whether or not any output is produced. Notice that the curve is very steep at first, indicating that in the beginning each additional unit of output is costly, because the production facility is not being used efficiently at low levels of output. For larger quantities of output, the curve becomes flatter, indicating that the original cost is falling. It becomes less costly to expand output when the facility is being used more efficiently. However, if output continues to be expanded, eventually capacity limits will start being reached. Then the marginal cost begins to rise, and the total cost curve becomes steeper again.

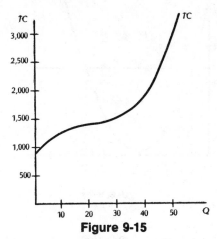

Figure 9-15

Here is the mathematical formula for the cost function shown in Figure 9-15:

$$TC(Q) = \frac{1}{15} Q^3 - 4Q^2 + 83Q + 800$$

Note that this function involves a term with Q raised to the third power. (Technically, the function is called a *third-degree polynomial in Q.*)

Suppose that the market price for the firm we are discussing remains constant at \$48. To choose the profit-maximizing quantity of output, we must find the quantity where the price equals marginal cost. To find the marginal cost, we need to take the derivative of the total cost function:

Term	Derivative with Respect to Q
$(1/15)Q^3$	$(1/5)Q^2$
$-4Q^2$	$-8Q$
$+83Q$	83
$+800$	0

Therefore, the marginal cost is given by this formula:

$$MC(Q) = \frac{1}{5} Q^2 - 8Q + 83$$

Figure 9-16 shows a graph of the marginal cost function. Now we set the marginal cost equal to the price:

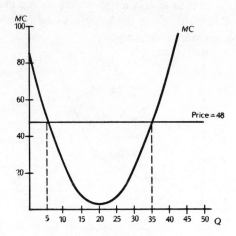

Figure 9-16

$$48 = \frac{1}{5} Q^2 - 8Q + 83$$

and rewrite this equation as follows:

$$\frac{1}{5} Q^2 - 8Q + 35 = 0$$

This is an example of a **quadratic equation**. To solve for Q, we need to use a formula called the **quadratic formula**. The general form of a quadratic equation can be written:

$$ax^2 + bx + c = 0$$

where a, b, and c are known (and $a \neq 0$), and x is unknown. Then there are two values for x that will solve this equation:

$$x = \frac{-b + \sqrt{b^2 - 4ac}}{2a} \qquad \text{or} \qquad x = \frac{-b - \sqrt{b^2 - 4ac}}{2a}$$

These equations can be written as a single formula, using the symbol "$\pm$", which means "plus or minus":

$$x = \frac{-b \pm \sqrt{b^2 - 4ac}}{2a}$$

If $b^2 - 4ac = 0$, then there is only one solution: $x = -b/2a$. If $b^2 - 4ac < 0$, then the formula requires us to take the square root of a negative number. In that case the two solutions are complex numbers, which we will not discuss in this book.

To solve our problem, we need to identify the constants in the problem with a, b, and c in the general formula for the quadratic equation. We find:

$$a = \frac{1}{5} = 0.2, \quad b = -8, \quad c = 35$$

We put these values into the quadratic formula:

$$Q = \frac{8 \pm \sqrt{64 - 4 \times 0.2 \times 35}}{2 \times 0.2}$$

$$= \frac{8 \pm \sqrt{36}}{0.4}$$

$$= \frac{8 \pm 6}{0.4}$$

$$Q = \frac{14}{0.4} \quad \text{or} \quad Q = \frac{2}{0.4}$$

$$Q = 35 \quad \text{or} \quad Q = 5$$

There are two values of Q where the marginal cost is equal to 48. (See Figure 9-16.) We need to determine which of these corresponds to the profit-maximizing point. The profit function can be written:

$$\text{profit}(Q) = 48Q - TC(Q)$$

The derivative of the profit function is

$$\text{profit}'(Q) = 48 - TC'(Q)$$
$$= 48 - \left(\frac{1}{5}Q^2 - 8Q + 83\right)$$

$$= 48 - \frac{1}{5}Q^2 + 8Q - 83$$

The second derivative of the profit function is

$$\text{profit}''(Q) = -\frac{2}{5}Q + 8$$

We evaluate the second derivative at the two critical points ($Q = 35$ and $Q = 5$):

$$\text{profit}''(5) = 6, \qquad \text{profit}''(35) = -6$$

The second derivative at $Q = 5$ is positive, so this point is the profit-*minimizing* point. We certainly do not want to produce that quantity. When $Q = 35$, the second derivative is negative, so this is the profit-*maximizing* point.

You need to be careful, since the derivative of the profit function will be zero (meaning that price equals marginal cost) at both the profit-maximizing point *and* the profit-minimizing point. That is why it is important to check the second derivative to make sure that you have found the maximum point.

There is another possibility we need to consider: a point with zero slope may be neither a maximum nor a minimum. Consider the function $y = y^3$. The derivative (which can be symbolized by y') is found from the formula $y' = 3x^2$. When $x = 0$, then $y' = 0$, and the curve has a flat spot. (See Figure 9-17.)

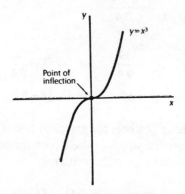

Figure 9-17

However, instead of being a maximum or a minimum, this is simply a place where the curve stops its ascent and momentarily becomes flat before it resumes its climb. If we calculate the second derivative: $y'' = 6x$, we find that it has the value zero when $x = 0$. (A point where the second derivative is zero is called an **inflection point**.)

Therefore, a point with zero first derivative that also has a zero value for the second derivative, may not be a maximum or a minimum. (However, a point with zero values for both the first and second derivatives may still be a maximum or minimum point. Consider the curve $y = x^4$. Then $y' = 4x^3$ and $y'' = 12x^2$. Both the first and second derivatives have the value zero at $x = 0$, but the point is still a minimum point.)

YOU SHOULD REMEMBER

Consider a function $f(x)$. Suppose that x_1 is a point where the derivative of that function is zero. Evaluate the second derivative of the function at that point.

- If the second derivative is positive, then the function reaches a relative minimum at the point where $x = x_1$.

- If the second derivative is negative, then the function reaches a relative maximum at that point.

- If the second derivative is zero, then the point may be a maximum, a minimum, or neither.

ABSOLUTE AND RELATIVE MAXIMUM POINTS

If the first derivative is zero and the second derivative is negative at a particular point, we know that point is higher than any of the surrounding points. Such a point is called a **relative maximum** or a **local maximum**. However, that point is not necessarily the highest point that the curve ever reaches. For example, consider the curve in Figure 9-18. Points *A*, *B*, and *C* are all local maximum points, but it is clear that point *B* is the highest point the curve ever reaches. Point *B* is called the **absolute maximum** or the **global maximum**. If a curve has several relative maxima, we will need to check each one to determine which is the absolute maximum.

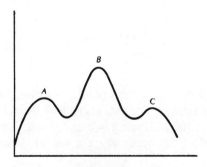

Figure 9-18

However, we also need to consider the possibility that the curve may go off to infinity, in which case there is no absolute maximum. Figure 9-19 shows an example of such a curve.

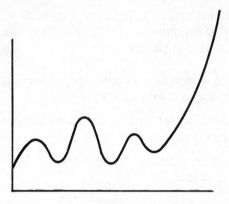

Figure 9-19

Sometimes we will be interested only in a curve within a particular range of values for the independent variable. For example, suppose that we want to find the absolute maximum of the curve

$$f(x) = x^3 - 2x^2 + x$$

in the interval from $x = 0$ to $x = 2$. We calculate the derivative:

$$f'(x) = 3x^2 - 4x + 1$$

and use the quadratic formula to find that the derivative becomes zero when $x = 1/3$ and $x = 1$. We calculate the second derivative: $f''(x) = 6x - 4$, and evaluate $f''(x)$ at the two critical points: $f''(1/3) = -2$; $f''(1) = 2$. Since $f''(1/3)$ is negative, $x = 1/3$ is the location of a relative maximum. Since $f''(1)$ is positive, $x = 1$ is the location of a **relative minimum** or **local minimum**. We evaluate the function when $x = 1/3$:

$$f(1/3) = \left(\frac{1}{3}\right)^3 - 2\left(\frac{1}{3}\right)^2 + \frac{1}{3} = 0.148$$

This is the only relative maximum point. However, we cannot tell whether this is the absolute maximum until we also check the values of the function at the two end points of the interval: $x = 0$ and $x = 2$. We find $f(0) = 0$, so the absolute maximum does not occur where $x = 0$. However, we find

$$f(2) = 2^3 - 2 \times 2^2 + 2 = 2$$

Therefore, the absolute maximum occurs where $x = 2$. (See Figure 9-20.)

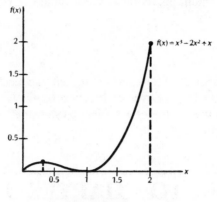

Figure 9-20

We follow the same procedure to locate the **absolute minimum** or **global minimum** for a function within a certain interval. We evaluate the function at all of the local minimum points, and then evaluate the function at the two end points of the interval. The smallest of these values is the minimum value of the function. For the function in Figure 9-20, there is a relative minimum at $x = 1$. There is a tie for the absolute minimum, since the value of the function is zero at both $x = 0$ and $x = 1$.

YOU SHOULD REMEMBER

The relative maximum and minimum points for a function will all occur at points where the derivative is zero.

To find the absolute maximum for the function in a particular interval, you need to check the value of the function at each of the relative maximum points and at each of the two end points of the interval. The largest of these values determines the point that is the absolute maximum.

Likewise, to find the relative minimum you need to choose the smallest value from among the local minimum points and the two end points of the interval.

Many of the practice exercises at the end of the chapter involve finding maximum and minimum points for functions that can be expressed as **polynomials**:

$$f(x) = a_n x^n + a_{n-1} x^{n-1} + \cdots + a_2 x^2 + a_1 x + a_0$$

You should work enough of the exercises so that you reach the point where you can solve derivatives for this type of function routinely. The appendix to the chapter contains some of the other rules that are used to find derivatives of more complicated functions.

APPENDIX TO CHAPTER 9

Here are some additional rules for calculating derivatives.

A. CHAIN RULE

Suppose that $h(x) = f(g(x))$. This means that x is the independent variable for the function $g(x)$. The result of the $g(x)$ function becomes the independent variable for the function $f(g(x))$. The result of that function becomes the value of $h(x)$. Then the derivative is found from the formula

$$\frac{dh}{dx} = \frac{df}{dg}\frac{dg}{dx}$$

This rule, called the **chain rule**, has intuitive appeal because it appears that the two dg's cancel each other out as if you were multiplying two fractions.

For example, suppose that $h(x) = (3x)^2$. Let $g(x) = 3x$, and $f(g) = g^2$. Then:

$$\frac{dg}{dx} = 3, \qquad \frac{df}{dg} = 2g, \qquad \frac{dh}{dx} = 3 \times 2g = 6g = 6 \times 3x = 18x$$

[Note that we could have found this derivative by using the power rule and rewriting $h(x)$ as $9x^2$.]

Here is another example:

$$h(x) = (ax^2 + bx + c)^n$$

Let $g(x) = ax^2 + bx + c$, and $f(g) = g^n$. Then:

$$\frac{dg}{dx} = 2ax + b, \qquad \frac{df}{dg} = ng^{n-1}$$

$$\frac{dh}{dx} = (2ax + b)(ng^{n-1})$$

$$= n(2ax + b)(ax^2 + bx + c)^{n-1}$$

B. PRODUCT RULE

Suppose that $h(x)$ consists of the product of two other functions, $f(x)$ and $g(x)$: $h(x) = f(x) \times g(x)$. Then:

$$h'(x) = [f(x) \times g'(x)] + [f'(x) \times g(x)]$$

In words, we can say: To find the derivative of a product, take the first factor multiplied by the derivative of the second, and then add the derivative of the first factor multiplied by the second factor.

For example, suppose that $f(x) = x^2$ and $g(x) = x^3$. Then $h(x) = x^5$; also, $f'(x) = 2x$ and $g'(x) = 3x^2$. Then:

$$h'(x) = x^2 3x^2 + 2x \times x^3 = 5x^4$$

(Note that in this case we could have found the derivative by using the power rule.)

Suppose that $h(x) = x\sqrt{1 - x^2}$. Let $f(x) = x$, and $g(x) = \sqrt{1 - x^2}$. Then:

$$\frac{df}{dx} = 1, \qquad \frac{dg}{dx} = \frac{1}{2}(1 - x^2)^{-(1/2)}(-2x) = -\frac{x}{\sqrt{1 - x^2}}$$

$$\frac{dh}{dx} = (x)\left(-\frac{x}{\sqrt{1 - x^2}}\right) + (1)\sqrt{1 - x^2}$$

C. LOGARITHM FUNCTIONS

If $y = b^x$, then x is said to be the **logarithm** of y to the base b. This is written as

$$\log_b y = x$$

For example, $\log_2 64 = 6$, since $2^6 = 64$. Also, $\log_{10} 10,000 = 4$, since

$10^4 = 10,000$. Logarithms to the base 10 are easy to work with, since we use a base-10 number system. However, in calculus it is best to work with logarithms to the base e, where e represents a special number approximately equal to 2.71828.

Logarithms to the base e are called *natural logarithms* and are often abbreviated as "ln". For example, $\ln 10 = 2.3026$ (rounded to four decimal places), since $e^{2.3026} = 10$. (Note that usually it is not possible to obtain exact decimal representation of natural logarithms.)

Logarithm functions obey the following properties for any positive numbers a and b and any real number n:

$$\log(ab) = \log a + \log b$$

$$\log\left(\frac{a}{b}\right) = \log a - \log b$$

$$\log(a^n) = n \log a$$

If $y = \ln x$, then $dy/dx = 1/x$.

D. EXPONENTIAL FUNCTIONS

If $y = a^x$, then y is said to be an **exponential function** of x. The derivative is found from the formula

$$\frac{dy}{dx} = (\ln a)(a^x)$$

If $y = e^x$, then:

$$\frac{dy}{dx} = (\ln e)(e^x)$$

Since $\ln e = 1$, we have:

$$\frac{dy}{dx} = e^x$$

The exponential function e^x has the unusual property that its derivative is equal to itself.

Sections C and D have provided very brief treatments of the use of logarithms and exponential functions in calculus; see a book on algebra for more information.

E. TRIGONOMETRIC FUNCTIONS

If $y = \sin x$, then $dy/dx = \cos x$.
If $y = \cos x$, then $dy/dx = -\sin x$.

KNOW THE CONCEPTS

DO YOU KNOW THE BASICS?
Test your understanding of Chapter 9 by answering the following questions:

1. If the marginal benefit of an activity is greater than the marginal cost, what should be done?
2. Can the maximum value for a function occur at a position where the derivative is not zero?
3. Does a curve reach a maximum or a minimum if the critical point occurs when the curve is oriented concave upward?
4. How many critical points can a function have?
5. Why can't Δx become zero in the original formula for the slope function?
6. State the intuitive reasoning why the total revenue decreases if the quantity of production is expanded far enough.
7. What is the inverse of the inverse of a function?
8. How does adding a constant to a function affect the derivative? Briefly explain.

TERMS FOR STUDY

absolute maximum
absolute minimum
calculus
chain rule
concave downward
concave upward
critical points
delta
dependent variable
derivative
exponential function
first derivative
fixed cost
function
global maximum
global minimum
independent variable

inflection point
inverse function
local maximum
local minimum
logarithm
marginal cost
marginal revenue
perfect competition
polynomial
quadratic equation
quadratic formula
relative maximum
relative minimum
secant line
second derivative
tangent line

PRACTICAL APPLICATION

COMPUTATIONAL PROBLEMS

For Exercises 1–5, find formulas for the derivative and the second derivative, and determine the values of x corresponding to maximum or minimum points. In each case, state whether the point is a maximum or minimum.

1. $y = -3x^2 + 5x - 9$

2. $y = 13x^2 + 4x + 19$

3. $y = 17x^2 + 11x - 10$

4. $y = 19x^2 - 10x + 18$

5. $y = -9x^2 + 16x + 9$

6. If the demand function for a good is given by the following formula:

$$Q = a - bP$$

calculate a formula for the total revenue (expressed as a function of the quantity produced) and the marginal revenue (that is, the derivative of the total revenue with respect to quantity). What should the quantity be to earn the maximum possible revenue?

7. The *elasticity* of demand for a good is a way of measuring how responsive the demand is when the price changes. If the elasticity is zero, then the buyers always buy the same quantity, regardless of the price. In general, the elasticity of demand at a particular point is given by the formula:

$$\text{elasticity} = \left| \frac{dQ}{dP} \frac{P}{Q} \right|$$

where the vertical lines stand for absolute value. Since the quality demand declines when the price increases, dQ/dP is negative. Because the absolute value is taken, the elasticity of demand will always be a positive number.

(a) If the demand curve is given by the formula $Q = a - bP$, determine a formula for the elasticity of demand at a particular quantity Q.

(b) What is the value of the elasticity at the revenue-maximizing quantity you found in Exercise 6?

8. (a) Derive a general formula for the marginal revenue, expressed in terms of the elasticity of demand and the price. (*Hint*: See the rules for derivatives in the appendix to the chapter.)

   (b) Using this formula, what will be true about the elasticity at the quantity where the revenue is at a maximum?

   (c) Show that, in general, an increase in quantity sold results in an increase in revenue if the elasticity is greater than 1.

9. Consider a retail store that chooses its price by setting the marginal revenue equal to the marginal cost. The marginal cost for each item is constant (equal to the amount that must be paid to the wholesaler to obtain the item). The markup percentage is equal to the difference between the price and the marginal cost, divided by the marginal cost:

$$\text{markup percentage} = \frac{P - MC}{MC}$$

   Derive a formula for the markup percentage in terms of the elasticity, and comment on the intuitive reasoning for the result.

10. Derive a formula for the elasticity for this demand function: $Q = aP^{-e}$.

For each of the problems Exercises 11–15, you are given the formula for the total cost and the market price for a perfectly competitive firm. Calculate the quantity of output that should be produced in order to earn the maximum possible profit. (Round the answer for the quantity to the nearest whole number.)

11. $TC = 0.01517Q^3 - 5.78375Q^2 + 751.3Q + 56, \quad P = 49$

12. $TC = 0.1105Q^3 - 51.5285Q^2 + 8020.65Q + 125, \quad P = 191$

13. $TC = 0.0165Q^3 - 5.06175Q^2 + 619.828Q + 96, \quad P = 110$

14. $TC = 0.05617Q^3 - 14.89475Q^2 + 1324.2Q + 285, \quad P = 173$

15. $TC = 0.00883Q^3 - 2.08975Q^2 + 175.184Q + 83, \quad P = 40$

16. The average cost of production is defined as the total cost divided by the quantity. Show that the average cost will increase when the quantity is increased if the marginal cost is greater than the average cost.

ANSWERS

KNOW THE CONCEPTS

1. The activity should be expanded as long as this condition is true.

2. If you are interested only in a certain range of values for the independent variable, the maximum may occur at one of the end points of the interval. Or, if the value of the function goes to infinity, there will not be a maximum. It is also possible that the maximum may occur at a point where the derivative does not even exist. For example, if a curve has a sharp corner, then no unique tangent line is defined at that point, so the derivative does not exist at that point. In this chapter we have not considered functions where the derivative does not exist.

3. Minimum.

4. There will be as many critical points as there are points where the value of the derivative is zero. If the function is a second-degree polynomial (called a *quadratic function*) such as $ax^2 + bx + c$, then the derivative will be a linear function and there will be one critical point. If the function is a polynomial of degree n, then the derivative will be a polynomial of degree $n - 1$, and there can be as many as $n - 1$ critical points. (See a book on algebra for more information on the solution to polynomial equations.) There are an infinite number of critical points for periodic functions such as $y = \sin x$.

5. Because the result would be 0/0.

6. When the quantity produced is expanded, sooner or later the price must be reduced in order to sell the entire quantity. If the price is reduced by a sufficient amount, revenue declines.

7. The function itself.

8. It has no effect. Adding a constant has the effect of shifting the curve representing the function up or down, but it does not change the slope of the curve at any point.

PRACTICAL APPLICATION

1. $y' = -6x + 5$; $y'' = -6$; maximum at $x = 0.833$

2. $y' = 26x + 4$; $y'' = 26$; minimum at $x = -0.154$

3. $y' = 34x + 11$; $y'' = 34$; minimum at $x = -0.324$

4. $y' = 38x - 10$; $y'' = 38$; minimum at $x = 0.263$

5. $y' = -18x + 16$; $y'' = -18$; maximum at $x = 0.889$

6.
$$P = \frac{a}{b} - \frac{Q}{b}, \quad TR = \frac{Qa}{b} - \frac{Q^2}{b}, \quad MR = \frac{a}{b} - \frac{2Q}{b}$$

Set $MR = 0$. Then:

$$\frac{a}{b} = \frac{2Q}{b}, \quad Q = \frac{a}{2}$$

7. (a) $\dfrac{dQ}{dp} = -b$

$$\text{elasticity} = \left| -\frac{bP}{Q} \right| = \left| -\frac{b(a/b - Q/b)}{Q} \right| = \left| -\frac{a}{Q} + 1 \right|$$

(b) When $Q = a/2$, elasticity $= 1$.

8. (a) $TR = PQ$

To find the marginal revenue, use the product rule for derivatives:

$$\frac{dTR}{dQ} = P\frac{dQ}{dQ} + Q\frac{dP}{dQ}$$

$$= P + Q\frac{dP}{dQ}$$

$$= P\left(1 + \frac{Q}{P}\frac{dP}{dQ}\right)$$

$(Q/P)(dP/dQ)$ is equal to $-1/e$, where e = elasticity.

$$MR = P\left(1 - \frac{1}{e}\right)$$

(b) The revenue is maximized where $MR = 0$, which means $P(1 - 1/e) = 0$, or the elasticity $= 1$.

(c) If the elasticity is less than 1, the marginal revenue is negative; if the elasticity is greater than 1, the marginal revenue is positive. This means that, if the elasticity of demand is less than 1, it is possible to increase the revenue by raising the price and reducing the quantity. However, if the elasticity is greater than 1, raising the price will cause the revenue to decline.

9. Use the formula from Exercise 8 for marginal revenue, and set marginal revenue equal to marginal cost:

$$MC = MR$$

$$= P\left(1 - \frac{1}{e}\right)$$

$$P = \frac{MC}{1 - 1/e} = \frac{eMC}{e - 1}$$

Solve for the markup:

$$\frac{P - MC}{MC} = \frac{eMC/(e - 1) - MC}{MC} = \frac{e}{e - 1} - 1 = \frac{e - (e - 1)}{e - 1}$$

$$= \frac{1}{e - 1}$$

If the elasticity is larger, the markup is smaller. This means that the buyers are more flexible, so the seller has less ability to charge higher prices.

10. $dQ/dP = -eaP^{-e-1}$

$$\text{elasticity} = \left|\frac{dQ}{dP}\frac{P}{Q}\right| = \left|\frac{-eaP^{-e-1}P}{Q}\right| = \left|\frac{-eaP^{-e}}{aP^{-e}}\right| = |-e| = e$$

This demand curve has the special property that the elasticity is the same at all points on the curve.

11. Take the derivative of the total cost to find the marginal cost:

$$MC = 0.0455Q^2 - 11.5675Q + 751.3$$

Set the marginal cost equal to the price:

$$49 = 0.0455Q^2 - 11.5675Q + 751.3$$

Rewrite the equation:

$$0.0455Q^2 - 11.5675Q + 702.3 = 0$$

Use the quadratic formula:

$$Q = \frac{11.5675 \pm \sqrt{11.5675^2 - 4 \times 0.0455 \times 702.3}}{2 \times 0.0455}$$

$$= 100.22 \text{ or } 154$$

By evaluating the second derivative of the function

$$49Q - (0.01517Q^3 - 5.78375Q^2 + 751.3Q + 56)$$

we find that the optimal quantity is 154.

12. $Q = 179$

13. $Q = 115$

14. $Q = 120$

15. $Q = 112$

16. $AC = TC/Q = TCQ^{-1}$

Use the product role for derivatives to find the derivative of the average cost with respect to quality.

$$\frac{dAC}{dQ} = TC\frac{d(Q^{-1})}{dQ} + Q^{-1}\frac{dTC}{dQ}$$

$$= TC(-Q^{-2}) + Q^{-1}MC$$

$$= \frac{-TC}{Q} \times \frac{1}{Q} + \frac{MC}{Q}$$

$$= \frac{MC - AC}{Q}$$

If $MC > AC$, then the derivative of the average cost with respect to quantity is positive, so the average cost will increase if quantity increases.

10

OPTIMAL VALUES OF MULTIVARIABLE FUNCTIONS

KEY TERMS

Kuhn-Tucker conditions a set of conditions for determining the optimum point for a nonlinear programming problem

Lagrange multiplier a variable that multiplies a constraint in a Lagrangian expression; the Lagrange multiplier represents the shadow price for that constraint

partial derivative the derivative of a multivariable function with respect to one of the independent variables, which is calculated by treating all other independent variables as constants

second-order conditions the conditions involving the second partial derivatives of a multivariable function that determine whether a critical point is a maximum point, a minimum point, or a saddle point

In Chapter 9 we considered functions with one independent variable. More realistically, we would expect that several factors will affect the quantities we are trying to maximize or minimize. Therefore, we will need to investigate optimizing techniques for functions with more than one independent variable.

PARTIAL DERIVATIVES

A store sells two grades of cleaning solutions: extra-strength and regular. Each unit of extra-strength costs \$4 to obtain from the wholesaler; each unit of regular costs \$3 to obtain. As would be expected, an increase in the price of each product will cause a decrease in the demand for that product. However, we also have to consider the fact that the price of extra-strength affects the quantity of regular that will be purchased, and the price of regular affects the quantity of extra-strength purchased. The two grades are substitute goods. An increase in the price of one grade will cause people to buy less of that grade and more of the other grade.

What is the profit-maximizing price of each product? The store has estimated that the demands for the two goods are given by these formulas:

$$Q_1 = 29 - 5P_1 + 2P_2, \qquad Q_2 = 13 - 7P_2 + 3P_1$$

where P_1 and Q_1 represent the price and the quantity of extra-strength and P_2 and Q_2 represent the price and the quantity of regular. We will use Z to represent the profit. (We cannot use P, since we have used P's to represent prices.) The profit will be total revenue minus total cost for both grades:

$$
\begin{aligned}
Z(P_1, P_2) &= (P_1 Q_1 - 4Q_1) + (P_2 Q_2 - 3Q_2) \\
&= P_1(29 - 5P_1 + 2P_2) - 4(29 - 5P_1 + 2P_2) \\
&\quad + P_2(13 - 7P_2 + 3P_1) - 3(13 - 7P_2 + 3P_1) \\
&= 29P_1 - 5P_1^2 + 2P_1 P_2 - 116 + 20P_1 - 8P_2 \\
&\quad + 13P_2 - 7P_2^2 + 3P_1 P_2 - 39 + 21P_2 - 9P_1 \\
&= 40P_1 + 26P_2 - 5P_1^2 - 7P_2^2 + 5P_1 P_2 - 155
\end{aligned}
$$

We have written the profit as $Z(P_1, P_2)$ to indicate that the profit is a function of two variables, P_1 and P_2. Now we need to choose values of P_1 and P_2 that maximize the profit. This problem is more complicated than the problems we did in Chapter 9 because we now have two variables. For the moment, let's make the problem simpler by pretending that the value of P_2 is fixed (in other words, that P_2 is not a variable). That leaves P_1 as the only variable, and we know how to choose the value of P_1 that will maximize the total profit: take the derivative of the total profit with respect to P_1, and then choose the value of P_1 that makes the derivative equal to zero.

According to the sum rule for derivatives, we need to take the derivative of each term in the profit function separately:

Term	Derivative with Respect to P_1
$40P_1$	40
$26P_2$	0
$-5P_1^2$	$-10P_1$
$-7P_2^2$	0
$5P_1 P_2$	$5P_2$
-155	0

Remember that we are treating P_2 as a constant. The final result for the derivative is

$$40 - 10P_1 + 5P_2$$

However, this derivative is not the same as the derivatives we calculated in Chapter 9 for functions of one variable. This type of derivative is called a **partial derivative**. To calculate the partial derivative of a multivariable function with respect to one of its variables, we pretend that all of the other variables are constants, and then proceed to calculate the derivative with respect to the variable in question. Therefore, if you know how to calculate ordinary derivatives, you already know how to calculate partial derivatives. The calculation mechanism is exactly the same.

We need a notation to represent a partial derivative. The ordinary derivative of y with respect to x is symbolized by dy/dx. We will use a similar symbol for a partial derivative, except that the upright part of the d curls backward:
$\frac{\partial y}{\partial x}$ represents the partial derivative of y with respect to x.
In our case, $\partial Z/\partial P_1$ represents the partial derivative of Z with respect to P_1:

$$\frac{\partial Z}{\partial P_1} = 40 - 10P_1 + 5P_2$$

We also used the notation $f'(x)$ to represent the derivative of a function f. We cannot use a prime symbol to represent a partial derivative, since we would not know which variable we are taking the partial derivative with respect to. To represent the partial derivative, we can write the independent variable as a subscript next to the name of the function. For example, if $f(x, y)$ is a function of the two variables x and y, then f_x represents the partial derivative with respect to x, and f_y represents the partial derivative with respect to y. In our case we could write

$$Z_{P_1} = 40 - 10P_1 + 5P_2$$

to represent the partial derivative of Z with respect to P_1.

The partial derivative represents the rate of change of the dependent variable when the independent variable in question changes, provided that all of the other independent variables remain fixed. If P_1 changes by a small amount ΔP_1, then the change in Z will be approximately

$$\Delta Z = \frac{\partial Z}{\partial P_1} \Delta P_1$$

This is the same result we found in Chapter 9 for ordinary derivatives, but now we must add the provision that all of the other independent variables remain constant.

YOU SHOULD REMEMBER

The partial derivative of a multivariable function with respect to one of the independent variables is found by treating all of the other independent variables as constants, and then determining the derivative of the function with respect to that variable. If $f(x_1, x_2, \ldots, x_n)$ is a function of n variables, then the partial derivative of f with respect to x_i is represented as

---

$$\frac{\partial f}{\partial x_i} \quad \text{or} \quad f_{x_i}$$

We can also calculate the partial derivative of the profit with respect to P_2. For the present, we will pretend that P_1 is a constant.

$$Z(P_1, P_2) = 40P_1 + 26P_2 - 5P_1^2 - 7P_2^2 + 5P_1P_2 - 155$$

Term	Derivative with Respect to P_2
$40P_1$	0
$26P_2$	26
$-5P_1^2$	0
$-7P_2^2$	$-14P_2$
$5P_1P_2$	$5P_1$
-155	0

Therefore, the partial derivative is

$$\frac{\partial Z}{\partial P_2} = 26 - 14P_2 + 5P_1$$

CRITICAL POINTS

Recall that a function of one variable can be illustrated by a curve or a line on a two-dimensional graph, with the value of the independent variable measured along the horizontal axis and the value of the dependent variable measured along the vertical axis. To graph a function with two independent variables, we need a three-dimensional diagram (or at least a perspective diagram that looks three-dimensional). The dependent variable is measured along the vertical axis, and the two independent variables are measured along the two horizontal axes. The function is represented by a hill. A place where the hill is higher corresponds to a place where the value of the function is larger. (Technically, this graph is called a **surface**.) Figure 10-1 illustrates the profit function:

$$Z(P_1, P_2) = 40P_1 + 26P_2 - 5P_1^2 - 7P_2^2 + 5P_1P_2 - 155$$

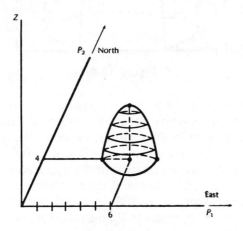

Figure 10-1

Note that the hill has a peak which corresponds to the maximum point.

To make it easier to talk about directions on this diagram, we will say that the P_1-axis points in the east direction and the P_2-axis points in the north direction.

The partial derivatives represent the slopes of cross sections of the hill. For example, suppose that we keep P_2 fixed with a value of 3. If we substitute this value in place of P_2 in the formula for Z, we can express the profit as a function of P_1:

$$Z = 55P_1 - 5P_1^2 - 140$$

Then the formula for the partial derivative with respect to P_1 becomes

$$40 - 10P_1 + 5 \times 3 = 55 - 10P_1$$

Suppose that we slice away a cross section of the hill along the east-west direction where $P_2 = 3$. (See Figure 10-2.) Then the partial derivative evaluated

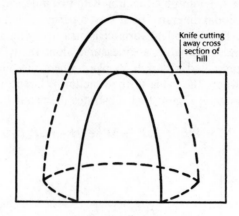

Figure 10-2

where $P_2 = 3$ will give the slope of the cross section for a particular value of P_1.

If the partial derivative with respect to P_1 is positive at a particular point, the cross section of the curve in the east-west direction slopes up, and we can increase the profits by increasing P_1. If $\partial Z/\partial P_1$ is negative, however, the cross section slopes down and we can increase profits by reducing P_1. Therefore, by the same reasoning we used in Chapter 9, the maximum value of the profit can occur only at a point where the partial derivative with respect to P_1 is zero. Exactly the same reasoning applies to P_2: the maximum value of the profit can occur only at a point where the partial derivative with respect to P_2 is zero.

Therefore, to find the maximum point for the function, we need to find a point where both $\partial Z/\partial P_1$ and $\partial Z/\partial P_2$ are equal to zero. A point where all of the partial derivatives of a function are zero is called a **critical point**. In the next section we'll see how to check whether a critical point is a maximum.

To find the point where both partial derivatives are zero, we need to solve this two-equation, two-variable system:

$$40 - 10P_1 + 5P_2 = 0$$
$$26 - 14P_2 + 5P_1 = 0$$

We can use the methods from Chapter 1. The solution values are as follows: $P_1 = 6$, $P_2 = 4$.

Therefore, to maximize profit, the price of the extra-strength cleaning solution should be \$6 and the price of the regular grade should be \$4. We can put these values in the formula for Z to determine that the profit will be \$17.

We can verify that this point is a relative maximum by observing what happens if either P_1 or P_2 is increased or decreased slightly from this level.

P_1	P_2	Profit
6	4	17
6.1	4	16.95
5.9	4	16.95
6	4.1	16.93
6	3.9	16.93

Any change in either price away from the point ($P_1 = 6$, $P_2 = 4$) will result in a reduction in profit.

SECOND-ORDER CONDITIONS

Recall the one-variable case, where a point with zero first derivative represented a flat spot on the curve. This flat spot could be either a maximum point, a minimum point, or neither. Likewise, a point where both first partial derivatives are zero is a flat spot on the hill, and this point can be either a maximum, a minimum, or neither. However, in the two-variable case it is more complicated to determine which the point is.

In the one-variable case we checked the second derivative to determine whether a critical point was a maximum or a minimum. Likewise, in the two-variable case we need to check the second partial derivatives. The conditions that we must check are called the **second-order conditions**.

For the store selling the cleaning products, we had this profit function:

$$Z = 40P_1 + 26P_2 - 5P_1^2 - 7P_2^2 + 5P_1P_2 - 155$$

with these partial derivatives:

$$Z_{P_1} = \frac{\partial Z}{\partial P_1} = 40 - 10P_1 + 5P_2, \qquad Z_{P_2} = \frac{\partial Z}{\partial P_2} = 26 - 14P_2 + 5P_1$$

We can calculate the derivative of $\partial Z/\partial P_1$ with respect to P_1, which we will represent as $\partial^2 Z/\partial P_1^2$ or $Z_{P_1P_1}$:

$$Z_{P_1P_1} = \frac{\partial^2 Z}{\partial P_1^2} = -10$$

The fact that the second partial derivative is always negative indicates that all cross sections of the curve cut in the east-west direction (parallel to the P_1-axis) are oriented so that they are concave downward. In that case, a flat spot (that is, a critical point) must be at the top of the curve, not the bottom.

We can also calculate the derivative of $\partial Z/\partial P_2$ with respect to P_2, which we will represent as $\partial^2 Z/\partial P_2^2$ or $Z_{P_2 P_2}$:

$$Z_{P_2 P_2} = \frac{\partial^2 Z}{\partial P_2^2} = -14$$

The value for this second derivative is always negative, so if we take a cross section of the curve along the north-south direction (parallel to the P_2-axis), it will always be oriented so that the concave part is downward.

Therefore, we expect that, if both $\partial^2 Z/\partial P_1^2$ and $\partial^2 Z/\partial P_2^2$ are negative, we will be at the top of a hill; this means that we are at a maximum point. However, the situation is a bit more complicated. The fact that both $\partial^2 Z/\partial P_1^2$ and $\partial^2 Z/\partial P_2^2$ are negative means that we are at the top of a hill if we take a cross section cut either directly north and south or directly east and west. There still is the possibility that the value of the function may turn up in some other direction.

For example, consider this function:

$$z(x, y) = -x^2 - y^2 + 3xy$$

Here are the partial derivatives:

$$\frac{\partial z}{\partial x} = -2x + 3y, \qquad \frac{\partial^2 z}{\partial x^2} = -2$$

$$\frac{\partial z}{\partial y} = -2y + 3x, \qquad \frac{\partial^2 z}{\partial y^2} = -2$$

There is a critical point where $x = 0$, $y = 0$, since both first derivatives are zero at that point. Both of the second derivatives, $\partial^2 z/\partial x^2$ and $\partial^2 z/\partial y^2$, are always negative, so we might be tempted to think that we have found a maximum point where the value of the function is $z = 0$. However, if we check the point $x = 0.001$, $y = -0.001$, the value of the function is 0.000001, which is greater than zero. Therefore, $(x = 0, y = 0)$ is not a relative maximum. If we were standing on the hill representing this function at the point $x = 0$ and $y = 0$, the hill would indeed slope down if we started walking north, south, east, or west. However, if we started walking directly northwest or directly southeast, the function would slope up.

This type of point is called a **saddle point**. A saddle point occurs where all of the first derivatives are zero, and the cross section of the curve is concave downward if you cut across the surface in some direction, but is concave upward if you cut across the surface in some other direction. There is a good intuitive reason for the term *saddle point*. Suppose that you were an ant standing in the middle of a saddle on a horse's back. If you walked along the saddle in a straight line toward the head of the horse, or toward the tail, the saddle would slope up. (The cross section of the saddle is concave upward if you cut the saddle with a vertical plane passing through the head and tail of the horse.) However, if you walked along the saddle in a straight line toward either side of the horse, you would be sloping downward. (The cross section of the saddle is concave downward if you cut the saddle with a vertical plane perpendicular to the horse.)

How can you tell the difference between saddle points and maximum points and minimum points? Here is an example of a curve that obviously has a saddle point:

$$z = x^2 - y^2$$

Calculate the partial derivatives:

$$\frac{\partial z}{\partial x} = 2x, \qquad \frac{\partial^2 z}{\partial x^2} = 2$$

$$\frac{\partial z}{\partial y} = -2y, \qquad \frac{\partial^2 z}{\partial y^2} = -2$$

The second partial derivative with respect to x is positive, so the cross section is concave upward if you cut the surface with a vertical plane along the x-axis. The second partial derivative with respect to y is negative, so the cross section is concave downward if you cut the surface with a vertical plane along the y-axis.

Figure 10-3 shows a graph of two cross sections of this curve. (You should note that saddle points are difficult to draw in two dimensions.)

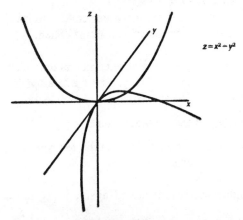

Figure 10-3

Therefore, a saddle point will occur if the two second partial derivatives with respect to x and y have different signs. However, we found with the function

$z = -x^2 - y^2 + 3xy$ that a saddle point can occur even if $\partial^2 z/\partial x^2$ and $\partial^2 z/\partial y^2$ have the same sign. To distinguish this situation, we need to check two other second partial derivatives: the partial derivative of $\partial z/\partial x$ with respect to y, and the partial derivative of $\partial z/\partial y$ with respect to x.

Here are the two first partial derivatives for the cleaning example:

$$Z_{P_1} = \frac{\partial Z}{\partial P_1} = 40 - 10P_1 + 5P_2, \qquad Z_{P_2} = \frac{\partial Z}{\partial P_2} = 26 - 14P_2 + 5P_1$$

We can calculate the derivative of $\partial Z/\partial P_1$ with respect to P_2, which we will represent as $\partial^2 Z/\partial P_1 \, \partial P_2$ or $Z_{P_1 P_2}$:

$$Z_{P_1 P_2} = \frac{\partial^2 Z}{\partial P_1 \, \partial P_2} = 5$$

We can also calculate the derivative of $\partial Z/\partial P_2$ with respect to P_1, which we will represent as $\partial^2 Z/\partial P_2 \, \partial P_1$ or $Z_{P_2 P_1}$:

$$Z_{P_2 P_1} = \frac{\partial^2 Z}{\partial P_2 \, \partial P_1} = 5$$

Note that the value of $Z_{P_1 P_2}$ is the same as the value of $Z_{P_1 P_2}$. This is not a coincidence; this result can be proved to be true for any well-behaved function of two variables. Therefore, we do not need to calculate both $Z_{P_1 P_2}$ and $Z_{P_2 P_1}$ separately. Once we have found one, we know that the other will be the same. This quantity is called the **cross partial**.

Here is the statement of the second-order condition involving cross partials: Evaluate f_{xx}, f_{yy}, and f_{xy} at the critical point. Then:

- If $f_{xx}f_{yy} > (f_{xy})^2$, there is a relative maximum or minimum. To tell the difference: if f_{xx} and f_{yy} are positive, you have a local minimum; if f_{xx} and f_{yy} are negative, you have a local maximum.

- If $(f_{xy})^2 > f_{xx}f_{yy}$, there is a saddle point.

- If $(f_{xy})^2 = f_{xx}f_{yy}$, you cannot tell from this test whether you have a maximum, a minimum, or a saddle point.

Here are the same conditions stated again, using the curly d (derivative) notation:

$$\frac{\partial^2 f}{\partial x^2} \times \frac{\partial^2 f}{\partial y^2} > \left(\frac{\partial^2 f}{\partial x \, \partial y} \right)^2 : \qquad \text{relative maximum or minimum}$$

$$\left(\frac{\partial^2 f}{\partial x\, \partial y}\right)^2 > \frac{\partial^2 f}{\partial x^2} \times \frac{\partial^2 f}{\partial y^2}: \quad \text{saddle point}$$

$$\left(\frac{\partial^2 f}{\partial x\, \partial y}\right)^2 = \frac{\partial^2 f}{\partial x^2} \times \frac{\partial^2 f}{\partial y^2}: \quad \text{can't tell from this test}$$

For the cleaning fluids example:

$$\frac{\partial^2 Z}{\partial P_1^2} = -10, \qquad \frac{\partial^2 Z}{\partial P_2^2} = -14, \qquad \frac{\partial^2 Z}{\partial P_1\, \partial P_2} = 5$$

$$\frac{\partial^2 Z}{\partial P_1^2} \times \frac{\partial^2 Z}{\partial P_2^2} = 140, \qquad \left(\frac{\partial^2 Z}{\partial P_1\, \partial P_2}\right)^2 = 25$$

Since 140 is greater than 25, we know that we are not at a saddle point. Since -10 and -14 are both negative, we know that we have a maximum, instead of a minimum.

For the $z = -x^2 - y^2 + 3xy$ example:

$$\frac{\partial^2 z}{\partial x^2} = -2, \qquad \frac{\partial^2 z}{\partial y^2} = -2, \qquad \frac{\partial^2 z}{\partial x\, \partial y} = 3$$

Since $3^2 = 9$, which is greater than $(-2) \times (-2) = 4$, this is a saddle point.

YOU SHOULD REMEMBER

A critical point for a multivariable function is a point where all of the partial derivatives of that function are zero. The second-order conditions can be used to determine whether a critical point is a maximum, a minimum, or a saddle point.

If there are more than two variables, then the second-order conditions are very complicated.

OPTIMIZATION IN THE PRESENCE OF CONSTRAINTS

So far in this chapter, we have looked for optimum values for functions in situations where the independent variables have been allowed to take on any possible values. However, we have seen that in reality many problems involve constraints that limit the feasible values. We need to develop some new methods to deal with this situation. First, we will look at cases where the constraints are expressed as equations; later, we will look at constraints that are inequalities.

Let's consider a typical situation where there is an objective function whose value is to be minimized, subject to a constraint. A business is trying to determine the least-cost method of producing a certain quantity of output. In many cases, there is considerable flexibility about the production process that can be used to produce a good. For example, one production method may use a great deal of labor and not much machinery; another method for producing the same quantity of output may use considerable machinery but not as much labor. An office building can be adequately heated either by using a lot of fuel and not much insulation, or by heavily insulating and not using as much fuel.

In each case the optimal choice will depend on the costs of the input goods used in the production process. For example, if heating fuel is very cheap and insulation is very expensive, then buildings will be built without much insulation, and they will require a lot of fuel. On the other hand, if fuel is expensive in relation to insulation, the buildings will have more insulation and consume less fuel.

For the present, we will consider situations where there are two input variables.

Example: Choosing the Optimal Mix of Inputs

A factory has found that two types of machinery are substitutes. It is possible to use a great deal of type x machinery and little of type y, or vice versa, or medium amounts of both.

The amount of output is given by this formula:

$$Q(x, y) = 60x^{2/3}y^{1/3}$$

This type of function is called a **production function**. In a production function the independent variables represent the amounts of the different inputs used in the production process, and the dependent variable is the amount of output that is produced.

This particular production function has a property called **constant returns to scale**, meaning that, if we doubled the amounts of both of the inputs, the amount of the output would exactly double. More generally, if we increased both of the inputs by a factor k, the amount of the output would also increase by factor k.

A function of the form $z = x^a y^b$ is called a **Cobb-Douglas** production function. A Cobb-Douglas production function will have constant returns to scale if the exponents add up to 1.

Earlier in the chapter we used perspective diagrams to illustrate functions of two variables. Another type of diagram we can use to illustrate a two-variable function is analogous to a contour map. A contour map contains curves that connect all points having the same elevation. On our diagram we will measure the two inputs along the two axes, and we will draw curves that connect all points that represent the same quantity of output. This type of diagram is called an **isoquant map**. (See Figure 10-4.) Each curve is called an **isoquant**. (The word *isoquant* means "same quantity.") Note that point A ($x = 8$, $y = 8$) represents a quantity of output of 480, since $60 \times 8^{2/3} \times 8^{1/3} = 480$. Point B ($x = 16$, $y = 2$) also represents a quantity of 480, so it is on the same isoquant as point A. Note that each isoquant is labeled by indicating the quantity of output that is represented by the points on that isoquant. If the quantities of both inputs are increased, then naturally the quantity of output will increase.

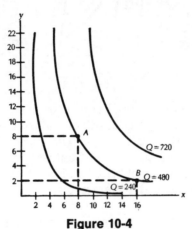

Figure 10-4

Suppose that the factory has made the decision that a quantity of 480 will be produced. (The optimal quantity occurs where the marginal revenue equals the marginal cost. We will assume that this calculation has already been made.) Therefore, we are subject to this constraint:

$$60x^{2/3}y^{1/3} = 480$$

We want to produce this output at the minimum possible cost. Each unit of x machinery costs 27; each unit of y machinery costs 4. Therefore, our problem is as follows:

Minimize $27x + 4y$
subject to $60x^{2/3}y^{1/3} = 480$

We can draw **isocost lines** for this situation. As in Chapter 2, an isocost line connects all points that have the same total cost. The slope of each isocost line is equal to the price of input x divided by the price of input y (in this case the slope is $-27/4$). (See Figure 10-5.)

The cost-minimizing solution can be found from the diagram. Clearly, none of the points on the isocost line with a total cost of \$108 is allowable, because none of these points crosses the isoquant corresponding to 480 units of output.

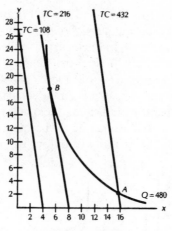

Figure 10-5

We would be glad to have a total cost of only $108 if we could, but it is impossible to produce a quantity of 480 at that level of cost.

Point *A* represents 480 units of output with a cost of $432. It is possible to produce the output with a cost of $432, but we can see that there are many points that are better. Any point below the isocost line corresponds to a lower value for the total cost, and there are many such points on the 480-unit isoquant.

Point *B* is the optimum. It is acceptable, because the output is 480. It represents a total cost of $216. None of the points with a total cost below $216 produces 480 units of output. In general, the least-cost production point occurs where an isocost line just touches (is tangent to) the isoquant representing the desired quantity of output. We can read from the diagram that this corresponds to $x = 5\frac{1}{3}$, and $y = 18$.

As we have seen before, graphical methods work only when there are two variables. Even then, finding the solution from a graph requires very careful graphing. Therefore, we need another method for finding optimum points of multivariable functions in situations where there are constraints.

LAGRANGE MULTIPLIERS

Imagine that we have been appointed by the local environmental protection agency to determine regulations concerning the location of a new waste-processing facility. The operators would like to locate the facility as close as possible to the city. We, on the other hand, would like the facility to be located along an industrial highway some distance away. Suppose that we have drawn a coordinate system where the location of the city is at the origin ($x = 0$, $y = 0$), and the industrial highway can be represented by the line $2x + y = 10$. (See Figure 10-6.) If the facility is located at a point (x, y), the operators face transportation costs equal to $x^2 + y^2$. (More realistically, the transportation costs would be proportional to $\sqrt{x^2 + y^2}$, the distance from the city to the facility. However, the mathematics is simpler if the cost is set equal to $x^2 + y^2$, and the optimal location of the factory turns out to be the same.)

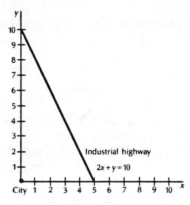

Figure 10-6

Here is the problem:

Minimize $x^2 + y^2$
subject to $2x + y = 10$

This is an example of a minimization problem in the presence of a constraint. We need a method that allows us to transform the problem into an unconstrained optimization problem so we can use the procedures we have already developed.

Suppose that we cannot force the operators to locate the facility along the main highway, but we can pay a bonus or impose a surcharge, depending on the location. We will charge a penalty if the facility is located too close to the city (if $2x + y < 10$). We will pay a bonus if the facility is located farther away (if $2x + y > 10$). The amount of the payment, either positive or negative, will be proportional to $(10 - 2x - y)$.

We do not intend to actually collect a surcharge or pay a bonus. Instead, we intend to set the surcharge at exactly the correct level so that the facility meets the constraint anyway.

Suppose that we set the surcharge equal to 3. Then the facility operators will minimize this function of two variables:

$$z(x, y) = x^2 + y^2 + 3(10 - 2x - y)$$

where $x^2 + y^2$ represents the cost of transportation, and $3(10 - 2x - y)$ equals the value of the penalty (if $2x + y < 10$) or the value of the bonus (if $2x + y > 10$).

We calculate the two partial derivatives:

$$\frac{\partial z}{\partial x} = 2x - 6, \qquad \frac{\partial z}{\partial y} = 2y - 3$$

Setting both of these equal to zero gives this two-equation, two-unknown system:

$$2x - 6 = 0$$
$$2y - 3 = 0$$

The solution is $x = 3$, $y = 3/2$. Unfortunately, these values do not satisfy the constraint $2x + y = 10$. We did not make the penalty for falling below the constraint line large enough, so the facility was located too close to the city.

Suppose instead we set the penalty equal to 5. Now this is the problem:

Minimize $z(x, y) = x^2 + y^2 + 5(10 - 2x - y)$

The solution turns out to be $x = 5$, $y = 2\frac{1}{2}$. This time the surcharge/bonus amount was too large. The operators found it profitable to locate the facility far enough from the city to collect the bonus.

We guess that the correct penalty amount must be between 3 and 5. We will try setting the penalty equal to 4. Then the facility operators will minimize this function:

$$z = x^2 + y^2 + 4(10 - 2x - y)$$

which has the optimum $x = 4$, $y = 2$. This point is located along the constraint line, so we have found the right amount for the penalty.

We cannot find the penalty amount by trial and error each time. There is a procedure that allows us to solve for the correct penalty amount, as well as the correct values for x and y. We write a new expression, called L, like this:

$$L(x, y, \lambda) = x^2 + y^2 + \lambda(10 - 2x - y)$$

This new expression is called the **Lagrangian**, after Joseph-Louis Lagrange, an eighteenth century mathematician. The symbol λ is the Greek letter **lambda**, which stands for a new quantity called a **Lagrange multiplier**. (It represents the penalty that must be paid for violating the constraint.) Note that the Lagrangian consists of the original objective function ($x^2 + y^2$ in this case) plus the Lagrange multiplier times a function that represents the constraint. If the constraint is written with a zero on one side of the equation and everything else on the other side. Our original constraint was

$$2x + y = 10$$

This can be written as

$$10 - 2x - y = 0$$

so you can see where that part of the Lagrangian expression comes from.

The use of the Lagrange multiplier method makes it possible to solve for the optimal value, subject to the constraint. The Lagrangian L is a function of three variables: x, y, and λ. We take the partial derivative of L with respect to each of these three variables:

$$\frac{\partial L}{\partial x} = 2x - 2\lambda, \qquad \frac{\partial L}{\partial y} = 2y - \lambda, \qquad \frac{\partial L}{\partial \lambda} = 10 - 2x - y$$

Now, we set up an equation system where each of these three partial derivatives is equal to zero.

$$2x - 2\lambda = 0$$
$$2y - \lambda = 0$$
$$10 - 2x - y = 0$$

Note that the last equation is the original constraint. Because of the way the Lagrangian expression is constructed, the equation formed by setting the partial derivative of the Lagrange multiplier equal to zero will always be the same as the constraint. Therefore, as long as this equation system is satisfied, the constraint will automatically be satisfied.

Here is the solution for our example:
From the first two equations, we have

$$2x = 2\lambda \qquad \text{and} \qquad 2y = \lambda$$

Therefore,

$$\lambda = x \qquad \text{and} \qquad x = 2y$$

We substitute $2y$ in place of x in the third equation:

$$10 - 2(2y) - y = 0$$
$$10 - 5y = 0$$
$$y = 2$$

Therefore, $x = 4$ and $\lambda = 4$.

Figure 10-7 illustrates the optimum by showing the constraint line and a contour curve that represents points that all have the same value for $x^2 + y^2$.

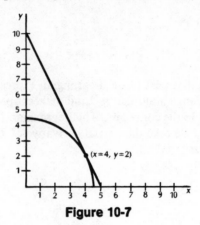

Figure 10-7

Now we can solve the factory cost-minimization problem on page 266 with Lagrange multipliers:

Minimize $27x + 4y$
subject to $60x^{2/3}y^{1/3} = 480$

We set up the Lagrangian:

$$L(x, y, \lambda) = 27x + 4y + \lambda(480 - 60x^{2/3}y^{1/3})$$

and take the partial derivatives of L with respect to x, y, and λ:

$$\frac{\partial L}{\partial x} = 27 - \frac{2}{3}\lambda 60\left(\frac{x^{2/3}y^{1/3}}{x}\right)$$

$$\frac{\partial L}{\partial y} = 4 - \frac{1}{3}\lambda 60\left(\frac{x^{2/3}y^{1/3}}{y}\right)$$

$$\frac{\partial L}{\partial \lambda} = 480 - 60x^{2/3}y^{1/3}$$

Now, we set up an equation system in which each of these partial derivatives is set equal to zero:

$$27 - \frac{2}{3}\lambda 60\left(\frac{x^{2/3}y^{1/3}}{x}\right) = 0$$

$$4 - \frac{1}{3}\lambda 60\left(\frac{x^{2/3}y^{1/3}}{y}\right) = 0$$

$$480 - 60x^{2/3}y^{1/3} = 0$$

Note that again the last equation is just a restatement of the original constraint.

This system does not consist of a set of linear equations, so there is no standard method for solving the system (as there was for the problems in Chapter 1).

Look at the first two equations:

$$27 = \frac{2}{3}\lambda 60\left(\frac{x^{2/3}y^{1/3}}{x}\right)$$

$$4 = \frac{1}{3}\lambda 60\left(\frac{x^{2/3}y^{1/3}}{y}\right)$$

If we divide the first equation by the second equation, most of the factors will cancel each other:

$$\frac{27}{4} = \frac{2y}{x}$$

Therefore, we know that at the optimum this equation will give the relation between y and x:

$$y = \frac{27x}{8}$$

Substituting this expression for y into the constraint equation gives

$$480 = 60x^{2/3}\left(\frac{27x}{8}\right)^{1/3}$$

$$\frac{480}{60} = x^{2/3}x^{1/3}\left(\frac{27}{8}\right)^{1/3}$$

$$8 = x\left(\frac{3}{2}\right)$$

$$x = \frac{16}{3}$$

Then we use the equation $y = 27x/8$ to find that $y = 18$.

Now we have the optimum: $x = 16/3$, $y = 18$, which will lead to a total cost of

$$27 \times \frac{16}{3} + 4 \times 18 = 216$$

This matches the graphical solution we found with the isoquant/isocost diagram.

We can use the second equation in the system to solve for λ, the value of the Lagrange multiplier:

$$4 = \frac{1}{3}\frac{\lambda}{y}(60x^{2/3}y^{1/3})$$

$$= \frac{1}{3}\frac{\lambda}{18}(480)$$

$$\lambda = \frac{4 \times 3 \times 18}{480}$$

$$= 0.45$$

Here is the interpretation for this value. The value of the Lagrange multiplier tells us how much we could reduce the cost if we could relax the constraint by 1 unit—that is, if it was acceptable to produce only 479, instead of 480. To show this, we solve the optimal values for x and y in this new situation:

$$479 = 60x^{2/3}\left(\frac{27x}{8}\right)^{1/3}$$

$$\frac{479}{60} = x^{2/3}x^{1/3}\left(\frac{27}{8}\right)^{1/3}$$

$$7.98333 = x\left(\frac{3}{2}\right)$$

$$x = \frac{2 \times 7.9833}{3} = 5.3222$$

Then we use the equation $y = 27x/8$ to find that $y = 17.9625$. The total cost is

$$27 \times 5.3222 + 4 \times 17.9625 = 215.55$$

Just as we suspected, the total cost has declined by 0.45.

The Lagrange multiplier acts as the shadow price for that constraint. The term *shadow price* rings a bell: we recall Chapter 6, where we found that the variables in the dual problem for a linear programming problem served as shadow prices for the constraints in the primal problem.

Here is the general procedure for using the Lagrange multiplier method. Note that there can be more than one constraint. Each constraint has its own Lagrange multiplier.

Consider this problem:

Maximize (or minimize) a function f of n variables

$$x_1, x_2, \ldots, x_n:$$
$$f(x_1, x_2, \ldots, x_n)$$

subject to a set of m constraints:

$$g_1(x_1, x_2, \ldots, x_n) = b_1$$
$$g_2(x_1, x_2, \ldots, x_n) = b_2$$
$$\cdots\cdots\cdots\cdots\cdots\cdots$$
$$g_m(x_1, x_2, \ldots, x_n) = b_m$$

To solve the problem, set up the Lagrangian expression, which consists of the objective function f, plus a function representing each constraint multiplied by its own Lagrange multiplier:

$$
\begin{aligned}
L = f(x_1, x_2, \ldots, x_n) &+ \lambda_1[b_1 - g_1(x_1, x_2, \ldots, x_n)] \\
&+ \lambda_2[b_2 - g_2(x_1, x_2, \ldots, x_n)] \\
&+ \cdots\cdots\cdots\cdots\cdots\cdots \\
&+ \lambda_m[b_m - g_m(x_1, x_2, \ldots, x_n)]
\end{aligned}
$$

The Lagrangian is a function of $n + m$ variables: $x_1, x_2, \ldots, x_n$, and $\lambda_1, \lambda_2, \ldots, \lambda_m$. Calculate the partial derivative with respect to each of these variables, and then set all of these partial derivatives equal to zero. The result will be a simultaneous equation system with $n + m$ equations and $n + m$ variables. Solve the system to determine the optimum. However, it may be difficult to solve the system. There is no guarantee that the equations will be linear equations, so the matrix methods used in Chapter 1 may not be applicable.

PRODUCTION FUNCTION WITH CAPITAL AND LABOR

Here is a general example of a cost-minimizing problem with two variables as inputs: labor (L) and capital (K). Let w represent the wage of labor, and r represent the rental price of capital.

Suppose that output is given by this Cobb-Douglas production function:

$$Q(K, L) = Qo\, K^a L^b$$

We need to produce a total output of Q^*. Our goal, then, is to minimize the total cost:

$$TC(L, K) = wL + rK$$

subject to the constraint

$$Qo\ K^a L^b = Q*$$

We set up the Lagrangian (we will use G to represent the Lagrangian, since we are already using L to represent labor):

$$G = wL + rK + \lambda(Q* - Qo\ K^a L^b)$$

We calculate the partial derivatives:

$$\frac{\partial G}{\partial K} = r - a\lambda\left(\frac{Qo\ K^a L^b}{K}\right), \qquad \frac{\partial G}{\partial L} = w - b\lambda\left(\frac{Qo\ K^a L^b}{L}\right),$$

$$\frac{\partial G}{\partial \lambda} = Q* - Qo\ K^a L^b$$

and set each of these partial derivatives equal to zero:

$$r - a\lambda\left(\frac{Qo\ K^a L^b}{K}\right) = 0$$

$$w - b\lambda\left(\frac{Qo\ K^a L^b}{L}\right) = 0$$

$$Q* - Qo\ K^a L^b = 0$$

We rewrite the first two equations:

$$r = \frac{a\lambda Qo\ K^a L^b}{K}$$

$$w = \frac{b\lambda Qo\ K^a L^b}{L}$$

Then we divide the first equation by the second equation, and cancel out everything that can be canceled:

$$\frac{r}{w} = \frac{aL}{bK}$$

This equation gives us a general rule: the optimal ratio of labor to capital will always be equal to

$$\frac{L}{K} = \frac{rb}{wa}$$

This formula makes intuitive sense. The ratio of labor to capital will increase if capital becomes more expensive in relation to labor (r/w becomes bigger) or if labor becomes more productive in relation to capital (b/a becomes larger).

NONLINEAR PROGRAMMING

The simplex method for linear programming problems allows us to solve problems that involve finding the optimal value of an objective function, subject to inequality constraints, provided that the objective function and the constraints are linear. The Lagrange multiplier method allows us to find the optimal value of an objective function subject to equality constraints, even if the objective function or the constraints are nonlinear. Now we turn to the trickiest situation: How do we find the optimal value for a function subject to inequality constraints, if the objective function and constraints are nonlinear? In other words, we will consider **nonlinear programming**.

Considering the two-variable case will be sufficient to indicate some of the difficulties. (Two-variable problems can be solved graphically. The problems that we will illustrate become much more complicated when there are more than two variables and it is not possible to graph the situation.) Figure 10-8 shows a problem where the constraints are all linear, so the feasible region has the same form as it does in a linear programming problem. Now, however, the objective function is nonlinear, so we have isoprofit curves instead of isoprofit lines. You can see that the optimal point no longer occurs at one of the corner points of the feasible region. Therefore, the simplex method, which is based on the fact that the solution to a linear programming problem occurs at one of the corners of the feasible region, will not work.

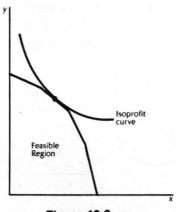

Figure 10-8

Figure 10-9 illustrates what can happen if the constraints are nonlinear. Even if the objective function is linear (as is represented by the straight isoprofit line in the figure), the optimum need not occur at a basic feasible solution. In the figure the optimum occurs at point *A*, which is not a point where two constraints intersect, so it is not a basic feasible solution.

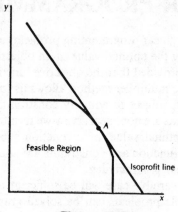

Figure 10-9

Matters become even worse if the feasible region is not a convex set. In a **convex set**, a line segment connecting any two points in the set will lie entirely within the set. For example, figure *A* in Figure 10-10 is a convex set. The line segment connecting points A_1 and A_2 is entirely within the set. If it is possible to draw a line segment that connects two points in the set in such a way that some of the points on the segment are not in the set, then the set is not a convex set. Figure *B* in Figure 10-10 is not a convex set. The line segment connecting points B_1 and B_2 passes outside the set. A nonconvex set has at least one dent in it.

Recall how the simplex method works: we keep moving from one feasible-region corner point (that is, a basic feasible solution) to another adjacent corner point, until we have reached a situation where we know that all of the adjacent

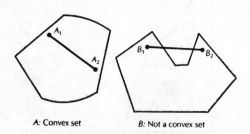

A: Convex set   *B:* Not a convex set

Figure 10-10

corner points have worse values for the objective function. Note that we do not check all of the corner points to see whether any of them has a better value of the objective function. Because the feasible region is convex, this is not necessary. If the feasible region is convex, and point *A* has a better value of the objective function than all of its adjacent corner points, then is must also have a better value of the objective function than all of the other corner points. (See Figure 10-11.) Because point *A* is on a higher isoprofit line than points *B* and *C*, it must also be on a higher isoprofit line than points *D*, *E*, and *F*.

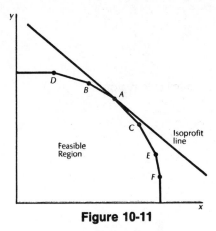

Figure 10-11

In a linear programming problem, the constraints are such that the feasible region must be a convex set. However, Figure 10-12 illustrates what can happen if the feasible region is not a convex set, as can occur if the constraints are nonlinear. Point *A* is on a higher isoprofit line than points *B* and *C*. However, point *D* is even better than point *A*. Because the feasible region is not convex,

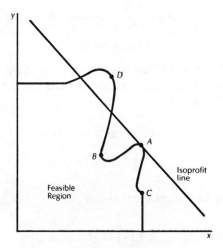

Figure 10-12

there is the possibility that a point that seems like the optimum may just be a high point surrounded by dents, with the true optimum on the other side of one of the dents.

We will work one example of a nonlinear programming problem:

Maximize xy
subject to

$$x^2 + y \leq 11$$
$$\frac{1}{3}x^2 + y \leq 5$$

$$x \geq 0, y \geq 0$$

Figure 10-13 illustrates the feasible region.

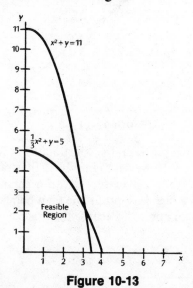

Figure 10-13

The solution method we will use is a combination of the Lagrange multiplier method and the simplex method. First, we rewrite the constraints so that zero is on one side of the inequality:

$$11 - x^2 - y \geq 0$$
$$5 - \frac{1}{3}x^2 - y \geq 0$$

Then we set up a Lagrangian expression:

$$L(x, y, \lambda_1, \lambda_2) = xy + \lambda_1(11 - x^2 - y) + \lambda_2\left(5 - \frac{1}{3}x^2 - y\right)$$

The Lagrangian consists of the objective function, plus a Lagrange multiplier times an expression representing each of the constraints.

In this case we have two Lagrange multipliers (λ_1 and λ_2) because we have two constraints. The Lagrange multipliers, as they did in the regular Lagrange multiplier calculations, represent the shadow price associated with each constraint—that is, how much we could improve the objective function if the constraint could be relaxed by 1 unit. Note that, in a linear programming problem, the dual variables served as the shadow prices for the constraints (see Chapter 6), so the connection with linear programming problems is beginning to appear. As in a linear programming problem, all of the variables (x, y, λ_1, and λ_2) are required to be nonnegative.

As we did in the regular Lagrange multiplier calculations, we take the partial derivative with respect to each of the four variables:

$$\frac{\partial L}{\partial x} = y - 2\lambda_1 x - \frac{2}{3}\lambda_2 x, \qquad \frac{\partial L}{\partial y} = x - \lambda_1 - \lambda_2,$$

$$\frac{\partial L}{\partial \lambda_1} = 11 - x^2 - y, \qquad \frac{\partial L}{\partial \lambda_2} = 5 - \frac{1}{3}x^2 - y$$

In the regular Lagrange multiplier situation we set all of the partial derivatives equal to zero. Now, however, the situation is more complicated. If the two partial derivatives $\partial L/\partial \lambda_1$ and $\partial L/\partial \lambda_2$ were set equal to zero, we would ensure that both of the constraints were met exactly with no excess capacity. However, there is no reason why this must be so, since both constraints involve inequalities.

Recall the role of the shadow prices in Chapter 6. If a constraint had excess capacity at the optimum, the value of the shadow price associated with that constraint was zero. On the other hand, if the shadow price was positive, the constraint had to be met exactly with no excess capacity. We have the same sort of conditions here, with the Lagrange multipliers playing the role of the shadow prices.

For the first constraint:

$$\text{either } \lambda_1 = 0 \qquad \text{or} \qquad \frac{\partial L}{\partial \lambda_1} = 0$$

(Recall that, if $\partial L/\partial \lambda_1$ is zero, then the first constraint is met exactly, with no excess capacity.)

For the second constraint:

$$\text{either } \lambda_2 = 0 \qquad \text{or} \qquad \frac{\partial L}{\partial \lambda_2} = 0$$

It turns out that the same conditions apply to both x and y:

$$\text{either } x = 0 \qquad \text{or} \qquad \frac{\partial L}{\partial x} = 0$$

$$\text{either } y = 0 \qquad \text{or} \qquad \frac{\partial L}{\partial y} = 0$$

THE KUHN-TUCKER CONDITIONS

We can make a complete list of all of the conditions that must be met at the optimum solution:

$$\frac{\partial L}{\partial x} \leq 0, \qquad \frac{\partial L}{\partial y} \leq 0, \qquad \frac{\partial L}{\partial \lambda_1} \geq 0, \qquad \frac{\partial L}{\partial \lambda_2} \geq 0$$

$$x\left(\frac{\partial L}{\partial x}\right) = 0, \qquad y\left(\frac{\partial L}{\partial y}\right) = 0$$

$$\lambda_1\left(\frac{\partial L}{\partial \lambda_1}\right) = 0, \qquad \lambda_2\left(\frac{\partial L}{\partial \lambda_2}\right) = 0$$

We also must satisfy the nonnegativity conditions:

$$x \geq 0, \qquad y \geq 0, \qquad \lambda_1 \geq 0, \qquad \lambda_2 \geq 0$$

These conditions are called the **Kuhn-Tucker conditions** and are the conditions for a maximization problem. The inequalities are reversed for a minimization problem (except for the nonnegativity conditions). These conditions provide substantial help in locating the optimum, although considerable work is left to do. Recall that in the regular Lagrange multiplier situation, the partial derivative of each variable was required to exactly equal zero. Now the partial derivatives with respect to x and y are required to be less than or equal to zero, and the partial derivatives with respect to λ_1 and λ_2 must be greater than or equal to zero.

The equation $x(\partial L/\partial x) = 0$ means that either $x = 0$ or $\partial L/\partial x = 0$. Therefore, the four equations for $x(\partial L/\partial x)$, $y(\partial L/\partial y)$, $\lambda_1(\partial L/\partial \lambda_1)$, and $\lambda_2(\partial L/\partial \lambda_2)$ given above are another way of stating that either a variable or the partial derivative of the Lagrangian with respect to that variable must be zero.

YOU SHOULD REMEMBER

The Kuhn-Tucker conditions must be met at the optimal solution to a nonlinear programming problem (provided that the feasible region is convex and the convex sides of the isoprofit curves are oriented toward the feasible region). The Kuhn-Tucker conditions state that at the optimum either a variable must be zero, or else the partial derivative of the Lagrangian with respect to that variable must be zero. If the partial derivative is not zero, then the Kuhn-Tucker conditions determine the sign that the partial derivative must have.

Unfortunately, these conditions do not tell us which of the variables, if any, will be zero. All we know is that, if a variable is nonzero, then its partial derivative must be zero. We have to resort to trial and error. First, let's suppose that all four variables (x, y, λ_1, and λ_2) have nonzero values at the optimum. Then we know that each partial derivative must be zero:

$$\frac{\partial L}{\partial x}: \quad y - 2\lambda_1 x - \frac{2}{3}\lambda_2 x = 0$$

$$\frac{\partial L}{\partial y}: \quad x - \lambda_1 - \lambda_2 = 0,$$

$$\frac{\partial L}{\partial \lambda_1}: \quad 11 - x^2 - y = 0$$

$$\frac{\partial L}{\partial \lambda_2}: \quad 5 - \frac{1}{3}x^2 - y = 0$$

The last two equations involve only x and y. Even though these are not linear equations (because x is raised to the second power), the elimination method will work in this case. We subtract the fourth equation from the third equation (to eliminate y). The resulting equation is

$$6 - \frac{2}{3}x^2 = 0$$

Therefore, $x = 3$, and we can find $y = 2$.

Now we substitute these values into the first two equations to solve for λ_1 and λ_2, and end up with this system:

$$2 - 6\lambda_1 - 2\lambda_2 = 0$$
$$3 - \lambda_1 - \lambda_2 = 0$$

Unfortunately, when we solve this system we find that $\lambda_1 = -1$ and $\lambda_2 = 4$. Since λ_1 is negative, the nonnegativity constraint has been violated. We cannot be at the optimum, so we have to start over.

Our first guess was that all variables had positive values. Now, let's guess that $\lambda_2 = 0$ at the optimum, and that x, y, and λ_1 are greater than zero. By assuming that $\lambda_2 = 0$, we are guessing that the second constraint $[(1/3)x^2 + y \le 5]$ will have some excess capacity at the optimum. This means that we can set the partial derivatives with respect to x, y, and λ_1 equal to zero:

$$\frac{\partial L}{\partial x}: \quad y - 2\lambda_1 x - \frac{2}{3}\lambda_2 x = 0$$

$$\frac{\partial L}{\partial y}: \quad x - \lambda_1 - \lambda_2 = 0$$

$$\frac{\partial L}{\partial \lambda_1}: \quad 11 - x^2 - y = 0$$

We can simplify the first two equations, since we are assuming that $\lambda_2 = 0$:

$$y - 2\lambda_1 x = 0$$
$$x - \lambda_1 = 0$$

The second equation says that $x = \lambda_1$. Then we can rewrite the first equation:

$$y - 2x^2 = 0$$

Adding the first equation and the third equation gives

$$3x^2 = 11$$

Therefore, $x = \sqrt{11/3}$, $\lambda_1 = \sqrt{11/3}$, and $y = 22/3$.

All of these values are positive. However, we have to check the first part of the Kuhn-Tucker conditions. We must have $\partial L/\partial \lambda_2 \ge 0$. If we insert the values we have obtained into the formula for $\partial L/\partial \lambda_2$:

$$\frac{\partial L}{\partial \lambda_2} = 5 - \frac{1}{3}x^2 - y$$

we end up with $(45 - 77)/9$. This is negative, so in this attempt we have violated the Kuhn-Tucker conditions. We can't be at the optimum.

We'll try another guess. We'll assume that $\lambda_1 = 0$, and the other variables are positive. This means we are guessing that the first constraint $(x^2 + y \le 11)$ will have excess capacity at the optimum. We must set three of the partial derivatives equal to zero:

$$\frac{\partial L}{\partial x}: \quad y - \frac{2}{3}\lambda_2 x = 0$$

$$\frac{\partial L}{\partial y}: \quad x - \lambda_2 = 0$$

$$\frac{\partial L}{\partial \lambda_2}: \quad 5 - \frac{1}{3}x^2 - y = 0$$

Remember that we can replace λ_1 with zero because of our assumption. The solution to this system turns out to be $x = \sqrt{5}$, $y = 10/3$, $\lambda_2 = \sqrt{5}$. So far, so good (the values are all positive). Now we need to check to see that $\partial L/\partial \lambda_1 \geq 0$:

$$\frac{\partial L}{\partial \lambda_1} = 11 - x^2 - y$$

$$= 11 - 5 - \frac{10}{3}$$

$$= \frac{8}{3}$$

This value is positive, so the Kuhn-Tucker conditions are satisfied. We have reached the optimum. The objective function has the value $\sqrt{5} \times 10/3 = 7.454$. Figure 10-14 illustrates a curve connecting all points with the same value for the objective function (an isoprofit curve). Note that the isoprofit curve just touches the feasible region at the optimum point.

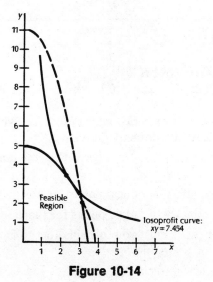

Figure 10-14

The trial and error method we used to find the optimum was tedious, but this method can be programmed on a computer. However, for a problem with many variables and constraints, there can be too many possibilities for even a computer to check in a reasonable amount of time. With the simplex method, we know that each step brings us closer to the optimum. We do not have that assurance in the nonlinear case.

The same method applies when there are more than two constraints and more than two variables. Write all constraints so that they contain zero on one side of the inequality, and all the remaining terms on the other side. If the problem is a maximization problem, set up the constraints in the form $g(x_1, \ldots, x_n) \geq 0$; if the problem is a minimization problem, set up the constraints in the form $g(x_1, \ldots, x_n) \leq 0$.

Set up the Lagrangian, including one Lagrange multiplier for each constraint. For each variable in the Lagrangian, it must be true at the optimum that either the variable is zero or the partial derivative of the Lagrangian with respect to that variable is zero. For a maximizing problem (as in our example), the partial derivative with respect to each choice variable must be less than or equal to zero; the partial derivative with respect to each Lagrange multiplier must be greater than or equal to zero. In a minimization problem, the signs are reversed: the partial derivative with respect to each original-choice variable must be greater than or equal to zero, and the partial derivative with respect to each Lagrange multiplier must be less than or equal to zero. However, the Kuhn-Tucker conditions apply only if the feasible region is a convex set and the isoprofit curves are oriented so that their concave sides point away from the feasible region. Both of these conditions were met in our example, but they may not be true for some problems.

KNOW THE CONCEPTS

DO YOU KNOW THE BASICS?

Test your understanding of Chapter 10 by answering the following questions:

1. How is the process for calculating partial derivatives different from the process for calculating ordinary derivatives?
2. Describe the geometry of partial derivatives for functions of two variables.
3. Describe the geometry of critical points for functions of two variables.
4. Describe the geometry of saddle points for functions of two variables.
5. How many equations must you solve in order to find the critical points for a function of n variables?
6. Why isn't it sufficient to check f_{xx} and f_{yy} if you are trying to determine whether a point is a minimum or a maximum?

7. If you take the partial derivative of the Lagrangian with respect to one of the Lagrange multipliers, what is the result?

8. How is a Lagrange multiplier similar to a dual variable in a linear programming problem?

9. Why it is difficult to solve a nonlinear programming problem if the feasible region is not convex?

10. What is the difference between the Kuhn-Tucker conditions and the conditions used to solve an ordinary Lagrange multiplier problem?

TERMS FOR STUDY

Cobb-Douglas production function
constant returns to scale
convex set
critical points
cross partial
isocost line
isoquant
isoquant map
Kuhn-Tucker conditions

Lagrange multiplier
lagrangian
lambda
nonlinear programming
partial derivative
production function
saddle point
second-order conditions
surface

PRACTICAL APPLICATION

COMPUTATIONAL PROBLEMS

For Exercises 1–5, locate the critical point and determine whether it is a maximum, minimum, or saddle point:

1. $3x^2 + xy + 2y^2 + 9x - 7y + 10$
2. $x^2 + 10xy + y^2 - x - 5y - 8$
3. $-x^2 - 2xy + 3y^2 + 8x - 4y - 17$
4. $-0.5x^2 + 0.2xy - 1.4y^2 + 1.8x - 1.2y + 0.75$
5. $x^3y + 2x - y$
6. A production function with two inputs (K and L) is given by the formula $Q = (L^{-2} + K^{-2})^{-(1/2)}$. (This is an example of a *constant elasticity of substitution* production function.) The profit is given by this formula:

$$Z(L, K) = PQ - wL - rK$$

where P, w and r are constants. Determine the profit-maximizing ratio between K and L. (Use the chain rule given in the appendix to Chapter 9.)

7. Consider this function of three variables:

$$f(x, y, z) = (x - 1)^2 + (y - 3)^2 + (z - 2)^2$$

Determine the coordinates of any critical points.

8. Consider a firm that sells two substitute products. The quantity demanded of product 1 is given by the formula:

$$q_1 = a_1 - b_1 p_1 + c_1 p_2$$

The quantity demanded of product 2 is

$$q_2 = a_2 - b_2 p_2 + c_2 p_1$$

The cost of producing each unit of product 1 is s_1, and the per-unit cost for product 2 is s_2. The total profit is given by the formula

$$\text{profit} = Z = p_1 q_1 - s_1 q_1 + p_2 q_2 - s_2 q_2$$

Derive a general formula for the values of p_1 and p_2 that maximize the profit. (*Hint:* express the result in terms of determinants.)

For Exercises 9–12, find, in each case, the optimal value of the indicated function, subject to the constraints that are given.

9. Maximize $x^3 y^2$ subject to $4x + 5y = 40$
10. Maximize xy subject to $x + 2y = 10$
11. Maximize $10xy - 2y^2$ subject to $x + y = 12$
12. Minimize $x^2 + y^2$ subject to $4x + 3y = 50$
13. Derive a general formula for the maximum or minimum point of the function

$$z(x, y) = ax^2 + bxy + cy^2 + dx + ey + f$$

subject to the constraint $mx + ny = k$. (You need not determine whether the point you find is a maximum or minimum.)

For Exercises 14–18, find, in each case, the maximum value of the given objective function, subject to these two constraints:

$$x^2 + y \le 11$$
$$\frac{1}{3} x^2 + y \le 5$$

14. $z = x + y$

15. $z = 8x + y$

16. $z = 3x + y$

17. $z = 6.2x + y$

18. $z = x^2y$

19. Here is another method for solving a problem that involves maximizing or minimizing an objective function with two variables subject to a constraint. First, use the constraint to write an expression for one of the variables in terms of the other. Then substitute that expression in the objective function. The result is a function of one variable, whose optimal value can be found by taking the derivative.

Use this method to solve the problem presented in the chapter: Minimize $x^2 + y^2$ subject to $2x + y = 10$.

ANSWERS

KNOW THE CONCEPTS

1. The process is the same. The only difference is that the other variables are assumed to remain constant while the derivative is calculated.

2. The partial derivative of a function evaluated at a particular point represents the slope of a cross section of the surface representing that function. If the partial derivative is taken with respect to x, then the cross section is cut in a direction parallel to the x-axis.

3. A critical point is a flat spot on the surface.

4. A saddle point is a flat spot on the surface such that the cross section of the surface is concave upward in one direction and concave downward in some other direction.

5. There will be a system of n equations with n variables.

6. By checking the values of f_{xx} and f_{yy}, you can determine whether the cross sections are concave upward or concave downward in the directions parallel to the x-axis and the y-axis. However, you also need to check whether the cross sections are concave upward or downward in other directions, and this is the reason why the second-order conditions require you to check the cross partial.

7. If the partial derivative with respect to a Lagrange multiplier is set equal to zero, then the resulting equation is the same as the constraint corresponding to that Lagrange multiplier.

8. They both represent shadow prices of their corresponding constraints.

9. If the feasible region is convex, then you know that a point with a higher value of the objective function than its neighboring points must have the

highest possible value for the objective function among all feasible points. If the feasible region is not convex, you cannot be sure of this.

10. The ordinary Lagrange multiplier conditions, which apply when the constraints are equalities, require that all the partial derivatives of the Lagrangian be set to zero. The Kuhn-Tucker conditions apply when the constraints involve inequalities. Either a variable or the partial derivative of the Lagrangian with respect to that variable must be zero, and there are also conditions on the signs of the partial derivatives.

PRACTICAL APPLICATION

For Exercises 1–5, let $D = z_{xx}z_{yy} - (z_{xy})^2$.

1. $x = -1.87$, $y = 2.217$, $D = 23$. D, z_{xx}, and z_{yy} are all positive, so this is a minimum point.

2. $x = 0.5$, $y = 0$, $D = -96$. D is negative, so this is a saddle point.

3. $x = 2.5$, $y = 1.5$, $D = -16$. D is negative, so this is a saddle point.

4. $x = 1.739$, $y = -0.304$, $D = 2.76$. D is positive, and z_{xx} and z_{yy} are negative, so this is a maximum point.

5. $x = 1$, $y = -2/3$, $D = -36$. D is negative, so this is a saddle point.

6.
$$\frac{\partial Z}{\partial L} = -\frac{1}{2}P(L^{-2} + K^{-2})^{-(3/2)}(-2L^{-3}) - w$$

$$\frac{\partial Z}{\partial K} = -\frac{1}{2}P(L^{-2} + K^{-2})^{-(3/2)}(-2K^{-3}) - r$$

Set the partial derivatives equal to zero and divide the first equation by the second equation:

$$\left(\frac{L}{K}\right)^{-3} = \frac{w}{r}$$

$$\frac{L}{K} = \left(\frac{w}{r}\right)^{-(1/3)}$$

7. $f_x = 2(x - 1)$, $f_y = 2(y - 3)$, $f_z = 2(z - 2)$
   The critical point is $x = 1$, $y = 3$, $z = 2$. This is an absolute minimum point.

8. Calculate the two partial derivatives:

$$\frac{\partial Z}{\partial p_1} = -2b_1p_1 + (c_1 + c_2)p_2 + (a_1 + b_1s_1 - c_2s_2)$$

$$\frac{\partial Z}{\partial p_2} = (c_1 + c_2)p_1 - 2b_2p_2 + (a_2 + b_2s_2 - c_1s_1)$$

Set both partial derivatives equal to zero. The result is a two-equation system with two variables (p_1 and p_1). The solution is

$$p_1 = \frac{\begin{vmatrix} (a_1 + b_1s_1 - c_2s_2) & (c_1 + c_2) \\ (a_2 + b_2s_2 - c_1s_1) & -2b_2 \end{vmatrix}}{\begin{vmatrix} -2b_1 & (c_1 + c_2) \\ (c_1 + c_2) & -2b_2 \end{vmatrix}}$$

$$p_2 = \frac{\begin{vmatrix} -2b_1 & (a_1 + b_1s_1 - c_2s_2) \\ (c_1 + c_2) & (a_2 + b_2s_2 - c_1s_1) \end{vmatrix}}{\begin{vmatrix} -2b_1 & (c_1 + c_2) \\ (c_1 + c_2) & -2b_2 \end{vmatrix}}$$

9. $L(x, y, \lambda) = x^3y^2 + \lambda(40 - 4x - 5y)$

Setting the three partial derivatives equal to zero gives this equation system:

$$3x^2y^2 - 4\lambda = 0$$
$$2x^3y - 5\lambda = 0$$
$$40 - 4x - 5y = 0$$

Divide the first equation by the second equation:

$$\frac{3y}{2x} = \frac{4}{5}$$

Put this equation back into the third equation. The solution is $x = 6$, $y = 16/5$.

10. $x = 5$, $y = 5/2$

11. $x = 7$, $y = 5$

12. $x = 8$, $y = 6$

13. Set up the Lagrangian:

$$L(x, y, \lambda) = ax^2 + bxy + cy^2 + dx + ey + f + \lambda(k - mx - ny)$$

Calculate the partial derivatives:

$$\frac{\partial L}{\partial x} = 2ax + by + d - \lambda m, \qquad \frac{\partial L}{\partial y} = 2cy + bx + e - \lambda n,$$

$$\frac{\partial L}{\partial \lambda} = k - mx - ny$$

Set each partial derivative equal to zero, and express the system using matrix notation:

$$\begin{pmatrix} 2a & b & -m \\ b & 2c & -n \\ m & n & 0 \end{pmatrix} \begin{pmatrix} x \\ y \\ \lambda \end{pmatrix} = \begin{pmatrix} -d \\ -e \\ k \end{pmatrix}$$

The solution can be expressed with determinants:

$$x = \frac{\begin{vmatrix} -d & b & -m \\ -e & 2c & -n \\ k & n & 0 \end{vmatrix}}{\begin{vmatrix} 2a & b & -m \\ b & 2c & -n \\ m & n & 0 \end{vmatrix}}, \quad y = \frac{\begin{vmatrix} 2a & -d & -m \\ b & -e & -n \\ m & k & 0 \end{vmatrix}}{\begin{vmatrix} 2a & b & -m \\ b & 2c & -n \\ m & n & 0 \end{vmatrix}}$$

$$\lambda = \frac{\begin{vmatrix} 2a & b & -d \\ b & 2c & -e \\ m & n & k \end{vmatrix}}{\begin{vmatrix} 2a & b & -m \\ b & 2c & -n \\ m & n & 0 \end{vmatrix}}$$

14. Set up the Lagrangian:

$$L(x, y, \lambda_1, \lambda_2) = x + y + \lambda_1(11 - x^2 - y) + \lambda_2\left(5 - \frac{1}{3}x^2 - y\right)$$

$$\frac{\partial L}{\partial x} = 1 - 2\lambda_1 x - \frac{2}{3}\lambda_2 x, \qquad \frac{\partial L}{\partial y} = 1 - \lambda_1 - \lambda_2,$$

$$\frac{\partial L}{\partial \lambda_1} = 11 - x^2 - y, \qquad \frac{\partial L}{\partial \lambda_2} = 5 - \frac{1}{3}x^2 - y$$

At the optimum, $\lambda_1 = 0$. (Determine this by trial and error.) Set the partial derivatives with respect to the other variables equal to zero:

$$0 = 1 - \frac{2}{3}\lambda_2 x$$

$$0 = 1 - \lambda_2$$

$$0 = 5 - \frac{1}{3}x^2 - y$$

Solve this system to find $x = 3/2$, $y = 4.25$, $\lambda_2 = 1$. After verifying that $\partial L/\partial \lambda_1$ is positive, we know this is the optimum.

15. At the optimum, $y = 0$ and $\lambda_2 = 0$. Set the partial derivatives of the other two variables equal to zero:

$$0 = 8 - 2\lambda_1 x$$
$$0 = 11 - x^2$$

Therefore, $x = \sqrt{11} = 3.317$ and $\lambda_1 = 1.206$. To show that this is the optimum, verify that $\partial L/\partial y$ is negative and $\partial L/\partial \lambda_2$ is positive.

16. At the optimum, all variables are positive, so the partial derivatives with respect to all four variables must be zero:

$$0 = 3 - 2\lambda_1 x - \frac{2}{3}\lambda_2 x$$

$$0 = 1 - \lambda_1 - \lambda_2$$
$$0 = 11 - x^2 - y$$
$$0 = 5 - \frac{1}{3}x^2 - y$$

The solution is $x = 3$, $y = 2$, $\lambda_1 = 1/4$, $\lambda_2 = 3/4$.

17. At the optimum, $\lambda_2 = 0$. Set the partial derivatives with respect to the other variables equal to zero:

$$0 = 6.2 - 2\lambda_1 x$$
$$0 = 1 - \lambda$$
$$0 = 11 - x^2 - y$$

The solution is $x = 3.1$, $y = 1.39$, $\lambda_1 = 1$. To show that this is the optimum, verify that $\partial L/\partial \lambda_2$ is positive.

18. At the optimum, $\lambda_1 = 0$. Set the partial derivatives with respect to the other variables equal to zero:

$$0 = 2xy - \frac{2}{3}\lambda_2 x$$

$$0 = x^2 - \lambda_2$$
$$0 = 5 - \frac{1}{3}x^2 - y$$

Divide both sides of the first equation by x. (We can do this because we are assuming that $x \neq 0$.)

$$2y = \frac{2}{3}\lambda_2$$

From the second equation we see that $\lambda_2 = x^2$, so substitute into the first equation, leaving these two equations:

$$2y = \frac{2}{3}x^2$$

$$0 = 5 - \frac{1}{3}x^2 - y$$

Multiply the second equation by 2, and then add the two equations to eliminate y. The solution is $x = \sqrt{30/4} = 2.739$, $y = 2.5$, $\lambda_2 = 7.5$.

19. $y = 10 - 2x$
Substitute into the objective function:

$$z = x^2 + y^2 = x^2 + (10 - 2x)^2 = x^2 + 100 - 40x + 4x^2$$
$$= 5x^2 - 40x + 100$$
$$\frac{dz}{dx} = 10x - 40$$

Set dz/dx equal to zero, and solve for x: $x = 4$. Then use the constraint equation to solve for y: $y = 2$.

11

PRINCIPLES OF PROBABILITY

KEY TERMS

combinations the number of combinations of n objects taken j at a time is the number of ways of selecting j objects from the group of n objects, when the order in which the objects are selected does not matter

conditional probability the probability that a particular event will occur, given that another event has occurred

independent events two or more events that do not affect each other

This chapter will investigate the principles of **probability** that have applications in fields such as game theory (Chapter 13), inventory theory (Chapter 14), queuing theory (Chapter 15), and decision theory (Chapter 16). Probability is also crucial in the development of statistical inference. We will not discuss that topic in this book, but it is covered in *Business Statistics* (Douglas Downing and Jeffrey Clark, Barron's Educational Series, Inc., 1985), which also includes a more detailed treatment of probability.

We will start by investigating the probabilities associated with easy-to-picture random phenomena involving games, such as cards, dice, and coin tossing. In these cases the probabilities can be determined by analyzing the nature of the process involved, and we have an intuitive understanding of these processes. Therefore, studying these processes provides a good way of learning the principles of probability. In applied problems, matters become more complicated because the probabilities usually cannot be derived by analyzing the situation. Then the probabilities must be estimated with statistical inference by examining past frequencies of occurrence, or they must be determined by subjective estimates.

PROBABILITY OF AN EVENT

Example: Rolling a Sum of 7

PROBLEM   If we roll two dice, what is the probability that the sum of the numbers that appear will be equal to 7?

SOLUTION   In this situation we can make a list of all of the possible **outcomes**. There are six possible results for the first die, and each of these possibilities can be matched with any of the six possibilities for the second die. Therefore, there are $6 \times 6 = 36$ possible results for tossing the dice. We can make a list of all of them (listing the number that appears on the first die first):

$$
\begin{array}{cccccc}
(1,1) & (1,2) & (1,3) & (1,4) & (1,5) & (1,6) \\
(2,1) & (2,2) & (2,3) & (2,4) & (2,5) & (2,6) \\
(3,1) & (3,2) & (3,3) & (3,4) & (3,5) & (3,6) \\
(4,1) & (4,2) & (4,3) & (4,4) & (4,5) & (4,6) \\
(5,1) & (5,2) & (5,3) & (5,4) & (5,5) & (5,6) \\
(6,1) & (6,2) & (6,3) & (6,4) & (6,5) & (6,6)
\end{array}
$$

Each of the possible outcomes is equally likely, so the probability of any individual outcome is 1/36. For example, the probability of rolling (6, 1) is equal to 1/36. The sum will be 7 if we roll (6, 1) but there are other ways of obtaining a 7. If we look closely at the table, we can see that altogether there are six ways of obtaining a sum of 7:

$$
\begin{array}{cccccc}
(6,1) & (5,2) & (4,3) & (3,4) & (2,5) & (1,6)
\end{array}
$$

The probability of rolling 7 is thus $6/36 = 1/6$.

In general, suppose that there are S possible outcomes for an experiment, which are all equally likely. Suppose that A represents an **event**. Let $N(A)$ represent the number of outcomes where event A occurs. Then the probability that event A will occur is equal to $N(A)/S$. This is symbolized as:

$$
\text{Pr}(A) = \frac{N(A)}{S}
$$

where $\text{Pr}(A)$ is read as "the probability of A."

In our example, A represents the event "7 appears as the sum on the two dice." There are six outcomes where A occurs, so $N(A) = 6$. There are $S = 36$ possible outcomes, so $\text{Pr}(A) = 6/36$.

Example: Rolling Doubles

What is the probability of rolling doubles?
There are six outcomes with doubles:

$$(1, 1) \quad (2, 2) \quad (3, 3) \quad (4, 4) \quad (5, 5) \quad (6, 6)$$

so the probability of rolling doubles is $6/36 = 1/6$.

Example: Rolling a Number Greater than or Equal to 9

What is the probability of rolling a number greater than or equal to 9?
There are 10 outcomes that correspond to this event:

			(3, 6)
		(4, 5)	(4, 6)
	(5, 4)	(5, 5)	(5, 6)
(6, 3)	(6, 4)	(6, 5)	(6, 6)

so the probability is $10/36 = 5/18$.

Example: Rolling 12

What is the probability of rolling 12?
There is only one outcome that corresponds to this event: (6, 6), so the probability is $1/36$. Note that the probability of rolling 12 is much less than the probability of rolling 7.

Example: Not Rolling 7

What is the probability of *not* rolling 7?
If we count all of the outcomes where the result is not 7, we find a total of 30. Therefore, the probability of not rolling 7 is equal to $30/36 = 5/6$.

There is a shorter way to find this result. We already found that the probability of rolling 7 was equal to $1/6$. Since we must either roll 7 or not roll 7, it follows that the probability of not rolling 7 must be 1 minus the probability of rolling 7:

$$\begin{aligned} \text{Pr(not rolling 7)} &= 1 - \text{Pr(rolling 7)} \\ &= 1 - 1/6 \\ &= 5/6 \end{aligned}$$

In general, where A is any event, the probability that A will not occur is equal to 1 minus the probability that A will occur:

$$\text{Pr(not } A) = 1 - \text{Pr}(A)$$

For example, if there is a 15 percent chance that a machine will jam when it is operated, then there is an 85 percent chance that the machine will not jam.

PROBABILITY OF *A* OR *B*

Example: Rolling 7 or 11

If we roll two dice, what is the probability that we will roll 7 or 11?

We know that Pr(rolling 7) = 6/36. There are two outcomes with a result of 11, so we find that Pr(rolling 11) = 2/36. Since there are eight outcomes where the result is either 7 or 11, we find that

$$Pr[(\text{rolling } 7) \text{ or } (\text{rolling } 11)] = 8/36$$

Note that the probability of rolling 7 or 11 is equal to the sum of the probabilities of these two events:

$$Pr[(\text{rolling } 7) \text{ or } (\text{rolling } 11)] = Pr(\text{rolling } 7) + Pr(\text{rolling } 11)$$

We might be tempted to state a general rule allowing us to add probabilities. However, we have to be careful. For example, here is incorrect reasoning: "Toss a coin twice. Since the probability of getting a head on the first toss is 1/2 and the probability of getting a head on the second toss is 1/2, the probability of getting a head on either the first toss or the second toss is equal to 1/2 + 1/2 = 1." Obviously, that is not the case. We need to determine when it is appropriate to add probabilities, and when it is not. Here is another example.

Example: Rolling Doubles or a Number Greater than or Equal to 9

If we roll two dice, what is the probability of rolling either doubles or a number greater than or equal to 9?

```
(1, 1)   (1, 2)   (1, 3)   (1, 4)   (1, 5)   (1, 6)
(2, 1)   (2, 2)   (2, 3)   (2, 4)   (2, 5)   (2, 6)
(3, 1)   (3, 2)   (3, 3)   (3, 4)   (3, 5)   (3, 6)
(4, 1)   (4, 2)   (4, 3)   (4, 4)   (4, 5)   (4, 6)
(5, 1)   (5, 2)   (5, 3)   (5, 4)   (5, 5)   (5, 6)
(6, 1)   (6, 2)   (6, 3)   (6, 4)   (6, 5)   (6, 6)
```

A line has been drawn around all of the outcomes with doubles (there are six of those outcomes). Likewise, all of the outcomes where the result is greater than or equal to 9 have been enclosed by a line (there are 10 outcomes). However, we can see that there are not 6 + 10 = 16 outcomes with doubles or 9 or greater. Therefore,

$$Pr[(\text{doubles}) \text{ or } (9 \text{ or greater})] \text{ does not equal}$$
$$Pr(\text{doubles}) + Pr(9 \text{ or greater})$$

Two of the outcomes, (5, 5) and (6, 6), represent both doubles and numbers greater than 9. These outcomes will be double-counted if we add 6 + 10. Therefore, we cannot simply add the probabilities of two events if some of the possible outcomes occur in both events.

We will say that two events are **disjoint events**, or **mutually exclusive events**, if both cannot occur at the same time. This means that there are no outcomes that correspond to both events. For example, the event of rolling 7 on the dice and the event of rolling 11 are disjoint events. There is no way for both to happen at the same time. We can now state a probability addition rule:

If _A_ and _B_ are two disjoint events, then:

$$Pr(A \text{ or } B) = Pr(A) + Pr(B)$$

(Mathematically, "_A_ or _B_" is called "_A_ union _B_," symbolized as $A \cup B$.)

For example, if there is a 30 percent chance that it will be raining at 3 P.M. tomorrow, and a 40 percent chance that it will be cloudy with no rain at that time, then there is a 70 percent chance that it will be either rainy or cloudy with no rain.

However, if _A_ and _B_ are not disjoint, then we cannot simply add the probabilities, because of the double-counting problem. Here is how to eliminate that problem. To find the probability of rolling doubles or 9 or greater, we will first add the two probabilities, but then, since this double-counts the outcomes that correspond to both events, we will subtract the probability of both occurring:

Pr[(doubles) or (9 or greater)]
 = Pr(doubles) + Pr(9 or greater) − Pr[(doubles) AND (9 or greater)]
   6/36 + 10/36 −   2/36
 = 14/36

We already found this to be the correct result, since we counted 14 outcomes with either doubles or a result greater than or equal to 9.

In general, for any two events _A_ and _B_:

$$Pr(A \text{ or } B) = Pr(A) + Pr(B) - Pr(A \text{ and } B)$$

PROBABILITY OF _A_ AND _B_

Example: Rolling an Even Number on Both Dice

If we roll two dice, what is the probability that we will roll an even number on both dice?

Let *A* be the event of rolling an even number on the first die, and *B* be the event of rolling an even number on the second die. We would like to find the probability that both *A* and *B* will occur.

To find the probability that *A* will occur, we list the six possible outcomes for the first die:

$$(1) \quad (2) \quad (3) \quad (4) \quad (5) \quad (6)$$

Three of these correspond to even numbers: (2), (4), and (6). Therefore,

$$Pr(\text{even number on first die}) = Pr(A) = 3/6 = 1/2$$

By the same reasoning, the probability of rolling an even number on the second die is also 1/2: $Pr(B) = 1/2$.

All of the outcomes where both numbers are even are circled below:

$$(1, 1) \quad (1, 2) \quad (1, 3) \quad (1, 4) \quad (1, 5) \quad (1, 6)$$
$$(2, 1) \quad \boxed{(2, 2)} \quad (2, 3) \quad \boxed{(2, 4)} \quad (2, 5) \quad \boxed{(2, 6)}$$
$$(3, 1) \quad (3, 2) \quad (3, 3) \quad (3, 4) \quad (3, 5) \quad (3, 6)$$
$$(4, 1) \quad \boxed{(4, 2)} \quad (4, 3) \quad \boxed{(4, 4)} \quad (4, 5) \quad \boxed{(4, 6)}$$
$$(5, 1) \quad (5, 2) \quad (5, 3) \quad (5, 4) \quad (5, 5) \quad (5, 6)$$
$$(6, 1) \quad \boxed{(6, 2)} \quad (6, 3) \quad \boxed{(6, 4)} \quad (6, 5) \quad \boxed{(6, 6)}$$

We can count nine outcomes where both numbers are even, so

$$Pr(A \text{ and } B) = 9/36 = 1/4$$

Note that $1/4 = 1/2 \times 1/2$. We might be tempted to think that it is possible to multiply two probabilities when we are looking for the probability that two events will both occur. That works in some cases, but again it does not work all the time. We need to specify when it does work.

Example: Rolling Doubles and a Number Greater than or Equal to 9

What is the probability of rolling a number greater than or equal to 9 and doubles?

We have found that

$$Pr(9 \text{ or greater}) = 10/36$$
$$Pr(\text{doubles}) = 6/36$$

The outcomes with both doubles and 9 or greater are circled below:

(1, 1)	(1, 2)	(1, 3)	(1, 4)	(1, 5)	(1, 6)
(2, 1)	(2, 2)	(2, 3)	(2, 4)	(2, 5)	(2, 6)
(3, 1)	(3, 2)	(3, 3)	(3, 4)	(3, 5)	(3, 6)
(4, 1)	(4, 2)	(4, 3)	(4, 4)	(4, 5)	(4, 6)
(5, 1)	(5, 2)	(5, 3)	(5, 4)	⟨(5, 5)⟩	(5, 6)
(6, 1)	(6, 2)	(6, 3)	(6, 4)	(6, 5)	⟨(6, 6)⟩

We can see that

$$\Pr[(\text{doubles}) \text{ AND } (9 \text{ or greater})] = 2/36$$

Since $10/36 \times 6/36 = 60/1{,}296 = .0463$, which does not equal $2/36 = .0556$, we can see that in this case we cannot simply multiply the two probabilities to find the probability that both events will occur.

Here is the difference between the two cases. The chance of rolling an even number on the second die is not affected by whether or not we rolled an even number on the first die. These two events are said to be **independent events**. When two events are independent, the probability that both will occur is equal to the product of their separate probabilities. However, the event of rolling doubles is not independent from the event of rolling a number greater than or equal to 9, since the probability of rolling doubles is changed if it is known that the number is greater than or equal to 9.

In general, if *A* and *B* are two independent events, then:

$$\Pr(A \text{ and } B) = \Pr(A) \times \Pr(B)$$

(Mathematically, "*A* and *B*" is called "*A* intersect *B*," which is symbolized as $A \cap B$.)

Example: Backup Information System

Suppose that your company maintains a backup information system in a separate building in case the primary system fails. Suppose you have estimated that the probability that the primary system will fail is equal to .01, and the probability that the backup system will fail is equal to .05. Also, suppose you have determined that these two events are independent: the failure of the primary system will have no affect on whether the backup system fails, and vice versa. Then the probability that both will fail is equal to .01 × .05 = .0005. The probability that both will fail is much smaller than the probability that either one individually will fail.

However, this result works only if the backup system truly is independent from the primary system. Suppose that the two systems are in the same building. Then the two events would not be independent. An event that damages the building could damage both systems. The probability of both systems failing is higher than it would be if they were independent.

YOU SHOULD REMEMBER

Two events are disjoint if they cannot both occur. If A and B are disjoint events, then

$$Pr(A \text{ or } B) = Pr(A) + Pr(B)$$

Two events are independent if they have no effect on each other, so that the occurrence of one of the events does not change the probability that the other event will occur. If A and B are independent events, then

$$Pr(A \text{ and } B) = Pr(A) \times Pr(B)$$

In general, if A and B are any two events, then:

$$Pr(A \text{ or } B) = Pr(A) + Pr(B) - Pr(A \text{ and } B)$$

CONDITIONAL PROBABILITY

If the occurrence of one event changes the likelihood that another event will occur, then the two events are not independent. For example, suppose that someone rolled two dice but did not let you see the results. If you knew nothing about the result, you would still know that the probability of rolling doubles is 1/6. If you were told that the result was greater than or equal to 9, but nothing else, you could figure that the probability of rolling doubles is now 2/10. You can arrive at this conclusion by noting that there are 10 outcomes with a result greater than or equal to 9:

			(3, 6)
		(4, 5)	(4, 6)
	(5, 4)	(5, 5)	(5, 6)
(6, 3)	(6, 4)	(6, 5)	(6, 6)

Of these 10 outcomes, two of them have doubles: (5, 5) and (6, 6).

This is an example of a **conditional probability**. Sometimes, the fact that one event has occurred will change the probability that another event will occur. In that case, you should revise your estimate of the probability to take into account the information about the event that has occurred.

The conditional probability that event A will occur, given that event B has occurred, is written as $\Pr(A \mid B)$. The vertical line is read as "given that."

Here is the formula for calculating conditional probabilities:

$$\Pr(A \mid B) = \frac{\Pr(A \text{ and } B)}{\Pr(B)}$$

Example: Drawing a King, Given That a Red Face Card Is Drawn

Suppose that one card is drawn at random from a deck of 52 cards. Let K be the event of drawing a king, and F be the event of drawing a red face card. Then

$$\Pr(K) = 4/52 = 1/13, \qquad \Pr(F) = 6/52, \qquad \Pr(K \text{ and } F) = 2/52$$

Here is the formula for the conditional probability that a king will be drawn, given that a red face card is drawn:

$$\Pr(K \mid F) = \frac{\Pr(K \text{ and } F)}{\Pr(F)} = \frac{2/52}{6/52} = 2/6 = 1/3$$

Example: Drawing a King, Given That a Red Card Is Drawn

Let R be the event of drawing a red card. Then

$$\Pr(R) = 26/52, \qquad \Pr(K \text{ and } R) = 2/52$$

$$\Pr(K \mid R) = \frac{\Pr(K \text{ and } R)}{\Pr(R)} = \frac{2/52}{26/52} = 2/26 = 1/13$$

Note that the probability of drawing a king, given that a red card was drawn, is the same as the unconditional probability of drawing a king. This result is true because the event of drawing a king is independent from the event of drawing a red card. In general, if A and B are two independent events, then:

$$\Pr(A \mid B) = \Pr(A)$$

Example: Factory Location

Suppose that a company is investigating 15 cities as possible sites for a new factory. As far as you can tell, the company is beginning the investigation with an open mind, so that each city is equally likely to be chosen. Therefore, the probability that your city will be chosen is 1/15. Let *A* represent the event that your city is chosen; then $\Pr(A) = 1/15$. Suppose you subsequently learn that the company has narrowed its choices to one of the six cities in your state. Let *B* be the event that the company chooses a city in your state; then $\Pr(B) = 6/15$.

Here is the formula for the conditional probability that your city will be chosen, given that a city in your state is chosen:

$$\Pr(A \mid B) = \frac{\Pr(A \text{ and } B)}{\Pr(B)} = \frac{1/15}{6/15} = 1/6$$

Since event *A* is part of event *B*, it follows that $\Pr(A \text{ and } B) = \Pr(A)$. Therefore, the probability that your city will be chosen, given that the factory will be located in your state, is equal to 1/6.

In general, if all of the outcomes in event *A* are included in event *B* (technically, *A* is said to be a *subset* of *B*), then:

$$\Pr(A \mid B) = \frac{\Pr(A)}{\Pr(B)}$$

On the other hand, if you learn that the choice for the new factory is located outside your state, then the probability that your city will be chosen is zero. Let *C* represent the event that the choice will be outside your state. Then *A* and *C* are clearly disjoint events, and $\Pr(A \mid C) = 0$.

Example: Heart Disease

Suppose you learned that the probability that a person will die form heart disease is .004. You are concerned that an acquaintance will succumb to heart disease. A probability of .004 does not give you nearly as much information as a conditional probability would. It would help to obtain information on the age, weight, and life-style of the person in whom you are interested. Then, if you knew the conditional probability of dying from heart disease for a person with these characteristics, you would have a much better idea as to whether your acquaintance was in jeopardy.

MULTIPLICATION PRINCIPLE

In situations where each outcome is equally likely, the probability of any event equals the number of outcomes in that event divided by the total number of possible outcomes. In the case of tossing two dice, it was easy to list all of the possible outcomes and then count the number of outcomes corresponding to any particular event. In many situations, however, the number of possible outcomes is far too large to list them all. What we need is a way of counting the number of outcomes without having to list them all. We will now cover several situations where there are formulas for the number of possibilities.

If we toss a coin, there are two possible outcomes (H, T). If we toss a coin twice, there are $2 \times 2 =$ four possible outcomes (HH, HT, TH, TT). For three tosses, there are $2 \times 2 \times 2 =$ eight possible outcomes (HHH, HHT, HTH, HTT, THH, THT, TTH, TTT). If the coin is tossed n times, the total number of possible outcomes is 2^n. You can see why the listing method is very cumbersome. Even if there were only 10 tosses, the number of possible outcomes would be $2^{10} = 1,024$.

In general, suppose that an experiment has m possible results, and that the experiment will be repeated n times. Assume that each trial is independent of the others (that is, no trial has any effect on the other trials). Then there are m^n possible outcomes. (This principle is called the **multiplication principle**.) For example, if we toss a set of dice, there are $m = 6$ possible results for each trial. Therefore, if we toss n dice, there are 6^n possible outcomes.

Example: Four-Letter Words

How many four-letter words are possible?
There are 26 possible choices for each letter, and four letters that will be chosen for each word, so there are $26^4 = 456,976$ possible four-letter words.

Example: License Plates

Suppose that the license plates in a particular state consist of three letters followed by three digits. How many possible license plates are there?
There are $26^3 = 17,576$ possible ways of choosing the three letters from the 26 possible letters, and $10^3 = 1,000$ ways of choosing the three digits from the 10 possible digits. Each possible way of selecting the letters can be matched with each possible way of selecting the digits, so there are $17,576 \times 1,000 = 17,576,000$ total ways of selecting the license plates.

Example: Clothing Store

A store sells coats that are available in four colors, three sizes, and six styles. If it wants to keep an inventory of all possible coats, how many items must it keep on hand?

$$4 \times 3 \times 6 = 72 \text{ items}$$

PERMUTATIONS

Example: Baseball Lineups

PROBLEM   An indecisive baseball manager decides to try all possible batting orders before deciding which order is the best. How many different orders are there? (Assume that there are only nine players, with no substitutes or designated hitters.)

SOLUTION   Clearly there are nine choices for the lead-off hitter. You might be tempted to think there will be 9^9 total possibilities, since nine batting positions must be chosen. However, the rules of baseball state firmly that no player may bat at more than one position in the nine-player order. Therefore, there are only eight choices for the second hitter, since the first hitter cannot bat again. There are only seven choices for the third batter, since the first two batters are no longer eligible. Finally, after the first eight positions have been filled, there is only one choice left for the final position. The total number of possible lineups is equal to

$$9 \times 8 \times 7 \times 6 \times 5 \times 4 \times 3 \times 2 \times 1 = 362,880$$

As you can see, the players will have retired long before the manager can test every possible order.

In general, suppose that we need to know the number of possible ways of putting n distinct objects in order. There are n choices for the first object, $n - 1$ choices for the second object, and so on. The total number of possibilities is:

$$n \times (n - 1) \times (n - 2) \times \cdots \times 3 \times 2 \times 1$$

This quantity appears frequently in probability formulas, so it is given a special name: the **factorial** of the number n. The factorial of a number is equal to the product of all of the whole numbers from 1 up to the number in question. You may be surprised at how quickly the results of the factorial function become very large. Perhaps to indicated this surprise, the factorial function is symbolized by an exclamation mark (!):

$$n! = n \times (n-1) \times (n-2) \times \cdots \times 3 \times 2 \times 1$$

Here are some examples:

$$1! = 1 \qquad 2! = 2 \qquad 3! = 3 \times 2 \times 1 = 6 \qquad 4! = 4 \times 3 \times 2 \times 1 = 24$$

$$5! = 120 \qquad 6! = 720$$

The exclamation mark is read as the word **factorial**. For example, "6!" is read as "six factorial," not "six!"

Here is an example that shows how rapidly the results of the factorial function become very large:

$$69! = 1.711 \times 10^{98}$$

The number of 10^{98} stands for the number consisting of a 1 followed by 98 zeros. A number expressed in this form is said to be written in *scientific notation* or *exponential notation*. It is much easier to write large numbers in scientific notation than in the long way.

There is one special rule for factorials: the factorial of zero is defined to be 1: $0! = 1$. This rule is necessary for the formulas to work. The intuition for this rule is that there is only one way to put zero objects in order.

Example: Shuffling a Deck of Cards

How many different ways are there of shuffling a deck of 52 cards?

There are 52 possibilities for the top card, 51 possibilities for the second card, and so on, so that altogether there are $52! = 8.07 \times 10^{67}$ ways of shuffling the deck.

Example: Putting Letter Blocks in Order

Suppose that we have 26 wooden blocks, each marked with a distinct letter of the alphabet. How many different ways can these blocks be put in order?

There are $26! = 4.033 \times 10^{26}$ different ways.

Now suppose that we randomly choose five of the letter blocks and set them on the table in the order that we choose them to see whether they form a word. How many possible ways are there of doing this?

There are 26 possibilities for the first block, 25 blocks left as possible choices for the second block, and so on. The total number of ways of making the choice is equal to

$$26 \times 25 \times 24 \times 23 \times 22 = 7,893,600$$

It would help to have a way of writing this expression using factorial notation. If we write 26!, we mean the product of all of the whole numbers from 26 down to 1. However, we want only to represent the product of the numbers from 26 to 22. We can cancel out all of the numbers from 21 to 1 by dividing 26! by 21!:

$$\frac{26!}{21!} = \frac{26 \times 25 \times 24 \times 23 \times 22 \times 21 \times 20 \times 19 \times 18 \times 17 \times 16 \times 15 \times 14 \times 13 \times 12 \times 11 \times 10 \times 9 \times 8 \times 7 \times 6 \times 5 \times 4 \times 3 \times 2 \times 1}{21 \times 20 \times 19 \times 18 \times 17 \times 16 \times 15 \times 14 \times 13 \times 12 \times 11 \times 10 \times 9 \times 8 \times 7 \times 6 \times 5 \times 4 \times 3 \times 2 \times 1}$$

$$= 26 \times 25 \times 24 \times 23 \times 22$$

In general, suppose that we are going to select j objects without replacement from a group of n objects. Then there are

$$\frac{n!}{(n-j)!}$$

ways of selecting the objects. Each way of selecting the objects is called a **permutation** of the objects, so the formula $n!/(n-j)!$ gives the number of permutations of n things taken j at a time. The number of permutations is also symbolized by $_nP_j$. We said that the selection would be made without replacement. This means that, once an object has been selected, we do not return it to the group it came from, so it has no chance of being selected again.

COMBINATIONS

Suppose that you are in a card game in which you will be dealt a hand of five cards from a deck of 52 cards. There are 52 possibilities for the first card you will be dealt, 51 possibilities for the second card, and so on. We can consider this an example of choosing a sample of size 5 without replacement from a population of 52 cards. (Once you've been dealt a card, you can't be dealt that particular card again.) Therefore, there are

$$\frac{52!}{(52-5)!} = \frac{52!}{47!}$$

$$= 52 \times 51 \times 50 \times 49 \times 48$$
$$= 311{,}875{,}200 \text{ ways of being dealt five cards}$$

However, in many card games it does not matter in what order you are dealt your five cards. In this case the permutations formula used above counts too many possibilities. When the permutations are counted, each possible ordering of the objects is counted separately. If we don't care about the order in which the objects are selected, the number of distinct possibilities will be much less.

How many different orderings of the five cards are there? We have already discussed this problem. Since there are five cards, there are 5! = 120 different ways of arranging the cards in different orders. In fact, for *every* possible hand there are 120 different orderings. Therefore, the permutations formula result (311,875,200) counts 120 times too many hands, so we must divide by 120. Therefore:

(total number of distinct five-card hands that can be dealt from a deck of 52 cards, not counting different orderings)

$$\frac{52!/(52-5)!}{5!} =$$

$$= \frac{311,875,200}{120}$$

$$= 2,598,960$$

In general, suppose that we select j items without replacement from a group of n items, and we're interested in the total number of possible ways of making the selection, without counting each ordering separately. Then the number of possibilities is given by the formula

$$\frac{n!}{(n-j)!j!}$$

The number of arrangements without regard to order is called the number of **combinations**. The formula $n!/[(n-j)!j!]$ is said to represent the number of combinations of n things taken j at a time. Note that the number of combinations is equal to the number of permutations divided by $j!$. The formula for the number of combinations is often symbolized as

$$\binom{n}{j}$$

Note that n, the total number of objects, is written above j, the number of objects being selected, in the symbol $\binom{n}{j}$, but that does not mean this is a fraction.

The formula for the number of combinations is also symbolized by $_nC_j$.

Example: Warehouse Location

PROBLEM   Suppose that we are planning to build five new warehouses, and we are considering 18 possible cities where the warehouses could be located. If we plan to investigate every possible way of locating the warehouses, how many possibilities must we look at?

SOLUTION   We use the formula for combinations, since we will be choosing five objects from a group of 18 objects:

$$\binom{18}{5} = \frac{18!}{5! \, 13!}$$

$$= \frac{18 \times 17 \times 16 \times 15 \times 14 \times 13 \times 12 \times 11 \times 10 \times 9 \times 8 \times 7 \times 6 \times 5 \times 4 \times 3 \times 2 \times 1}{5 \times 4 \times 3 \times 2 \times 1 \times 13 \times 12 \times 11 \times 10 \times 9 \times 8 \times 7 \times 6 \times 5 \times 4 \times 3 \times 2 \times 1}$$

Many of the factors cancel:

$$\binom{18}{5} = \frac{18 \times 17 \times 16 \times 15 \times 14}{5 \times 4 \times 3 \times 2 \times 1}$$

$$= 8,568$$

By carefully noting which factors cancel, you can save yourself work while computing the number of combinations. Nevertheless, it is usually best to have a computer perform the calculations if the numbers are very large.

Example: Committee Assignment

PROBLEM   A club is planning to organize five committees. Each member will be on three committees. No member is supposed to have exactly the same committee assignments as any other member. How many choices are there for committee assignments?

SOLUTION   We use the formula for combinations, since we are choosing three objects from a group of five objects:

$$\binom{5}{3} = \frac{5!}{3! \, 2!} = \frac{5 \times 4}{2 \times 1} = 10$$

If the five committees are labeled *A, B, C, D,* and *E*, here are the 10 ways of making the choice:

ABC	ABD	ABE	ACD	ACE
ADE	BCD	BCE	BDE	CDE

Therefore, if the club has more than 10 members, it will not be possible for each member to have committee assignments distinct from those of any other member.

Example: Basic Solutions to Linear Programming Problems

PROBLEM   Suppose that we have a linear programming problem with n total variables (including slack variables) and m constraints. (Assume that $n > m$, as will always be the case if we have added slack variables.) Recall from Chapter 3 that a basic solution is a solution where the number of nonzero variables is equal to the number of constraints. How many basic solutions will there be?

SOLUTION   This question is the same as asking, How many ways are there to choose m nonzero variables from the set of n total variables? We can use the formula

$$\frac{n!}{m!(n-m)!}$$

For example, if there are $n = 6$ variables and $m = 4$ constraints, then the number of basic solutions is:

$$\frac{6!}{4!(6-4)!} = \frac{6 \times 5 \times 4 \times 3 \times 2 \times 1}{4 \times 3 \times 2 \times 1 \times 2 \times 1} = \frac{6 \times 5}{2 \times 1} = \frac{30}{2} = 15$$

Suppose that there are $m = 15$ constraints and $n = 25$ variables. Then we can calculate that the number of basic solutions is 3,268,760. You can see why it would be impracticable to check all of the basic solutions. We are fortunate to have the simplex method, which makes it unnecessary to check them all.

Example: Card Selection

If you draw five cards from a 52-card deck, what is the probability that you will draw ace, king, queen, jack, ten, all of hearts?

There is only one way of drawing this set of cards, so the probability is

$$\frac{1}{\binom{52}{5}} = \frac{1}{2,598,960} = 3.848 \times 10^{-7}$$

What is the probability of drawing ace, king, queen, jack, ten, with all five cards of the same suit?

There are four possibilities, so the probability is

$$\frac{4}{\binom{52}{5}} = \frac{4}{2,598,960} = 1.539 \times 10^{-6}$$

What is the probability of drawing three hearts and two cards that are not hearts?

There are $\binom{13}{3}$ ways of drawing the three hearts, and $\binom{39}{2}$ ways of drawing the two nonhearts. Since each possible way of drawing the hearts can be matched with each possible way of drawing the nonhearts, the total number of hands with exactly three hearts is

$$\binom{13}{3} \times \binom{39}{2}$$

Therefore, the probability is

$$\frac{\binom{13}{3} \times \binom{39}{2}}{\binom{52}{5}} = \frac{286 \times 741}{2,598,960} = .082$$

Here are four special cases of the combination formula:

$$\binom{n}{0} = \frac{n!}{0!n!} = 1$$

$$\binom{n}{1} = \frac{n!}{1!(n-1)!} = n$$

$$\binom{n}{n-1} = \frac{n!}{(n-1)!1!} = n$$

$$\binom{n}{n} = \frac{n!}{n!0!} = 1$$

YOU SHOULD REMEMBER

If an experiment has *m* possible outcomes, and it is repeated *n* times, where each trial is independent of the others, then there are m^n total possible outcomes.

The factorial of a number *n*, symbolized by *n!*, is the product of all of the whole numbers from 1 to *n*.

If *j* objects are to be selected without replacement from a group of *n* objects, then there are

$$\frac{n!}{(n-j)!}$$

ways of making the selection, if each possible ordering is counted separately. Each possible selection is called a *permutation*.

If *j* objects are to be selected without replacement from a group of *n* objects, then there are

$$\binom{n}{j} = \frac{n!}{j!(n-j)!}$$

ways of making the selection, if each possible ordering is not counted separately. Each possible selection is called a *combination*.

KNOW THE CONCEPTS

DO YOU KNOW THE BASICS?

Test your understanding of Chapter 11 by answering the following questions:

1. When should the probabilities of two events be multiplied?
2. When should the probabilities of two events be added?
3. Can two events be both independent and disjoint? (Do not consider unusual events, such as those that have zero probability of occurring or that are certain to occur.)
4. What is $\Pr(A \mid B)$ if A and B are independent?
5. What is $\Pr(A \mid B)$ if A and B are disjoint?
6. Explain the formula that gives the number of distinct ways of putting n objects in order.
7. If j objects are to be selected from a group of n objects, are there more permutations or more combinations?

TERMS FOR STUDY

combinations
conditional probability
disjoint events
event
factorial
independent events

multiplication principle
mutually exclusive events
outcome
permutations
probability

PRACTICAL APPLICATION

COMPUTATIONAL PROBLEMS

1. If you roll two dice,
   (a) what is the probability that at least one of the two numbers will be greater than or equal to 5?
   (b) what is the probability that both numbers will be greater than or equal to 5?
   (c) what is the probability that one and only one of the two numbers will be greater than or equal to 5?

2. (a) If you roll two dice, what is the probability that there will be at least one 6 among the n numbers?

   (b) If you roll n dice, what is the probability that there will be at least one 6 among the n numbers?

3. If you fly on Ultra-No-Frill Airline, whose slogan is "We put excitement back into flying," there is a 10 percent chance that you will lose your luggage and a 30 percent chance that your flight will arrive late. Assume that these two events are independent.

   (a) What is the probability that you will both arrive late and lose your luggage?

   (b) What is the probability that you will arrive late or lose your luggage, or both?

   (c) What is the probability that you will either arrive late or lose your luggage, but not both?

4. Suppose that you are managing a data processing system where there is a 6 percent chance that the data in your data bank will be lost because of some unforeseen event. Therefore, you maintain several copies of your data in separate locations. You will be all right as long as the data in at least one of the data banks survive, but it would be catastrophic if all of the banks failed at the same time. How many data banks will you need in order to make sure that the probability of all data banks failing is less than 1/10 of 1 percent (.001)?

5. Suppose that you are drawing a card from a standard 52-card deck.

   (a) What is the conditional probability of drawing a 5, given that the card drawn is not a face card?

   (b) What is the conditional probability of drawing a diamond, given that a red card is drawn?

   (c) What is the conditional probability of drawing a red card, given that a diamond is drawn?

   (d) What is the conditional probability of drawing a club, given that a red card is drawn?

   (e) What is the conditional probability of drawing a black card, given that a face card is drawn?

6. If you draw two cards from a standard 52-card deck, what is the probability that you will draw two 5's, given the fact that the first card you draw is a 5?

7. Suppose that the probability of an earthquake is .005, and the probability of a fire, given that an earthquake occurs, is .20. What is the probability that there will be both an earthquake and a fire?

8. Suppose that five people (Anderson, Bertoli, Clark, Diaz, and Eisenberg) are at a meeting. Two of them will be selected to give presentations.

(a) Give a formula showing the number of combinations of possible ways of selecting the two people.

(b) List all of the combinations. (Each person can be identified by the first letter of the name.)

(c) Give a formula showing the number of permutations for the number of possible ways of selecting the two people.

(e) List all of the permutations.

9. Suppose that your company has 10 locations, and you would like each location to be directly connected to every other location. How many connections are needed?

10. A combination lock consists of three numbers from 1 to 30. What is the probability that you could randomly guess the combination?

ANSWERS

KNOW THE CONCEPTS

1. If you are looking for the probability that both of two independent events will occur.

2. If you are looking for the probability that either one of two disjoint events will occur.

3. No. If they are disjoint, then they must have some effect on each other, because the occurrence of one prevents the occurrence of the other.

4. $\Pr(A)$.

5. Zero.

6. There are $n!$ (n factorial) ways, since there are n choices for the first object, $n - 1$ choices for the second object, and so on.

7. There are more permutations, since the number of permutations counts each possible ordering of the objects separately.

PRACTICAL APPLICATION

1. Let A be the event of getting a 5 or greater on the first die, and B be the event of getting a 5 or greater on the second die. Then $\Pr(A) = \Pr(B) = 1/3$, and A and B are independent. Solve (b) first.

    (b) $\Pr(A \text{ and } B) = 1/3 \times 1/3 = 1/9$

    (a) $\Pr(A \text{ or } B) = 1/3 + 1/3 - 1/9 = 5/9$

    (c) $\Pr(A \text{ or } B) - \Pr(A \text{ and } B) = 5/9 - 1/9 = 4/9$

2. (a) Let A be the event of not getting a 6 on the first die, and B be the event of not getting a 6 on the second die. Then $\Pr(A) = \Pr(B) = $

5/6, and A and B are independent. The probability of getting at least one 6 is equal to

$$1 - [\Pr(A \text{ and } B)] = 1 - \Pr(A) \times \Pr(B) = 11/36$$

(b) $1 - (5/6)^n$

3. Let A be the event of losing the luggage, and B be the event of arriving late.
   (a) $\Pr(A \text{ and } B) = \Pr(A) \times \Pr(B) = .10 \times .30 = .03$
   (b) $\Pr(A \text{ and } B) = \Pr(A) + \Pr(B) - \Pr(A \text{ and } B) = .37$
   (c) $\Pr(A \text{ or } B) - \Pr(A \text{ and } B) = .34$

4. If each data bank is independent, the probability that they will all fail is $.06^n$, where n is the number of data banks. You will need three data banks, since $.06^3 = .000216$, which is less than .001.

5. (a) 1/10
   (b) 1/2
   (c) 1
   (d) 0
   (e) 1/2 (These two events are independent.)

6. 3/51

7. $.005 \times .2 = .001$

8. (a) $\binom{5}{2} = \dfrac{5!}{3! \, 2!} = \dfrac{5 \times 4}{2 \times 1} = 10$

   (b) | AB | BC | CD | DE |
       |----|----|----|----|
       | AC | BD | CE | |
       | AD | BE | | |
       | AE | | | |

   (c) $\dfrac{5!}{3!} = 5 \times 4 = 20$

   (d) | — | BA | CA | DA | EA |
       |----|----|----|----|----|
       | AB | — | CB | DB | EB |
       | AC | BC | — | DC | EC |
       | AD | BD | CD | — | ED |
       | AE | BE | CE | DE | — |

9. $\binom{10}{2} = \dfrac{10 \times 9}{2 \times 1} = 45$

10. $1/30^3 = 1/27{,}000$

12

RANDOM VARIABLES

It often happens in probability that the events in which we're interested involve counting something or measuring something. For example, at times we've been interested in the numbers that appear on a pair of dice or the number of times that a head appears when we toss a coin several times. In more practical situations, random variables include:

- the number of customers that arrive at a store in an hour

- the amount of time it takes to provide service to a customer

- the rate of return on a portfolio of financial assets

Example: The Number That Appears When Two Dice Are Rolled

Suppose that we let X represent the sum of the numbers that appear when two dice are tossed. We would like a list of the probabilities for all of the possible values for X. Here is a list showing the 36 possible outcomes:

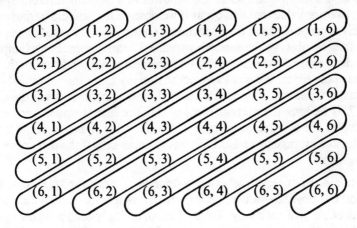

We can calculate the probability for each of the possible values of X:

$$\Pr(X = 2) = 1/36 \qquad \Pr(X = 8) \ = 5/36$$
$$\Pr(X = 3) = 2/36 \qquad \Pr(X = 9) \ = 4/36$$
$$\Pr(X = 4) = 3/36 \qquad \Pr(X = 10) = 3/36$$
$$\Pr(X = 5) = 4/36 \qquad \Pr(X = 11) = 2/36$$
$$\Pr(X = 6) = 5/36 \qquad \Pr(X = 12) = 1/36$$
$$\Pr(X = 7) = 6/36$$

The first line in the left-hand column is read as "The probability that X will equal 2 is 1/36."

X is called a **discrete random variable**. A random variable is a variable whose value depends on the outcome of some type of random process; it is customary to use capital letters to represent random variables. In this case the value of X is determined by the outcome of the toss of the dice. A discrete random variable is a random variable for which all of the possible values can be listed. Later, we will discuss continuous random variables, for which it is not possible to make a list of the possible values.

The behavior of a discrete random variable can be characterized by listing the probability for each possible value. The sum of the probabilities for all of the possible values must be equal to 1, since the random variable must take one of its possible values. However, the result of the random variable on any particular observation is unpredictable.

THE EXPECTATION OF A RANDOM VARIABLE

Often we would like to summarize the behavior of a random variable by calculating the average value that will occur if we observe the random variable many times. This average is called the **expectation** or the **expected value** or the **mean**. Suppose that we observe the random variable X many times. For example, we toss two dice, write down the result, toss the dice again, and repeat the same procedure many times. We would expect that many times the result will be less than 7, many times it will be greater than 7, and sometimes it will be exactly equal to 7. If we took the average of all of those results, it would seem reasonable to expect the average to be near 7. On the other hand, it would be very unlikely for the average to be 12. That would occur only if the dice came up 12 every single roll.

To calculate the expected value for a discrete random variable, we take the average of the possible values, giving greater weight to values that have a greater probability of occurring. To do this, we multiply each possible value by its probability of occurrence, and then add. We will use $E(X)$ to symbolize the expectation of X. Suppose that $x_1, x_2, \ldots, x_n$ are the possible values for X. Then:

$$E(X) = x_1 \text{Pr}(X = x_1) + x_2 \text{Pr}(X = x_2) + \cdots + x_n \text{Pr}(X = x_n)$$

The expected value (or mean) is also symbolized by the Greek letter mu: μ.

Here is a table showing the calculation of the expected value when X represents the sum of the numbers that appear when two dice are tossed:

Probability	Value	Probability Times Value
1/36	2	2/36
2/36	3	6/36
3/36	4	12/36
4/36	5	20/36
5/36	6	30/36
6/36	7	42/36
5/36	8	40/36
4/36	9	36/36
3/36	10	30/36
2/36	11	22/36
1/36	12	12/36
Total: 1		252/36

$$E(X) = \frac{252}{36} = 7$$

Example: Coin Tossing

Toss a coin 3 times, and let Y represent the number of heads that appear. Here are the probabilities:

$$\Pr(Y = 0) = 1/8$$
$$\Pr(Y = 1) = 3/8$$
$$\Pr(Y = 2) = 3/8$$
$$\Pr(Y = 3) = 1/8$$

All the probabilities add up to 1, as they must. Calculate the expectation:

$$E(Y) = 0 \times 1/8 + 1 \times 3/8 + 2 \times 3/8 + 3 \times 1/8$$
$$= 12/8$$
$$= 1.5$$

Note that the expectation for a random variable does not have to be one of the possible values for that random variable.

When the probabilities for a random variable are symmetric about a central value, as they are in the two preceding examples with dice and coins, it is intuitively clear that the expected value should be that central value. Here is a case where the probabilities are not symmetric.

Example: Lottery

Suppose that you enter a lottery where a ticket costs \$1. You choose six numbers from 1 to 48. Six numbers will be randomly drawn; if you choose the correct ones, you win \$1 million; otherwise you simply lose the \$1 ticket cost. There are

$$\binom{48}{6} = \frac{48!}{6! \; 42!} = 12{,}271{,}512$$

ways that the numbers can be selected, so the probability of winning is $1/12{,}271{,}512 = 8.149 \times 10^{-8}$.

Let Z represent your profit from buying the ticket. Then:

$$\Pr(Z = -1) \qquad = .99999992$$
$$\Pr(Z = 1{,}000{,}000) = .00000008$$

The expected value is $E(Z) = -0.9185$. Therefore, if you play the game every week for 100 weeks, your expected loss is \$91.85.

Here are two properties of expectations:
First, if x and Y are two random variables, then

$$E(X + Y) = E(X) + E(Y)$$

For example, toss two dice, letting X be the number that appears on the first die, Y be the number that appears on the second die, and Z be the sum of the two numbers. Then

$$E(X) = 3.5 \quad \text{and} \quad E(Y) = 3.5$$

$Z = X + y$, so

$$E(Z) = E(X) + E(Y) = 7$$

Second, if X is a random variable and c is a constant (not a random variable), then

$$E(cX) = cE(X)$$

For example, toss two dice, and let X be the sum of the two numbers. Let Z be the average of the two numbers:

$$Z = \frac{1}{2}X$$

Then $E(X) = 7$. Using the formula, with $c = 1/2$, you find $E(Z) = 3.5$.

YOU SHOULD REMEMBER

A discrete random variable can be characterized by listing the probabilities that it takes on all of its possible values. However, any single observation of the random variable is unpredictable.

The expectation (also called the *expected value*, *mean*, or *weighted average*) of a random variable is the average value that would appear if the random variable was observed many times. If $x_1, x_2, \ldots, x_n$ are the possible values for the discrete random variable X, then the expectation [symbolized as $E(X)$ or μ] is found from the formula

$$E(X) = x_1\Pr(X = x_1) + x_2\Pr(X = x_2) + \cdots + x_n\Pr(X = x_n)$$

THE VARIANCE OF A RANDOM VARIABLE

Knowing the expectation for a random variable tells you what value you would expect to see, on average, when that random variable is observed. However, it doesn't tell how unpredictable the random variable is. Consider these two random variables, representing the profits from different investments:

U: profit from a relatively safe investment

$\Pr(U = 0)\quad = .30$

$\Pr(U = 100) = .40$

$\Pr(U = 200) = .30$

$E(U) = 0 \times .30 + 100 \times .40 + 200 \times .30 = 100$

V: profit from a risky investment

$\Pr(V = 0)\qquad\qquad = .95$

$\Pr(V = 2{,}000)\qquad\quad = .05$

$E(V) = 0 \times .95 + 2{,}000 \times .05 = 100$

Both U and V have the same expectation, but they are clearly quite different. The value of U is much more likely to be near its expected value of 100. To measure the degree of unpredictability of a random variable, we need to investigate the average distance between the value of the random variable and its expected value. If, on average, the value of the random variable is close to its expected value, the random variable is not very unpredictable. It turns out to be most convenient to measure the expected value of the square of the distance from the random variable to its mean. This quantity is called the **variance** of the random variable. Here are the steps to calculate the variance of a random variable (after you have already calculated the expected value):

1. Calculate the distance between each possible value and the expected value.

2. Square that distance.

3. Multiply the squared distance by the probability that the random variable will take on that value.

4. Add the products obtained in step 3.

Remember that the mean was found by taking a weighted average, where each possible value was multiplied by its probability of occurrence. Now we are taking a weighted average for the square of the distance from the mean. We will use the notation $\text{Var}(X)$ to represent the variance of X. If $x_1, x_2, \ldots, x_n$ are the possible values, we can write the formula for the variance:

$$\mathrm{Var}(X) = [x_1 - E(X)]^2 \mathrm{Pr}(X = x_1) + [x_2 - E(X)]^2 \mathrm{Pr}(X = x_2)$$
$$+ \cdots + [x_n - E(X)]^2 \mathrm{Pr}(X = x_n)$$

The square root of the variance is called the **standard deviation**. Like the variance, the standard deviation is a measure of the unpredictability of the random variable. Obviously, if the variance becomes larger, the standard deviation becomes larger. The standard deviation is often more convenient to work with than the variance, because the size of the standard deviation is more convenient. Also, the standard deviation of X is measured in the same units that X is measured in, whereas the variance is measured in units that are the squares of the units used to measure X.

The standard deviation is symbolized by the lowercase Greek letter sigma: σ. Since the variance is equal to the square of the standard deviation, the variance is often symbolized as σ^2 (read as "sigma-squared"). We can write the formula for the variance using the Greek letters sigma and mu:

$$\sigma^2 = [x_1 - \mu]^2 \mathrm{Pr}(X = x_1) + [x_2 - \mu]^2 \mathrm{Pr}(X = x_2) + \cdots + [x_n - \mu]^2 \mathrm{Pr}(X = x_n)$$

Here are the calculations for the variance for U and V:

$$\begin{aligned}
\mathrm{Var}(U) &= .30(0 - 100)^2 + .40(100 - 100)^2 + .30(100 - 200)^2 \\
&= .30 \times 10{,}000 + .40 \times 0 + .30 \times 10{,}000 \\
&= 6{,}000 \\
\sigma &= \sqrt{6{,}000} = 77.46 \\
\mathrm{Var}(V) &= .95(0 - 100)^2 + .05(2{,}000 - 100)^2 \\
&= .95 \times 10{,}000 + .05 \times 3{,}610{,}000 \\
&= 190{,}000 \\
\sigma &= \sqrt{190{,}000} = 435.89
\end{aligned}$$

It is often more convenient to calculate the variance using this formula:

$$\mathrm{Var}(X) = E(X^2) - [E(X)]^2$$

where $E(X^2)$ represents the expectation of X^2. To calculate $E(X^2)$, multiply each possible value of X^2 by its probability of occurrence, and then add all of these probabilities. In other words, you calculate the expectation of X^2 just the same as you calculate the expectation of X, except that you multiply the probabilities by the possible values of X^2, instead of the possible values of X.

You can use this formula to calculate $\mathrm{Var}(U)$ and $\mathrm{Var}(V)$:

$$\begin{aligned}
E(U^2) &= .30 \times 0^2 + .40 \times 100^2 + .30 \times 200^2 \\
&= .30 \times 0 + .40 \times 10{,}000 + .30 \times 40{,}000 \\
&= 4{,}000 + 12{,}000
\end{aligned}$$

$$= 16,000$$
$$\text{Var}(U) = E(U^2) - [E(U)]^2$$
$$= 16,000 - 100^2$$
$$= 6,000$$

$$E(V^2) = .95 \times 0^2 + .05 \times 2,000^2$$
$$= .05 \times 4,000,000$$
$$= 200,000$$
$$\text{Var}(V) = E(V^2) - [E(V)]^2$$
$$= 200,000 - 10,000$$
$$= 190,000$$

Here are two properties of the variance:
If X is a random variable and c is a constant:

$$\text{Var}(cX) = c^2\,\text{Var}(X)$$

If X and Y are two independent random variables:

$$\text{Var}(X + Y) = \text{Var}(X) + \text{Var}(Y)$$

Two random variables are independent if knowledge of the value of one of the variables does not give you any information about the value of the other variable. (See the discussion of independent events in Chapter 11.)

COVARIANCE

If two random variables are not independent, matters become more complicated. It is possible that $\text{Var}(X + Y)$ may be less than $\text{Var}(X) + \text{Var}(Y)$, or it may be greater; it depends on how the two random variables are related. In the extreme case, it is possible that the variability in X may exactly cancel out the variability in Y, so that $\text{Var}(X + Y)$ is zero. For example, if X is the number that appears on the top of a die, and Y is the number that appears on the bottom of the die, then $X + Y$ is always equal to 7, so $\text{Var}(X + Y) = 0$.

The quantity that measures the relationship between two random variables is called the **covariance**. If two random variables have a negative covariance, then a large value of one of the variables is more likely to be associated with a small value of the other. If the variables have a positive covariance, then a large value of one is likely to be associated with a large value of the other. The covariance is zero if the two random variables are independent.

Here is an example of two random variables with a positive covariance. Suppose that A represents your earnings from a purchase of stock in an airline company, and B represents your earnings from a purchase of stock in a hotel company. Suppose too that, if firm A is doing well, then firm B will also be doing well; and if one does poorly, then the other will also do poorly. Here is a list of probabilities for the two random variables:

$$\Pr(A = 20 \text{ and } B = 10) = .3$$
$$\Pr(A = 20 \text{ and } B = 100) = .1$$
$$\Pr(A = 200 \text{ and } B = 10) = .2$$
$$\Pr(A = 200 \text{ and } B = 100) = .4$$

(Probabilities in situations such as this often must be determined by subjective estimates.)

We can arrange these results in a table:

		A		
		20	200	
B	10	.3	.2	.5
	100	.1	.4	.5
		.4	.6	

The numbers at the right, which are the totals for the two rows, are the probabilities for the possible values of B. The numbers at the bottom, which are the totals for the two columns, are the probabilities for the possible values of A.

$$\Pr(A = 20) = .4$$
$$\Pr(A = 200) = .6$$
$$\Pr(B = 10) = .5$$
$$\Pr(B = 100) = .5$$

We can calculate the expected value and the variance for A and for B:

$$
\begin{aligned}
E(A) &= .4 \times 20 + .6 \times 200 = 128 \\
E(A^2) &= .4 \times 400 + .6 \times 40,000 = 24,160 \\
\text{Var}(A) &= 24,160 - 128^2 = 7,776 \\
E(B) &= .5 \times 10 + 5 \times 100 = 55 \\
E(B^2) &= .5 \times 100 + .5 \times 10,000 = 5,050 \\
\text{Var}(B) &= 5,050 - 55^2 = 2,025
\end{aligned}
$$

Let C represent your total profit from your stock purchases; in the two companies $C = A + B$. We can calculate the probability for each of the possible values of C:

$$\Pr(C = 30) \ = .3$$
$$\Pr(C = 120) = .1$$
$$\Pr(C = 210) = .2$$
$$\Pr(C = 300) = .4$$

Now we can calculate the expected value and variance:

$$E(C) = .3 \times 30 + .1 \times 120 + .2 \times 210 + .4 \times 300$$
$$= 183$$
$$E(C^2) = .3 \times 900 + .1 \times 14{,}400 + .2 \times 44{,}100 + .4 \times 90{,}000$$
$$= 46{,}530$$
$$\mathrm{Var}(C) = 46{,}530 - 183^2$$
$$= 13{,}041$$

We could have calculated the variance of C by calculating the covariance. The covariance of two random variables is found from this formula:

$$\mathrm{Cov}(A, B) = E(AB) - [E(A)][E(B)]$$

To calculate $E(AB)$, we need to multiply each possible value for AB by its probability of occurrence, and then add:

$$E(AB) = .3 \times (20 \times 10) + 1.1 \times (20 \times 100) + .2 \times (200 \times 10) + .4 \times (200 \times 100)$$
$$= 60 + 200 + 400 + 8{,}000$$
$$= 8{,}660$$

Now we can use the formula to find the covariance:

$$\mathrm{Cov}(A, B) = E(AB) - [E(A)][E(B)]$$
$$= 8{,}660 - 128 \times 55$$
$$= 1{,}620$$

Once we know the covariance of two random variables, we can calculate the variance of their sum from this formula:

$$\mathrm{Var}(A + B) = \mathrm{Var}(A) + \mathrm{Var}(B) + 2\mathrm{Cov}(A, B)$$

We can use this formula for our example:

$$\mathrm{Var}(A + B) = 7{,}776 + 2{,}025 + 2 \times 1{,}620$$
$$= 13{,}041$$

This is the same answer we found before.

In this case the two stocks have a positive covariance, so the profits have a large variance. In selecting a portfolio, it usually is better to choose stocks that have negative covariances. This means that, if one stock is doing poorly, the other stock is likely to be doing well. In this way you can reduce your risk. This mathematical result is summed up in the proverb "Don't put all your eggs in one basket."

YOU SHOULD REMEMBER

The variance of a random variable is a measure of how unpredictable the random variable is. It can be found from the formula

$$\text{Var}(X) = E(X^2) - [E(X)]^2$$

The square root of the variance is called the **standard deviation** symbolized by σ.

The convariance of two random variables indicates how the random variables are related. If the covariance is negative, large values of one variable are likely to be associated with small values of the other variable. If the covariance is positive, large values of one variable are more likely to be associated with large values of the other. If the random variables are independent, their covariance is zero.

If X and Y are two random variables, then the covariance is given by this formula:

$$\text{Cov}(X, Y) = E(XY) - [E(X)][E(Y)]$$

The variance of $X + Y$ is given by this formula:

$$\text{Var}(X + Y) = \text{Var}(X) + \text{Var}(Y) + 2\text{Cov}(X, Y)$$

Several general classes of random variable distributions are commonly used and have been given special names.

THE BINOMIAL DISTRIBUTION

Suppose that you are manager for a company with five identical machines. By observing past data and using statistical inference, you have estimated that each machine has a 15 percent chance of becoming jammed. Looking at the bright side, there is an 85 percent chance that a particular machine will *not* become jammed. You need to know: What is the probability that none of the machines will become jammed? Also, what is the probability that—horror of horrors—all five machines will become jammed?

In general, suppose that X is a random variable equal to the number of machines that do not become jammed. The possible values of X are 0, 1, 2, 3, 4, and 5. We would like to know the probability for each of these possible values.

First, let's look at the probability that machine A and machine B will both work. Assume that the machines are independent, that is, that a jamming of one machine has no effect on whether any other machine becomes jammed. Since the machines are independent, and we want to find the probability that both of these two events will occur (that is, machine A will work and so will machine B), we can multiply the two probabilities:

$$Pr[(\text{machine } A \text{ works}) \text{ and } (\text{machine } B \text{ works})]$$
$$= Pr(\text{machine } A \text{ works}) \times Pr(\text{machine } B \text{ works})$$
$$= .85 \times .85$$
$$= .7225$$

By the same reasoning, the probability that all five machines will work is equal to the product of the five probabilities:

$$Pr[(A \text{ works}) \text{ and } (B \text{ works}) \text{ and } (C \text{ works}) \text{ and } (D \text{ works}) \text{ and } (E \text{ works})]$$
$$= Pr(A \text{ works}) \times Pr(B \text{ works}) \times Pr(C \text{ works}) \times Pr(D \text{ works}) \times Pr(E \text{ works})$$
$$= .85 \times .85 \times .85 \times .85 \times .85$$
$$= .85^5$$
$$= .4437$$

We can see that, even though there is an 85 percent probability that any one particular machine will work, the chance that all five machines will work is less than half.

To find the probability that all five machines will jam, we must multiply the probabilities that the individual machines will jam:

$$Pr[(A \text{ jams}) \text{ and } (B \text{ jams}) \text{ and } (C \text{ jams}) \text{ and } (D \text{ jams}) \text{ and } (E \text{ jams})]$$
$$= Pr(A \text{ jams}) \times Pr(B \text{ jams}) \times Pr(C \text{ jams}) \times Pr(D \text{ jams}) \times Pr(E \text{ jams})$$
$$= .15^5$$
$$= .0000759 = 7.59 \times 10^{-5}$$

Fortunately, the probability that all five machines will jam is very small.

It is a little more complicated to calculate the probability that exactly one machine will jam. Here is the probability that machine A will jam while the other four machines work:

$$Pr[(A \text{ jams}) \text{ and } (B \text{ works}) \text{ and } (C \text{ works}) \text{ and } (D \text{ works}) \text{ and } (E \text{ works})]$$

$= \text{Pr}(A \text{ jams}) \times \text{Pr}(B \text{ works}) \times \text{Pr}(C \text{ works}) \times \text{Pr}(D \text{ works}) \times \text{Pr}(E \text{ works})$
$= .15 \times .85 \times .85 \times .85 \times .85$
$= .0783$

The same reasoning can be applied to calculate the probability that machine B will jam while the other four work:

$\text{Pr}[(A \text{ works}) \text{ and } (B \text{ jams}) \text{ and } (C \text{ works}) \text{ and } (D \text{ works}) \text{ and } (E \text{ works})]$
$= \text{Pr}(A \text{ works}) \times \text{Pr}(B \text{ jams}) \times \text{Pr}(C \text{ works}) \times \text{Pr}(D \text{ works}) \times \text{Pr}(E \text{ works})$
$= .85 \times .15 \times .85 \times .85 \times .85$
$= .0783$

Likewise:

$$\text{Pr}(\text{only } C \text{ jams}) = .0783$$
$$\text{Pr}(\text{only } D \text{ jams}) = .0783$$
$$\text{Pr}(\text{only } E \text{ jams}) = .0783$$

Now, we calculate the probability that exactly one machine will jam:

$\text{Pr}(\text{one and only one machine jams})$
$= \text{Pr}(\text{only } A \text{ jams}) + \text{Pr}(\text{only } B \text{ jams}) + \text{Pr}(\text{only } C \text{ jams})$
$\qquad + \text{Pr}(\text{only } D \text{ jams}) + \text{Pr}(\text{only } E \text{ jams})$
$= .0783 + .0783 + .0783 + .0783 + .0783$
$= .3915$

Now we need to calculate the probability that exactly two machines will jam. First, we calculate the probability that machines A and B will jam while the other three work:

$\text{Pr}[(A \text{ jams}) \text{ and } (B \text{ jams}) \text{ and } (C \text{ works}) \text{ and } (D \text{ works}) \text{ and } (E \text{ works})]$
$= \text{Pr}(A \text{ jams}) \times \text{Pr}(B \text{ jams}) \times \text{Pr}(C \text{ works}) \times \text{Pr}(D \text{ works}) \times \text{Pr}(E \text{ works})$
$= .15 \times .15 \times .85 \times .85 \times .85$
$= .0138$

To find the probability that exactly two machines will jam, we need to add the probabilities for all of these events:

$\text{Pr}(\text{only } A, B \text{ jam}) + \text{Pr}(\text{only } A, C \text{ jam}) + \text{Pr}(\text{only } A, D \text{ jam}) + \text{Pr}(\text{only } A, E \text{ jam})$
$\qquad + \text{Pr}(\text{only } B, C \text{ jam}) + \text{Pr}(\text{only } B, D \text{ jam}) + \text{Pr}(\text{only } B, E \text{ jam})$
$\qquad\qquad + \text{Pr}(\text{only } C, D \text{ jam}) + \text{Pr}(\text{only } C, E \text{ jam})$
$\qquad\qquad\qquad + \text{Pr}(\text{only } D, E \text{ jam})$
$= 10 \times .0138$
$= .138$

There are 10 possible ways for exactly two machines to jam, because there are 10 ways of selecting two objects from a group of five objects, according to the combination formula from Chapter 11:

$$\binom{5}{2} = \frac{5!}{2!3!} = \frac{5 \times 4 \times 3 \times 2 \times 1}{2 \times 1 \times 3 \times 2 \times 1} = \frac{5 \times 4}{2 \times 1} = \frac{20}{2} = 10$$

After we have completed the probability calculations, we can make this tabulation of the probabilities for X, the number of machines that will work:

$$\Pr(X = 0) = .00008 \qquad \Pr(X = 3) = .13818$$
$$\Pr(X = 1) = .00215 \qquad \Pr(X = 4) = .39150$$
$$\Pr(X = 2) = .02438 \qquad \Pr(X = 5) = .44371$$

The type of situation we have just discussed occurs often. In general, suppose that we observe n trials for an "experiment" that has two results: "success" and "failure." (For this purpose, you can call any process with two outcomes an "experiment," and it doesn't matter which of the two outcomes you call "success.") Suppose there is a probability of p that any particular trial will be a success. Assume that this probability is constant for all trials, and that the trials are independent, so that the outcome of one trial has no effect on the outcomes of any other trials. Let X be a random variable equal to the number of successes that occur during the n trials. Then the possible values for X are the whole numbers from 0 to n. X is said to have the **binomial distribution** with parameters n and p.

The probability for each of the possible values is calculated from this formula:

$$\Pr(X = i) = \binom{n}{i} p^i (1 - p)^{n-i} = \frac{n!}{i!(n-i)!} p^i (1 - p)^{n-i}$$

(provided that $0 \le i \le n$).

If you compare this formula with the calculations in the preceding section, you will see where it comes from.

Here are two special cases of the formula:

$$\Pr(X = n) = \binom{n}{n} p^n (1 - p)^0 = p^n$$

$$\Pr(X = 0) = \binom{n}{0} p^0 (1 - p)^{n-0} = (1 - p)^n$$

These formulas give the probabilities that all trials will be successes and that all trials will be failures, respectively.

Example: *Coin Tossing*

Tossing a coin can be considered an experiment that is a success if the result is a head. If the coin is fair, then the probability of success is equal to 1/2. Therefore, if we toss a coin *n* times, we can use the binomial distribution:

$$\Pr(X = i) = \binom{n}{i}\left(\frac{1}{2}\right)^i\left(1 - \frac{1}{2}\right)^{n-i} = \binom{n}{i}\left(\frac{1}{2}\right)^n$$

This formula can be used for any experiment where the probability of success is equal to 1/2.

If we toss a fair coin 100 times, we expect to see about 50 heads. In general, we expect that the number of heads will tend to be about half of the number of tosses. It can be shown that, if a coin is tossed *n* times, the expected value for the number of heads is equal to $(1/2)n$.

If we conduct an experiment 100 times, where each trial has a 75 percent chance of success, we expect to see about 75 successes. Here is the general formula for the expectation for a random variable with a binomial distribution:

$$E(X) = np$$

This formula agrees with our intuition. A larger value of *p* will lead to a higher expected value for the number of successes. In the extreme case where $p = 1$, we know for sure that all trials will succeed, so the expected value must be equal to *n*.

Here is the formula for the variance of a random variable with the binomial distribution:

$$\text{Var}(X) = np(1 - p)$$

Note that, if *p* is equal to either 0 or 1, the variance becomes zero. In either of these two cases there is no uncertainty. The experiment is either a sure failure or a sure success. For a given value of *n*, the variance will be largest if *p* is equal to 1/2. In that case there is the greatest amount of uncertainty about the results of the experiment.

Example: Airline Overbooking

PROBLEM Suppose you are running an airline that flies planes seating 200 people each. On average, 7 percent of the people who make reservations fail to show up for their flights. It seems wasteful to take only 200 reservations for each flight, because you know that there will probably be some empty seats. You decide to gamble by taking more than 200 reservations. If more than 200 people show up however, you will be in big trouble.

Suppose you have decided that you are willing to run a 5 percent risk of having too many people show up for a flight. How many reservations can you accept while still keeping the probability of an overflow less than 5 percent?

SOLUTION We can regard each reservation as a "trial," and we can call each time a person with a reservation shows up for the flight a "success." (We are assuming that no people show up without making reservations.) If we let X be the number of people who show up for a particular flight, then X has a binomial distribution, where n is the number of reservations and $p = .93$.

Suppose that you take 210 reservations. Then we can calculate these probabilities:

	Binomial Probability with $n = 210$ and $p = .93$
$Pr(X = 201)$	.034
$Pr(X = 202)$	.020
$Pr(X = 203)$	.011
$Pr(X = 204)$	.005
$Pr(X = 205)$	.002
$Pr(X = 206)$	.001

The probability that X will be greater than 206 is negligible. There will be an overflow if 201 or more people show up, so by adding up all of the probabilities in our table we find that the probability of an overflow is about 7 percent. We want the overflow probability to be less than 5 percent, however, so we must take fewer than 210 reservations. We can repeat the same calculations for 209 reservations; we find that the overflow probability is about 4 percent.

Therefore, you should take 209 reservations for each flight since that is the largest number you can take and still have less than a 5 percent chance of an overflow.

YOU SHOULD REMEMBER

Suppose that you conduct an experiment n times. The probability of success for any trial is p, and all of the trials are independent. Let X be a random variable representing the number of successes that occur. Then X is said to have a binomial distribution with parameters n and p.

The probabilities for X are given by the formula

$$\Pr(X = i) = \binom{n}{i} p^i (1 - p)^{n-i}$$

The expectation and the variance for X are given by these formulas:

$$E(X) = np, \qquad \text{Var}(X) = np(1 - p)$$

THE POISSON DISTRIBUTION

Let X be the number of telephone calls that arrive at a particular office in an hour. X is a random variable, and it turns out that X often has a distribution called the **Poisson distribution**. Here is the formula for the probability that X will take on a particular value i:

$$\Pr(X = i) = \frac{e^{-\lambda}\lambda^i}{i!}$$

(provided that $i \geq 0$).

The symbol λ is the Greek letter lambda, which represents the mean of the random variable X. A random variable with a Poisson distribution has the unusual property that its variance is equal to its mean, so λ is also equal to the variance of X.

The letter e represents a special number equal to about 2.71828, which is important in mathematics.

For example, suppose a study has determined that the number of phone calls arriving every hour at the office referred to above can be represented by a Poisson random variable with mean $\lambda = 5$. Then we can calculate the probabilities for X:

i	Pr$(X = i)$ (Probability of Getting Exactly i Phone Calls)	i	Pr$(X = i)$ (Probability of Getting Exactly i Phone Calls)
0	.006	7	.104
1	.033	8	.065
2	.084	9	.036
3	.140	10	.018
4	.175	11	.008
5	.175	12	.003
6	.146		

Note that the probability is very small that there will be no (zero) phone call. The probabilities increase, reaching a maximum near the value of the mean ($i = 5$). After that, the probabilities decline; the probability of 12 or more phone calls is small. This pattern agrees with our intuition.

Other examples where a Poisson distribution is applicable include the following:

* the number of novae in our galaxy in a given decade

* the number of appointments made to the Supreme Court in a given decade

* the number of movies to gross over $25 million in a year

* the number of people who have bought this book who bought it in New York City

In Chapter 15 there is a discussion of the application of the Poisson distribution to queuing theory.

YOU SHOULD REMEMBER

The random variable X is said to have a Poisson distribution with parameter λ if the probabilities are given by this formula:

$$\Pr(X = i) = \frac{e^{-\lambda}\lambda^i}{i!}$$

The expectation and the variance are both equal to λ.

THE HYPERGEOMETRIC DISTRIBUTION

Suppose that a box contains eight working components and six defective components. If we randomly select five components from the box, what is the probability that exactly three of the components will work and the other two will be defective?

Since we will be selecting five objects at random from a group of 14 objects, the total number of possible ways of making the selection is given by the formula for combinations:

$$\binom{14}{5} = \frac{14!}{5!9!} = \frac{14 \times 13 \times 12 \times 11 \times 10}{5 \times 4 \times 3 \times 2 \times 1} = 2{,}002$$

Now we need to calculate the number of these possibilities that have exactly three working components. There are 56 ways of choosing three working components from the eight working components in the box:

$$\binom{8}{3} = \frac{8 \times 7 \times 6}{3 \times 2 \times 1} = 56$$

There are 15 ways of choosing two defective components from the six defective components in the box:

$$\binom{6}{2} = \frac{6 \times 5}{2 \times 1} = 15$$

To find the total number of possibilities with three working components and two defective components, we must multiply: $56 \times 15 = 840$. (Any possible way of selecting the three working components can be paired with any of the possible ways of selecting the two defective components.) Therefore, the probability of obtaining exactly two defective components is $840/2{,}002 = .420$.

In general, suppose that we will be randomly selecting a sample of n objects from a population of N objects. The N objects in the population are divided into two classes: M are in the "desired" class, and the other $N - M$ are in the "undesired" class. Let X represent the number of objects in our sample that are in the desired class. Then X is a random variable with a distribution called the **hypergeometric distribution**. The probability that X will be equal to a particular value i is found from this formula:

$$\Pr(X = i) = \frac{\binom{M}{i}\binom{N - M}{n - i}}{\binom{N}{n}}$$

(provided that $0 \le i \le n$).

The expressions in the parentheses again represent the formula for combinations. The mean of X is equal to nM/N. This matches our intuition. If n is larger, then we would expect X to be larger. Also, we would expect X to be larger if the fraction of population objects in the desired state (M/N) becomes larger. The variance of X is given by the formula

$$\text{Var}(X) = n\left(\frac{M}{N}\right)\left(1 - \frac{M}{N}\right)\left(\frac{N-n}{N-1}\right)$$

In the preceding example, we had $N = 14$, $M = 8$, and $n = 5$. Therefore,

$$E(X) = 2.86 \quad \text{and} \quad \text{Var}(X) = 0.848$$

The hypergeometric distribution is applicable in situations where a random sample is selected without replacement from a population. Calculations involving the hypergeometric distribution, however, are very cumbersome. Fortunately, in many cases the binomial distribution can be used as an approximation for the hypergeometric distribution. This approximation is reasonable as long as N (the number of items in the population) is much larger than n (the number of items in the sample). In the next section we will discover that an even more convenient approximation is available in the *normal distribution*, which can be used as an approximation for the binomial distribution.

YOU SHOULD REMEMBER

Consider a population of N objects, consisting of M objects of type A and $N - M$ objects of type B. Choose n objects at random from the population, and let X represent the number of type A objects in the sample of n objects. Then X is a random variable having a hypergeometric distribution with parameters n, N, and M.

The probabilities are given by this formula:

$$\Pr(X = i) = \frac{\dbinom{M}{i}\dbinom{N-M}{n-i}}{\dbinom{N}{n}}$$

The expectation and the variance can be found from these formulas:

$$E(X) = \frac{nM}{N}, \quad \text{Var}(X) = n\left(\frac{M}{N}\right)\left(1 - \frac{M}{N}\right)\left(\frac{N-n}{N-1}\right)$$

THE NORMAL DISTRIBUTION

There are many quantities, such as heights, test scores, and experimental errors, where extreme values are less likely than moderate values. The distribution of these quantities often can be represented by a bell-shaped curve, known as the **normal distribution**.

The normal distribution is a new type of distribution: a **continuous random variable** distribution. Previously we discussed discrete random variable distributions, where it is possible to make a list of all of the possible values. (In the case of the Poisson distribution, there is an infinite number of possible values: all whole numbers greater than zero. We could list all of these values if we had an infinite amount of time. The technical description for that situation is that there is a **countably infinite** number of possible values.) However, we cannot list the possible values for a variable which measures a quantity that can vary over a continuous range. For example, if X is the amount of time until the next customer enters a store, X could have the value 40 seconds or 40.01 seconds or 40.001 seconds or 40.000001 seconds, and so on. When a quantity can take on values over a continuous range such as this, it is not possible to list the possible values. Between any two possible values there is always an infinite number of other possible values.

A continuous random variable is a random variable that can take on any value in a continuous range. In that case we cannot discuss the probability that the random variable will have a particular value. In fact, the probability of a continuous random variable taking any specific value is zero. However, we really are not interested in the probability that the variable will take the value 1.000001 as opposed to the value 1.000002. Instead, we are interested in the probability that the variable will be within a certain range. For example, we may need to know the probability that the variable will be between 1.1 and 1.2.

The behavior of a continuous random variable is characterized by a function called the **density function**. Figure 12-1 shows the graph of a density function for a continuous random variable with a normal distribution. The density function has this property: The probability that the value of the random variable will be between two values a and b is equal to the area under the curve, to the right of the line $x = a$, to the left of the line $x = b$, and above the x-axis.

The value of a density function is always nonnegative (so the curve representing the density function is always above the x-axis). Also, the total area under the curve must be equal to 1.

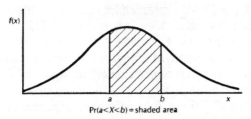

Pr(a<X<b) = shaded area

Figure 12-1

It is necessary to use calculus to determine the area under a curve. If $f(x)$ represents the density function, then the area under the curve $f(x)$, to the right of the line $x = a$, to the left of the line $x = b$, and above the x-axis, is symbolized in this way:

$$\int_a^b f(x)\,dx$$

This symbol is called the *definite integral*. The process of calculating the integral for a function is the opposite of calculating the derivative for that function. We will not go into detail here. The book *Calculus the Easy Way* (Douglas Downing, Barron's Educational Series, Inc., 1982) provides an introduction to calculus, including integrals. In the case of the normal distribution, there is no formula that gives the area under the density function, so we will have to use a table to calculate the area.

The expectation for a continuous random variable has the same meaning as does the expectation for a discrete random variable: it is the average value that would be expected to appear if you observed the random variable many times. However, the calculation process is different for a continuous random variable. If $f(x)$ represents the density function for a random variable X, then the expected value of X is given by the following definite integral:

$$E(X) = \int_{-\infty}^{\infty} x f(x)\,dx$$

As in the case of discrete random variables, the variance of a continuous random variable measures the degree of unpredictability. If you have calculated the expected value of X and the expected value of X^2, then the variance of X can again be found from the formula

$$\mathrm{Var}(X) = E(X^2) - [E(X)]^2$$

The formula for the density function for the normal distribution is

$$\frac{1}{\sqrt{2\pi}\sigma} \exp\left[-\frac{1}{2}\left(\frac{x - \mu}{\sigma}\right)^2\right]$$

In the formula, μ represents the mean and σ represents the standard deviation. The expression exp (A) represents e^A, where $e = 2.71828. \ldots$ There are many different normal distributions. Each one can be identified by specifying the mean and the variance (or standard deviation). The mean is located at the peak of the distribution. The variance determines the shape of the distribution—whether it will be spread out or whether most of the area will be concentrated near the peak. Figure 12-2 shows four normal distributions that have the same variance but different means.

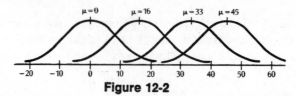

Figure 12-2

Figure 12-3 shows four normal distributions that have the same mean but different variances. The area under each of these curves is 1, as it must be for a continuous probability distribution. The curve never touches the axis. Therefore, the normal random variable could conceivably have any value, including values far away from the mean. However, you can see that there is not much area under the curve far from the mean, so the chance that the observed value will appear far from the mean is remote.

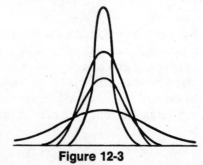

Figure 12-3

An important property of a normal random variable is the addition property. If X is a normal random variable with mean μ and variance σ^2, and $Y = aX + b$, where a and b are two constants, then Y has a normal distribution with mean $a\mu + b$ and variance $a^2\sigma^2$.

Also, suppose that X and Y are two independent random variables with normal distributions, and that

$$E(X) = \mu_x, \qquad \text{Var}(X) = \sigma_x^2, \qquad E(Y) = \mu_y, \qquad \text{Var}(Y) = \sigma_y^2$$

If we form a new random variable by adding X and Y together, $V = X + Y$, then V will also have a normal distribution, with

$$E(V) = \mu_x + \mu_y, \qquad \text{Var}(V) = \sigma_x^2 + \sigma_y^2$$

For example, suppose that you decide to enter the hamburger business by opening restaurants at two different locations. The number of hamburgers sold each day at the downtown location is given by a normal random variable with mean 200 and variance 1,600. The number of hamburgers sold at the suburban location has a normal distribution with mean 100 and variance 400. Then the total number of hamburgers that you will sell at both restaurants has a normal distribution with mean 300 and variance 2,000.

THE STANDARD NORMAL DISTRIBUTION

We need to look in a table to find the area under the normal curve. It is impossible to prepare a separate table for every normal distribution with every possible mean and every possible variance. Fortunately, we can find the results for any normal distribution by looking at a table for the normal distribution that has mean $\mu = 0$ and variance $\sigma^2 = 1$. This special normal distribution is called the **standard normal distribution**.

Let Z be a random variable with a standard normal distribution. Figure 12-4 shows a graph of the density function for Z. Suppose we need to know the probability that Z is less than 0. From Table 12-1 we can see that $\Pr(Z < 0)$ is .5. This matches our intuition. Also, we can see from Figure 12-4 that the density function is symmetric about the line $x = 0$; therefore, the area to the left of $x = 0$ is equal to the area to the right of $x = 0$.

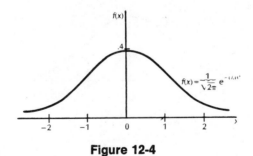

Figure 12-4

To find the probability that Z will be less than 1, we look in the table:

$$\Pr(Z < 1) = .8413$$

Likewise, we can use Table 12-1 to find the probability that Z will be less than any positive value a. Note that the table does not go past $a = 3.5$. The probability that a standard normal random variable will be less than 3.5 is equal to .9998. Therefore, the chance that Z will be greater than 3.5 is equal to .0002.

The probability that the value of Z will be larger than 3.5 is so remote that there is no point in extending the table to that range.

Suppose we want to find the probability that Z will be greater than 1. This probability is simply 1 minus the probability that Z will be less than 1:

$$\Pr(Z > 1) = 1 - \Pr(Z < 1) = 1 - .8413 = .1587$$

In general, if X is a continuous random variable and a is a constant, then

$$\Pr(X > a) = 1 - \Pr(Z < a)$$

This property holds true for continuous random variables, because X must be either greater than a or less than a. However, this property does not hold true for discrete random variables, because a discrete random variable may be exactly equal to a.

Table 12-1 does not give values for $\Pr(Z < a)$ if a is negative. However, we can find these probabilities because the normal distribution is symmetric:

$$\Pr(Z < -a) = \Pr(Z > a)$$

(See Figure 12-5.)

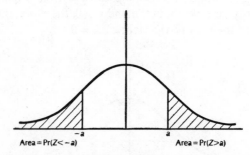

Area = Pr(Z< – a)   Area = Pr(Z>a)

Figure 12-5

For example:

$$\Pr(Z < -1.2) = \Pr(Z > 1.2)$$
$$= 1 - \Pr(Z < 1.2)$$
$$= 1 - .8849$$
$$= .1151$$

Now suppose we need to find the probability that Z is between 0.6 and 1. From Figure 12-6, we can see that the area betwen 0.6 and 1 is equal to the area to the left of 1, minus the area to the left of 0.6:

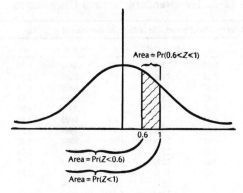

Figure 12-6

$$Pr(0.6 < Z < 1) = Pr(Z < 1) - Pr(Z < 0.6)$$
$$= .8413 - .7257$$
$$= .1156$$

In general, we can find the probability that Z will be between two values by subtracting:

$$Pr(a < Z < b) = Pr(Z < b) - Pr(Z < a)$$

(provided that $a < b$).

We can use Table 12-1 for the standard normal distribution to find the probabilities for any random variable with the normal distribution. For example, suppose that Y has a normal distribution with mean 6 and standard deviation 3, and we need to know the probability that Y will be between 5 and 8. We create the random variable Z:

$$Z = \frac{Y - 6}{3}$$

which will have a normal distribution with mean 0 and variance 1, because of the addition property for normal random variables. It should be clear that, if Y is between 5 and 8, then Z will be between $-1/3$ and $2/3$. Now we can look up the probabilities in the table:

$$Pr(5 < Y < 8) = Pr(-1/3 < Z < 2/3)$$
$$= Pr(Z < 0.667) - Pr(Z < -0.333)$$
$$= .7486 - (1 - .6293)$$
$$= .7486 - .3707$$
$$= .3779$$

Table 12-1. The Standard Normal Distribution

If Z has a standard normal distribution, the table gives the value of $\Pr(Z < z)$

z	$\Pr(Z < z)$	z	$\Pr(Z < z)$	z	$\Pr(Z < z)$	z	$\Pr(Z < z)$
0.01	.5040	0.60	.7257	1.19	.8830	1.78	.9625
0.02	.5080	0.61	.7291	1.20	.8849	1.79	.9633
0.03	.5120	0.62	.7324	1.21	.8869	1.80	.9641
0.04	.5160	0.63	.7357	1.22	.8888	1.81	.9649
0.05	.5199	0.64	.7389	1.23	.8907	1.82	.9656
0.06	.5239	0.65	.7422	1.24	.8925	1.83	.9664
0.07	.5279	0.66	.7454	1.25	.8944	1.84	.9671
0.08	.5319	0.67	.7486	1.26	.8962	1.85	.9678
0.09	.5359	0.68	.7517	1.27	.8980	1.86	.9686
0.10	.5398	0.69	.7549	1.28	.8997	1.87	.9693
0.11	.5438	0.70	.7580	1.29	.9015	1.88	.9699
0.12	.5478	0.71	.7611	1.30	.9032	1.89	.9706
0.13	.5517	0.72	.7642	1.31	.9049	1.90	.9713
0.14	.5557	0.73	.7673	1.32	.9066	1.91	.9719
0.15	.5596	0.74	.7704	1.33	.9082	1.92	.9726
0.16	.5636	0.75	.7734	1.34	.9099	1.93	.9732
0.17	.5675	0.76	.7764	1.35	.9115	1.94	.9738
0.18	.5714	0.77	.7794	1.36	.9131	1.95	.9744
0.19	.5753	0.78	.7823	1.37	.9147	1.96	.9750
0.20	.5793	0.79	.7852	1.38	.9162	1.97	.9756
0.21	.5832	0.80	.7881	1.39	.9177	1.98	.9761
0.22	.5871	0.81	.7910	1.40	.9192	1.99	.9767
0.23	.5910	0.82	.7939	1.41	.9207	2.00	.9773
0.24	.5948	0.83	.7967	1.42	.9222	2.01	.9778
0.25	.5987	0.84	.7995	1.43	.9236	2.02	.9783
0.26	.6026	0.85	.8023	1.44	.9251	2.03	.9788
0.27	.6064	0.86	.8051	1.45	.9265	2.04	.9793
0.28	.6103	0.87	.8079	1.46	.9279	2.05	.9798
0.29	.6141	0.88	.8106	1.47	.9292	2.06	.9803
0.30	.6179	0.89	.8133	1.48	.9306	2.07	.9808
0.31	.6217	0.90	.8159	1.49	.9319	2.08	.9812
0.32	.6255	0.91	.8186	1.50	.9332	2.09	.9817
0.33	.6293	0.92	.8212	1.51	.9345	2.10	.9821
0.34	.6331	0.93	.8238	1.52	.9357	2.11	.9826
0.35	.6368	0.94	.8264	1.53	.9370	2.12	.9830
0.36	.6406	0.95	.8289	1.54	.9382	2.13	.9834
0.37	.6443	0.96	.8315	1.55	.9394	2.14	.9838
0.38	.6480	0.97	.8340	1.56	.9406	2.15	.9842
0.39	.6517	0.98	.8365	1.57	.9418	2.16	.9846
0.40	.6554	0.99	.8389	1.58	.9429	2.17	.9850
0.41	.6591	1.00	.8413	1.59	.9441	2.18	.9854
0.42	.6628	1.01	.8438	1.60	.9452	2.19	.9857
0.43	.6664	1.02	.8461	1.61	.9463	2.20	.9861
0.44	.6700	1.03	.8485	1.62	.9474	2.25	.9878
0.45	.6736	1.04	.8508	1.63	.9484	2.30	.9893
0.46	.6772	1.05	.8531	1.64	.9495	2.35	.9906
0.47	.6808	1.06	.8554	1.65	.9505	2.40	.9918
0.48	.6844	1.07	.8577	1.66	.9515	2.50	.9938
0.49	.6879	1.08	.8599	1.67	.9525	2.60	.9953
0.50	.6915	1.09	.8621	1.68	.9535	2.70	.9965
0.51	.6950	1.10	.8643	1.69	.9545	2.80	.9974
0.52	.6985	1.11	.8665	1.70	.9554	2.90	.9981
0.53	.7019	1.12	.8686	1.71	.9564	3.00	.9987
0.54	.7054	1.13	.8708	1.72	.9573	3.10	.9990
0.55	.7088	1.14	.8729	1.73	.9582	3.20	.9993
0.56	.7123	1.15	.8749	1.74	.9591	3.30	.9995
0.57	.7157	1.16	.8770	1.75	.9599	3.40	.9997
0.58	.7190	1.17	.8790	1.76	.9608	3.50	.9998
0.59	.7224	1.18	.8810	1.77	.9616		

In general, if X is a normal random variable with mean μ and variance σ^2, then $(X - \mu)/\sigma$ is a standard normal random variable. For example, suppose we would like to know the probability that you will sell more than 230 hamburgers at your downtown restaurant (see page 341). Let X represent the number of hamburgers. In this case,

$$\mu = 200, \qquad \sigma^2 = 1{,}600, \qquad \text{and} \qquad \sigma = 40$$

We create the standard normal random variable Z:

$$Z = \frac{X - 200}{40}$$

If X is greater than 230, then Z is greater than 3/4. Table 12-1 tells us that the probability of this occurring is

$$1 - \Pr(Z < 0.75) = 1 - .7734 = .2266$$

Now, suppose we would like to know the probability that you will sell more than 330 hamburgers at the two locations. Let X be the total number of hamburgers. Then

$$\mu = 300, \qquad \sigma^2 = 2{,}000, \qquad \text{and} \qquad \sigma = 44.72$$

We can calculate:

$$\Pr(X > 330) = \Pr\left(\frac{X - 300}{44.72} > \frac{330 - 300}{44.72}\right)$$

Let $Z = (X - 300)/44.72$. Then:

$$\Pr(X > 330) = \Pr\left(Z > \frac{330 - 300}{44.72}\right)$$
$$= \Pr(Z > 0.671)$$
$$= 1 - \Pr(Z < 0.671)$$
$$= .2514$$

The normal distribution has many applications. It can often be used to describe quantities where extreme values are less likely than moderate values. If n (the number of trials) is large enough, then, as mentioned earlier, the normal distribution can be used as an approximation for the binomial distribution. This approximation is very helpful because the calculations with the normal distribution are easier than the calculations with the binomial distribution. The approximation works even though the normal distribution is a continuous distribution, while the binomial distribution is a discrete distribution.

If $X_1, X_2, \ldots, X_n$ are random variables that all are independent and all have the same distribution, then their sum will have a normal distribution if n is large enough. This theorem is called the *central limit theorem*. The amazing fact is that it works no matter what the distribution of $X_1, X_2, \ldots, X_n$ happens to be.

YOU SHOULD REMEMBER

The normal distribution is a continuous random variable distribution with a bell-shaped density function. The area under the density function curve between two values is equal to the probability that the random variable will be between these two values. The peak of the curve occurs at the mean of the distribution, and the shape of the curve is determined by the standard deviation.

If X has a normal distribution with mean μ and standard deviation σ, then

$$Z = \frac{X - \mu}{\sigma}$$

has a normal distribution with mean 0 and standard deviation 1 (which is called the *standard normal distribution*). The probability that Z will be less than a particular value can be found in Table 12-1.

THE EXPONENTIAL DISTRIBUTION

If you operate a retail business, you can never be sure when your next customer will arrive. Let X be a continuous random variable that represents the amount of time until the arrival of the next customer. We expect that very large intervals between customers are unlikely, so the density function for X will decline for larger values of X. A distribution known as the **exponential distribution** can often be applied in this type of situation. The density function is given by

$$\lambda e^{-\lambda x}$$

(provided that $x > 0$).

The Greek letter lambda (λ) is used as the parameter for this distribution, as it was for the Poisson distribution. Figure 12-7 shows a graph of the density function for an exponential distribution. The expectation of the exponential random variable is equal to $1/\lambda$, and the variance is $1/\lambda^2$.

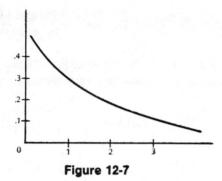

Figure 12-7

It is possible to use calculus to derive a formula for the probability that X will have a value less than a specified value a:

$$\Pr(X < a) = 1 - e^{-\lambda a}$$

and therefore

$$\Pr(X > a) = e^{-\lambda a}$$

For example, suppose that we have found that the exponential distribution is appropriate, and the mean interval between customer arrival times is 5 minutes. Then $\lambda = 1/5$, and therefore

$$\Pr(X > a) = e^{-(1/5)a}$$

For example, the probability that X will be greater than 10 minutes is

$$\Pr(X > 10) = e^{-(10/5)} = .135$$

(*Note:* To solve this type of problem it is necessary to have a calculator that will automatically calculate the exponential function e^x. Fortunately, many readily available calculators have this capability.)

The exponential function has an interesting property called the *lack of memory* property. Suppose that you have already waited 15 minutes since the last customer, and you want to know the probability that you will have to wait at least 10 additional minutes for the next customer.

We need to calculate the conditional probability that X will be greater than 25, given that X is already greater than 15:

$$\Pr[(X > 25) \,|\, (X > 15)]$$

The vertical line means "given that" (see Chapter 11).
Using the formula for conditional probability, we have

$$\Pr[(X > 25) \,|\, (X > 15)] = \frac{\Pr[(X > 25) \text{ and } (X > 15)]}{\Pr(X > 15)}$$

The probability that X will be both greater than 25 and greater than 15 is the same as the probability that X will be greater than 25:

$$\Pr[(X > 25) \,|\, (X > 15)] = \frac{\Pr(X > 25)}{\Pr(X > 15)}$$

$$= \frac{e^{-(25/5)}}{e^{-(15/5)}}$$

Using the properties of exponents gives

$$\Pr[X > 25) \,|\, (X > 15)] = e^{-(25/5) - [-(15/5)]} = e^{-(10/5)}$$
$$= .135$$

Note that the conditional probability that X will be greater than 25, given that X is already greater than 15, is the same as the unconditional probability that X will be greater than 10. This seems to be intuitive; the potential customers out there have no way of knowing how long it has been since the last customer, so there is nothing to make them more likely to appear sooner just because more than 15 minutes have elapsed since the last customer.

YOU SHOULD REMEMBER

A continuous random variable distribution called the *exponential distribution* can often be applied to situations involving arrival times. The density function is given by the formula

$$\lambda e^{-\lambda x}$$

If X has an exponential distribution, then

$$\Pr(X < a) = 1 - e^{-\lambda a}$$
$$E(X) = \frac{1}{\lambda}, \qquad \text{Var}(X) = \frac{1}{\lambda^2}$$

KNOW THE CONCEPTS

DO YOU KNOW THE BASICS?

Test your understanding of Chapter 12 by answering the following questions:

1. Why must the probabilities for all of the possible values for a discrete random variable add up to 1?

2. Why must the total area under the density function for a continuous random variable be equal to 1?

3. If X is a random variable, is $\Pr(X < a) = \Pr(X \leq a)$?

4. What value of p causes the variance of a random variable with the binomial distribution to take its largest possible value? Explain intuitively.

5. What assumptions are required to apply to binomial distribution?

TERMS FOR STUDY

binomial distribution	exponential distribution
continuous random variable	hypergeometric distribution
countably infinite	mean
convariance	normal distribution
density function	Poisson distribution
discrete random variable	standard deviation
expectation	standard normal distribution
expected value	variance

PRACTICAL APPLICATION

COMPUTATIONAL PROBLEMS

1. Suppose that two dice are tossed. Let X be the product of the two numbers that appear. Calculate $E(X)$ and $\mathrm{Var}(X)$.

2. Suppose that two dice are tossed. Let X be the sum of the two numbers that appear. Calculate $\mathrm{Var}(X)$. (We already found that $E(X) = 7$.)

3. You have the following information on three investment projects. In each case there is uncertainty. There are three possible values for the net present value for each project; the table shows the probability associated with each possible value.

Project A	Possible Value	Probability
	500	.25
	600	.50
	700	.25

Project B	Possible Value	Probability
	500	.33
	600	.34
	700	.33

Project C	Possible Value	Probability
	450	.25
	550	.50
	650	.25

(a) Calculate the expected value and the standard deviation of the net present value for each project.

(b) Suppose that you are risk averse. This means that, if you have a choice between two projects with the same expected net present value, you will choose the one with less risk (smallest standard deviation). You would also like the expected value of the net present value to be as large as possible. Which of these projects will you choose?

4. Suppose that you have a machine that has a 60 percent chance of working each time it is operated, and that you operate the machine six times. Assume that each time is independent from the others.

(a) What is the probability that the machine will work all six times?

(b) What is the probability that the machine will fail all six times?

(c) What is the probability that the machine will work two times and fail four times?

(d) Let X be a random variable equal to the number of times that the machine works. What is $E(X)$ and $Var(X)$?

5. (a) Consider a situation with two roommates who live in a room with one phone. There is a probability of .25 that one of the roommates will want to use the phone at 6 P.M. on Friday night. The probability of .25 is the same for both roommates, and the probability that one roommate will want to use the phone is not affected by whether or not the other roommate is using the phone. What is the probability that both will want to use the phone at 6 P.M. this Friday night?

   (b) Consider a situation with four roommates who live in a house with two phones. There is a probability of .25 that one of the roommates will want to use the phone at 6 P.M. on Friday night. The probability of .25 is the same for all roommates, and the probability that one roommate will want to use the phone is not affected by whether or not another roommate is using the phone. What is the probability that two or more roommates will want to use the phone at 6 P.M. this Friday night?

   (c) Consider the same situation as in part (b). What is the probability that three or more roommates will want to use the phone at 6 P.M. this Friday night?

6. There is a 25 percent chance that bad weather will cause a delay for flights landing at a particular airport. During the next year you will be taking eight flights that land at this airport. Assume that each flight can be considered independently—in other words, the weather on the day that one flight lands has no effect on the weather on the days when any of the other flights land.

   (a) Calculate the probability for each of the possible values of X, the number of flights that will be delayed.

   (b) What is the probability that at least five flights will be delayed?

   (c) Calculate $E(X)$ and $Var(X)$.

7. Suppose that the number of phone calls that arrive at your office in an hour is a random variable having a Poisson distribution with mean 10. Calculate the probabilities of receiving k phone calls, for values of k from 5 to 15.

8. Suppose that Z is a random variable with a standard normal distribution.

   (a) What is the probability that Z will be less than 0.8?

   (b) What is the probability that Z will be less than -1.2?

   (c) What is the probability that Z will be greater than 0.7?

9. (In each case give a formula, not a numerical answer.) Your company has 90 employees. Of these, 60 would like the walls painted red and 30 would like the walls painted blue. Suppose that you conduct a survey by asking 20 randomly selected employees what their preferences are.

   (a) How many different ways can this sample be chosen?

   (b) What is the probability that all 20 people in the sample will prefer blue walls?

(c) What is the probability that all 20 people in the sample will prefer red walls?

(d) What is the probability that 14 people in the sample will prefer red walls and six people in the sample will prefer blue walls?

10. The size of the total daily withdrawals at a bank has a normal distribution with a mean of $6,000 and a standard deviation of $2,000. The size of the total daily deposits has a normal distribution with a mean of $6,500 and a standard deviation of $2,500. The amount of withdrawals is independent from the amount of deposits.

(a) What is the probability that the withdrawals will be between $4,000 and $8,000?

(b) What is the probability that the withdrawals will be greater than $8,500?

(c) What is the probability that the withdrawals will be between $7,000 and $8,000?

(d) What is the probability that withdrawals will be greater than deposits by at least $500?

11. The lifetime of a brand X battery has a normal distribution with mean = 60 hours and standard deviation = 15 hours. You have purchased two of these batteries. The two batteries are identical, and they are independent.

(a) What is the probability that both batteries will last at least 70 hours?

(b) What is the probability that at least one of the batteries will last 70 hours?

(c) What is the probability that one of the batteries will last at least 70 hours, while the other one will last less than 70 hours?

12. That hat sizes of the people in a city follow a normal distribution with mean $\mu = 7$ and standard deviation $\sigma = 2$. Suppose that you select an individual at random.

(a) What is the probability that this individual will have a hat size between 5 and 9?

(b) What is the probability that this individual will have a hat size greater than 8?

(c) What is the probability that this individual will have a hat size less than 4?

13. You are told that the number of days until a crucial component is delivered to your firm is given by a random variable having a normal distribution with mean = 25 days and standard deviation = 5 days.

(a) What is the probability that the number of days until the part is delivered will be between 20 and 30?

(b) What is the probability that the number of days until the part is delivered will be between 15 and 35?

(c) What is the probability that the number of days until the part is delivered will be less than 21?

(d) What is the probability that the number of days until the part is delivered will be greater than 32?

The correlation between two random variables A and B is defined to be $\text{Cov}(A, B)/\sqrt{\text{Var}(A)\,\text{Var}(B)}$. *For Exercises 14–16, calculate* $\text{Cov}(A, B)$, $\text{Var}(A)$, $\text{Var}(B)$, $\text{Var}(A + B)$, *and the correlation between A and B.*

14. $\Pr[(A = 5) \text{ and } (B = 2)] = .04$ $\Pr[(A = 8) \text{ and } (B = 4)] = .10$
     $\Pr[(A = 5) \text{ and } (B = 4)] = .35$ $\Pr[(A = 12) \text{ and } (B = 2)] = .30$
     $\Pr[(A = 8) \text{ and } (B = 2)] = .15$ $\Pr[(A = 12) \text{ and } (B = 4)] = .06$

15. $\Pr[(A = 0) \text{ and } (B = 0)] = .38$ $\Pr[(A = 1) \text{ and } (B = 0)] = .07$
     $\Pr[(A = 0) \text{ and } (B = 1)] = .15$ $\Pr[(A = 1) \text{ and } (B = 1)] = .40$

16. $\Pr[(A = 2) \text{ and } (B = 4)] = .12$ $\Pr[(A = 3) \text{ and } (B = 4)] = .28$
     $\Pr[(A = 2) \text{ and } (B = 5)] = .18$ $\Pr[(A = 3) \text{ and } (B = 5)] = .42$

17. Suppose that the arrival time between customers in a store is given by a random variable having an exponential distribution with mean 20 minutes.
    (a) What is the probability that the time until the next customer will be more than 20 minutes?
    (b) What is the probability that the time will be more than 30 minutes?
    (c) What is the probability that the time will be less than 10 minutes?

ANSWERS

KNOW THE CONCEPTS
  1. The probability is 1 that the random variable will take on one of its possible values.

  2. The total area is equal to the probability that the random variable will be between negative infinity and positive infinity. There is a probability of 1 that the random variable will be somewhere in this range.

  3. This property is true if X is a continuous random variable, but not if X is a discrete random variable.

  4. $p = .5$. In this case there is the greatest uncertainty as to whether a particular trial will be a success or a failure.

  5. Each trial is independent, and the probability is the same for all trials.

PRACTICAL APPLICATION
  1. Here are the probabilities for all of the possible values:
    $\Pr(X = 1) = 1/36$ $\Pr(X = 12) = 4/36$
    $\Pr(X = 2) = 2/36$ $\Pr(X = 15) = 2/36$
    $\Pr(X = 3) = 2/36$ $\Pr(X = 16) = 1/36$

$$\Pr(X = 4) = 3/36 \qquad \Pr(X = 18) = 2/36$$
$$\Pr(X = 5) = 2/36 \qquad \Pr(X = 20) = 2/36$$
$$\Pr(X = 6) = 4/36 \qquad \Pr(X = 24) = 2/36$$
$$\Pr(X = 8) = 2/36 \qquad \Pr(X = 25) = 1/36$$
$$\Pr(X = 9) = 1/36 \qquad \Pr(X = 30) = 2/36$$
$$\Pr(X = 10) = 2/36 \qquad \Pr(X = 36) = 1/36$$

$$E(X) = \frac{441}{36} = 12.25, \qquad E(X^2) = \frac{8{,}281}{36} = 230.0278$$
$$\text{Var}(X) = 79.9653$$

2. $E(X^2) = (2^2 \times 1/36) + (3^2 \times 2/36) + (4^2 \times 3/36) + (5^2 \times 4/36)$
$\qquad + (6^2 \times 5/36) + (7^2 \times 6/36) + (8^2 \times 5/36) + (9^2 \times 4/36),$
$\qquad + (10^2 \times 3/36) + (11^2 \times 2/36) + (12^2 \times 1/36)$
$\qquad = 54.833$
$\text{Var}(X) = 5.833$

3. (a) A: expected value 600   standard deviation 70.71
         B: expected value 600   standard deviation 81.24
         C: expected value 550   standard deviation 70.71
   (b) Choose project A.

4. (a) $.6^6 = .0467$
   (b) $(1 - .6)^6 = .0041$

   (c) $\binom{6}{2} \times .6^2 \times .4^4 = .1382$

   (d) X has a binomial distribution with parameters $n = 6$ and $p = .6$.

   $$E(X) = 6 \times .6 = 3.6, \qquad \text{Var}(X) = 6 \times .6 \times .4 = 1.44$$

5. (a) These two events are independent, so multiply the probabilities: $.25 \times .25 = .0625$.
   (b) Use the binomial distribution with $n = 4$, $p = .25$:

   $$\Pr(X = 4) = \binom{4}{4}.25^4 \times .75^0 = .0039$$

   $$\Pr(X = 3) = \binom{4}{3}.25^3 \times .75^1 = .0469$$

   $$\Pr(X = 2) = \binom{4}{2}.25^2 \times .75^2 = .2109$$

   $\Pr(X = 2 \text{ or more}) = .2109 + .0469 + .0039 = .2617$
   (c) $\Pr(X = 3 \text{ or more}) = .0469 + .0039 = .0508$

6. (a) Use *the binomial* distribution with $n = 8$ and $p = .2500$:

i	$Pr(X = i)$	i	$Pr(X = i)$
0	.10011	5	.02307
1	.26697	6	.00385
2	.31146	7	.00037
3	.20764	8	.00002
4	.08652		

(b) .0273

(c) $E(X) = 2,$ $Var(X) = 0.5$

k	$Pr(X = k)$	k	$Pr(X = k)$
5	.0378	11	.1137
6	.0631	12	.0948
7	.0901	13	.0729
8	.1126	14	.0521
9	.1251	15	.0347
10	.1251		

8. (a) .7881

(b) .1152

(c) .242

9. (a) $\dbinom{90}{20}$

(b) $\dfrac{\dbinom{30}{20}}{\dbinom{90}{20}}$

(c) $\dfrac{\dbinom{60}{20}}{\dbinom{90}{20}}$

(d) $\dfrac{\dbinom{60}{14} \times \dbinom{30}{6}}{\dbinom{90}{20}}$

10. Let Z represent a random variable with a standard normal distribution.

(a) $Pr(-1 < Z < 1) = .68$

(b) $Pr(X > 8,500) = Pr[(X - 6,000)/2,000 > (8,500 - 6,000)/2,000]$
$= Pr(Z > 1.25) = .1056$

(c) $Pr(0.5 < Z < 1) = .1498$

(d) Let $W - D$ = withdrawals minus deposits. $W - D$ has a normal distribution with

$$E(W - D) = E(W) - E(D) = 6,000 - 6,500 = -500$$

$$Var(W - D) = Var(W) + (-1)^2 Var(D) = 4,000,000 + 6,250,000$$
$$= 10,250,000$$

standard deviation $= 3{,}201.56$

$$\Pr[(W - D) > 500] = \Pr\{Z > [500 - (-500)]/3{,}201.56\}$$
$$= \Pr(Z > 0.31) = .3783$$

11. To find the probability that one of the batteries will last longer than 70 hours:

$$\Pr(X > 70) = \Pr[Z > (70 - 60)/15] = \Pr(Z > 0.67) = .2514$$

Let $A =$ event that battery A lasts >70 hours; let $B =$ event that B lasts >70 hours.

(a) Since they are independent:

$$\Pr(A \text{ and } B) = \Pr(A) \times \Pr(B) = .2514 = .0632$$

(b) $\Pr(A \text{ or } B) = \Pr(A) + \Pr(B) - \Pr(A \text{ and } B)$
$$= .2514 + .2514 - .0632 = .4396$$

(c) Let $C =$ event that exactly one battery lasts >70 hours.
Let $D =$ event that both batteries last >70 hours (A and B).
Let $E =$ event that at least one battery lasts >70 hours (A or B).
$E = C$ union D; C and D are disjoint.

$$\Pr(E) = \Pr(C) + \Pr(D)$$
$$\Pr(C) = \Pr(E) - \Pr(D) = .4396 - .0632 = .3764$$

12. (a) $\Pr(5 < X < 9) = \Pr(-1 < Z < 1) = .68$
(b) .3085
(c) .0668

13. (a) .68
(b) .9546
(c) .2119
(d) $1 - .9192 = .0808$

14. $E(AB) = 23.08,$ $E(a) = 8.27,$ $E(B) = 3.02$
$\text{Var}(A) = 9.1971, \text{Var}(B) = 0.9996$
$\text{Cov}(A, B) = 23.08 - 8.27 \times 3.02 = -1.8954,$ correlation $= -.625$
$\text{Var}(A + B) = 9.1971 + 0.9996 - 2 \times 1.8954 = 6.4059$

15. $E(AB) = 0.40,$ $E(A) = 0.55,$ $E(B) = 0.47$
$\text{Var}(A) = 0.2475,$ $\text{Var}(B) = 0.2491$
$\text{Cov}(A, B) = 0.47 - 0.40 \times 0.55 = 0.1415,$ correlation $= .5699$
$\text{Var}(A + B) = 0.7796$

13 GAME THEORY

KEY TERMS

equilibrium point a payoff in a payoff matrix that is optimal for both players in the following sense: given Player I's choice, Player II can do no better with another choice, and vice versa

game an activity wherein each of a group of players is faced with a fixed set of choices, and each possible combination of choices among the players has a fixed outcome

payoff matrix a matrix displaying the payoffs in a two-person, zero-sum game

value a number associated with a two-person, zero-sum game: the best that Player I can expect to do, and the least that Player II can expect to lose, on the average, if both play intelligently

zero-sum game a game where the sum of the payoffs to all of the players is zero

---

INTRODUCTION

In business and diplomacy, situations often arise where the outcomes depend on the choices of more than one individual or group.

- Two gas stations face each other across a road. If one station lowers its price significantly, it will probably take away some of its competitor's business. What if the other station then lowers its prices to regain its share of the market? Both sides could end up with their original shares of the market but lower profits. The first station could not control the outcome from its price change; that outcome depended on the second station's reaction.

- A popular children's game is "paper, stone, and scissors." Each player extends either a flat hand ("paper"), a fist ("stone"), or two fingers ("scissors"). Paper covers and thus beats stone, stone bends and thus beats scissors, and scissors cut and thus beat paper. The loser (if there is one) then gives the winner a penny. When I play, if my opponent always sticks out two fingers for scissors, it is in my best interest to extend a fist for stone. My strategy in the game depends on my understanding of my opponent's behavior. In turn, my opponent may react to my constant choice of stone, and start choosing paper.

A **game** involves a set of players, each with a fixed set of choices, where each possible combination of choices among the players has a fixed outcome. (The outcomes are often numbers—profit, cost, and so on. Then they're called *payoffs*.)

Two-person games are those with two players. They are the easiest to analyze, and such a game can be described by a **game diagram** (see Figure 13-1).

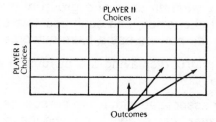

Figure 13-1

THE PRISONER'S DILEMMA

The **prisoner's dilemma** is a type of game situation that often applies in business when one firm is concerned about the actions of its rivals. Here is the situation: Smith and Jones have been arrested. The district attorney suspects that they are guilty of a major crime, but there is not enough hard evidence to convict them of that crime. However, there is enough evidence to convict both Smith and Jones of a minor crime. The district attorney would like to get a confession to the major crime. If neither Smith nor Jones confesses, then each will get 1 year in jail for the minor crime. If both confess, then each will get 5 years in jail for the major crime. If only one confesses, then the DA is willing to drop the charges against that suspect in exchange for testimony against the other suspect, who will get 10 years in jail.

Each suspect has two possible options: confess and not confess. Therefore, we can set up a two-by-two array that lists the possible outcomes of the game:

		Smith confess	Smith don't confess
Jones	confess	S: 5 J: 5	S: 10 J: 0
	don't confess	S: 0 J: 10	S: 1 J: 1

The outcome listed is the number of years in jail (the lower, the better, with 0 meaning that the person goes free). Now we have to figure out: What will happen?

After carefully examining the table, we can see that the best that can happen for both Smith and Jones is 1 year in jail, which will occur if neither confesses. There is no way that both can go free. If they have an opportunity to meet with each other before they are questioned, there is a good chance that they will reach an agreement not to confess; and, indeed, this is what happens.

However, suppose that they are then separated and brought in for questioning, without the other being present. Smith starts thinking that 1 year in jail doesn't look appealing. Since he knows that Jones has agreed not to confess, it suddenly strikes Smith that confessing is a good idea: Jones will get 10 years in jail, but Smith will go free. After thinking it over a bit further, though, Smith feels remorse and decides that double-crossing Jones would be a mean, deceitful thing to do. Therefore, Smith plans to stick to the bargain he made with Jones and not confess. Suddenly, however, panic strikes Smith. What if Jones has been thinking along exactly the same lines? Smith suddenly realizes that, if Jones confesses and Smith doesn't, then Smith will get 10 years in jail. Now Smith thinks, "I would stick with the agreement not to confess if I could be sure that Jones will—but how do I know that Jones won't double-cross me? I better confess to avoid the possibility of 10 years in jail."

Therefore, there are two ways that the agreement may break down: one prisoner may break the agreement out of a deliberate plan to double-cross the other, or one may break it out of fear of being double-crossed. There is no way to know with certainty what will happen.

The structure of the prisoner's dilemma game is the same as that of many real situations. There is one strategy that everyone should follow to achieve the best result for the group. In the prisoner's case, this would be for neither to confess. However, once this strategy has been agreed to, each individual has an incentive to break away from the group agreement. If one person breaks away and the others don't, the person who breaks away reaps a big benefit. In the prisoner's case, the one who confesses goes free if the other sticks to the agreement. However, since all those involved have the incentive to break away, there is the possibility that all will do so. In that case, every member of the group ends up worse off than if all had stuck with the agreement. In the prisoner's case, each gets 5 years in jail if they both confess, which is much worse than the 1 year each would get if both had stuck with the agreement.

There is no way to predict the result of the prisoner's dilemma situation without knowing more about certain factors. One is the personalities of Smith and Jones. If they are good friends who care about each other, then they will probably stick to the agreement not to confess. On the other hand, if they dislike each other, then it is much more likely that they will both confess. Another factor to consider is possible future consequences. If Jones is the leader of a powerful crime organization, Smith may fear that confessing will lead to future retaliation. The circumstances under which the prisoners are questioned can also make a big difference. It is in the DA's best interest to keep them separated as much as possible to prevent them from reaching an agreement and coordinating their answers.

The economic application of the prisoner's dilemma situation occurs in a market where there is a small number of sellers. This type of market is known as an **oligopoly**. (This contrasts with a **monopoly**, where there is only one seller; and **perfect competition**, where there are many sellers, all of them so small that no individual seller has a noticeable effect on the market.) The best strategy for the oligopolists as a group is to get together and agree to raise their prices and restrict their quantities of production. If they are well coordinated, it is possible for the sellers to earn the level of profits that a monopolistic seller would. If the oligopoly firms have set up a formal organization to administer the high price/ restricted quantity agreement, then the organization is called a **cartel**. [The Organization of Petroleum Exporting Countries (OPEC) is an example of a cartel.]

However, once all sellers have raised their prices and reduced their quantities sold to the levels agreed upon, then each individual seller has an incentive to break away from the group and undercut the others. To make a high level of profits, the cartel must have raised the price noticeably above the cost of production. Therefore, any individual seller can charge a price slightly lower than the others, still make a profit for every item sold, and sell to a much larger market share by taking customers away from the other, higher priced cartel members. However, they can't all increase their market shares by charging a lower price than their rival firms. If all members break away from the price agreed upon, the result will be worse for all of them—prices and profits will be lower. (However, here is one important point to remember: the tendency of a cartel to break up may be bad news for its members, but it is good news for consumers because they will pay lower prices.)

Here is an example of an oligopoly market with two sellers:

	Firm *A* keep price high	lower price
Firm *B* keep price high	*A*: high profits *B*: high profits	*A*: very high profits *B*: low profits
lower price	*A*: low profits *B*: very high profits	*A*: mediocre profits *B*: mediocre profits

As in the situation with the two prisoners, there is no way to predict with certainty how the sellers in an oligopoly market will behave. This depends on psychological factors. If the individual firms realize their common interest, then they will be more likely to keep prices high. If there is animosity among the different firms, then they are less likely to act in the best interests of the group. If there are more than three or four sellers, then it will be harder for them to coordinate their prices. The tendency of the sellers to break away from a price agreement has led most cartels to try to adopt a formal structure for enforcing such agreements, but these attempts have not always worked.

In the United States the law is designed to make it difficult for a group of sellers to coordinate a price increase. Section 1 of the Sherman Anti-Trust Act makes it illegal for sellers to agree to raise price and restirct output. This is analogous to a requirement that the prisoners in the prisoner's dilemma situation be kept apart and not be allowed to coordinate their strategy.

Example: Battery Advertising

Here is another business example of a prisoner's dilemma situation. There are two general effects that a business can expect from its advertising: (1) expand the total market for a product (including, it is hoped, the market for that particular firm's product) and (2) expand the share of the market that is purchased from that firm (which means taking customers away from rival firms). In many cases advertising can be expected to have both effects. Advertising that expands the entire market for a product will be beneficial for all of the firms in that market. However, advertising aimed to expand the market share for a particular firm does not help the firms as a group.

A good example of advertising designed only to expand market share is the advertising by the battery industry. An advertisement for a particular brand of batteries probably has little effect on the total demand for batteries. (When was the last time a battery advertisement convinced you to buy a battery, and you then wandered around the store looking for something to put the battery into?)

The total profit of all of the firms in the battery industry would probably increase if all of them drastically reduced their advertising. However, if all did that, then each individual firm would have an incentive to start advertising again, to try to make its batteries stand out and thereby increase its market share at the expense of the other firms. Again we find the prisoner's dilemma situation: each individual has an incentive to break away from the strategy that is best for the whole group.

As we have seen, the outcome of the prisoner's dilemma game cannot be predicted conclusively. We can identify the strategy that is best for the group to follow, but other factors that we cannot predict, such as the friendliness or animosity of the participants, will play a role in determining whether all will stick with the best strategy for the group.

ZERO-SUM GAMES

In the rest of the chapter we will deal with a restricted class of games in which it is easier to determine an optimal strategy for each participant. First, we will restrict our attention to two-person games. (Note that the prisoner's dilemma situation can apply to more than two participants.) Second, we will consider only games where the amount one person wins is the amount that the other person loses. This is clearly not the case for the prisoner's dilemma, in which there is one outcome where both participants do well, and one where both do poorly. Therefore, the prisoner's dilemma is not a game where one person "wins" and the other person "loses."

A game in which one person's gain is the other person's loss is called a **zero-sum** game. The matrix describing a zero-sum game is much simpler than the matrix for the prisoner's dilemma, since we need only to list the outcomes for one of the players; we know that the outcomes for the second player will be negative of the outcomes for the first player. In the rest of this chapter we will restrict our attention to two-person, zero-sum games.

The **payoff matrix A** for the "paper, stone, and scissors" game is as follows:

		Player II		
		paper	stone	scissors
	paper	0	1	−1
Player I	stone	−1	0	1
	scissors	1	−1	0

The values in the cells represent the payoff to Player I.

This chapter will show how to use the simplex algorithm to devise the best way of playing a two-person, zero-sum game.

EQUILIBRIUM

Look at the following payoff matrix **A**:

		Player II 1	2	3	4
	1	1	2	−5	−7
Player I	2	1	−2	6	−3
	3	1	3	3	0
	4	1	2	1	−1

If Player I were to play his first choice, then Player II would want to play her fourth choice, to get a payoff of $-(-7) = 7$, the largest possible in the first row.

But if Player I knew that Player II was playing her fourth choice, he would play his third choice, to get the largest possible payoff, zero, in the fourth column.

Now, if Player II knew that Player I was going to play his third choice, it wouldn't change her strategy at all—her fourth choice would still be the best one for the third row.

The payoff of zero in the third row and fourth column is called an **equilibrium point**—Player I can't do any better by playing any other row, and Player II can't do any better by playing any other column.

Not every payoff matrix has an equilibrium point, and some have more than one.

PURE AND MIXED STRATEGIES

A **pure strategy** is a fixed choice on the part of one player. If I am Player II in the two-person, zero-sum game whose payoff matrix is as follows:

		Player II A	B
Player I	a	−1	1
	b	−1	1

I will always select choice A, since then Player I will always end up paying me 1 unit (remember: the −1 column A refers to the payoff for Player I). If I always choose A any time I play this game, then I am using a pure strategy. I would be stupid to do otherwise.

In the "paper, stone, and scissors" game, however, a pure strategy is clearly a mistake. If I, as Player I, always choose paper, my opponent will figure this out and start choosing scissors all of the time. If I always choose stone, my opponent will choose paper; and if I always choose scissors, my opponent will choose stone.

Rather than play a pure strategy, I could try mixing them. Suppose that I decide to play paper half the time and stone half the time. (I would do this by flipping a coin or in some other random fashion. If I just alternated paper and stone, my opponent could soon figure this out and predict my moves as easily as if I played a pure strategy.)

A strategy whereby I play each choice a fixed fraction of the time (in a random way) is called a **mixed strategy**. A mixed strategy is represented by a probability vector, whose entries are the probabilities corresponding to each choice.

Since my mixed strategy for the "paper, stone, and scissors" game calls for me to play paper half of the time, stone half of the time, and scissors none of the time, my probability vector will be

$$\mathbf{p} = \begin{pmatrix} 1/2 \\ 1/2 \\ 0 \end{pmatrix}$$

What will my opponent's reaction be? If we play the game long enough, she can get a good idea what my mixed strategy is by counting how often I choose paper, how often stone, and so on. She still can't tell what my next choice will be, but she won't be helpless.

If I choose paper half the time, and stone half the time, then she knows that, if she chooses paper, my average payoff will be

$$\frac{1}{2}(0) + \frac{1}{2}(-1) = -\frac{1}{2}$$

Similarly, if she chooses stone, my average payoff will be

$$\frac{1}{2}(1) + \frac{1}{2}(0) = \frac{1}{2}$$

and if she chooses scissors, my average payoff will be

$$\frac{1}{2}(-1) + \frac{1}{2}(1) = 0$$

With my mixed strategy, the payoff matrix, on the average, will be as follows:

		Player II		
		paper	stone	scissors
Player I	**p**	$-1/2$	$1/2$	0

Note that this matrix is merely $\mathbf{p'A}$, as will be true in general. (Remember that $\mathbf{p'A}$ is the matrix product of the one-row matrix $\mathbf{p'}$, the transpose of $\mathbf{p}$, and the matrix $\mathbf{A}$.)

Since the numbers represent what my opponent pays me, if she constantly chooses paper, and I play my mixed strategy, she will win an average of half a cent from me per game.

YOU SHOULD REMEMBER

A pure strategy is a decision to play one choice.
A mixed strategy is a decision to play various choices at various probabilities, and is described by a probability vector.

VALUE OF A GAME

I can do better than lose half a cent per game in the "paper, stone, and scissors" game. If I use the mixed strategy

$$\mathbf{p} = \begin{pmatrix} 1/3 \\ 1/3 \\ 1/3 \end{pmatrix}$$

(That is, play each of the choices one third of the time), then the payoff matrix will become $\mathbf{p'A}$, that is,

		Player II		
		paper	stone	scissors
Player I	**p**	0	0	0

and no matter what my opponent does, on the average we will break even. An optimal strategy, if there is one, must now guarantee me that I will at least break even on the average.

What if my opponent plays a mixed strategy, like this one?

$$\mathbf{q} = \begin{pmatrix} 2/3 \\ 0 \\ 1/3 \end{pmatrix}$$

If I choose paper, my payoff will, on the average, be

$$\frac{2}{3}(0) + \frac{1}{3}(-1) = -\frac{1}{3}$$

If I choose stone, I will average

$$\frac{2}{3}(-1) + \frac{1}{3}(1) = -\frac{1}{3}$$

and if I choose scissors, I will average

$$\frac{2}{3}(1) + \frac{1}{3}(0) = \frac{2}{3}$$

The payoff matrix will become

		Player II
		q
	paper	$-1/3$
Player I	stone	$-1/3$
	scissors	$2/3$

which is just **Aq**. If I always choose scissors, I will aveage two thirds of a cent per game.

This is not my opponent's best strategy. If she chooses my strategy of playing each choice one third of the time, and

$$\mathbf{q} = \begin{pmatrix} 1/3 \\ 1/3 \\ 1/3 \end{pmatrix}$$

then the payoff matrix becomes

		Player II
		q
	paper	0
Player I	stone	0
	scissors	0

and my opponent can guarantee that she will at least break even.

Since I can guarantee that I will at least break even no matter what my opponent does (whether she uses a pure strategy, uses a mixed strategy, or reads tea leaves), and she can guarantee the same thing, then, if we both play intelligently, we will break even on the average.

If I can find a strategy that guarantees that I will gain, on the average, ω (cents, dollars, etc.) per game, no matter what my opponent does, and if my opponent can find a strategy that guarantees that she will pay me at most ω per game on the average, no matter what I do, then ω is called the **value** of the game. If we both play intelligently, I will gain ω per game.

We have showed that the value of the "paper, stone, and scissors" game is 0, and that

$$\begin{pmatrix} 1/3 \\ 1/3 \\ 1/3 \end{pmatrix}$$

is an optimal strategy for both players. It is a mixed strategy that works, on the average, as well as or better than any other strategy, be it pure, mixed, or otherwise.

We will show in the next section that every two-person, zero-sum game has a value, and how linear programming can be used to find both the value and the optimal mixed strategies for the two players.

THE LINEAR PROGRAMMING PROBLEM

Given **A**, an m by n payoff matrix, we want to find ω (the value of the game), **p** (an optimal mixed strategy for Player I), and **q** (an optimal mixed strategy for Player II). Strategy **p** has m entries, and **q** has n entries.

In order for **p** to be an optimal strategy for Player I, we require that tne payoff matrix corresponding to **p**, that is, $\mathbf{p'A}$, have no entry less than ω. This can be written as $\mathbf{p'A} \geq \omega$.

Likewise, for **q** to be an optimal strategy for Player II, we require that $\mathbf{Aq} \leq \omega$.

Finally, we require that **p** and **q** represent probabilities, that is, that the entries for the two vectors be nonnegative and sum to 1, respectively.

Assume for the time being that every entry of $\mathbf{A}$ is positive. Then ω, if it exists, is positive. Our problem is as follows:

$$\mathbf{p}'\mathbf{A} \geq \omega$$
$$\mathbf{A}\mathbf{q} \leq \omega$$
$$p_1 + p_2 + \cdots + p_m = 1$$
$$\mathbf{p} \geq 0$$
$$q_1 + q_2 + \cdots + q_n = 1$$
$$\mathbf{q} \geq 0$$

This is not yet normal form for a linear programming problem, but we are close. Let $\mathbf{x} = \mathbf{p}/\omega$ and $\mathbf{y} = \mathbf{q}/\omega$ (this is why we needed to have $\omega > 0$). Then our problem becomes

$$\mathbf{x}'\mathbf{A} \geq 1$$
$$\mathbf{A}\mathbf{y} \leq 1$$
$$x_1 + x_2 + \cdots + x_m = \frac{1}{\omega}$$
$$\mathbf{x} \geq 0$$
$$y_1 + y_2 + \cdots + y_n = \frac{1}{\omega}$$
$$\mathbf{y} \geq 0$$

This problem actually consists of two linear programming problems, which are duals of each other.

Problem I: $\mathbf{x}'\mathbf{A} \geq 1, \mathbf{x} \geq 0$, and $x_1 + x_2 + \cdots + x_m = 1/\omega$ at a minimum (since Player I wants to make ω as large as possible).

Problem II: $\mathbf{A}\mathbf{y} \leq 1, \mathbf{y} \geq 0$, and $y_1 + y_2 + \cdots + y_n = 1/\omega$ at a maximum (since Player II wants to make ω as small as possible).

Problem I has a feasible solution: since each entry of $\mathbf{A}$ is positive, we just choose the entries of $\mathbf{x}$ large enough to make $\mathbf{x}'\mathbf{A} \geq 1$.

Problem II has a feasible solution: $\mathbf{y} = 0$.

By what we showed in Chapter 6 for the dual problem, we know that, since both Problems I and II have feasible solutions, they both have optimal solutions, with both optimal values being $1/\omega$.

Thus, if we solve Problem I for $\mathbf{x}$ and $1/\omega$, we obtain

$$\omega = \frac{1}{1/\omega} \quad \text{and} \quad \mathbf{p} = \omega\mathbf{x}$$

Likewise, we can obtain $\mathbf{q} = \omega\mathbf{y}$ by solving Problem II. (To put Problem I in normal standard form, we note that the transpose of the row vector $\mathbf{x}'\mathbf{A}$ is the column vector $\mathbf{A}'\mathbf{x}$. Problem I becomes $\mathbf{A}'\mathbf{x} \geq 1, \mathbf{x} \geq 0$, and $-x_1 - x_2 - \cdots - x_m$ is at a maximum.)

What if **A** has a nonpositive entry? Let M be a number large enough that **A** + M (that is, the matrix obtained by adding M to each entry of **A**) has all of its entries positive. This is like Player II just handing Player I M units at the start of each game. This new game has a value ω and optimal strategies **p** and **q**. If Player I hands the M units back after the game, we will have the original payoff matrix **A**. The strategies **p** and **q** will still be optimal, but our value will now be $\omega = \omega - M$.

Example: Finding **p** *and* ω

Let the payoff matrix **A** be

$$\begin{pmatrix} 3 & 8 & 4 \\ 9 & 4 & 6 \end{pmatrix}$$

Let's find **p** and ω.

Every entry of **A** is positive, so we don't have to worry about choosing an M.
We want to solve $\mathbf{A}'\mathbf{x} \geq 1, \mathbf{x} \geq 0$, so that $-x_1 - x_2$ is at a maximum. Plugging this into our simplex method, we get

$$\mathbf{x} = \begin{pmatrix} 1/16 \\ 1/8 \end{pmatrix}$$

Then

$$\frac{1}{\omega} = \frac{1}{16} + \frac{1}{8} = \frac{3}{16}, \quad \omega = \frac{16}{3}, \quad \text{and} \quad \mathbf{p} = \omega\mathbf{x} = \begin{pmatrix} 1/3 \\ 2/3 \end{pmatrix}$$

As a check, $\mathbf{p}'\mathbf{A} = (7, 16/3, 16/3) \geq \omega = 16/3$.

Example: Finding **q** *and* ω

Let the payoff matrix **A** be

$$\begin{pmatrix} 1 & 2 & -1 & -2 \\ 0 & 3 & -1 & 0 \\ 0 & -2 & 4 & 1 \end{pmatrix}$$

Let's find **q** and ω.
Not all of the entries of **A** are positive, so we set

$$\mathbf{A}' = \mathbf{A} + 3 = \begin{pmatrix} 4 & 5 & 2 & 1 \\ 3 & 6 & 2 & 3 \\ 3 & 1 & 7 & 4 \end{pmatrix}$$

all of whose entries are positive.

Solving $A'y \le 1$, $y \ge 0$, to maximize $y_1 + y_2 + y_3 + y_4$ yields

$$y = \begin{pmatrix} 11/54 \\ 1/54 \\ 0 \\ 5/54 \end{pmatrix}$$

Then

$$\frac{1}{\omega'} = \frac{11}{54} + \frac{1}{54} + 0 + \frac{5}{54} = \frac{17}{54}, \qquad \omega' = \frac{54}{17}$$

$$q = \omega'y = \begin{pmatrix} 11/17 \\ 1/17 \\ 0 \\ 5/17 \end{pmatrix}, \qquad \text{and} \qquad \omega = \omega' - 3 = \frac{3}{17}$$

As a check,

$$Aq = \begin{pmatrix} 3/17 \\ 3/17 \\ 3/17 \end{pmatrix} \le \omega = \frac{3}{17}$$

YOU SHOULD REMEMBER

To calculate the value and optimal strategies of a two-person, zero-sum game, with payoff matrix A:

If $A \ge 0$, solve $A'x \ge 1$, $x \ge 0$, and $\Sigma_i x_i$ at a minimum. Then

$$\omega = \frac{1}{\sum_i x_i}, \qquad \text{and} \qquad p = \omega x.$$

To find q, solve $Ay \le 1$, $y \ge 0$, and $\Sigma_i y_i$ at a maximum. Then

$$\omega = \frac{1}{\sum_i y_i}, \qquad \text{and} \qquad q = \omega y.$$

If A has a nonpositive entry, use $A + M$ (where M is large enough that $A + M > 0$). Then p and q are as above, and the value is

$$\omega = \omega' - M$$

(where ω' is the value found for $A + M$).

KNOW THE CONCEPTS

DO YOU KNOW THE BASICS?
Test your understanding of Chapter 13 by answering the following questions:

1. Is poker a game as we have defined "game"?
2. Can a game with more than two players be a zero-sum game?
3. Is a mixed strategy also a pure strategy? Vice versa?
4. If the value of a two-person, zero-sum game is negative, is it more profitable to be the first or the second player?
5. If one choice always pays off less than another, what can you say about an optimal mixed strategy for the game in question?
6. If a game diagram for a two-person, zero-sum game has only one equilibrium point, what will the optimal strategies for the two players be? What will the value of the game be?
7. If a two-person game had payoffs that sum to 2 instead of 0 (that is, two-sum game), how would our method of finding optimal strategies change? What about the value?
8. Is it possible to have different optimal strategies (with the same value) for a two-person, zero-sum game?
9. If there are n choices for a player, how many pure strategies are there? How many mixed strategies? How many symmetric mixed strategies (that is, mixed strategies where all of the entries are the same)?
10. Would the optimal strategies for a two-person, zero-sum game change if the payoff matrix were multiplied by 2? By -5?

TERMS FOR STUDY

cartel	payoff matrix
equilibrium point	perfect competition
game	prisoner's dilemma
game diagram	pure strategy
mixed strategy	value
monopoly	zero-sum game
oligopoly	

PRACTICAL APPLICATION

COMPUTATIONAL PROBLEMS

Find the equilibrium points, if any, for the payoff matrices in Exercises 1–5.

1. $\begin{pmatrix} 1 & -3 & 4 & 1 \\ 5 & 2 & -6 & -5 \\ 8 & -2 & 3 & 0 \end{pmatrix}$

4. $\begin{pmatrix} 1 & 0 & 1 & 0 \\ 0 & -1 & 0 & -1 \\ 1 & 0 & 1 & 0 \end{pmatrix}$

2. $\begin{pmatrix} 1 & -7 & 9 \\ -5 & 6 & 3 \\ 0 & 1 & 5 \\ 6 & 2 & 4 \end{pmatrix}$

5. $\begin{pmatrix} 1 & 2 & 3 \\ 4 & -2 & 6 \\ -3 & 1 & 2 \\ 0 & -2 & 5 \end{pmatrix}$

3. $\begin{pmatrix} 1 & 2 & 4 & 8 \\ -4 & -3 & -2 & -1 \end{pmatrix}$

Find an optimal mixed strategy **p** *for Player I and the value* ω *for each of the payoff matrices in Exercises 6–10.*

6. $\begin{pmatrix} 1 & -3 & 1 \\ 2 & 4 & -3 \end{pmatrix}$

9. $\begin{pmatrix} 1 & 2 \\ 2 & 1 \\ 0 & 3 \end{pmatrix}$

7. $\begin{pmatrix} 2 & 1 & -2 \\ 4 & -5 & 3 \\ -1 & 0 & 4 \end{pmatrix}$

10. $\begin{pmatrix} 1 & 2 & 3 \\ 8 & 9 & 4 \\ 7 & 6 & 5 \end{pmatrix}$

8. $\begin{pmatrix} 2 & -1 & -9 \\ 4 & -2 & 2 \\ -1 & 3 & 0 \\ -3 & 5 & 6 \end{pmatrix}$

Find an optimal mixed strategy $\mathbf{q}$ *for Player II and the value* ω *for each of the payoff matrices in Exercises 11–15.*

11. $\begin{pmatrix} 1 & 2 & -4 & 9 \\ 6 & 0 & -3 & -5 \\ 5 & 8 & 2 & 1 \end{pmatrix}$

14. $\begin{pmatrix} -1 & 0 & 0 \\ 6 & -2 & 6 \\ 8 & 2 & -3 \\ 0 & 4 & 5 \end{pmatrix}$

12. $\begin{pmatrix} 1 & 0 \\ -3 & 2 \\ 1 & -5 \end{pmatrix}$

15. $\begin{pmatrix} 1 & -2 & 3 \\ -2 & 2 & -4 \\ 3 & -4 & 5 \end{pmatrix}$

13. $\begin{pmatrix} 0 & 2 & 4 \\ 1 & -5 & 6 \\ -8 & 1 & 9 \end{pmatrix}$

ANSWERS

KNOW THE CONCEPTS

1. No, because poker, when played honestly, depends on random chance.

2. Yes, as long as, given any set of choices for each player, the sum of the payoffs is 0.

3. A mixed strategy isn't a pure strategy (since more than one choice is used), but a pure strategy is a mixed strategy (where one entry in the probability vector is 1 and the rest are 0's).

4. Since the payoff matrix represents what Player II pays to Player I, a negative value will benefit Player II in the long run.

5. The lesser choice would never be chosen, and the corresponding probability in the mixed strategy would be 0.

6. The equilibrium point will be the value, and the optimal strategies will be pure strategies for its row and column. The two strategies will guarantee for each player that the other player can do no better than the equilibrium point.

7. Such a game would be equivalent to a game whose payoffs were decreased by 1 (and thus would sum to 0), where each player was given 1 at the beginning of each game. The optimal strategies would be the same as those for this new zero-sum game, and the expected payoffs would then sum to twice the value of the zero-sum game.

8. Yes, as easily seen for the following payoff matrix with value 0:

$$\begin{pmatrix} 0 & 0 & 0 \\ 0 & 0 & 0 \\ 0 & 0 & 0 \end{pmatrix}$$

9. There are n pure strategies and an infinite number of mixed strategies, but only one symmetric mixed strategy, where each entry is equal to $1/n$.

10. The optimal strategies would stay the same if the stakes were doubled; but if they were multiplied by -5, inequalities would be reversed and the strategies could change.

PRACTICAL APPLICATION

1. No equilibrium points.
2. No equilibrium points.
3. One equilibrium point in the first row and the first column.
4. Four equilibrium points: in the first row, the second and fourth entries; and in the third row, the second and fourth entries.
5. No equilibrium points.

6. $\mathbf{p} = \begin{pmatrix} 7/11 \\ 4/11 \end{pmatrix}, \qquad \omega = -5/11$

7. $\mathbf{p} = \begin{pmatrix} 4/7 \\ 0 \\ 3/7 \end{pmatrix}, \qquad \omega = 4/7$

8. $\mathbf{p} = \begin{pmatrix} 0 \\ 14/34 \\ 19/34 \\ 1/34 \end{pmatrix}, \qquad \omega = 1$

9. $\mathbf{p} = \begin{pmatrix} 0 \\ 3/4 \\ 1/4 \end{pmatrix}, \qquad \omega = 3/2$

10. $\mathbf{p} = \begin{pmatrix} 0 \\ 0 \\ 1 \end{pmatrix}, \qquad \omega = 5$

11. $\mathbf{q} = \begin{pmatrix} 0 \\ 0 \\ 4/7 \\ 3/7 \end{pmatrix}, \qquad \omega = 11/7$

12. $\mathbf{q} = \begin{pmatrix} 1/3 \\ 2/3 \end{pmatrix}, \qquad \omega = 1/3$

13. $\mathbf{q} = \begin{pmatrix} 7/8 \\ 1/8 \\ 0 \end{pmatrix}, \qquad \omega = 1/4$

14. $\mathbf{q} = \begin{pmatrix} 25/71 \\ 28/71 \\ 18/71 \end{pmatrix}, \qquad \omega = 202/71$

15. $\mathbf{q} = \begin{pmatrix} 3/8 \\ 4/8 \\ 1/8 \end{pmatrix}, \qquad \omega = -1/4$

14

INVENTORY THEORY

INTRODUCTION

Inventory decisions are among the most important made by businesses. A store that runs out of an item may lose potential customers. On the other hand, if the store keeps in stock too much of an item, it will have higher storage and insurance costs.

Inventory theory attempts to minimize the costs associated with inventories by identifying all of the pertinent factors, and mathematically deriving the best values for these factors.

Inventory decisions may be complicated by various factors. Because of transportation or manufacturing delays, there may be a significant delay (called a **lead time**) between when an order is placed and when it arrives. Items may come in fixed-size lots. Demand may fluctuate. An institution or business may need to ensure that it will never run out of an item (for example, hospital supplies) by always keeping extra on hand (called a **buffer inventory**).

INVENTORY PARAMETERS

We may use several different strategies for ordering new supplies.

In an **order quantity inventory**, the order size stays constant. Whenever our supply reaches a fixed minimum, we place another order. Thus, while the order size stays fixed, the time when we order varies according to supply.

On the other hand, if we want to keep a minimal inventory, we can use a **variable order quantity inventory**. In that case we base our order size on customer demand.

If we place orders monthly or on some other regular basis, we use a **fixed period inventory** strategy. Then, of course, our order sizes will vary. The other possibility is a **variable period inventory** strategy.

These strategies are not independent. Often, in practice, a combination of them is used.

There are various costs associated with maintaining an inventory. **Acquisition costs** are costs associated with acquiring the items—trucking, accounting, and so on. **Holding costs**, usually expressed as a fraction of the corresponding purchase costs and denoted by I, include insurance, rent, maintenance, and the like. **Outage costs** are costs associated with running out of an item, and can represent costs due to rush orders or lost customers.

If L is the lead time, and U is the average rate of usage (in items per unit time), then between order and arrival we will deplete our inventory by UL items.

We will denote by R the number of items used in a given period (annually, monthly, etc.)

Then our total cost (TC) for inventory in that period will come from three sources:

1. The cost of the items themselves. If the cost of each item is C, this cost is RC.

2. The inventory carrying cost. This is I times the cost of the average size of the inventory over the period, or CI times the average size of the inventory.

3. The ordering cost. If we assume that the acquisition cost is relatively constant per order, say A, then the ordering cost is A times the number of orders in the given period. If the order size is fixed at Q, then there are R/Q orders in the period, and the ordering cost is RA/Q.

ECONOMIC ORDER QUANTITY

If we assume, further, that stock depletion is constant and known, and that we stock just what we need, we will then order $Q = UL$ at regular intervals, and our stock size will look like that depicted in Figure 14-1. Our average stock size will be $Q/2$. Then

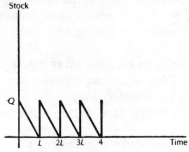

Figure 14-1

$$TC = \text{cost of items} + \text{inventory-carrying cost} + \text{ordering costs}$$

$$= RC + \left(\frac{Q}{2}\right)CI + \frac{RA}{Q}$$

If R, C, I, and A are all known, we can use calculus to solve for an optimal Q.

$$\left(\frac{d}{dQ}\right)TC = \frac{CI}{2} - \frac{RA}{Q^2} = 0$$

when the total cost is at a minimum, and

$$\frac{CI}{2} = \frac{RA}{Q^2}, \qquad Q^2 = \frac{2RA}{CI}, \qquad \text{and} \qquad Q = \sqrt{\frac{2RA}{CI}}$$

choosing the positive root. Also,

$$\left(\frac{d^2}{dQ^2}\right)TC = \frac{2RA}{Q^3}$$

which is positive for this value of Q and thus gives us a minimal total cost. This value of Q is called the **economic order quantity**, abbreviated as **EOQ**. Thus

$$EOQ = \sqrt{\frac{2RA}{CI}}$$

and the number of orders per period becomes

$$\frac{R}{EOQ} = \sqrt{\frac{RCl}{2A}}$$

Because of the square root, small errors in the values of R, A, C, or l will not affect the value of EOQ greatly.

Example 14-1: Calculating the EOQ

PROBLEM   Suppose that Johnson's Emporium sells 9,000 yo-yos per year Each yo-yo costs $2.50, the holding cost is 8 percent, and the ordering cost is $9 per order.

What is the EOQ, and how often should Johnson order yo-yos per year?

SOLUTION $R = 9,000$, $A = \$9$, $C = \$2.50$,   and $l = 0.08$

$$EOQ = \sqrt{\frac{2 \times 9,000 \times 9}{2.50 \times 0.08}} = 900$$

and Johnson should order

$$\frac{R}{EOQ} = \frac{9,000}{900} = 10 \text{ times per year}$$

YOU SHOULD REMEMBER

$$EOQ = \sqrt{\frac{2RA}{CI}}$$

is the order size that will minimize total cost when the demand is constant, where R = demand per period, A = acquisition cost per order, C = cost per item, and I = inventory cost (fraction of the cost per item).

VARIABLE DEMAND

It may well be that the demand is no longer constant, and varies enough that we don't fully trust the EOQ. We will then want to take into account how the demand varies, in determining how large Q should be, and when we should reorder.

Since the demand is now variable, it is possible that we will have a stockout (that is, run out of stock) if we don't order enough. Let's assume that the cost of a stockout is constant, and call it d.

To minimize costs, we want to place orders that are a little larger than the demand we expect. Let S stand for the stock demand during the lead time, and let $E(S)$ be the expected demand. If our demand were constant, as before, we would reorder when supply fell so that $E(S) = S$. Now, since S varies, we want to reorder when our supply falls to $E(S) + SS$, where SS is our **safety stock**. We call

$$E(S) + SS = ROP$$

our **reorder point**, that is, the size of the stock when we want to place our new order.

Given no other costs, we might want to set SS very high to minimize our risk of stockout. Unfortunately, storage and insurance costs again enter the picture. Recall that the inventory-carrying cost per unit is CI.

We have to balance off, somehow, the risk of stockout and its associated cost against inventory-carrying cost. Once again, we turn to our total cost equation. Now the inventory-carrying cost is

$$\left(\frac{Q}{2} + SS\right)CI = \left[\frac{Q}{2} + ROP - E(S)\right]CI$$

on the average. Our cost of items and ordering costs will stay the same. We have a new cost, the expected stockout cost, to consider.

The cost per stockout is d. The number of lead times during whch a stockout can occur is R/Q. We will call the average number of stockouts per lead time $E(SPL)$. Then the expected stockout cost will be $d[E(SPL)](R/Q)$.

We now need to be able to compute $E(SPL)$. Stockouts occur when the demand S exceeds the supply ROP at the time of reordering, and thus

$$E(SPL) = \sum_{S > ROP} (S - ROP)\Pr(S)$$

Note that $E(SPL)$ depends on both the probabilities $\Pr(S)$ and the quantity ROP.

Example 14-2: Calculating E(SPL)

PROBLEM   Suppose that Joe's Piano Store has in the past experienced the following demands in pianos per lead time:

S	Pr(S)	Pr(demands ≥ S)
0	.60	.40
1	.15	.25
2	.13	.12
3	.12	0
	$E(S) = 0.77$	

What should Joe's order size, Q, be?

SOLUTION If Joe tries the following ROP's, he will have the following $E(SPL)$'s:

ROP	E(SPL)
0	$(1-0)(.15) + (2-0)(.13) + (3-0)(.12) = 0.77$
1	$(2-1)(.13) + (3-1)(.12) = 0.37$
2	$(3-2)(.12) = 0.12$
3	0

Joe's total cost, in general will be

$$TC = RC + \left[\frac{Q}{2} + ROP - E(S)\right]Cl + \frac{RA}{Q} + d[E(SPL)]\left(\frac{R}{Q}\right)$$

This depends on both Q and ROP, given the probabilities $\Pr(S)$. To minimize costs, we would want to set $\partial TC/\partial Q = 0$ and $\partial TC/\partial ROP = 0$. Then

$$\frac{\partial TC}{\partial Q} = \frac{Cl}{2} - \frac{RA}{Q^2} - \frac{d[E(SPL)]R}{Q^2} = 0$$

$$\frac{Cl}{2} = \frac{RA + d[E(SPL)]R}{Q^2}$$

$$Q^2 = \frac{2R(A + d[E(SPL)])}{Cl}$$

(1)

$$Q = \sqrt{\frac{2R(A + d[E(SPL)])}{Cl}}$$

$$\frac{\partial TC}{\partial ROP} = Cl + \left(\frac{dR}{Q}\right)\left[\frac{\partial E(SPL)}{\partial ROP}\right]$$

$$\frac{\partial E(SPL)}{\partial ROP} = -\sum_{S>ROP} \Pr(S) = -\Pr(S > ROP)$$

$$0 = Cl + \left(\frac{dR}{Q}\right)[-\Pr(S > ROP)]$$

$$\frac{dR[\Pr(S > ROP)]}{Q} = Cl$$

(2)
$$\Pr(S > ROP) = \frac{ClQ}{dR}$$

Now, given C, l, d, R, and A, we would still be hard put to solve for Q and ROP. Given $\Pr(S > ROP)$, we could solve for ROP from our given probabilities, but the equation for Q contains $E(SPL)$, which depends on ROP, and the equation for $\Pr(S > ROP)$ contains Q.

The way around this difficulty is to calculate EOQ as in the preceding section. This value for Q assumes a constant demand, and thus is an approximation to the Q we seek. It also has the virtue of being insensitive to variations in C, l, R, and A.

Therefore, we take this value of Q, insert it into equation (2), and solve for $\Pr(S > ROP)$. Now, near the optimal value for $\Pr(S > ROP)$,

$$E(SPL) = \sum_{S>ROP} (S - ROP)\Pr(S)$$

is dominated by the first term, where $S - ROP = 1$. For this reason, $E(SPL)$ is approximately equal to

$$\sum_{S>ROP} (1)\Pr(S) = \Pr(S > ROP)$$

and we can use our value of $\Pr(S > ROP)$ for $E(SPL)$ in equation (1).

We then take this value of Q, calculate $\Pr(S > ROP)$ again with equation (2), and repeat until the values of Q and $\Pr(S > ROP)$ remain constant. Thus we can use our cumulative probabilities to calculate ROP.

Example 14-3: Calculating Order Size for Variable Demand

PROBLEM   In Example 14-2, assume that Joe pays $10,000 per piano to his
distributor, sells 100 pianos per year, and has a 2 percent inventory
cost, a $100 per stockout cost (for having to place rush orders with
his distributor), and an acquisition cost of $5 per order. Then

$$C = 10,000, \quad R = 100, \quad l = 0.02,$$
$$A = 100, \quad \text{and} \quad d = 100$$

What should the order size be?

SOLUTION
$$EOQ = \sqrt{\frac{2RA}{Cl}} = \sqrt{\frac{2(100)(100)}{(10,000)(0.02)}} = 10$$

Inserting this value for Q into equation (2) gives

$$\Pr(S > ROP) = \frac{(10,000)(0.02)(10)}{(100)(100)} = .2$$

Inserting this value into equation (1) for $E(SPL)$ gives

$$Q = \sqrt{\frac{2(100)[100 + (100)(0.2)]}{(10,000)(0.02)}} = 10.954$$

$$\Pr(S > ROP) = \frac{(10,000)(0.02)(10.954)}{(100)(100)} = .2191$$

$$Q = \sqrt{\frac{2(100)[100 + (100)(0.2191)]}{(10,000)(0.02)}} = 11.041$$

$$\Pr(S > ROP) = \frac{(10,000)(0.02)(11.041)}{(100)(100)} = .2208$$

$$Q = \sqrt{\frac{2(100)[100 + (100)(0.2208)]}{(10,000)(0.02)}} = 11.049$$

$$\Pr(S > ROP) = \frac{(10,000)(0.02)(11.049)}{(100)(100)} = .2210$$

$$Q = \sqrt{\frac{2(100)[100 + (100)(0.2210)]}{(10,000)(0.02)}} = 11.050$$

$$\Pr(S > ROP) = \frac{(10,000)(0.02)(11.050)}{(100)(100)} = .2210$$

Since $\Pr(S > ROP)$ stays the same, so will Q, and we have our optimal values. We round Q down to 11, and looking at Example 14-2, we see that this value of $\Pr(S > ROP)$ corresponds to $ROP = 1$. At these values, our expected total cost is

$$TC = (100)(10,000) + \left(\frac{11}{2} + 1 - 0.77\right)(10,000)(0.02)$$

$$+ \frac{(100)(100)}{11} + (100)(0.37)\left(\frac{100}{11}\right)$$

$$= \$1,002,392$$

The values of Q and $\Pr(S > ROP)$ converged relatively quickly because the value of Q did not depend greatly on the value of $E(SPL)$.

YOU SHOULD REMEMBER

Given values for the following quantities: R = demand per period, A = acquisition cost per order, d = stockout cost per unit, C = cost per item, and I = inventory cost, then, to calculate Q = order size and ROP = reorder point when demand varies, first approximate Q by

$$EOQ = \sqrt{\frac{2RA}{CI}}$$

Then use this value for Q in

(a) $$\Pr(S > ROP) = \frac{CIQ}{dR}$$

and use $E(SPL) = \Pr(S > ROP)$ in

(b) $$Q = \sqrt{\frac{2R(A + d[E(SPL)])}{CI}}$$

Repeat (a) and (b) until the values of $\Pr(S > ROP)$ and Q stop changing. Use the cumulative probabilities for $\Pr(S)$ to find ROP.

KNOW THE CONCEPTS

DO YOU KNOW THE BASICS?

Test your understanding of Chapter 14 by answering the following questions:

1. What are the costs associated with understocking and overstocking?
2. How could you calculate the probabilities associated with a variable demand?
3. Can a constant demand inventory be analyzed as if it were a variable demand inventory?
4. Why do small variations in R, A, C, and I not affect the EOQ greatly?
5. In Example 14-3, why did we stop our calculations when $\Pr(S > ROP)$ stayed constant?

TERMS FOR STUDY

acquisition cost

buffer inventory

economic order quantity (EOQ)

fixed period inventory

holding cost

inventory theory

lead time

order quantity inventory

outage cost

reorder point (ROP)

safety stock

variable order quantity inventory

variable period inventory

PRACTICAL APPLICATION

COMPUTATIONAL PROBLEMS

Assuming a constant demand, calculate the EOQ (rounded to the nearest integer) for each problem in Exercises 1–5.

1. Jones Air Conditioners sells 1,000 deluxe air conditioners per year at $250 each. Each order costs $50, and the inventory cost is 5 percent.
2. Jefferson's Quality Tombstones sells 55 tombstones per year at $200 each. Each order costs $10, and the inventory cost is 1 percent.
3. Smith's Music Emporium sells 600 oboe reeds per year at $1 each. Each order costs $20, and the inventory cost is 2.5 percent.
4. Redburn's Furniture Store sells 100 patio umbrellas per year at $70 each. Each order costs $7, and the inventory cost is 10 percent.
5. George's Doorknob Supply House sells 75 Model K doorknobs per year at $35 each. Each order costs $3, and the inventory cost is 6 percent.

In Exercises 6–10, calculate, in each case, the ROP and optimal order size Q (rounded to the nearest integers), given the indicated values for R, A, d, C, l, and P(S).

6.

S	Pr(S)	$R = 100$
0	.10	$A = \$20$
1	.20	$d = \$15$
2	.25	$C = \$75$
3	.20	$I = 6$ percent
4	.15	
5	.10	

7.

S	Pr(S)	$R = 15$
0	.50	$A = \$5$
1	.30	$d = \$10$
2	.10	$C = \$25$
3	.07	$I = 10$ percent
4	.03	

8.

S	Pr(S)	$R = 30$
0	.2	$A = \$10$
1	.5	$d = \$15$
2	.2	$C = \$10$
3	.1	$I = 1$ percent

9.

S	Pr(S)	$R = 50$
0	.10	$A = \$5$
1	.30	$d = \$10$
2	.25	$C = \$8$
3	.30	$I = 5$ percent
4	.05	

10.	S	Pr(S)	$R = 60$
	0	.05	$A = \$12$
	1	.10	$d = \$20$
	2	.15	$C = \$30$
	3	.20	$I = 2$ percent
	4	.30	
	5	.20	

ANSWERS

KNOW THE CONCEPTS

1. Understocking results in lost customers and rush orders. Overstocking results in less space available for other inventory and in higher insurance and maintenance costs.

2. If the company has kept records, you could examine past demands. Other companies with similar products could be observed, and customers could be polled.

3. Yes, where Pr(S_0) = 1 for the constant demand S_0, and Pr(S) = 0 elsewhere.

4. The square root dampens small perturbations, lessening their effect.

5. If we had performed the calculation for Q, we would have obtained the same value as for the previous Q calculation. From this point on, 0 and Pr($S > ROP$) will not change.

PRACTICAL APPLICATION

1. 89
2. 23
3. 980
4. 14
5. 13

6. $Q = 31$, $ROP = 4$
7. $Q = 9$, $ROP = 2$
8. $Q = 78$, $ROP = 3$
9. $Q = 36$, $ROP = 3$
10. $Q = 50$, $ROP = 5$

15 QUEUING THEORY

KNOW THE TERMS

arrival rate (λ) the average number of arrivals in a queue per unit time

queuing theory the study of the parameters involved in units having to wait to be serviced

service rate (μ) the average number of units serviced per unit time

steady-state queue a queue for which the probabilities associated with queue length remain constant

INTRODUCTION

A queue is a line, pure and simple. This line can consist of

- people lined up at a cash register in a grocery store

- cars being assembled in an automobile factory

- ships waiting to use a docking facility

Usually, the faster a line moves, the better for the business. If people see that the lines are too long in a particular grocery store, they will not shop there. In that case the owner may want to increase the number of registers and thus shorten the lines. This reasoning, however, can be taken to an absurd extreme—no owner wants to have more registers operating than there are customers in the store.

Various costs, such as a cashier's salary, have to be taken into account when planning how to service queues. **Queuing theory** attempts to analyze these quantities and provide enough data for an informed decision.

QUEUE PARAMETERS

There are many different kinds of queues. A single cashier in a movie theater results in a **single-channel queue**, while cashiers in a supermarket deal with a **multiple-channel queue**.

A queue can be served in different orders. Most cashiers serve **first-in, first-out (FIFO)**. An "in" basket's contents, on the other hand, are processed **last-in, first-out (LIFO)**. Any procedure for determining what person or item is served next is called a *queuing discipline*. Some queuingdisciplines, such as the procedure used at a hospital admissions desk, assign *priorities*.

Most servicing facilities deal with a fairly large number of potential customers—in other words, an *infinite population*. On the other hand, NASA services only a small number of space shuttles. This organization deals with a *finite population* and allocates its resources accordingly.

The **queue length** is the largest number of items that could possibly be waiting to be serviced. If there is no restriction on the possible length of the queue, we say that the queue length is *infinite* (for example, ships at a docking facility). Otherwise, the queue length is infinite (for example, a barber shop which has only a finite number of chairs for seating customers while they wait).

The **arrival rate**, λ, is the average number of items arriving in the system per unit time. The value of λ may fluctuate, but often we can count on its staying fairly constant. If, in addition, we assume that the probability of two items arriving simultaneously is negligible, then the number of items arriving in a single-channel, FIFO queue with an infinite population in a given interval follows a *Poisson distribution with parameter λ* (see Chapter 12).

Similarly, the **service rate**, μ, is the average number of items serviced per unit time. Again, μ may fluctuate; but if it stays constant, then, for a single-channel, FIFO queue with an infinite population, the service time satisfies an *exponential distribution with parameter μ* (see Chapter 12).

We now assume that our queue is a single-channel, FIFO queue with an infinite population. Not only does this simplify the mathematics of the model, but also the behavior of many other kinds of queues can be deduced from this system's behavior.

The arrival/service ratio, ρ, is just λ/μ. In order that a queue will not increase in length indefinitely, we want to assume that λ is less than μ, that is, $\rho < 1$.

A queue may be in a **transient state** if the servicing has not settled into a regular pattern. A store that has just opened for the day is in a transient state in its service of its customers. As the morning progresses, the service achieves a **steady state**—a regular pattern of service is established. The length of the queue may still fluctuate, but the owner can tell what the odds are that a queue will be of a certain length. If we set $P_n(t)$ equal to the probability that the system at time t will have n people in it, then, for a queue in a steady state,

$$\left(\frac{d}{dt}\right)[P_n(t)] = 0$$

that is, $P_n(t) = P_n$ is independent of the time, t. $P_0(t)$ is the fraction of the time that the servicing center is idle.

The mean number of units in the system is labeled L, and the mean number of units in the queue is called L_q. W is the mean wait in the system before leaving, and W_q is the mean wait in the queue.

STEADY-STATE QUEUES OF INFINITE LENGTH

If we can determine $P_n = P_n(t)$ for each n, we will be able to tell a great deal about the queue.

Between time t and time $t + \Delta t$, where Δt is small, there is a probability of $\lambda \Delta t$ that there will be an arrival of $1 - \lambda \Delta t$ that there will be no arrival, of $\mu \Delta t$ that an item will be serviced, and of $1 - \mu \Delta t$ that an item will not be serviced. Assuming that arrivals and servicings are independent, and that Δt^2 is negligibly small, we have four possibilities to consider:

1. The queue may have an arrival but no servicings, and the queue length increases by 1. The probability of this happening is

    $$\lambda \Delta t(1 - \mu \Delta t) = \lambda \Delta t - \lambda\mu \Delta t^2 = \lambda \Delta t$$

2. If there is at least one item in the system, an item may be serviced, but nothing may arrive, and the queue length decreases by 1. The probability of this happening is

    $$\mu \Delta t(1 - \lambda \Delta t) = \mu \Delta t - \lambda\mu \Delta t^2 = \mu \Delta t$$

3. There are no arrivals or servicings, and the queue length stays the same. The probability of this happening is

    $$(1 - \lambda \Delta t)(1 - \mu \Delta t) = 1 - \lambda \Delta t - \mu \Delta t + \lambda\mu \Delta t^2 = 1 - \lambda \Delta t - \mu \Delta t$$

4. There are both an arrival and a servicing, and the queue length stays the same. The probability of this happening is

    $$(\lambda \Delta t)(\mu \Delta t) = \lambda\mu \Delta t^2 = 0$$

This is depicted in Figure 15-1. Thus

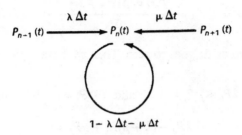

Figure 15-1

$$P_n(t + \Delta t) = (\lambda \, \Delta t)P_{n-1}(t) + (1 - \lambda \, \Delta t - \mu \, \Delta t)P_n(t) + (\mu \, \Delta t)P_{n+1}(t)$$

and

$$\frac{P_n(t + \Delta t) - P_n(t)}{\Delta t} = \lambda P_{n-1}(t) - (\lambda + \mu)P_n(t) + \mu P_{n+1}(t)$$

As Δt approaches zero, the expression on the right-hand side of the last equation approaches zero, since in a steady state the probabilities do not change with time. We have

$$\lambda P_{n-1} - (\lambda + \mu)P_n + \mu P_{n+1} = 0$$

If $n = 0$, the situation is as depicted in Figure 15-2. The queue will have no

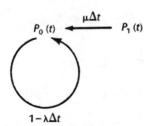

Figure 15-2

new arrivals with probability $1 - \lambda \, \Delta t$, and will service 1 unit, if it has a unit, with probability $\mu \, \Delta t$. Then

$$P_{n+1}(t + \Delta t) = (1 - \lambda \, \Delta t)P_0(t) + (\mu \, \Delta t)P_1(t)$$

and

$$\frac{P_0(t + \Delta t) - P_0(t)}{\Delta t} = -\lambda P_0(t) + \mu P_1(t)$$

which goes to zero as Δt goes to zero. Then we have

$$-\lambda P_0 + \mu P_1 = 0 \quad \text{and} \quad P_1 = \left(\frac{\lambda}{\mu}\right) P_0 = \rho P_0$$

$$\lambda P_0 - (\lambda + \mu) P_1 + \mu P_2 = 0$$

$$P_2 = \left(\frac{1}{\mu}\right)[(\lambda + \mu) P_1 - \lambda P_0)]$$

$$= \left(\frac{1}{\mu}\right)\left[(\lambda + \mu)\left(\frac{\lambda}{\mu}\right) P_0 - \lambda P_0\right]$$

$$= \left(\frac{\lambda^2}{\mu^2}\right) P_0 = \rho^2 P_0$$

Continuing the same way with

$$\lambda P_1 - (\lambda + \mu) P_2 + \mu P_3 = 0, \quad \text{etc.}$$

we see that $P_n = \rho^n P_0$ in general. We now need to determine P_0.
Since the probabilities for all possible cases must add up to 1,

$$\sum_n P_n = \sum_n \rho^n P_0 = P_0 \sum_n \rho^n = \frac{P_0}{1 - \rho} = 1$$

(where Σx means summation over all n) and

$$P_0 = 1 - \rho, \quad P_n = \rho^n (1 - \rho)$$

(The smaller $\rho = \lambda/\mu$ is, the less likely the queue is to be very long; this agrees with out intuition.)

$$L = \sum_n n P_n = \sum_n n \rho^n (1 - \rho) = (1 - \rho) \sum_n n \rho^n$$

Now, for $0 < |x| < 1$, we know that

$$\sum_n x^n = \frac{1}{1-x}$$

$$\frac{1}{(1-x)^2} = \left(\frac{d}{dx}\right)\left(\frac{1}{1-x}\right) = \left(\frac{d}{dx}\right)\sum_n x^n = \sum_n nx^{n-1} = \left(\frac{1}{x}\right)\sum_n nx^n$$

and

$$\sum_n nx^n = \frac{x}{(1-x)^2}$$

(which is also true if $x = 0$). Thus

$$L = (1-\rho)\sum_n n\rho^n = \frac{\rho}{1-\rho} = \frac{\lambda}{\mu - \lambda}$$

$L_q = L - ($ the fraction of the time that a unit is being serviced$)$

$$= L - (1 - P_0) = L - \rho = \frac{\rho^2}{1-\rho} = \frac{\lambda^2}{\mu(\mu - \lambda)}$$

For a steady state, the average wait in the system is the average number of items in the system, divided by the average arrival rate (not the average servicing rate, since the servicing center is idle part of the time). Thus

$$W = \frac{L}{\lambda} = \frac{1}{\mu - \lambda}$$

and similarly

$$W_q = \frac{L_q}{\lambda} = \frac{\lambda}{\mu(\mu - \lambda)}$$

Example 15-1: An Infinite-Length, Steady-State Queue

Suppose that a car wash can wash only one car at a time, and can wash 15 cars per hour. Suppose also that cars arrive at the rate of 12 per hour on the average. When the car wash achieves a steady state, we have

$$\lambda = 12 \text{ per hour}, \qquad \mu = 15 \text{ per hour}, \qquad \rho = \frac{\lambda}{\mu} = 0.8$$

and

$$P_n = \rho^n(1-\rho) = (0.8)^n(0.2)$$

Then

$$L = \frac{\rho}{1 - \rho} = \frac{0.8}{0.2} = 4 \text{ cars}$$

$$L_q = \frac{\rho^2}{1 - \rho} = \frac{(0.8)^2}{0.2} = 3.2 \text{ cars}$$

and

$$W = \frac{L}{\lambda} = \frac{4}{12/\text{hour}} = \frac{1}{3} \text{ hour} = 20 \text{ minutes}$$

$$W_q = \frac{L_q}{\lambda} = \frac{3.2}{12/\text{hour}} = \frac{4}{15} \text{ hour} = 16 \text{ minutes}$$

Thus the average number of cars in the car wash is 4, the average number in line is 3.2, the average time that a car is at the car wash is 20 minutes, and the average wait in line is 16 minutes.

STEADY-STATE QUEUES OF FINITE LENGTH

If the system can hold at most M units, then $P_n = 0$ for $n \geq M$. We have

$$1 = \sum_n P_n = \sum_{0 \leq n \leq M} \rho^n P_0 = P_0 \sum_{0 \leq n \leq M} \rho^n = \frac{P_0(1 - \rho^{M+1})}{1 - \rho}$$

and

$$P_0 = \frac{1 - \rho}{1 - \rho^{M+1}}, \qquad P_n = \frac{\rho^n(1 - \rho)}{1 - \rho^{M+1}} \quad \text{for } 0 \leq n \leq M$$

Now

$$L = \sum_n n P_n = \frac{\sum_{0 \leq n \leq M} n\rho^n(1 - \rho)}{1 - \rho^{M+1}} = \left(\frac{1 - \rho}{1 - \rho^{M+1}}\right) \sum_{0 \leq n \leq M} n\rho^n$$

Again, we find $\Sigma_{0 \le n \le M} n\rho^n$ using derivatives:

$$\left(\frac{d}{dx}\right)\left(\frac{1-x^{M+1}}{1-x}\right) = \frac{1-(M+1)x^M + Mx^{M+1}}{(1-x)^2}$$

$$= \left(\frac{d}{dx}\right)\sum_{0 \le n \le M} x^n = \sum_{0 \le n \le M} nx^{n-1} = \left(\frac{1}{x}\right)\sum_{0 \le n \le M} nx^n$$

and

$$\sum_{0 \le n \le M} nx^n = \frac{x-(M+1)x^{M+1} + Mx^{M+2}}{(1-x^2)} \left(\frac{1-\rho}{1-\rho^{M+1}}\right)\sum_{0 \le n \le M} n\rho^n$$

$$= \frac{\rho-(M+1)\rho^{M+1} + M\rho^{M+2}}{(1-\rho)(1-\rho^{M+1})}$$

$$= \frac{\rho}{1-\rho} - \frac{(M+1)\rho^{M+1}}{1-\rho^{M+1}}$$

$$L_q = L - (1-P_0) = \frac{\rho}{1-\rho} - \frac{(M+1)\rho^{M+1}}{1-\rho^{M+1}} - 1 + \frac{1-\rho}{1-\rho^{M+1}}$$

Before we calculate the average waiting times, we have to determine the **effective arrival rate**, λ_e. If the system is full, with M items in it, then new units or customers will be turned away. The probability of this happening is P_M, and $\lambda_e = \lambda(1 - P_M)$. Then

$$W = \frac{L}{\lambda_e} = \frac{L}{\lambda(1-P_M)}$$

$$W_q = \frac{L_q}{\lambda_e} = \frac{L_q}{\lambda(1-P_M)}$$

Example 15-2: A Finite-Length, Steady-State Queue

If, in addition, the car wash in Example 15-1 has room for only a total of 10 cars on its premises, we then have a queue of finite length with $M = 10$. Also, $\rho = 08$.

$$P_0 = \frac{1-0.8}{1-(0.8)^{11}} = .2188$$

$$P_n = \rho^n P_0 = (.2188)(0.8)^n \quad \text{for } 0 \le n \le 10$$

$$L = \frac{\rho}{1-\rho} - \frac{(M+1)\rho^{M+1}}{1-\rho^{M+1}} = 2.966$$

$$L_q = L - (1 - P_0) = 2.185$$

$$P_{10} = .02349$$

$$\lambda_e = \lambda(1 - P_{10}) = (12/\text{hour})(1 - .02349) = 11.72/\text{hour}$$

$$W = \frac{L}{\lambda_e} = 0.2531 \text{ hour} = 15.19 \text{ minutes}$$

$$W_q = \frac{L_q}{\lambda_e} = 0.1865 \text{ hour} = 11.19 \text{ minutes}$$

Because fewer customers can be accommodated, we have significantly cut the average length and waiting time.

YOU SHOULD REMEMBER

The probability P_n that a steady-state queue of infinite length will contain n units is $\rho^n(1-\rho)$, where $\rho = \lambda/\mu$ is the ratio of the arrival rate to the service rate.

The probability P_n that a steady-state queue of finite length M will contain n units is $\rho^n(1-\rho)/(1-\rho^{M+1})$, for $0 \le n \le M$.

The effective arrival rate, λ_e, is obtained by multiplying the arrival rate by the probability that a unit will not be turned away because the queue is full, that is, $\lambda_e = \lambda(1 - P_M)$.

KNOW THE CONCEPTS

DO YOU KNOW THE BASICS?

Test your understanding of Chapter 15 by answering the following questions:

1. Does a steady-state queue contain a fixed number of units?
2. Is the effective arrival rate for a finite-length queue larger or smaller than the real arrival rate?
3. What would happen if $\lambda > \mu$?
4. What kind of queuing discipline is used by someone washing dishes that are piling up in a sink?

5. Is it likely or unlikely that a store will be in a steady state when it opens in the morning?

TERMS FOR STUDY

arrival rate

effective arrival rate

first-in, first-out (FIFO)

last-in, first out (LIFO)

multiple-channel queue

queue length

queuing discipline

queuing theory

service rate

single-channel queue

steady-state queue

transient-state queue

PRACTICAL APPLICATION

COMPUTATIONAL PROBLEMS

In Exercises 1–5, use the given values of λ and μ to calculate, in each case, ρ, P_n, L, L_q, W, and W_q for an infinite-length, steady-state, single-channel queue.

    1. $\lambda = 8$ per hour, $\mu = 15$ per hour

    2. $\lambda = 200$ per hour, $\mu = 300$ per hour

    3. $\lambda = 5$ per hour, $\mu = 10$ per hour

    4. $\lambda = 100$ per hour, $\mu = 400$ per hour

    5. $\lambda = 60$ per hour, $\mu = 100$ per hour

    In Exercises 6–10, use the given values of M, λ, and μ to calculate, in each case, ρ, P_n, L, L_q, λ_e, W, and W_q for a finite-length, steady-state, single-channel queue.

    6. $M = 5$, $\lambda = 8$ per hour, $\mu = 15$ per hour

    7. $M = 10$, $\lambda = 200$ per hour, $\mu = 300$ per hour

    8. $M = 6$, $\lambda = 5$ per hour, $\mu = 10$ per hour

    9. $M = 5$, $\lambda = 100$ per hour, $\mu = 400$ per hour

    10. $M = 10$, $\lambda = 60$ per hour, $\mu = 100$ per hour

---

ANSWERS

KNOW THE CONCEPTS

    1. Not necessarily. All that is required of a steady-state queue is that the probability P_n be constant for each n.

2. Since some customers may be turned away from a finite-length queue, λ_e will be less than or equal to λ.

3. Since more customers would arrive than would be serviced, the number of customers in the queue would increase indefinitely.

4. Probably last-in, first-out (LIFO).

5. The store is probably not in a steady-state condition upon opening, since customers would not yet be in the queue.

PRACTICAL APPLICATION

1. $\rho = 0.533$, $P_n = (0.466)(0.533)^n$, $L = 1.14$, $L_q = 0.610$, $W = 0.143$ hour, $W_q = 0.0762$ hour

2. $\rho = 0.667$, $P_n = (0.333)(0.667)^n$, $L = 2.00$, $L_q = 1.33$, $W = 0.0100$ hour, $W_q = 0.00667$ hour

3. $\rho = 0.500$, $P_n = (0.500)(0.500)^n$, $L = 1.00$, $L_q = 0.500$, $W = 0.200$ hour, $W_q = 0.100$ hour

4. $\rho = 0.250$, $P_n = (0.750)(0.250)^n$, $L = 0.333$, $L_q = 0.0833$, $W = 0.00333$ hour, $W_q = 0.000833$ hour

5. $\rho = 0.600$, $P_n = (0.400)(0.600)^n$, $L = 1.50$, $L_q = 0.900$, $W = 0.0250$ hour, $W_q = 0.0150$ hour

6. $\rho = 0.533$, $P_n = (0.478)(0.533)^n$ for $0 \leq n \leq 5$, $L = 1.00$, $L_q = 0.479$, $\lambda_e = 7.84$ per hour, $W = 0.128$ hour, $W_q = 0.0612$ hour

7. $\rho = 0.67$, $P_n = (0.337)(0.667)^n$ for $0 \leq n \leq 10$, $L = 1.87$, $L_q = 1.21$, $\lambda_e = 199$ per hour, $W = 0.00941$ hour, $W_q = 0.00608$ hour

8. $\rho = 0.500$, $P_n = (0.504)(0.500)^n$ for $0 \leq n \leq 6$, $L = 0.945$, $L_q = 0.449$, $\lambda_e = 4.96$ per hour, $W = 0.190$ hour, $W_q = 0.0905$ hour

9. $\rho = 0.250$, $P_n = (0.750)(0.250)^n$ for $0 \leq n \leq 5$, $L = 0.332$, $L_q = 0.0821$, $\lambda_e = 99.9$ per hour, $W = 0.00332$ hour, $W_q = 0.000821$ hour

10. $\rho = 0.600$, $P_n = (0.401)(0.600)^n$ for $0 \leq n \leq 10$, $L = 1.46$, $L_q = 0.861$, $\lambda_e = 59.9$ per hour, $W = 0.0244$ hour, $W_q = 0.0144$ hour

16

DECISION THEORY

KEY TERMS

decision theory the study of making decisions designed to achieve some objective, often under conditions of uncertainty

decision tree a diagram that illustrates all possible consequences of different decisions in different states of nature

expected payoff the expected value of the payoff resulting from a decision

---

Every day of our lives, we are faced with decisions. Many of them involve outcomes where the difference between the possible results is inconsequential. If I use the "wrong" toothpaste, my teeth may not be as white but are unlikely to be drastically affected. If I put my shoes on before my socks in the morning, I waste several minutes in correcting my error, and risk stretching my socks, but eventually my feet will be conventionally shod. In business, however, decisions usually have more important consequences. A company choosing one manufacturing process over another may go bankrupt if the choice was wrong. Thus it is important to come up with some rules, based on **decision theory**, that will help us to make the best decision possible, given the information that we have.

Statisticians distinguish among three different kinds of decisions:

1. **Decisions under certainty.** These are decisions where you have all the information you need and can calculate precisely the outcome of every choice you make. This doesn't necessarily mean that you know exactly what to do: there may be more data than a person can comprehend. For example, you may wish to maximize the production of a certain chemical while simultaneously satisfying 531 related Environmental Protection Agency regulations. In cases like this, it is usually best to use an appropriate algorithm, such as linear programming, to evaluate the data and select the best outcome.

2. **Decisions under conflict.** These are decisions where you have to take into account what a competitor may do. A company has to consider what its

competitors may charge for an item when deciding its own price. This category of decisions is dealt with by game theory (see Chapter 13).

3. Decisions under uncertainty. These are decisions where you have to take chance into account, without worrying about what a competitor may be doing, just you and Nature. Here, intuition about what random chance may be up to comes into play. A farmer may have to choose what crops to grow on the basis of what he thinks the weather will be like. He will probably base his decision on past weather and long-range forecasting.

DECISION TREE

Before trying to make an intelligent decision, it is a good idea to have all of the possible choices and their outcomes charted for you. One way of doing this is to use a **decision tree**.

Suppose that you want to manufacture an item and have k different processes, $A_1, \ldots, A_k$, to choose from. Then you start out going from left to right with k branches (see Figure 16-1).

For each of the processes, there are different possible outcomes that we call **states of nature**. A state of nature is a chance result, usually unpredictable beforehand, such as the number rolled on a die or a particular day's weather.

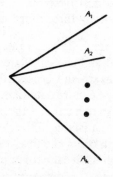

Figure 16-1

We'll call the states of nature $B_1, \ldots, B_l$. For example B_1 might be the outcome where the item manufactured came out perfect, B_2 the outcome where the item came out flawed, B_3 the outcome where the plant blew up, and so on. These are depicted as additional branches (see Figure 16-2).

Now you may have further decisions, $C_1, \ldots, C_m$, to make as a result of these outcomes, for example, to improve the process, rebuild the factory, or declare bankruptcy. These can be shown as more branches (see Figure 16-3).

The branching can be carried out as far as you wish, depending on how many levels you wish to analyze. The branches alternate between your choices and states of nature.

YOU SHOULD REMEMBER

Many business decisions must be made in environments of uncertainty. The field of decision theory provides guidance in such cases.

A decision tree is a diagram listing all possible outcomes for each possible decision and each possible state of nature.

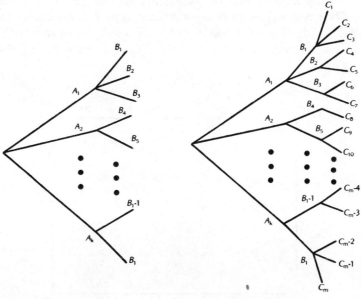

Figure 16-2   **Figure 16-3**

OBJECTIVE VARIABLES

We need to have some way of deciding which outcomes are better than others. A yo-yo manufacturer may think it best to make blue yo-yos because they sell better than yo-yos of other colors, or because blue is her favorite color.

Sales figures are examples of **objective variables**. They provide a way of comparing outcomes that mean the same to you, me, or anybody else. If item A sells more than item B, this is true no matter who reads the sales report. Other examples of objective variables include profits and production.

Color preference is not an objective variable.

PAYOFF TABLE

In the simplest decision trees, we have one level of choices, one level of states of nature, and, for each choice, the same states of nature to consider. Then we can form a table (see Figure 16-4).

Of course, it looks a little empty now. If we have an objective variable X, then we can enter its values (see Figure 16-5). Here X_{ij} is the value of the objective variable corresponding to the ith choice and the jth state of nature. This array is then called the *payoff table*.

The payoff table may be huge, and it would be helpful if we could simplify it. One way is to reject **dominated** or **inadmissible actions**. These are choices that should not be made because there are other choices that are always better. More accurately, A_i is dominated by A_j if, for all k, X_{ik} is less than or equal to X_{jk}, and there is at least one value of k such that $X_{ik} < X_{jk}$. Thus we would never choose

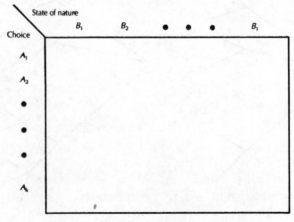

Figure 16-4

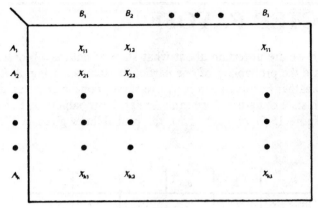

Figure 16-5

	B_1	B_2	B_3	B_4	B_5
A_1	1	2	5	8	3
A_2	2	2	5	2	7
A_3	3	9	8	7	6
A_4	0	1	3	2	4

Figure 16-6

A_i because A_j would always be better for us. For example, see Figure 16-6, where A_4 is dominated by A_2 and A_3 and thus is inadmissible.

Once we've eliminated any inadmissible actions, we've done just about all we can do with complete certainty.

YOU SHOULD REMEMBER

An objective variable is a variable that you are trying to maximize or minimize in making a decision.

A payoff table lists the payoff (the value of the objective variable) that would result for each possible decision and each possible state of nature.

EXPECTED PAYOFF

Even though we are uncertain about what state of nature will occur, we can often estimate the probability of one particular state occurring. A farmer can check past weather history, a company can survey consumer tastes, and so on. Then to each state of nature B_j we can associate a probability p_j. For the above example (Figure 16-6) we might have the probabilities given in Figure 16-7.

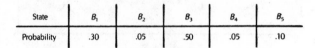

State	B_1	B_2	B_3	B_4	B_5
Probability	.30	.05	.50	.05	.10

Figure 16-7

Naturally we require that the p_j's add up to 1.

Even though the probabilities are at best estimates, we can still take the expected values of the objective variable for a given choice. Thus, for A_1

$$E(X_{1j}) = 1(.3) + 2(.05) + 5(.5) + 8(.05) + 3(.1) = 3.6$$

Similarly, $E(X_{2j}) = 4.0$, $E(X_{3j}) = 6.3$, and we don't bother to check choice A_4 since it is inadmissible.

The expected value of the objective variable for a given choice is called the **expected payoff**. If we compare expected payoffs, we see that A_3 has the highest, and we might want to choose it over A_1 and A_2 (again, A_4 is out of the running). Such a decision is said to be based on the **maximum expected payoff criterion**. This is not the only criterion for making a decision, but it is usually helpful.

Example: Using the Maximum Expected Payoff Criterion

State Choice	2	3	4	5	6	7	8	9	10	11	12
A_1	5	7	26	9	29	-6	8	15	4	-6	23
A_2	12	8	5	7	13	3	11	14	7	8	6
A_3	9	23	15	24	9	22	13	13	-5	-6	0
A_4	22	-3	-7	5	4	15	9	12	4	-2	6

Figure 16-8

PROBLEM   Suppose you have the following payoff table for a board game, where your choices are options available to you on your present turn, and the states of nature are the numbers your opponent may roll with two six-sided dice (see Figure 16-8). Which option should you choose, according to the maximum expected payoff criterion?

SOLUTION   It's reasonable to assume that the dice are fair, and we have the following probabilities for the states of nature (see Figure 16-9).

State	2	3	4	5	6	7	8	9	10	11	12
Probability	1/36	2/36	3/36	4/36	5/36	6/36	5/36	4/36	3/36	2/36	1/36

Figure 16-9

Then

$$E(X_{1j}) = 10.14, \qquad E(X_{2j}) = 8.56, \qquad E(X_{3j}) = 12.86$$

and

$$E(X_{4j}) = 6.44$$

Thus, using the maximum expected payoff criterion, you would choose option A_3.

OPPORTUNITY LOSS

Looking at the payoff table in Figure 16-6, we see that the best payoff that we can hope for with B_1 is 3, if we choose A_3. If we choose A_1 instead, the payoff is 1 instead of 3, a difference of 2. We call this the **opportunity loss** of A_1 at B_1. The opportunity loss of A_i at B_j, in general, is (the largest X_{kj} over all k) $- X_{ij}$, and is always nonnegative. The opportunity losses for the payoff table in Figure 16-6 are given in Figure 16-10.

	$B_1 \square$	$B_2 \square$	$B_3 \square$	$B_4 \square$	B_5
A_1	2	7	3	0	4
A_2	1	7	3	6	0
A_3	0	0	0	1	1
A_4	3	8	5	6	3

Figure 16-10

The opportunity loss tells us how much better we could have done for a given state of nature. Clearly, we'd like to have the opportunity loss as small as possible.

Since, however, the opportunity loss depends on the state of nature, there's not much that we can do to make it small. We can calculate the *expected opportunity loss* for a choice A_1 (written as EOL_1) if we have a set of probabilities for the states of nature.

Thus, using the probabilities in Figure 16-7, we have

$$EOL_1 = 2(.3) + 7(.05) + 3(.5) + 0(.05) + 4(.1) = 2.85$$
$$EOL_2 = 2.45, \qquad EOL_3 = 0.15, \qquad \text{and} \qquad EOL_4 = 4.4$$

If we choose A_3, with the smallest EOL_1, we are using the **minimum expected opportunity loss criterion.**

It is not by coincidence that the maximum expected payoff criterion and the minimum expected opportunity loss criterion point to the same choice, A_3, in this example. You may notice that for each one

$$EOL_1 = 6.45 - E(X_{ij})$$

Where does this 6.45 come from? Another way of writing the last equation is

$$6.45 = EOL_1 + E(X_{ij})$$

$$= \sum_j p_j \, (\text{opportunity loss of } A_1 \text{ at } B_j) + \sum_j p_j X_{ij}$$

$$= \sum_j p_j \, ((\text{largest } X_{kj} \text{ over all } K) - X_{ij}) + \sum_j p_j X_{ij}$$

$$= \sum_j p_j \, (\text{largest } X_{kj} \text{ over all } K)$$

In general, we call this the **expected payoff under certainty.** Why? Suppose that we had some way of knowing with certainty before we made our choice what the state of nature was going to be. If we knew in the above example that B_4 was going to occur, we would certainly choose A_1 to maximize our payoff. Thus, under certainty, we would gain 8 if state B_4 occurred.

Thus, the expected payoff under certainty is derived by using the probabilities of the various states occurring to average our payoffs under certainty.

Example: Expected Payoff under Certainty

Suppose that we had the payoff matrix given in Figure 16-11, with the probabilities given in Figure 16-12. Then our payoffs under certainty are those given in Figure 16-13, and our expected payoff under certainty is

$$8(.1) + 8(.05) + 7(.3) + 7(.2) + 9(.2) + 7(.15) = 7.55$$

	B_1 ☐	B_2 ☐	B_3 ☐	B_4 ☐	B_5 ☐	B_6
A1	1	8	3	7	2	0
A_2	3	0	7	7	9	7
A_3	8	6	5	4	3	1

Figure 16-11

State	B_1	B_2	B_3	B_4	B_5	B_6
Probability	.1	.05	.3	.2	.2	.15

Figure 16-12

State	B_1	B_2	B_3	B_4	B_5	B_6
Payoff under certainty	8	8	7	7	9	7

Figure 16-13

Our opportunity losses are given in Figure 16-14, and our expected opportunity losses in Figure16-15. Using our minimum expected opportunity loss criterion, we would choose A_2.

For A_2, our expected payoff is $7.55 - 0.9 = 6.65$.

	B_1	B_2	B_3	B_4	B_5	B_6
A_1	7	0	4	0	7	7
A_2	5	8	0	0	0	0
A_3	0	2	2	3	6	6

Figure 16-14

Choice	EOL_1
A_1	4.35
A_2	0.9
A_3	3.4

Figure 16-15

YOU SHOULD REMEMBER

The sum of the expected value and the opportunity loss is the expected payoff under certainty.

ROLLBACK ANALYSIS

Let's return to our decision tree. Suppose that, through some sort of estimation, we have found the probability for each state of nature, and an objective variable whose value is known at the end of each branch. Suppose further that we are using exclusively the maximum expected payoff criterion to decide which choice to make at each stage.

If, at any stage, we know the expected payoffs for all choices, then we know by this criterion which choice we will make. We no longer have to worry about the branch that follows this choice, and we can use its expected payoff as a new objective variable. Thus we can repeatedly "trim off" branches of our decision tree, until we have a strategy of choices mapped out. This process is called **rollback analysis**.

Example: Rollback Analysis

Suppose that we are given the decision tree in Figure 16-16, with the objective variable values and probabilities indicated. We can then calculate the expected payoff for each C_i (see Figure 16-17). We choose C_2 over C_1, C_3 by default, C_4 over C_5, C_6, C_7, C_8, and C_9 by default, and C_{11} over C_{10}.

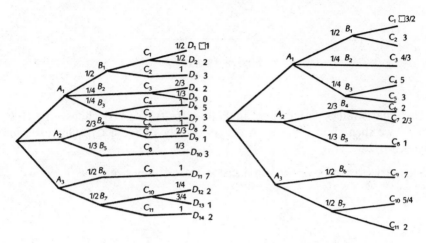

Figure 16-16   **Figure 16-17**

Then we have a value (the expected payoff of each of these choices) for each B_j (see Figure 16-18). From these values, we have an expected payoff for each A_i (see Figure 16-19). We would want to choose A_3.

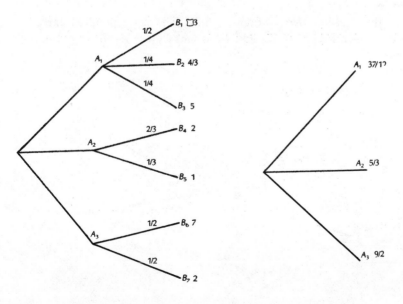

Figure 16-18   **Figure 16-19**

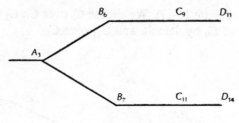

Figure 16-20

Our final strategy is indicated in Figure 16-20. We first choose A_3. If B_6 occurs, we then choose C_9. If B_7 occurs, we then choose C_{11}. Our expected payoff is 9/2.

This process can be applied to decision trees of any size.

SENSITIVITY ANALYSIS

If the probabilites for a given decision tree are being estimated roughly, we need to be careful that a small error in the probabilities doesn't cause us to make the wrong choice.

Consider the decision tree in Figure 16-21. The corresponding expected payoffs are given in Figure 16-22, and we would choose A_2. If we are wrong

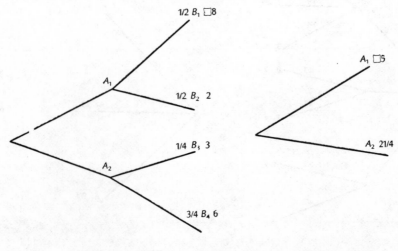

Figure 16-21   **Figure 16-22**

about the probabilities for B_1 and B_2, and they are in fact those given in Figure 16-23, then the expected payoff for A_1 is 28/5, and we should have chosen A_1 instead.

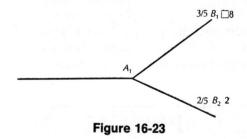

Figure 16-23

Always check in rollback analysis to see which choices would be altered if the probabilities were slightly off, and be mindful of this possibility (perhaps to try to verify the sensitive probabilities). This process of checking is known as **sensitivity analysis.**

YOU SHOULD REMEMBER

It is important to perform sensitivity analysis to be aware how much rollback analysis depends on the accuracy of the data.

KNOW THE CONCEPTS

DO YOU KNOW THE BASICS?

Test your understanding of Chapter 16 by answering the following questions:

1. How do you determine the probabilities used when evaluating business decisions?
2. Why are inadmissible choices ruled out?
3. What is the value of a decision tree?
4. If two decisions provide the same expected return, how do you think you would choose between them?
5. Consider two stocks, one very safe and one very risky. Which do you think will provide the greater expected return?
6. In what way does rollback analysis depend on the maximum expected payoff criterion?

TERMS FOR STUDY

decision theory
decision tree
dominated actions
expected payoff
expected payoff under certainty
inadmissible actions
maximum expected payoff criterion

minimum expected
    opportunity loss criterion
objective variables
opportunity loss
rollback analysis
sensitivity analysis
state of nature

PRACTICAL APPLICATION

COMPUTATIONAL PROBLEMS

1. In the following payoff table, which of the choices are inadmissible?

		State				
		I	II	III	IV	V
	A	4	3	6	9	7
	B	1	5	7	6	8
Choice	C	0	2	-2	6	3
	D	1	5	4	6	8

2. If you estimate that the probabilities of the states in Exercise 1 are as follows:

I	II	III	IV	V
.2	.3	.1	.2	.2

what is the expected payoff for each choice?

3. Draw a decision tree relating the weather to the way you dress. How many outcomes can you list?

4. You are playing blackjack alone with the dealer, who has two 10's, and you have been dealt a queen and a 6. Draw a decision tree for your response.

5. Construct a payoff table for the first level of Exercise 4, with the state of nature being the next card to be dealt, using the following objective variables: −1 if you lose, 0 if your turn continues, and 1 if you win. (Remember that the dealer wins all ties and cannot draw another card on 20.)

6. Which is (are) the inadmissible choice(s) in Exercise 4?

7. Assuming that the two 10's, the queen, and the 6 (Exercise 4) are the only cards drawn from a regular 52-card deck, calculate the probabilities for the states of nature (Exercise 5), and calculate the expected payoffs for the choices.

8. Suppose that you play the following game: You pick a number from 1 to 12 and roll two six-sided dice. If the number you pick is bigger than the number you roll, you lose in points the number you picked. If the number you pick is smaller than the number you roll, you gain in points the number you picked. If you pick the number you roll, you get 10 points. Construct a payoff table for this game.

9. Calculate the expected payoffs for the game described in Exercise 8.

10. List five objective variables.

Perform rollback analyses upon the decision trees shown in Exercises 11 and 12 to find the optimal strategies, and determine, in each case, the expected payoff with the optimal strategy.

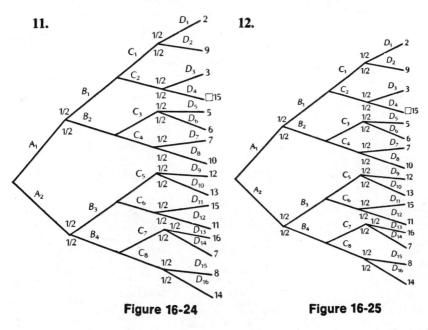

11.

12.

Figure 16-24   **Figure 16-25**

ANSWERS

KNOW THE CONCEPTS

1. Often these probabilities are subjective estimates.
2. There is one choice that is better in all circumstances.

3. A decision tree illustrates the consequences of many different types of actions in different states of nature.

4. If you are like most people, you would probably choose the decision with the lower risk.

5. If the stocks provided the same expected return, few people would want to buy the risky stock. Therefore, the risky stock must promise a higher expected return.

6. At each stage, the expected payoffs for the remaining branches are calculated. The branch with the greatest expected payoff is chosen, and the rest of the branches are discarded.

PRACTICAL APPLICATION

1. C and D.

2. 5.5 for A, 5.2 for B, 2.2 for C, 4.9 for D

3.

Weather	Dress

Rain
— Wear a raincoat.
— Carry an umbrella.
— Wear rubber boots.

Cold, dry
— Wear a heavy coat.
— Wear thermal underwear.

Windy, mild, dry
— Wear a windbreaker.
— Wear long sleeves

Hot, dry ——— Wear short sleeves.

(Feel free to add more branches to this tree. There is no limit to the number of possibilities.)

4. Here is part of the tree:

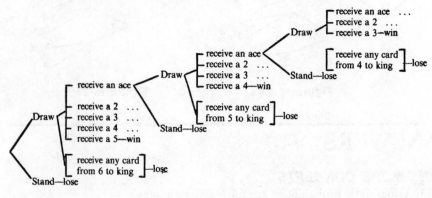

5.

	A	2	3	4	5	6	7	8	9	10	J	Q	K
Draw	0	0	0	0	1	−1	−1	−1	−1	−1	−1	−1	−1
Stand	−1	−1	−1	−1	−1	−1	−1	−1	−1	−1	−1	−1	−1

6. Stand

7. The probabilities of the states of nature are as follows:

A	4/48	6	3/48	J	4/48
2	4/48	7	4/48	Q	3/48
3	4/48	8	4/48	K	4/48
4	4/48	9	4/48		
5	4/48	10	2/48		

The expected value for draw is $-1/2$, and that for stand is -1.

8.
Roll

	2	3	4	5	6	7	8	9	10	11	12
2	10	2	2	2	2	2	2	2	2	2	2
3	−3	10	3	3	3	3	3	3	3	3	3
4	−4	−4	10	4	4	4	4	4	4	4	4
5	−5	−5	−5	10	5	5	5	5	5	5	5
6	−6	−6	−6	−6	10	6	6	6	6	6	6
7	−7	−7	−7	−7	−7	10	7	7	7	7	7
8	−8	−8	−8	−8	−8	−8	10	8	8	8	8
9	−9	−9	−9	−9	−9	−9	−9	10	9	9	9
10	−10	−10	−10	−10	−10	−10	−10	−10	10	10	10
11	−11	−11	−11	−11	−11	−11	−11	−11	−11	10	11
12	−12	−12	−12	−12	−12	−12	−12	−12	−12	−12	10

9. The expected payoff for each choice is as follows:

2	80/36	8	−38/36
3	116/36	9	−140/36
4	138/36	10	−240/36
5	140/36	11	−332/36
6	116/36	12	−410/36
7	60/36		

10. Profit, cost, efficiency, quantity, electricity used, etc.

11. Choose A_2. If B_3, then C_4. If B_4, then C_6. The expected payoff is 163/25.

12. Choose A_2. If B_3, then C_6. If B_4, then C_7. The expected payoff is 49/4.

1

APPENDIX

GLOSSARY

absolute maximum   the point where the value of a function attains its largest value; also called *global maximum*

absolute minimum   the point where the value of a function attains its smallest value; also called *global minimum*

acquisition costs   costs associated with obtaining orders (for example, trucking and accounting costs)

arrival rate (λ)   the average number of arrivals in a queue per unit time

assignment problem   a special kind of transportation problem in which all supplies and demands are equal to 1 (for example, where individuals are to be assigned different jobs)

auxiliary tableau   a tableau consisting of a prospective new basis vector, RHS, and the inverse of the matrix whose columns are the basis vectors; used in cases of degeneracy to decide where to pivot

basic feasible solution   a basic solution that is also feasible (that is, all variables are nonnegative); the basic feasible solutions correspond to the corner points of the feasible region

basic solution   a solution to the Constraint Simultaneous Equation (CSE) system for a linear programming problem where the number of nonzero variables is the same as (or, in exceptional cases, less than) the number of constraints

basis set   a set of entries in a vector **x** representing a basic solution that contains all of the nonzero entries

basis vectors   the columns of the constraint matrix **A** that correspond to the basis set

binomial distribution   the discrete probability distribution that applies when an experiment is conducted n times with each trial having a probability p of success and each trial being independent of every other trial

branch-and-bound   an algorithm for solving integer programming problems

buffer inventory   surplus inventory maintained to avoid running out of an item

calculus   a branch of mathematics that involves the study of derivatives (which measure the rate of change of functions with respect to their independent variables) and integrals (which represent the reverse process of calculating derivatives)

cartel   a formal organization set up by an oligopoly to reduce the quantity sold and maintain high prices

chain rule   a rule for determining the derivative of a function of the form $y = f(g(x))$, where f and g are two functions

Cobb-Douglas production function   a production function of the form

$$Q = Q_0 x_1^{a_1} x_2^{a_2} \times \cdots \times x_n^{a_n}$$

where x_1 to x_n represent the quantity of the n inputs

coefficient   a quantity that multiplies another quantity

column vector   a matrix with one column

combinations   the number of combinations of n objects taken j at a time is the number of ways of selecting j objects from the group of n objects, when the order in which the objects are selected does not matter

complementary slackness   a set of conditions that asserts that, if the optimal value of a variable for the dual to a linear programming problem is greater than zero, then the corresponding slack variable in the primal problem will be zero at the optimum

concave downward   a concave downward curve is a curve oriented as shown in Figure 9-14

concave upward   a concave upward curve is a curve oriented as shown in Figure 9-14

conditional probability   the probability that a particular event will occur, given that another event has occurred

constant returns to scale   a production function has constant returns to scale if increasing all inputs by the same proportion causes the output to increase by that same proportion

constraint ratio   in a simplex tableau, the values found by dividing each value in the right-hand-side column by each of the values in the pivot column; the row with the smallest positive value of the constraint ratio is the pivot row

consumption function a function that expresses the amount of consumption spending as a function of after-tax income

continuous random variable a random variable that can take on any real-number value within a certain range; it is characterized by a density function such that the area under the curve between two numbers represents the probability that the random variable will be between these two numbers

convex set a set in which the line segment connecting any two points in the set never passes outside the set

countably infinite a set has a countably infinite number of members if it has an infinite number of members and each element in the set can be assigned to a unique positive integer; for contrast, the set of real numbers has an infinite number of members but is not countably infinite

convariance a quantity that measures the relation between two random variables; it is zero if the two random variables are independent

critical point a point where the slope of a curve (that is, the derivative) is zero; for multivariable functions, the critical points are the points where all of the partial derivatives are equal to zero

cross partial if f is a well-behaved function of x and y, then the cross partial is the derivative of $\partial f / \partial x$ with respect to y, written as $\partial^2 f / \partial x \, \partial y$, also equal to the derivative of $\partial f / \partial y$ with respect to x

CSE system abbreviation for Constraint Simultaneous Equation system; a set of equations in a linear programming problem formed by adding slack variables so that the constraints of the problem can be represented as equations; a solution to the CSE system with all variables nonnegative is a feasible solution to the linear programming problem

decision theory the study of making decisions designed to achieve some objective, often under conditions of uncertainty

decision tree a diagram that illustrates all possible consequences of different decisions in different states of nature

degeneracy a situation that arises in a linear programming problem when more than one row of the simplex tableau gives the same constraint ratio, or the constraint ratio is zero

delta the Greek capital letter delta (Δ), used to represent "change in"

density function for a discrete random variable, the probability density function at a specific value is the probability that the random variable will have that value; for a continuous random variable, the probability density function is represented by a curve such that the area under the curve, above the axis, and between two numbers is equal to the probability that the random variable will be between these two numbers

dependent variable   in the function $y = f(x)$, y is the dependent variable; its value depends on the value of the independent variable

derivative   the derivative of a function $f(x)$ is a function $f'(x)$ whose value at a particular point is equal to the slope of the curve representing $f(x)$ at that point; it measures the rate of change of the dependent variable with respect to the independent variable

determinant   a quantity that characterizes the nature of a matrix; if the determinant of the matrix of coefficients for an equation system is zero, then the matrix does not have an inverse and the equation system is either redundant or contradictory

discrete random variable   a random variable with either a finite or a countably infinite number of possible values

disjoint events   two events that cannot both happen; also called *mutually exclusive events*

dominated actions   choices that are worse than other choices and thus should never be chosen; also called *inadmissable actions*

dot product   if **a** is a 1 by n row vector and **b** is an n by 1 column vector, then the dot product of **a** and **b** (written as **a** · **b**) is

$$a_1b_1 + a_2b_2 + \cdots + a_nb_n$$

where a_i and b_i represent the components of **a** and **b**, respectively

dual problem   the dual problem for a linear programming problem is a new linear programming problem formed by interchanging the features of the original problem; each variable in the dual problem corresponds to one of the constraints in the original problem

economic order quantity (*EOQ*)   an order quantity that minimizes total costs, given a constant demand

effective arrival rate (λ_e)   the arrival rate, adjusted to take into account customers who are turned away from a finite-length queue

element   in a matrix, one of the individual numbers or variables contained in that matrix

elimination method   a method for solving a system of equations where multiples of one equation are added to another equation to eliminate some of the variables from that equation, thereby making the system easier to solve

equilibrium point   a payoff in a payoff matrix that is optimal for both players in the following sense: given Player I's choice, Player II can do no better with another choice, and vice versa

event a set of outcomes; if all possible outcomes are equally likely, then the probability that an event will occur is equal to the number of outcomes in that event divided by the total number of outcomes

expectation the average value that would appear if a random variable was observed many times; also called the *expected value* or *mean*

expected payoff the expected value of the payoff resulting from a decision

expected payoff under certainty the expected value of the largest payoff for each state of nature

expected value See **expectation**.

exponential distribution a continuous random variable distribution with the density function $\lambda e^{-\lambda x}$ (if $x > 0$)

exponential function a function consisting of a quantity (called the *base*) raised to a variable exponent (for example, e^x)

factorial for a particular whole number, the product of all the whole numbers from 1 to that number

feasible region a set of points that satisfy all of the constraints in a linear programming problem

feasible solution a point that satisfies all of the constraints in a linear programming problem

first derivative the derivative of a function

first-in, first-out (FIFO) a queuing discipline whereby items are serviced in the order in which they arrive

fixed cost a cost that must be paid regardless of the level of production

fixed period inventory an inventory where orders are placed on a regular basis

function a rule that associates each value of the independent variable (or variables) with a value of the dependent variable

game an activity wherein each of a group of players is faced with a fixed set of choices, and each possible combination of choices among the players has a fixed outcome

game diagram a rectangular diagram corresponding to a two-person game, plotting the choices of Player I on the left, the choices of Player II on the top, and the outcomes for each pair of choices inside the rectangle

global maximum See **absolute maximum**.

global minimum See **absolute minimum**.

holding cost the cost (expressed as a fraction of the item's cost) incurred in storing an item

hypergeometric distribution the discrete probability distribution that applies when a group of items is selected without replacement

inadmissable actions See **dominated actions**.

identity matrix a square matrix with 1's on the main diagonal from the upper left corner to the lower right corner, and 0's everywhere else; multiplying any other matrix by an identity matrix leaves the other matrix unchanged

independent events two or more events that do not affect each other

independent variable in the function $y = f(x)$, x is the independent variable

inflection point a point where the second derivative is zero

integer programming the study of linear programming problems in which all numbers are required to be integers

inventory theory the study of the costs involved in storing and ordering items

inverse function the inverse function for a function is the function that does exactly the opposite of what the original function does

inverse matrix if A is a square matrix, then its inverse matrix (written as A^{-1}, if it exists) is the matrix such that the product of A^{-1} and A is an identity matrix

isocost line a line passing through points that represent combinations with the same total cost

isoprofit line a line passing through points that represent combinations with the same total profit

isoquant a curve passing through points that represent input combinations that result in the same quantity of output

isoquant map a diagram showing several isoquants

iterative procedure a procedure that keeps repeating the same steps until a solution is found

Kuhn-Tucker conditions a set of conditions for determining the optimum point for a nonlinear programming problem

Lagrange multiplier a variable that multiplies a constraint in a Lagrangian expression; the Lagrange multiplier represents the shadow price for that constraint

Lagrangian an expression formed by taking the objective function and adding terms consisting of a Lagrange multiplier multiplied by an expression representing a constraint

lambda the Greek letter lambda (λ), used to represent Lagrange multipliers; it is also used to represent the parameters in Poisson and exponential distributions

last-in, first-out (LIFO) a queuing discipline whereby items that have arrived most recently are serviced first

lead time the time elapsed between the placing of an order and its arrival

linear equation an equation in which no variable is raised to any power other than 1, and no variables are multiplied together

linear programming the study of problems where the goal is to maximize (or minimize) a particular linear function, called the *objective function*, subject to a set of constraints that are expressed as linear equations or inequalities

linearly dependent a set of vectors ($\mathbf{v}_1, \mathbf{v}_2, \ldots, \mathbf{v}_n$) is linearly dependent if there are numbers $c_1, c_2, \ldots, c_n$, not all zero, such that

$$c_1\mathbf{v}_1 + c_2\mathbf{v}_2 + \cdots + c_n\mathbf{v}_n = \mathbf{0}$$

local maximum See **relative maximum.**

local minimum See **relative minimum.**

logarithm the equation $y = a^x$ can be written as $x = \log_a y$, which means "x is the logarithm of y to the base a"

marginal cost the derivative of the total function with respect to the quantity produced; in some cases defined as the amount that cost increases when 1 more unit is produced

marginal net gain the rate of change in the value of the objective function in a linear programming problem caused by bringing in a new basis vector

marginal revenue the derivative of the total revenue function with respect to the quantity produced; in some cases defined as the amount that revenue increases when 1 more unit is produced

matrix a rectangular table of numbers or variables arranged in rows and columns

maximum expected payoff criterion a strategy consisting of selecting the choice with the greatest expected payoff

mean See **expectation.**

minimum expected opportunity loss criterion a strategy consisting of selecting the choice with the least expected opportunity loss

mixed strategy a strategy calling for each choice to be played a fixed fraction of the time (in a random manner so as to be unpredictable)

monopoly a market with one seller

multiple-channel queue a queue with more than one servicing area

multiplication principle a principle that states: If there are m possible outcomes of the first experiment and n possible outcomes of the second experiment, then there are mn possible combined outcomes of both experiments (if the two experiments are independent)

mutually exclusive events See **disjoint events.**

nonlinear programming the study of problems that involve finding the maximum or minimum value of an objective function, subject to constraints that may be written as inequalities, where the objective function and the constraints are allowed to contain expressions that are not linear expressions

nonnegativity constraints the constraints in a linear programming problem that require the value of each variable to be greater than or equal to zero

normal distribution the most important continuous random variable distribution; its density function is bell-shaped

normal form a linear programming problem has been converted into normal form when it can be expressed as follows: maximize $\mathbf{cx}$, subject to $\mathbf{Ax} = \mathbf{R}$, where all of the elements of $\mathbf{R}$ are nonnegative and all of the variables in $\mathbf{x}$ are required to be nonnegative

northwest corner rule a method for determining a basic feasible solution to a transportation problem

objective function a function of several variables in a situation where the goal is to determine values of these variables that maximize or minimize the value of the objective function, subject to meeting a set of constraints

objective variables ways of comparing outcomes that are unbiased

oligopoly a market containing a small number of sellers

opportunity loss the difference in the payoff between a given choice and the best choice, for a given state of nature

order quantity inventory an inventory where order size stays constant

outage cost the cost associated with running out of an item

outcome one of the possible results of a probability experiment

partial derivative   the derivative of a multivariable function with respect to one of the independent variables, which is calculated by treating all other independent variables as constants

payoff matrix   a matrix displaying the payoffs in a two-person, zero-sum game

perfect competition   a market containing many sellers, all of which are so small as to have no noticeable effect on the market

permutations   the number of different ways of selecting j objects from a group of n objects, when each distinct way of ordering the chosen objects counts separately

phase I   the first phase of the simplex method, which consists of finding an initial basic feasible solution

phase II   the second phase of the simplex method, which consists of moving from the initial basic feasible solution to the optimal basic feasible solution

pivoting   the process of adjusting the simplex tableau to remove one variable from the basis and add another variable to the basis

Poisson distribution   a discrete probability distribution where the probability that the variable takes a particular value k is equal to $e^{-\lambda}\lambda^k/k?$, where λ is the mean and $e = 2.71828\ldots$

polynomial   a polynomial in x is an algebraic expression of the form
$$a_n x^n + a_{n-1} x^{n-1} + \cdots + a_3 x^3 + a_2 x^2 + a_1 x + a_0$$
where $a_n, a_{n-1}, \ldots, a_0$ are constants that are the coefficients of the polynomial

primal problem   the original problem in a linear programming situation; the term is used to distinguish this from the dual problem

prisoner's dilemma   a game wherein each player, by trying to optimize his or her individual payoff, worsens the overall payoffs

probability   the study of chance phenomena

production function   a function where the independent variables represent the quantities of the inputs used in the production process and the dependent variable is the quantity of output produced

pure strategy   in game theory, a fixed choice on the part of one player

quadratic equation   an equation of the form $ax^2 + bx + c = 0$

quadratic formula   a formula that gives the solution for x to the equation $ax^2 + bx + c$:
$$x = \frac{-b \pm \sqrt{b^2 - 4ac}}{2a}$$

queue length the largest number of items that could possibly be waiting to be serviced

queuing discipline a procedure for determining who or what is to be serviced next

queuing theory the study of the parameters involved in units having to wait to be serviced

redundancy a situation that arises in a linear programming problem when some of the constraint equations can be derived from other constraint equations

redundancy equation an equation used to eliminate variables that must be zero for all feasible solutions; used when Phase I calculations provide a nonbasic feasible solution

relative maximum a point where the value of a function is greater than at surrounding points; also called *local maximum*

relative minimum a point where the value of a function is less than at surrounding points; also called *local minimum*

reorder point (*ROP*) a lower bound for inventory that minimizes cost; the point at which a new order should be placed

rollback analysis a procedure for determining the optimal strategy for a given decision tree (with associated probabilities for the various states of nature and payoffs), repeatedly using the maximum expected payoff criterion

row vector a matrix with one row

saddle point a critical point for a function of two variables such that the cross section of the surface is concave upward in one direction and concave downward in some other direction (see Figure 10-3)

safety stock (*SS*) the size of the buffer inventory

scalar product same as **dot product**

secant line a line that crosses a section of a curve at two points

second derivative the derivative of the derivative

second-order conditions the conditions involving the second partial derivatives of a multivariable function that determine whether a critical point is a maximum point, a minimum point, or a saddle point

sensitivity analysis the examination of how small changes in the estimation of probabilities would affect a strategy

service rate (μ) the average number of units serviced per unit time

SES form abbreviation for Standard Easily Solvable form; an equation system where each variable occurs in one and only one of the equations, and the coefficient for the variable is equal to 1 in the equation where it does occur

shadow prices the shadow price associated with each constraint in a linear programming problem tells how much the value of the objective function would be improved if that constraint was relaxed by 1 unit; the shadow prices are equal to the optimal values of the variables for the dual to the original problem

simplex an n-simplex is a convex set containing n vertices that exists in a space with $n - 1$ dimensions; for example, a 3-simplex is a triangle and a 4-simplex is a tetrahedron (pyramid); the feasible region to a linear programming problem consists of a set of simplexes

simplex method a method for solving linear programming problems that involves moving from one basic feasible solution to another basic feasible solution with a better value for the objective function, continuing to repeat this process until the optimum is found

simplex tableau a table used to arrange the data utilized in the simplex linear programming algorithm

single-channel queue a queue with one servicing area

slack variable a variable included in a linear programming problem that measures the excess capacity associated with a particular constraint; the inclusion of slack variables converts inequality constraints into equations

slope a quantity that measures the steepness of a line; a horizontal line has a slope of zero and a vertical line has an infinite slope

square matrix a matrix where the number of rows is the same as the number of columns

standard deviation the square root of the variance

standard normal distribution a normal distribution with mean equal to 0 and standard deviation equal to 1

state of nature in decision theory, an unpredictable outcome

steady-state queue a queue for which the probabilities associated with queue length remain constant

stepping-stone algorithm a method for moving from one basic feasible solution of a transportation problem to another of lower cost, and determining whether a basic feasible solution is optimal

substitution method a method for solving a system of equations by solving one of the equations in terms of one of the variables, and then substituting the resulting expression in place of that variable in the other equations

surface a two-dimensional curved object that can exist in a space of three (or more dimensions); for example, if you curl a piece of paper, the result is a surface

tangent line a line that just touches a portion of a curve at one point without crossing the curve

transient-state queue a queue whose servicing has not yet settled into a regular pattern

transportation problem a problem that involves transporting goods from where they are stored to where they are needed in a way that minimizes cost

transpose if x is the element in row i, column j in a matrix **A**, then x will be located in row j, column i in the matrix that is the transpose of **A**

value a number associated with a two-person, zero-sum game: the best that Player I can expect to do, and the least that Player II can expect to lose, on the average, if both play intelligently

variable order quantity inventory an inventory where order size depends on customer demand

variable period inventory an inventory where orders are placed as customer demand requires

variance the expected value of the square of the distance from a random variable to its mean; it indicates the degree of unpredictability of the random variable

vertical intercept the point where a line crosses the vertical axis

zero-sum game a game where the sum of the payoffs to all of the players is zero

2 APPENDIX

COMPUTER PROGRAMS

Here is a BASIC program for performing the simplex method for small-scale linear programming problems. The program is written in Microsoft BASIC (also known as IBM PC BASIC). The program will solve either minimization problems (using the two-phase simplex method) or maximization problems. The user specifies the type of problem to be solved and has the option of looking only at the results or of looking at each stage of the simplex tableau. (Of course, if the problem is too big, the tableaus will be too wide to fit on the screen.)

This program writes the output to a disk file, which gives the user the option of subsequently displaying the output on the screen, printing the result, or saving it for future use. All of the statements with "PRINT # 1," can be replaced with "PRINT" and then the output will be directed to the screen. (In that case lines 10 to 20 can be eliminated, and line 4099 can be replaced with END.)

Following the simplex method program is a program for solving systems of simultaneous linear equations.

```
1   REM    SIMPLEX LINEAR PROGRAMMING METHOD
2   REM    WRITTEN IN MICROSOFT BASIC
5   DEF FNST$(X)=MID$(STR$(X),2,LEN(STR$(X))-1) :REM CONVERT NUM. TO STRING
10  PRINT "Type in name of file where output will be sent:";
15  INPUT F$
20  OPEN"O",#1,F$
25  PRINT "Type 1 to see the tableaus, otherwise type 0:"
30  INPUT DEM
32  IF DEM=1 THEN INPUT "Enter number of decimal places to display:";DECPLC
35  PRINT "Type 1 for minimization problem, 2 for maximization problem:";
40  INPUT PROBTYPE
50  IF PROBTYPE=1 THEN GOTO 200 ELSE IF PROBTYPE=2 THEN GOTO 500
51  GOTO 35
197 '
198 '
199 '
200 REM READ IN VALUES FOR MINIMIZATION PROBLEM
205 INPUT "Number of choice variables:";NO
210 INPUT "Number of constraints:";M
215 T=NO+2*M+1   : REM NUMBER OF COLUMNS IN TABLEAU
220 GOSUB 5000   : REM DIMENSION ARRAYS
225 FOR I=1 TO M
```

```
230    PRINT "Enter coefficients for constraint ";I
240    FOR J=1 TO N0
250      PRINT "  ";J;": ";
255      INPUT A(I,J)
260    NEXT J
265    INPUT "Enter right hand side value:";A(I,T)
270  NEXT I
275  FOR I=1 TO M  :REM  FILL IN -1 COEFFICIENTS FOR SURPLUS VARIABLES
280    A(I,(N0+I))=-1:NEXT I
285  FOR I=1 TO M  :REM  FILL IN 1 COEFFICIENTS FOR EXTRA VARIABLES ADDED
286               REM   IN PHASE 1
290    A(I,(N0+M+I))=1
295    INBAS(N0+M+I)=1   :NEXT I
300  FOR J=1 TO N0+M:TOPROW(J)=0:NEXT J
305  FOR J=(N0+M+1) TO (N0+2*M):TOPROW(J)=-1:NEXT J
308  PHASE=1
309  REM  FILL IN VARIABLE NAMES
310  FOR J=1 TO N0:VARLIST$(J)="X"+FNST$(J):NEXT J
312  FOR J=(N0+1) TO (N0+M):VARLIST$(J)="S"+FNST$(J-N0):NEXT J
313  FOR J=(N0+M+1) TO (N0+2*M):VARLIST$(J)="S'"+FNST$(J-N0-M):NEXT J
315  GOTO 1000 : REM START PHASE 1 CALCULATIONS
320  REM -- START PHASE 2 CALCULATIONS
321  REM           THE COMPUTER WILL ARRIVE HERE AFTER IT HAS FOUND THE
322  REM           PHASE 1 SOLUTION  (LINE 4095)
330  PRINT "Input Objective Function Coefficients:"
340  FOR J=1 TO N0
345      PRINT J;": ";
350      INPUT C:TOPROW(J)=-C
355  NEXT J
360  REM  REMOVE EXTRA PHASE 1 VARIABLES
365  FOR I=1 TO M
370    A(I,(N0+M+1))=A(I,T)
375  NEXT I
380  T=T-M
385  PHASE=2
390  GOTO 1000  :REM  START PHASE 2 CALCULATIONS
497 '
498 '
499 '
500  REM READ IN VALUES FOR MAXIMIZATION PROBLEM
510    INPUT "Number of choice variables:";N0
511    REM  NOTE -- N0 DOES NOT INCLUDE THE SLACK VARIABLES
520    INPUT "Number of constraints:";M
530    T=M+N0+1 : REM NUMBER OF COLUMNS IN TABLEAU
540  GOSUB 5000   :REM DIMENSION ARRAYS
550    FOR I=1 TO M
555      PRINT "Enter coefficients for constraint ";I
560      FOR J=1 TO N0
570        PRINT "  ";J;": ";
580        INPUT A(I,J)
590      NEXT J
600    INPUT "Right hand side value:";A(I,T)
610    NEXT I
650  FOR I=1 TO M  :REM FILL IN 1 COEFFICIENTS FOR SLACK VARIABLES
655    INBAS(N0+I)=1
660    A(I,(N0+I))=1 : NEXT I
700  PRINT "Input objective function coefficients:"
710  FOR J=1 TO N0:PRINT J;": ";:INPUT TOPROW(J):NEXT J
720  FOR J=1 TO N0:VARLIST$(J)="X"+FNST$(J):NEXT J
730  FOR J=(N0+1) TO (N0+M):VARLIST$(J)="S"+FNST$(J-N0):NEXT J
740  PHASE=2
750  GOTO 1000 : REM START CALCULATIONS
997 '
998 '
999 '
1000 REM START NEW ITERATION
1005 SOLFOUND=0
1010 GOSUB 2000   :REM CALCULATE MARGINAL NET GAIN
1015 GOSUB 2200 : REM CHECK TO SEE WHICH NEW VARIABLES
```

```
1016                    REM SHOULD BE INCLUDED IN BASIS
1017                    REM IN OTHER WORDS, WHICH COLUMN TO PIVOT ON
1025 IF SOLFOUND=1 THEN GOTO 4000   :REM OPTIMAL SOLUTION FOUND
1030 GOSUB 2400   :REM DETERMINE WHICH ROW TO PIVOT ON
1035 IF DEM=1 THEN GOSUB 3000 :REM PRINT TABLEAU
1040 GOSUB 2600   :REM CARRY OUT PIVOT OPERATION
1050 GOTO 1000
1997 '
1998 '
1999 '
2000 REM CALCULATE MARGINAL NET GAIN
2010 FOR J=1 TO T
2020 IF INBAS(J)<>1 THEN GOTO 2090
2030    REM DETERMINE CJ VALUE
2040    FOR I=1 TO M
2050       IF A(I,J)=1 THEN GOTO 2070
2060    NEXT I
2070    C(I)=TOPROW(J)
2080    BASISLIST$(I)=VARLIST$(J)
2090 NEXT J
2095 RETURN
2197 '
2198 '
2199 '
2200 REM  CHECK TO SEE WHICH NEW VARIABLES SHOULD
2201 REM  BE INCLUDED IN BASIS
2210 MAXNETGAIN=0 : MAXNGNUM=1 :ALLNEG=1
2220 FOR J=1 TO T-1
2230 IF INBAS(J)=1 THEN BOTROW(J)=0:GOTO 2290 :REM THIS VAR. IS IN BASIS
2240    NETGAIN=TOPROW(J)   :REM NETGAIN TELLS HOW MUCH WOULD BE
2241                        REM GAINED IF THIS VARIABLE WENT UP BY 1
2250    FOR I=1 TO M
2260       NETGAIN = NETGAIN - A(I,J) * C(I)
2270    NEXT I
2274    BOTROW(J)=NETGAIN
2276    IF NETGAIN>0 THEN ALLNEG=0
2280    IF NETGAIN>MAXNETGAIN THEN MAXNETGAIN=NETGAIN:MAXNGNUM=J
2281    REM MAXNGNUM WILL GIVE US THE COLUMN NUMBER OF THE VARIABLE
2282    REM THAT GIVES THE MAXIMUM NET GAIN
2290 NEXT J
2295 PIVCOL=MAXNGNUM   :REM  THE PIVOT COLUMN WILL BE THE COLUMN OF THE
2296                    REM  VARIABLE WITH THE MAXIMUM NET GAIN
2298    IF ALLNEG=1 THEN SOLFOUND=1
2299    RETURN
2397 '
2398 '
2399 '
2400 REM DETERMINE WHICH ROW TO PIVOT ON
2410 MINRATIO=1E+30 : MINRNUM=1
2420 FOR I=1 TO M
2430    IF A(I,PIVCOL)<>0 THEN RATIO=A(I,T)/A(I,PIVCOL) ELSE GOTO 2450
2435    IF RATIO<0 THEN GOTO 2450
2440    IF RATIO<MINRATIO THEN MINRATIO=RATIO : MINRNUM=I
2450 NEXT I
2460 PIVROW=MINRNUM
2499 RETURN
2597 '
2598 '
2599 '
2600 REM CARRY OUT PIVOT OPERATION
2602 FOR J=1 TO T-1:IF INBAS(J)=0 THEN GOTO 2606
2603 IF A(PIVROW,J)=1 THEN OLDSOLVAL=J:GOTO 2610
2606 NEXT J
2610 PIVELEM=A(PIVROW,PIVCOL)
2618 REM  DIVIDE THE PIVOT ROW BY THE PIVOT ELEMENT TO MAKE
2619 REM  THE VALUE IN THE PIVOT POSITION EQUAL TO 1
2620 FOR J=1 TO T
2630    A(PIVROW,J)=A(PIVROW,J)/PIVELEM
2640 NEXT J
```

```
2700    REM
2720    FOR I=1 TO M
2730      IF I=PIVROW THEN GOTO 2770
2735      KEYVAL=A(I,PIVCOL)/A(PIVROW,PIVCOL)
2740      FOR J=1 TO T
2750       A(I,J)=A(I,J)-KEYVAL*A(PIVROW,J)
2760      NEXT J
2770    NEXT I
2780    INBAS(PIVCOL)=1:INBAS(OLDSOLVAL)=0
2799    RETURN
3000    REM PRINT TABLEAU
3003    FW=7   'FIELD WIDTH (WIDTH OF COLUMNS)
3008    BLANKCOL$=SPACE$(FW)
3010    PRINT#1, "----------------------------"
3013    FOR J=1 TO T-1
3014    IF INBAS(J)=1 THEN PRINT#1,  "    ****"; ELSE PRINT#1, "
3015    NEXT J:PRINT#1," "
3020    FOR J=1 TO T-1:Z0=TOPROW(J):GOSUB 9000   'PRINT TOPROW(J);
3025      NEXT J
3030    PRINT#1," << Obj. Fn. Coeff."
3035    PRINT#1," "
3040    FOR J=1 TO T-1:PRINT#1,SPC(FW-LEN(VARLIST$(J)));VARLIST$(J);
3045    NEXT J
3047    PRINT#1,"    RHS BASISVRS CBV    RATIO"
3049    REM  PRINT THE CENTRAL PART OF THE TABLEAU
3050    FOR I=1 TO M
3070      FOR J=1 TO T
3080        Z0=A(I,J):GOSUB 9000   'PRINT A(I,J);
3090      NEXT J
3092      PRINT#1,SPC(FW-LEN(BASISLIST$(I)));BASISLIST$(I);
3095      Z0=C(I):GOSUB 9000    ' PRINT C(I);
3097      IF SOLFOUND=1 THEN PRINT#1," ":GOTO 3110
3098      IF A(I,PIVCOL)<>0 THEN Z0=A(I,T)/A(I,PIVCOL):GOSUB 9000
3099      IF I=PIVROW THEN PRINT#1,"<<" ELSE PRINT#1," "
3110    NEXT I
3128    PRINT#1," "
3129    REM -- PRINT THE BOTTOM ROW -- THE NET GAIN FIGURES
3130    FOR J=1 TO T-1
3131      Z0=BOTROW(J)
3132      IF ((J<>PIVCOL) OR (SOLFOUND=1)) THEN GOSUB 9000:GOTO 3138
3134      FW=6:GOSUB 9000:PRINT#1,"^";:FW=7
3138    NEXT J
3140    PRINT#1,"  << Marginal Net Gains"
3150    IF SOLFOUND<>1 THEN PRINT#1,"Pivot: Row ";PIVROW;", Column ";PIVCOL
3199    RETURN
3998    '
3999    '
4000    REM SOLUTION FOUND
4005    IF DEM=1 THEN GOSUB 3000   'PRINT TABLEAU
4010    PRINT#1,"    Solution:"
4020    OBJVAL=0
4030    FOR J=1 TO T-1
4040      IF INBAS(J)<>1 THEN GOTO 4070
4050      PRINT#1,VARLIST$(J);" = ";
4055      FOR I=1 TO M
4060      IF A(I,J)<>1 THEN GOTO 4065
4062      PRINT#1, A(I,T)
4063      OBJVAL=OBJVAL+TOPROW(J)*A(I,T)
4065      NEXT I
4070    NEXT J
4080      PRINT#1,"Objective function value: ";OBJVAL
4082    IF PHASE=2 THEN GOTO 4099   'END
4095    GOTO 320   :REM BEGIN PHASE 2 CALCULATION
4099    CLOSE#1
4100    END
4997    '
4998    '
4999    '
5000    REM DIMENSION ARRAYS
```

```
5010 DIM A(M,T) :REM  ARRAY THAT HOLDS ELEMENTS OF SIMPLEX TABLEAU
5020 DIM INBAS(T): REM INBAS(I) IS 1 IF VARIABLE IN COLUMN I IS IN BASIS
5030 DIM TOPROW(T): REM  TOP ROW OF TABLEAU -- OBJECTIVE FN. COEFFICIENTS
5040 DIM BOTROW(T): REM  BOTTOM ROW OF TABLEAU -- MARGINAL NET GAINS
5050 REM  NOTE -- ALL VARIABLES ARE ASSUMED TO HAVE THE VALUE 0
5051 REM  AT THE START
5060 RETURN
8997 '
8998 '
8999 '
9000 REM PRINT VALUE OF Z0 WITH APPROPRIATE NUMBER OF DECIMAL PLACES
9005 FMT$=LEFT$("###################",FW)
9006 REM FW STANDS FOR FIELD WIDTH -- WHICH NORMALLY IS 7
9007 Z2=ABS(Z0)
9008 IF (Z2-INT(Z2))<.001  THEN PRINT#1,USING FMT$;Z0;:RETURN
9060 MID$(FMT$,(FW-DECPLC),1)="."
9070 PRINT#1,USING FMT$;Z0;
9080 RETURN



10  REM  THIS MICROSOFT BASIC PROGRAM SOLVES AN EQUATION SYSTEM
11  REM  WITH N LINEAR EQUATIONS AND N UNKNOWNS
100  REM READ IN COEFFICIENTS
110  INPUT "Number of Equations:";N
120  DIM M(N,(N+1)),X(N)
130  FOR I=1 TO N
140    PRINT "Enter coefficients for equation ";I
150    FOR J=1 TO N
155      PRINT J;": ";:INPUT M(I,J)
160    NEXT J
170    INPUT "Right hand side constant:";M(I,(N+1))
180  NEXT I
197  '
198  '
199  '
200  REM  BEGIN CALCULATIONS
210  FOR B= 1 TO (N-1)
220    FOR A=N TO (B+1) STEP -1
230      C=-M(A,B)/M(B,B)
240      FOR J=1 TO (N+1)
250        M(A,J)=M(A,J)+C*M(B,J)
260      NEXT J
270    NEXT A
280  NEXT B
299  '
300  X(N)=M(N,N+1)/M(N,N)
310  FOR K=(N-1) TO 1 STEP -1
320    T = 0
330    FOR J=(K+1) TO N
340      T=T+X(J)*M(K,J)
350    NEXT J
360    X(K)=(M(K,N+1)-T)/M(K,K)
370  NEXT K
397  '
398  '
399  '
400  REM OUTPUT
410  FOR I= 1 TO N
420    PRINT "X";I;"=";X(I)
430  NEXT I
440  END
449  '
450  REM -- NOTE: THIS PROGRAM WILL NOT WORK IF THERE ARE ZEROS
455  REM    IN THE COEFFICIENT MATRIX AT PLACES THAT REQUIRE
460  REM    DIVISION BY ZERO.  HOWEVER, IF THE COEFFICIENT MATRIX
465  REM    CONTAINS ZEROS THEN THE OTHER SOLUTION METHODS, SUCH
470  REM    AS THE SUBSTITUTION METHOD OR CRAMER'S RULE, BECOME EASIER
```

INDEX

More selected BARRON'S titles:

DICTIONARY OF ACCOUNTING TERMS
Joel Siegel and Jae Shim
Approximately 2500 terms are defined for accountants, business managers, students, and small business persons.
Paperback, $8.95, Canada $12.95/ISBN 3766-9

DICTIONARY OF ADVERTISING AND DIRECT MAIL TERMS
Jane Imber and Betsy-Ann Toffler
Approximately 3000 terms are defined as reference for ad industry professionals, students, and consumers.
Paperback, $8.95, Canada $12.95/ISBN 3765-0

DICTIONARY OF BUSINESS TERMS
Jack P. Friedman, general editor
Over 6000 entries define a wide range of terms used throughout business, real estate, taxes, banking, investment, more.
Paperback, $8.95, Canada $12.95/ISBN 3775-8

DICTIONARY OF COMPUTER TERMS
Douglas Downing and Michael Covington
Over 600 key computer terms are clearly explained, and sample programs included. Paperback, $8.95, Canada $12.95/ISBN 2905-4

DICTIONARY OF INSURANCE TERMS, *by Harvey W. Rubin*
Approximately 2500 insurance terms are defined as they relate to property, casualty, life, health, and other types of insurance.
Paperback, $8.95, Canada $12.95/ISBN 3722-3, 448 pages

BARRON'S BUSINESS REVIEW SERIES
Self-instruction guides cover topics taught in a college-level business course, presenting essential concepts in an easy-to-follow format.
Each book paperback $9.95, Canada $13.95, approx. 228 pages
ACCOUNTING, *by Peter J. Eisen*/ISBN 3574-7
BUSINESS LAW, *by Hardwicke and Emerson*/ISBN 3495-3
BUSINESS STATISTICS, *by Downing and Clark*/ISBN 3576-3
ECONOMICS, *by Walter J. Wessels*/ISBN 3560-7
FINANCE, *by A. A. Groppelli and Ehsan Nikhbakht*/ISBN 3561-5
MANAGEMENT, *by Montana and Charnov*/ISBN 3559-3
MARKETING, *by Richard L. Sandhusen*/ISBN 3494-5
QUANTITATIVE METHODS, *by Downing and Clark.* $10.95, Canada $15.95/ISBN 3947-5

BARRON'S TALKING BUSINESS SERIES:
BILINGUAL DICTIONARIES
Five bilingual dictionaries translate about 3000 terms not found in most foreign phrasebooks. Includes words related to accounting, sales, banking, computers, export/import and finance.
Each book paperback, $6.95, Canada $9.95, approx. 256 pages
TALKING BUSINESS IN FRENCH, *by Beppie LeGal*/ISBN 3745-6
TALKING BUSINESS IN GERMAN, *by Henry Strutz*/ISBN 3747-2
TALKING BUSINESS IN ITALIAN, *by Frank Rakus*/ISBN 3754-5
TALKING BUSINESS IN JAPANESE, *by C. & N. Akiyama*/3848-7
TALKING BUSINESS IN KOREAN, *by Un Bok Cheong*/ISBN 3992-0
TALKING BUSINESS IN SPANISH, *by Fryer and Faria*/ISBN 3769-3

All prices are in U.S. and Canadian dollars and subject to change without notice. At your bookseller, or order direct adding 10% postage (minimum charge $1.50), N.Y. residents add sales tax.

Barron's Educational Series, Inc.
250 Wireless Boulevard, Hauppauge, NY 11788
Call toll-free: 1-800-645-3476, in NY 1-800-257-5729
In Canada: 195 Allstate Parkway, Markham, Ontario L3R4T8